INDIA'S
FINANCE
MINISTERS

Celebrating 35 Years of
Penguin Random House India

INDIA'S
FINANCE
MINISTERS

From Independence to Emergency
(1947–1977)

A.K. BHATTACHARYA

PENGUIN
BUSINESS

An imprint of Penguin Random House

PENGUIN BUSINESS

USA | Canada | UK | Ireland | Australia
New Zealand | India | South Africa | China | Singapore

Penguin Business is part of the Penguin Random House group of companies
whose addresses can be found at global.penguinrandomhouse.com

Published by Penguin Random House India Pvt. Ltd
4th Floor, Capital Tower 1, MG Road,
Gurugram 122 002, Haryana, India

First published in Penguin Business by Penguin Random House India 2023

Copyright © A.K. Bhattacharya 2023

Illustrations by Binay Sinha

ISBN 9780670094165

Typeset in Garamond by MAP Systems, Bengaluru, India
Printed at Replika Press Pvt. Ltd, India

www.penguin.co.in

For Dada (Jayanta) and Bani

Contents

Introduction

Independent India has so far seen twenty-five finance ministers, each of whom stayed long enough in the saddle to have presented at least one full Budget. The role of a finance minister is uniquely important and critical in governance and policymaking in any nation. Understanding the manner in which a nation's finance ministers deal with policy matters is also another way of revisiting its economic history. A finance minister's job is not just to present the annual statement of government finances or the Budget. It is also to provide leadership to all the key economic policies pertaining to the finances of the government and its policies on trade and industry. Politically also, the finance minister is a key member of a government's top policymaking team, or the Cabinet. The finance minister's relationship with the prime minister is a key element when it comes to the manner in which the economic policies of a government are framed and implemented. Indeed, the quality of the relationship between the prime minister and the finance minister often determines the quality of policy and economic governance in a country. India is no exception.

In an ideal world, the performance and exploits of all the twenty-five finance ministers of India so far should be captured in a single volume for ease of access and readability. However, the sheer scale of what these finance ministers achieved and the economic policy challenges each faced and tried to address is difficult to compress in a single volume without doing injustice to most of them. Hence, the present volume focuses only on ten finance ministers, who led the Indian government's exchequer from 1947 to 1977. It is interesting to note that during this period two prime ministers (Jawaharlal Nehru and Indira Gandhi) presented a full Budget each while holding additional charge of the finance ministry.

These thirty years were not only eventful for India's economy and its many public institutions involved in economic governance, but they were also witness to the new direction the finance ministers during that period gave to India's economic development.

It is important to note that this period broadly corresponds with the longest uninterrupted rule of the Congress at the Centre for three decades when there were three prime ministers: Jawaharlal Nehru, Lal Bahadur Shastri and Indira Gandhi. Politically, this is an important phase, as it captures a period that began with India gaining independence in 1947 and ended with it hurtling into the Emergency in 1975, when the democratic rights of Indians remained suspended for the next nineteen months. It is needless to point out that economic policies too reflected the swinging political mood in these three decades.

The Journey Begins

We begin our journey with the start of the Nehru era on 15 August 1947. The reign of Nehru as prime minister was the longest. He had served India for sixteen years and 286 days before his death on 27 May 1964. Nehru was succeeded by Lal Bahadur Shastri, who also died suddenly, in January 1966, after which Indira Gandhi took charge of the Congress government. Of the thirty years covered in this volume, almost seventeen were under Nehru, less than twenty months under Shastri and a little over eleven years under Indira Gandhi. Nehru worked with as many as five different finance ministers—R.K. Shanmukham Chetty, John Matthai, C.D. Deshmukh, T.T. Krishnamachari and Morarji Desai. Shastri had worked with Krishnamachari for about a year and a half before Sachindra Chaudhuri became his finance minister. Shastri shared only a few days with him. Gandhi spent her days with Chaudhuri, Desai, Yashwantrao Balwantrao Chavan and Chidambaram Subramaniam, each of whom acted as finance minister during her tenure as prime minister. In these thirty years, Nehru had presented one of the Budgets when he donned the hat of finance minister in 1958 and presented the Budget for 1958–59.

His daughter, Indira Gandhi, also had presented one Budget in 1970. That was for 1970–71. Both the occasions when the prime minister had to take charge of the finance ministry and present a Budget were preceded by major controversies that led to the sudden removal of the incumbent finance ministers.

Nehru and His Finance Ministers

Nehru was a towering personality. During his seventeen-year tenure as prime minister, he even took upon himself the additional responsibility of the finance portfolio for a few months and even presented a Budget. But the finance ministers he worked with were no pygmies; each was a highly accomplished person in his respective field and well-regarded, be it in the world of politics or economics. But the average time each of his five ministers spent at the job turns out to be just a little over three years. Even these stints were split for two of the five finance ministers. In short, the longevity of finance ministers under Nehru was relatively poor. Shanmukham Chetty quit after one year. Matthai left after less than two years. Krishnamachari had two stints as finance minister. In his first stint, under Nehru, he could not even complete two years, singed as he was by the Mundhra scandal. His second stint with Nehru was for less than a year as the latter died in May 1964. Only two of Nehru's finance ministers were at the post for more than five years—Deshmukh, for about six years, and Desai, for about five years.

Each of Nehru's finance ministers either quit in a huff or was made to resign under unusual circumstances. Shanmukham Chetty and Krishnamachari resigned in the wake of scandals. Neither was accused of financial misconduct, but they committed procedural mistakes— Shanmukham Chetty sought the withdrawal of some of the names being investigated by an income-tax commission even as he was seeking Parliamentary sanction for a change in the relevant law, while Krishnamachari allowed the recently nationalized life insurance company to make investments in a controversial businessman's company. Neither finance minister was accused of having financially gained from their decisions, but both offered to resign in the wake of the controversies and Nehru accepted their resignations, even though the prime minister believed that Krishnamachari was not guilty.

The other two resignations by Nehru's finance ministers were triggered by their policy differences with the prime minister. Matthai quit because he was extremely unhappy with the way Nehru decided to set up the Planning Commission. And Deshmukh quit in a huff over the manner in which Nehru had handled the question of reorganization of the state of Maharashtra. While Nehru's differences with Matthai were understandable, as they were over a policy approach and those differences had indeed become irreconcilable, why Nehru allowed Deshmukh to quit the government remained a mystery. Deshmukh had opposed the original idea of Nehru's reorganization of the state of Maharashtra. Eventually, Nehru did not implement his original idea of trifurcating Maharashtra. Yet, he did not persuade Deshmukh to stay back either. Had he had enough of Deshmukh as his finance minister after six years and was looking for a fresh face for the post? Or was it the influence of other political personalities that had worked on Nehru?

Whatever those factors were, there is little doubt that of all his finance ministers, Nehru liked Krishnamachari the most. Indeed, the man who succeeded Deshmukh as finance minister was Krishnamachari. He and Nehru shared a strong bond. Nehru went along with Krishnamachari, supporting him even when it meant diluting the independence of the governor of the Reserve Bank of India. When Krishnamachari was indicted by the M.C. Chagla Commission for his role in the Mundhra scandal, Nehru took all the necessary steps to ensure that his finance minister was exonerated of the charges levelled against him. And that is how he made sure that Krishnamachari was back in North Block as the finance minister as soon as there was an opportunity to bring him in—which came his way in 1963—even if that meant sacrificing the reigning finance minister.

That was exactly how Morarji Desai lost his job as finance minister in 1963. It was a consequence of the famous 'Kamaraj Plan' that envisaged deployment of senior ministers in the Nehru Cabinet in organizational work, removing them from their ministerial roles. Nehru's relations with Desai were always strained. Desai was a formidable leader with a strong, popular base. He was also an inflexible leader and had his own views on economic and political issues. There were plenty of differences between the two. But that they went along as prime minister and finance minister as part of a team for about five years is also a reflection of the political culture that prevailed during that time.

Finance Ministers under Shastri and Indira Gandhi

This kind of mutual understanding or tolerance was missing in the relationship between the other two prime ministers and their finance ministers. Lal Bahadur Shastri's appearance as a mild-mannered leader was quite deceptive. When it came to dealing with economic policy issues or his finance minister, Shastri was quite firm. If Krishnamachari differed with Shastri on the question of devaluation and economic reforms, then the finance minister had to pay the price. That was what saw Krishnamachari quit by the end of December 1965. Shastri's political astuteness was also in evidence when he chose a person like Sachindra Chaudhuri to be the next finance minister. Indeed, Indira Gandhi also decided to have Chaudhuri stay on as her finance minister as there could be no other more understanding and pliable finance minister than he to take on the responsibility of presiding over the devaluation of the Indian rupee by 57 per cent in June 1966—a decision on which he had little say.

Morarji Desai's run with a difficult prime minister does not end with Nehru. When Indira Gandhi won the 1967 general elections and was exploring the options for her Cabinet, she looked to Morarji Desai to be her finance minister. Desai was extremely reluctant, and indeed apprehensive, about joining Indira Gandhi's Cabinet. Eventually, he did join the Cabinet when she agreed to his condition that he be made the deputy prime minister with the responsibility of the finance ministry.

Indira Gandhi as Finance Minister

Desai's tenure as finance minister under Gandhi was stressful. It ended in 1969, when Gandhi decided to divest Desai of the finance ministry and she herself became the finance minister. That ended Desai's second stint as finance minister.

This also marked the beginning of one of India's most dramatic years of economic policy making leading to a political storm. Indira Gandhi stayed as finance minister for less than a year but presided over the nationalization of fourteen private-sector banks, ushering in a new era of socialism and state control over economic activities. But before that decision was taken, there was intense debate and political contestation of the idea of bank nationalization within and outside the ruling party. This was remarkable and reflective of the political environment that prevailed in India those days. She brought in Y.B. Chavan as her successor in the finance ministry in the latter half of 1970. The leftward lurch of economic policy continued under Chavan, who brought about significant amendments to the Foreign Exchange Regulation Act in 1973 and made its provisions even more draconian, and began raising income-tax rates. Chavan's tenure as finance minister coincided with the Indian economy coming under a huge economic burden as a result of the war with Pakistan and the millions of refugees that came from erstwhile East Pakistan. By 1974, the economic situation had got better even though the challenges were still daunting. Chavan was replaced by C. Subramaniam in the latter half of 1974. Thus, it was Subramaniam, who had to steer the government's finances when Indira Gandhi declared internal Emergency in the country suspending all civil liberty laws including the freedom of the media. Budget making during those two years was full of challenges, and how Subramaniam managed those challenges is an eye-opener.

The Role of Finance Minister in a Developing Economy

While describing the work of India's finance ministers during the first thirty years of independent India, this volume also traces how the finance ministry's clout and importance in governance matters increased over the years. The finance minister played a critical role in every major economic policy decision taken by the government. Naturally, over these years, the importance of the finance minister too increased within the government. Even after the formation of the Planning Commission, the finance ministry and the finance minister continued to wield the kind of power within government that few other ministers in the Cabinet would have, particularly in the area of economic policymaking. The notion that finance ministers became more important only in post-reforms India, after 1991, is completely false. The finance ministers of India of the first thirty years following Independence were no less important and powerful than those that came after 1991.

It will be unfair to ignore those finance ministers who had very short tenures in that important position in the Union Cabinet and yet made a significant impact on governance. Thus, the very first section of this volume examines the role of Shanmukham Chetty, the first finance minister of India after Independence. Shanmukham Chetty shepherded the delicate fiscal situation of the country immediately after Independence and Partition.

Equally important was the contribution of John Matthai, who, as finance minister, witnessed his prime minister's gradual accordance of primacy to the state in the economic activities of the nation. But when Nehru decided to set up the Planning Commission, Matthai could not agree with him. Although he was the one who announced Nehru's decision to create the Planning Commission to oversee economic development across the country, he quit the Cabinet immediately afterwards. No less important is the short stint of Sachindra Chaudhuri as finance minister. A decision that had tremendous impact on the economy was taken by him—devaluation of the Indian rupee. Yet, little was known of him before he became the finance minister, and even less after he was replaced by Morarji Desai at the end of the general elections in 1967.

The longest uninterrupted tenure of any finance minister in India after Independence is captured in the third section. C.D. Deshmukh was the country's finance minister for six long years, without a break. He was a retired Indian Civil Services officer and came to North Block after having steered the Reserve Bank of India as its first Indian Governor. Having been a career bureaucrat, he set a precedent to be followed on more than one occasion in the following seven decades.

Deshmukh's entry was as controversial as his stint of six years was eventful. It was under his charge as finance minister that the newly independent country moved towards a new industrial policy and saw the nationalization of a couple of private-sector companies operating in key sectors of the economy. How Deshmukh oversaw all these major changes in economic policy is a fascinating story. While Deshmukh had to quit the government over Nehru's move on reorganization of the Indian states, the relations between the two had not really soured. Over the next few years, Deshmukh would continue to be involved in government projects. Indeed, he was Nehru's choice to be the next managing director of the International Monetary Fund, an offer that Deshmukh declined. But other jobs came his way, like the chairmanship of the University Grants Commission.

Morarji Desai holds a record as a finance minister that is yet to be equalled or surpassed. In his two stints as finance minister, separated by about four years, Desai presented as many as ten Union Budgets, including two Interim Budgets. Desai was finance minister under two different prime ministers—Jawaharlal Nehru and his daughter Indira Gandhi. He was also the first finance minister who became the country's prime minister, a feat repeated by V.P. Singh and Manmohan Singh, several years later.

The economy under Desai's finance-ministership underwent significant transformation. A strict disciplinarian himself, Desai was not very popular as the finance minister. Himself a pro-business person, Desai, however, had a difficult time working under his two prime ministers, who were ideologically not in tune with his views. As a consequence, both his stints ended abruptly, but during the years that he steered the finance ministry, he left an indelible mark on the country's economic policies. This section dwells on those economic policy high points as well as the political low points.

The Idea behind This Volume

The purpose of this volume is to present the economic history of India during the thirty years following Independence through the prism of ten finance ministers, relying significantly on the various Budget speeches they delivered during their tenure. The events unfolding in these pages are largely presented as they were seen from the perspective of these finance ministers. Thus, the volume focuses primarily on how the finance ministers dealt with the major economic policy challenges under the specific political circumstances that prevailed during their time. Understandably, their evaluation of the economy would be substantially influenced by their subjective perspectives and may not always be similar to independent assessments.

A central premise here is that finance ministers do not operate outside the realm of politics. Even though they are influenced by inputs from technocrats and economic counsel from experts, they often have to tailor their decisions in light of the prevailing political reality. The decisions these finance ministers actually took after critically gauging the advice they received provide us material for a comprehensive study of the country's political economy. In some cases, these finance ministers followed the technical advice they received, but in many cases they went by their own political gut, even when they had to sacrifice their job as a consequence.

We also consider the social, economic and political backgrounds of India's finance ministers of those thirty years. Except for Morarji Desai, T.T. Krishnamachari, Y.B. Chavan and C. Subramaniam, none of the others had a huge political following (we do not consider Nehru and Gandhi here as they were prime ministers holding additional charge of the finance ministry). Shanmukham Chetty and Matthai were not even part of the Congress. Deshmukh did not have any political training either, before becoming the finance minister. Sachindra Chaudhuri was a lawyer and a politician, but he was a lightweight. Not surprisingly, therefore, the resignations of Krishnamachari and Desai made a bigger impact on the country's politics than those of Shanmukham Chetty or Matthai.

This volume follows a chronological sequence in outlining how the different finance ministers during the first three decades after India's independence influenced the course of the Indian economy. This chronological sequencing of the narrative will also help present the various issues and economic developments as they unfolded and, therefore, provide a proxy for a contemporary economic history of India after Independence. This is a narrative that relies a lot on anecdotes, sourced from research and interviews. Each segment is self-contained, in the sense that readers will be able to understand the context of developments from each of the individual chapters and sections themselves. The objective is to make India's economic history—through the eyes of its finance ministers—during those thirty years a little more accessible.

R.K. Shanmukham Chetty
(Finance Minister, 1947–1948)

A Victim of a Procedural Lapse

At the age of fifty-five, Sir Ramasamy Chetty Kandasamy Shanmukham Chetty, better known as R.K. Shanmukham Chetty, became the first finance minister of India after it gained independence on 15 August 1947. The choice of Chetty as the finance minister was a surprise, though there were no questions about his competence, given the many responsibilities he had discharged in the national and international arena.

Born in Coimbatore in 1892, Shanmukham Chetty studied economics at Madras Christian College and later joined Madras Law College. But he chose not to take up the legal profession. Instead, he initially joined his family-owned textile business and later embraced politics. He was a member of both the Swaraj Party, a nationalist outfit, and the Justice Party. By 1917, he had become a councillor in the Coimbatore municipality and as its vice-chairman was responsible for bringing about many reforms in its administration. He widened his area of operation by winning the elections in 1920 to become a member of the Madras Presidency legislative council. He quit his council seat two years later.

The Swaraj Party was born in January 1923, following the Congress party's annual session at Gaya in December 1922. Shanmukham Chetty was among the first to join the Swaraj Party, which was a movement that demanded self-governance and political freedom for the Indian people from the British government. About a year later, in 1924, he was elected to the central legislative assembly, and from 1931 to 1935 he served the assembly as its deputy president.

This was also the time when Shanmukham Chetty represented India at international forums. For three years—in 1928, 1929 and 1932—he represented Indian employers at the sessions of the International Labour Conference in Geneva. And he was an Indian delegate at the Imperial Economic Conference held in Ottawa in 1932. The Imperial Economic Conference, also known as the British Empire Economic Conference, was a gathering of representatives of British colonies to deliberate on the implications of the Great Depression of 1930. It adopted the ideas propounded by British economist Lord Maynard Keynes to lower interest rates, increase money supply and expand government spending. Shanmukham Chetty signed the Ottawa Pact at the end of the conference, a decision that could not have pleased the Congress party at home.

At the central legislative assembly, Shanmukham Chetty became its president in 1934, succeeding Sir Ibrahim Rahimtoola. But he had quit the assembly in 1935 after he lost the elections that year. However, the electoral loss did not diminish his public profile. He was appointed as the Diwan of Cochin in 1935, which essentially meant he functioned as its chief minister and stayed in that post till 1941. His six-year tenure was known for the many reforms he brought about, including reorganization of the administrative structure in Cochin for greater efficiency of functioning. He also brought about operational improvements in the running of Cochin Port. Although he was busy with his administrative responsibilities as the Diwan of Cochin, he found time to visit Geneva in 1938 as an Indian delegate to the League of Nations, and later to Bretton Woods in the US in 1944 to attend as India's delegate at the World Monetary Conference, which laid the road map for the setting up of international financial institutions like the World Bank and the International Monetary Fund to rescue the developed world from the economic crisis after the Great Depression and the Second World War. It was around this time that Shanmukham Chetty tried to revive the Justice Party, which operated mainly from Madras Presidency. But he made little progress.

A Multifaceted Personality

Being a multifaceted personality—a lawyer, an economist and a politician—Chetty took upon himself many other responsibilities. He was appointed as constitutional adviser to the Nawab of Bhopal and also served as the president of the Indian Tariff Board. But what eluded him was a position in the Constituent Assembly, perhaps because of his pro-British views and strong links with industry. He had played a key role in the formation of the South India Mills Association, South India Textile Research Association and the Indian Chamber of Commerce and Industry.

Yet, Shanmukham Chetty became finance minister in the first Cabinet that Jawaharlal Nehru formed after Independence. Was he Nehru's choice? Weren't Nehru and indeed Mahatma Gandhi too upset with Shanmukham Chetty for having signed the Ottawa Pact? And what influenced them to opt for a man who was not even a member of the Congress as the country's first finance minister?

Madras Courier, a publication launched in 1785 and which was the first newspaper to be published from the Madras Presidency of British India, remarked that 'Shanmukham Chetty was a brilliant economist', and quoted historian Ramachandra Guha, who described him as 'one of the best financial minds in India', with a 'good record of public service' and a 'great reputation in political life'.[1] Perhaps it was all this that changed Gandhi's and Nehru's attitude towards Chetty. Gandhi was fully convinced that Shanmukham Chetty's understanding of economic matters made him an ideal choice as the finance minister. Nehru agreed to this suggestion from the Father of the Nation.

The other contender for the finance minister's post was John Matthai, who was the finance member for a few months in the interim government before Independence. But Vallabhbhai Patel was not too pleased with Matthai as he had endorsed the Budget proposals presented by Liaqat Ali Khan earlier in the year. The proposals had caused the Gujarat leader a lot of anguish as he believed a few clauses in the Budget had targeted Hindu business leaders from Gujarat in particular. That put paid to any hope of Matthai getting the nod for the finance minister's post. Gandhi's support of Shanmukham Chetty's candidature clinched the issue.

The choice of a non-Congress man as the first finance minister for the newly independent country also reflected the maturity and non-partisan thinking of Gandhi and Nehru. They chose someone they thought was the most qualified for the role, irrespective of his political affiliations or indeed his economic or political views. They needed a man who could represent India on economic policy matters on international platforms with competence and conviction. They needed a man who could settle the pending Partition-related economic disputes with Pakistan. That Shanmukham Chetty was of a different thinking or was a man with British leanings or was not a member of the Congress did not matter. He became India's first finance minister because he was the most capable man at that time. That was a different era!

The First Budget of India

Just three and a half months after India gained independence from British rule, Shanmukham Chetty presented the first Union Budget of the government on 26 November 1947. From a procedural point of view, there was no need for Shanmukham Chetty to present that Budget, with just about four months remaining of that financial year. A Budget for the full financial year of 1947–48 had been approved in March 1947 before India gained independence. It was possible for the nation to have continued with that Budget till March 1948. But there were demands from influential sections within the country that an independent country must operate under a fresh Budget presented and approved by its Parliament. The Budget Shanmukham Chetty presented in November 1947 was thus largely aimed at fulfilling this public demand. Hence, the first Budget did not contain any taxation proposals, which always are and would become a key feature of all Budgets that would be presented in subsequent years.

A good part of the Budget speech was devoted to outlining how India was coping with the consequences of Partition. The need for economic and political adjustments after India was partitioned into two different dominions, as Shanmukham Chetty noted, was of utmost importance. Attributes like 'time, patience, goodwill and mutual understanding to effect the adjustments necessitated by the economic consequences of Partition' would be crucially important. The finance minister even referred to the complementarities between India and Pakistan and underlined the need to exploit them to mutual advantage. While the Partition Council, set up to resolve the differences between the two countries relating to Partition, was on the job, the finance minister also listed out the key areas that still required some mature handling. Chetty said:

Among the important issues on which it has not been possible to reach an agreement, I may mention the allocation of debt between the two Dominions, the method of discharging the pensionary liability, the valuation of the Railways, the division of the assets of the Reserve Bank of India and the division of the movable stores held by the Army.

The Budget played a key role in providing a clear roadmap for the manner in which financial and monetary powers would be enjoyed or shared between India and Pakistan. As far as the existing taxes and duties were concerned, they would continue as before and there would be free movement of trade between India and Pakistan without any border controls even as the import and exchange controls for the two countries would be coordinated by the respective authorities. The Budget also announced that a common currency system, managed by the Reserve Bank of India, would prevail in both India and Pakistan till September 1948. But Pakistan would begin printing currency notes and minting its coins from April 1948 itself. On the crucial question of revenues, Shanmukham Chetty said, '. . . each Dominion will ordinarily retain what it collects but in respect of income tax on assessments for 1946-47 and earlier years and uncollected demands on the date of the Partition, an arrangement for sharing the receipts arising in both the Dominions has been arrived at'. Though the Budget was not playing its traditional role of levying new taxes or raising revenues, it provided the much-needed clarity on how financial and monetary issues between the two newly created countries would be handled.

Shanmukham Chetty's first Budget for the country also lent clarity to the process of planning for reconstitution of the armed forces. The armed forces too had to be divided between the two countries after Partition. Based on the reconstitution plan, the total strength of the pre-Partition army, at 4,10,000 troops, were shared in the following ratio: India got 2,60,000 troops, or about 63 per cent, and Pakistan was allocated the remaining 1,50,000 troops. This was one area where implementation of the reconstitution plan took place much faster than scheduled. This exercise was to be completed by March 1948, but Shanmukham Chetty told the nation at the end of November 1947 that the headquarters of the two Dominions had already taken over the administrative responsibilities of their respective troops. For the British officers in service in pre-Partition India, a new arrangement was put in place. Since the Supreme Commander's Office was to be wound up by the end of December 1947, Shanmukham Chetty announced in his speech that British officers had been serviced a three-month notice with effect from 1 October 1947. Clearly, the Budget was playing a role much larger than the traditional accounting of the government's finances.

The Partition saw millions of refugees cross the newly created borders between India and Pakistan, both on the western and the eastern fronts. The Budget gave a fair idea of the significant financial burden the task of managing and rehabilitating the refugees had imposed on the exchequer. Shanmukham Chetty revealed that the Budget had already earmarked an expenditure of Rs 22 crore for evacuation of and relief for the refugees— an amount which was more than a fifth of the Union government's total civil expenditure that year. The finance minister made it clear that the modalities of sharing the burden of refugee rehabilitation would not come in the way of ensuring that the pain of the displaced people was addressed adequately.

There was, of course, the customary reference to the worrying food availability situation and the rise in the inflation rate. While the country had managed to overcome a serious threat of a breakdown of its food rationing system, the government planned to import more food grain and make it available to people, said the Budget. The interim recommendations of a committee created to examine the food situation in the country had been received by the government, which were being examined for quick implementation. (It was interesting that the committee was headed by industry leader Purshottamdas Thakurdas.) On the price front, the finance minister noted that the inflation index had risen by 7 points between April and August 1947 and that there was a need for improvement in the domestic availability of goods by means of increased domestic production.

Lord Keynes and his expansionary fiscal policies, following which many countries lowered interest rates to sustain demand in their recession-hit economies, also figured in Shanmukham Chetty's Budget speech. Conceding that the Indian authorities had also embraced the easy money policy, Shanmukham Chetty noted the need for keeping a balance between the demands of the government and those of the private sector for undertaking industrial activities when it came to borrowings. Shetty announced:

Our borrowing programme will be such as will enable us to obtain the funds required by the Government as cheaply as possible without in any way affecting the flow of investment into industry. It is also my intention to reorganize the small savings movement, which was considerably expanded during the war years, so that it might be retained as a peacetime organisation with the primary purpose of encouraging savings among the middle classes.

The finance minister also expressed his concern about the rapidly declining sterling balances, which constituted the country's entire foreign exchange reserves at that time. He urged the need for restricting imports, particularly of those commodities that were not essential, and of luxury goods. He announced the government's intention to follow a more restrictive import policy from the second half of 1947 by dividing goods under three categories—free, restricted and prohibited—laying down a template for classifying imports that would be followed for many decades to come. The era of foreign exchange shortages and restrictive import policies had begun.

Like all finance ministers, Shanmukham Chetty was a worried man when it came to the continuing and expanding deficit level in the government finances. For the eighth consecutive year, the government could not avoid a deficit budget. But in the 1947–48 Budget, Shanmukham Chetty showed greater understanding and appreciation of the fiscal deficit. He acknowledged that the uncovered deficit had largely arisen because of higher expenditure on account of the most unusual circumstance of a country having been partitioned and millions of people being displaced from their homes. So he let the uncovered deficit remain as it was and did not make any additional tax mobilization effort to cover it.

The only additional tax effort he made was with respect to export duty on cotton cloth and yarn, which was raised to fetch an additional annual revenue of Rs 8 crore, but which still left a final deficit of Rs 25 crore for the full year.

But looking ahead, Shanmukham Chetty underlined the need for revamping the taxation structure that prevailed in the country. The latest annual report of the Reserve Bank of India had noted that the severity of the last Budget was hindering the formation of capital for productive purposes. Shanmukham Chetty assured the nation that the government had no desire to have a taxation policy that would stifle industrial growth. He gave an assurance that the private sector would have an adequate role to play in India's economic growth in the coming years and promised that before he presented the next annual Budget, he would examine the 'consequences of our taxation policy and endeavour to make any adjustments that may be necessary to instil confidence in private enterprise'.

A Tax Plan to Contain Deficit

In his second Budget, which he presented about three months later, Shanmukham Chetty kept his promise of making the taxation structure more friendly towards the Indian private sector. The Budget was presented just about a month after the tragic assassination of Mahatma Gandhi. Quite ironically, Gandhi's assassination was preceded by his decision to go on an indefinite fast on 13 January 1948 to protest against the stand that Shanmukham Chetty had taken, with the support of Home Minister Vallabhbhai Patail, to hold back the cash balances that were to be transferred to Pakistan. As the fast continued, Shanmukham Chetty and Patel came under pressure to reconsider their stand and released the cash balances to be paid to Pakistan. Gandhi ended his fast on 18 January. Twelve days later, he was shot dead by Nathuram Godse. Appropriately, Shanmukham Chetty's Budget speech on 28 February 1948 began with the paying of respects to the departed leader.

In his Budget, Shanmukham Chetty, however, stayed true to the promise he had made three months ago of unveiling his taxation plan and measures to contain the deficit. In addition, the finance minister also provided a broad outline of the state of the Indian economy. The mass migration of people between West Pakistan and India was posing a big challenge for India. Millions had to be rehabilitated. An estimated Rs 22 crore was provided for this during 1947–48. Chetty also informed Parliament about the successful conclusion of India's financial settlement with Pakistan, which had become a contentious issue.

Adding to the stress on the economy was the food situation, which had worsened, causing anxiety in many regions, including the Madras Presidency, following the failure of the monsoon. Inflation rose as a result, creating another pressure point and underlining the need for increasing domestic production—both industrial and agricultural.

The balance of payments situation also worsened as a result of a sharp rise in imports. Demand for consumer goods, plants and equipment rose as the economy came out of the shadow of the Second World War. And imports of food grain went up as domestic production was not adequate to meet the demand. The finance minister became acutely conscious of the need to increase domestic food production if India's dependence on imports had to come down. Indeed, he concluded that as long as the pressure of food imports was not reduced, the problem of 'an adverse balance of payments and disequilibrium in our economy will persist'. For the short term, however, the foreign exchange accommodation that India received from the United Kingdom would meet the country's external financing needs. But that was temporary, and not a sustainable solution.

In a bid to provide the promised incentives for saving and investment, Shanmukham Chetty's second Budget rolled out a series of taxation changes. He did not withdraw the controversial business profits tax, introduced in March 1947, even though there had been a promise made by the previous finance minister that the new tax would be effective only for a year. But while continuing with it, Chetty allowed abatement at a rate by which the effective incidence of the business profits tax would come down by 10 per cent, thus considerably reducing the burden of that tax on the targeted group.

His second proposal pertained to reduction of the super-tax, both on earned and unearned incomes. Similarly, the tax on undistributed profits for companies was reduced by 6.25 per cent. The income-tax on companies with an income of Rs 25,000 and below was halved so that smaller companies got a boost and encouragement.

Ushering in the idea of taxing foreign companies more than Indian companies for the first time in India after Independence, Chetty raised the corporation tax rate on foreign companies not paying dividends in India from 12.50 per cent to 18.75 per cent. Foreign companies that declared and distributed their dividends in India were to enjoy a rebate of 6.25 per cent. The logic of differential tax rates was simple. The finance minister said:

> Honourable Members are aware that under the law as it stands, we are entitled to recover super-tax on dividends paid by companies incorporated outside this country to their shareholders abroad in respect of their Indian business. For this purpose, it is necessary to ascertain from the companies particulars about their shareholders abroad and

the dividends distributed to them. This information is rarely available in full, with the result that very little of the tax due is collected. It is necessary that some effective arrangement should be made to protect our revenue against this leakage and I think that this can best be done by raising the general rate of Corporation Tax and giving an appropriate rebate on their income to those companies which declare and pay their dividends in India.

On the indirect taxes front, Chetty was fairly conservative. He levied export duties by varying margins on oilseeds, vegetable oils and manganese. Customs duties on motor cars, cigars, cigarettes and manufactured tobacco were raised. And excise duties were increased on tobacco, cigarettes, tea, coffee, vegetable products and tyres.

Chetty's net additional taxes were to mobilize an estimated Rs 27 crore, reducing the overall deficit to about Rs 1 crore only, a big reduction from the deficit of Rs 6.5 crore in 1947–48, which in itself represented a downward revision from the earlier deficit estimate of Rs 24.5 crore.

India's first finance minister was quite cautious about keeping the deficit well within the prudential norms of the day. But his second Budget stood out also because of some of the long-term fiscal policy principles that he laid down in his speech in Parliament. He noted that inflationary pressure on the economy arose out of 'too much money chasing too few goods . . . and there is no indication that a reversal of this trend is in sight'. The Budget surplus, therefore, needed to be achieved in a way that curtailed wasteful spending and created incentives for increasing production. In his vision, the tax burden must be met by reducing expenditure on consumption and not by saving less. 'Similarly, the borrowing made must be from genuine savings and not from inflated bank credit,' he noted, outlining the early contours of fiscal policy for the newly independent country.

Chetty's second Budget also made notable progress in the area of the tax mix in the economy. It became clear that the finance minister had not lost sight of the principle of equity in taxation. The traditional view has been that direct taxes are more equitable, since the taxes are paid by the income earners, depending on their income or profits earned. In contrast, indirect taxes are iniquitous, as the tax burden is borne equally by all at the same rate, irrespective of whether the taxpayer is rich or poor. Shanmukham Chetty noted that in 1937–38, the share of direct taxes in the government's total revenues was only 21 per cent. But for 1948–49, Shanmukham Chetty raised the share of direct taxes in total revenues to almost 51 per cent, which was just short of the 52 per cent direct taxes share of total tax revenues in the United Kingdom. This was a commendable achievement for the finance minister of a country with a relatively poor industrial economy and which was in the early stages of industrialization.

Even with respect to the share of the government's overall debt in the national economy, Shanmukham Chetty was acutely conscious of the need to remain prudent. According to his calculations, the government's total debt was estimated at around Rs 2231 crore, which was less than 50 per cent of the size of the national economy, estimated at about Rs 4500 crore. This was much better than the situation in advanced economies like the United States, where the debt was almost one and a half times the national income; the same debt ratio for the United Kingdom was as high as three times the national income. Chetty also drew comfort from the fact that the government's net interest burden, at Rs 27 crore, was only about 10 per cent of its total anticipated revenue of Rs 257 crore.

The finance minister's purpose in outlining these figures was obvious. Almost at the end of his Budget speech, Shanmukham Chetty said:

> The inference that may legitimately be drawn from these figures is that we could carry even a larger volume of debt and that there is still a large source available here for financing the development of the country. The savings of the community could be mobilized on a very much larger scale for financing productive schemes of development. I appealed earlier in my speech for public cooperation in the borrowing programme of the Government. The picture of our financial position which I have unfolded before this House will, I hope, have a reassuring effect on the public and instill a spirit of confidence all round.

The Sudden End of the Tenure

The tenure of India's first finance minister was very short, just about one year. It was at Mahatma Gandhi's insistence that Nehru had agreed to appoint Shanmukham Chetty as finance minister, even though he had differences with Chetty. When Gandhi was assassinated in January 1948,

Chetty now had to deal with the prime minister without the support he may have indirectly enjoyed from Gandhi. How different Chetty was in his thinking from the Congress leaders could be gauged from a section in the final paragraph of his first Budget speech, delivered just three and a half months after India gained freedom:

> While we have secured freedom from foreign yoke, mainly through the operation of world events, and partly through a unique act of enlightened self-abnegation on behalf of the erstwhile rulers of the country, we have yet to consolidate into one unified whole the many discordant elements in our national life.

No Congress leader could have been pleased with that statement of the government's finance minister, although the spirit of what Shanmukham Chetty said could not be questioned.

But why did Shanmukham Chetty resign just after one year in office, on 17 August 1948? There is lack of clarity on actually how and why the finance minister quit so soon after his appointment. M.O. Mathai, personal assistant to Nehru, wrote in his memoirs that Vallabhbhai Patel, home minister, had persuaded Shanmukham Chetty to

> . . . delete a few names of Gujarati businessmen and industrialists from the list of those who were to be proceeded against on the basis of the findings of the Commission (Income Tax Investigation Commission set up about a year ago). When this became known, there was a furore in Parliament and Patel found himself in a tight corner. He kept quiet and let down the man, who did his bidding and did not lose a wink of sleep in the process. Nehru asked for and received Chetty's resignation.[2]

But there is no corroboration of this account by Mathai elsewhere. Instead, the official records of communication among the three—Nehru, Patel and Chetty—seem to suggest a different sequence of developments leading to the finance minister's resignation. The original cause, of course, had emerged from the same earlier decision, taken around the time of Independence, to set up an Income Tax Investigation Commission to examine cases of income-tax arrears of industrialists. It was headed by Justice Srinivas Varadachariar, who was a former acting chief justice of the

Federal Court of India. Justice Varadachariar accepted the assignment only on the condition that there would be no interference from the executive in the Commission's functioning.[3] But, as subsequent events unfolded, there was a series of controversies that eventually led to the resignation of the finance minister.

The work of the Commission and the manner in which the finance ministry, under the charge of Shanmukham Chetty, was bringing industrialists under the scope of tax investigation had become a bone of contention. As early as on 28 January 1948, Prime Minister Nehru wrote to his home minister and deputy prime minister, Sardar Vallabhbhai Patel, informing him that Finance Minister Shanmukham Chetty had made a suggestion that additional powers should be given to the Income Tax Investigation Commission. Nehru had concurred with his finance minister and informed Patel about it accordingly. 'Otherwise the Commission might as well be wound up. There appeared to be no half-way house,' he wrote. But Patel was not pleased with this approach of Nehru's. While agreeing with the prime minister that such an approach was inevitable, he expressed caution about the whole exercise: 'The cumulative effect would be lack of confidence in the business world.'[4]

The crux of the controversy was that some cases under investigation had been withdrawn by the finance minister just before the government had introduced an amendment to the relevant law making withdrawal of cases subject to approval by the Commission. An additional point of friction arose between Vallabhbhai Patel and Shanmukham Chetty over the manner in which the tax department had begun sending out notices on investigations to industrialists. Patel was already unhappy about the government's inclination to start tax investigations, which industrialists feared would dampen business confidence at a time private investment in the economy had to pick up to increase domestic production and meet shortages.

Dealing with an Unhappy Patel

On 16 July 1948, Patel wrote a long letter to Chetty:

> I am enclosing a copy of a letter which I have received through the post and which purports to have been issued from the office of the Commissioner of Income-Tax, Bombay. You will notice that it

requires preparation of a list of cases for the Income-Tax Investigation Commission as widely as possible. Indeed, some sentences can be construed to mean that, even if some innocent persons are included, it won't much matter and that the Income-Tax officers should err on the side of indiscretion and indiscriminate entries, rather than caution and careful consideration. This sort of procedure is bound to affect the money market and the industrialists, who are already in a somewhat panicky frame of mind due, I regret to say, to some indiscreet remarks of high-placed persons. You are fully aware of our tight monetary position and the shy capital for industrial enterprise. I do not think we can afford to create further lack of confidence, and I would advise you to see that such improper instructions are not issued and that the harassment of innocent persons is avoided. As far as I can see, the intention was to refer the cases to the Investigation Commission after careful scrutiny, and only where it was established to the satisfaction of the Government prima facie that an evasion of tax had taken place. I hope it will be possible for you to set matters right.[5]

Patel was also disturbed by a panic-stricken telegram he had received from leading industrialist Kasturbhai Lalbhai, pleading with the government to not proceed with the proposed amendment in the Income-Tax Investigation Commission Act as it would 'create indefinite successive assessments and will seriously interfere [with] business and industrial enterprises'. Not surprisingly, Patel also informed the prime minister that he had asked the finance minister to take quick corrective action on what he considered high-handed investigative action by the finance ministry's revenue department.

A Procedural Lapse

Eventually, what actually led to Shanmukham Chetty's resignation was not the attack from Patel or the misapprehensions of industry leaders. It was, in fact, a technical point as to whether the finance ministry should have moved for withdrawal of some cases before introducing an amendment bill that would allow such withdrawals only after obtaining the Commission's green signal.

In his explanation to the prime minister on 15 August 1948, Chetty clarified that he had done no wrong. The withdrawal of cases pertained to a period well before the amendment of the law had been mooted. He told Nehru:

> A number of cases had to be sent to the Commission before 31 December 1947, according to the provisions of the Act as it then stood, and there was no time to make a detailed examination as to whether there was a prima facie case in relation to each one of them. It was the intention of the Central Board of Revenue to examine these in detail, and then withdraw such of the cases in which it was found there was no prima facie case. It was as a result of such examination that these groups of cases were withdrawn. However, the cases have now been referred back to the Commission, and the reference has been followed up by a request for withdrawal with the consent of the Commission terms of Section 5 of the Act.[6]

A mild note of complaint and even regret was also evident in the letter Chetty wrote to the prime minister. He told Nehru that the entire procedure followed by him was adopted after obtaining his (Nehru's) 'full concurrence'. Hence, he was surprised that this matter had been brought up once again at the Congress party meeting on 13 August, with some members raising questions on the date of withdrawal of the cases. Shanmukham clarified that oral instructions for withdrawal of the cases were issued on 19 February 1948, after consultation with the chairman of the Central Board of Revenue, although the written order was issued later, on 12 March 1948.

In his letter, Chetty recalled an earlier conversation with the prime minister in which he had argued that such minor procedural issues could become problematic only when the finance minister's bona fides were under doubt. And if the prime minister had any doubts about his integrity, then he should be allowed to tender his resignation. He recalled that the prime minister had assured him then that there were no doubts as to his bona fides and had mentioned that once again before the start of the Congress party meeting on 13 August. But he was surprised by the trend of the discussion at the meeting, and in particular by Nehru's announcement at the end of the meeting that he would like to review the matter and take a decision. In light of this, Shanmukham Chetty ended his letter to the prime minister with these words: 'With a view to enable you to reach a decision without any embarrassment, I herewith place my resignation in your hands.'

A day later, Nehru accepted his resignation. While reiterating that he did not doubt the bona fides of his finance minister, Nehru also explained the logic behind his acceptance of the resignation:

I feel . . . that in the circumstances when you had already sponsored the Bill before the Cabinet, with the express provision that no withdrawal should take place without the consent of the Commission, and this Bill was on the point of being introduced into the Assembly, there should have been no withdrawal without reference to the Commission. In view of the fact that mention was made about the possibility of withdrawals in the Assembly debate, information about the steps already taken should have been placed before the Select Committee of the Assembly. I feel sure myself that this was an error of judgement, and you had not applied your mind to this matter. This error has naturally led many members to think that the ignoring of the Assembly in regard to this particular matter was a discourtesy.[7]

Nehru went on to elaborate further on why he accepted Chetty's resignation:

If this aspect (of discourtesy to the Assembly) had struck you, you would no doubt have informed the Assembly, and referred the withdrawals to the Commission for their consent. It was unfortunate that you had not thought of this at the time, and thus a certain degree of misapprehension has arisen. I have given deep thought to this matter. While there is no question in my mind of your bona fides being challenged, I feel that an error of this type having been committed, it is right, as you yourself have done, that you should place your resignation in my hands. I think you have acted perfectly correctly. As you told me in the course of your talk, you feel yourself that this mistake should not have occurred and that it was essential for us to maintain the highest standards of public conduct in our work. I am sure that my colleagues in the Cabinet as well as the members of the Assembly will appreciate the action you have taken.[8]

Nehru was of course deeply regretful of the manner in which he was letting a highly competent finance minister go. He wrote to Chetty saying:

I am accepting your resignation, but I do so with deep regret. During the year we have worked together in the Government of India, I have admired your ability and your application to the heavy and intricate work that you have had to face. We shall miss you in the Cabinet and in the Government . . . Pending such other arrangements as we might make, you might hand over charge of your portfolio to Neogy (K.C. Neogy was then the minister for relief and rehabilitation in the Cabinet). I am informing him of this.

That is how India's first finance minister lost his job, for discourtesy shown to Parliament and for an error of judgement, but with no mala fide intentions. K.C. Neogy took temporary charge of the finance ministry from 17 August. But by September 20, Nehru had found a replacement in John Matthai, who had agreed to take charge of the finance ministry. For Matthai, the shift from railways to finance was equally eventful.

Ironically, Patel had been keen on Shanmukham Chetty at the time of Nehru forming the first Cabinet after Independence. Not because he had any special preference for him, but primarily because Nehru was reportedly planning to bring in John Matthai as the finance minister. As mentioned earlier, Patel had reservations about Matthai, who had supported the plan of Liaqat Ali Khan, the finance minister in the provisional government before 1947, to set up the Income Tax Investigation Commission. Matthai had even influenced Nehru to agree to the idea of the Commission. Gandhi's idea of appointing Chetty as the finance minister was quickly lapped up by Patel.[9] But, as events in the following year showed, issues pertaining to the same Commission created a rift between Patel and Chetty, leading to the latter's resignation.

After he resigned from the finance ministry, Chetty moved back to Madras and was involved in state politics. He fought the Madras state legislative assembly elections in 1952 and won as an independent candidate. But, with the scar of a scandal having caused his exit from the Union government as the finance minister, Shanmukham Chetty was a deeply disheartened man. He did not live too long after that. On 3 May 1953, he suffered a massive heart attack. He could not fully recover from that and suffered a second attack two days later, on 5 May, to which he succumbed.

John Matthai (Finance Minister, 1948–1950)

The Finance Minister Who Quit over Planning Commission

The invitation from Prime Minister Jawaharlal Nehru to John Matthai on 20 September 1948 to become the finance minister was not the first time that the accomplished economist was being asked to take charge of the government's finances. In 1946, when Nehru had to suggest a few names to be part of the interim government in the run-up to India becoming an independent country, the name of John Matthai had figured among the fourteen ministers that were to take oath to take charge of the ministries. Viceroy Wavell, Nehru and Jinnah . . . all were in favour of Matthai becoming the finance minister in the interim government. However, that stint lasted only about a month. Matthai was sworn in as the finance member (ministers were designated as 'members' in the interim government) on 9 September 1946. But within a month the Muslim League decided to join the interim government, and its representative, Liaquat Ali Khan, became the finance member. However, even during that short stint, Matthai had left his mark as an administrator by quickly abolishing the controversial salt duty, which had become a bone of contention during British rule. After Liaquat Ali Khan took charge of the finance portfolio, Matthai was asked to look after the industries and supplies portfolio in the interim government from 26 October 1946 to 14 August 1947. In the first government formed by Nehru after Independence, Matthai became a Cabinet minister for railways and transport.

In the process, Matthai had lost the opportunity of producing the Budget for the interim government in March 1947. That was presented by Liaquat Ali Khan. It was the same Budget that had mooted the idea of setting up an Income Tax Investigation Commission to probe cases of tax evasion by companies. Matthai played a role in this, even though he was not the finance member. Viceroy Wavell had mandated that the Budget proposals would be vetted by a committee consisting of himself, Liaquat Ali Khan, Nehru and Matthai. But that did not prevent an outcry against the Budget proposals, particularly from Congress members, led, among others, by Vallabhbhai Patel. Congress members alleged that the proposal was primarily aimed at Hindu business leaders. And their target of attack was John Matthai, because he was among those who had approved the proposal when it came up for review by the committee headed by Wavell.

Matthai Takes Charge as Finance Minister

For leaders like Matthai, opportunities knock at their door not just once but several times. That is exactly what happened in September 1948 after Chetty quit suddenly after the controversy over the manner in which some names to be probed by the Income Tax Investigation Commission had been withdrawn by the finance ministry. The irony for Patel was that the man whose appointment as finance minister was opposed by him just about fourteen months ago was back in the reckoning. As far as Nehru was concerned, he was getting the man he had originally wanted as his finance minister.

Born on 10 January 1886, John Matthai hailed from a well-to-do and widely respected Syrian Christian family based in Travancore. A brilliant student, he graduated from Madras Christian College and also completed his law degree from Madras Law College before he went to Oxford for higher education. He completed his doctoral research at the London School of Economics, specializing in the cooperative movement and village government in British India. But before he went to Oxford for higher studies, he had practised as a lawyer in India for about four years. On his return to India, he joined the Madras government in 1918 to serve in its cooperative department as an officer on special duty for about two years. Subsequently, he took to teaching, and taught economics at Presidency College. He remained in government service till 1940 in different capacities, such as member and chairman of the Tariff Board, and later as the director-general of Commercial Intelligence and Statistics. In 1940, he also worked for the private sector as a director with the Tata group and had been in charge of Tata Chemicals for about two years.

Matthai was one of the authors of the famous Bombay Plan that had laid out the investment programme and policy priorities that India must adopt after Independence. The two-part document—'A Brief Memorandum Outlining a Plan of Economic Development for India'— was brought out in 1944–45 and was produced by Matthai and seven other leading industrialists and bankers of the day. They were J.R.D. Tata, Ghanshyam Das Birla, Ardeshir Dalal, Lala Shri Ram, Kasturbhai Lalbhai, Ardeshir Darabshaw Shroff and Purshottamdas Thakurdas. When the British government offered Matthai a place in the executive council as a finance member of the interim government, it was appointing not just a well-regarded economist, teacher and administrator, but also a man with a clear vision for India's economic development.

The economy Matthai inherited when he took charge of the finance ministry in September 1948, was not in good shape. The adverse effects of the Second World War and Partition were still troubling the economy. Inflation was on the rise and India had to rely on higher food imports, which created stress for the country's foreign exchange reserves or its sterling balances. Owing to the failure of crops in India because of poor rains, food imports had risen—from about 2 million tonnes, at Rs 110 crore, in 1947–48 to 2.8 million tonnes in 1948–49, at Rs 130 crore. Floods in Bihar and the United Provinces (erstwhile Uttar Pradesh), cyclone damages in Bombay and outbreak of famine in parts of Gujarat, Saurashtra, Rajasthan and Kutch were threatening to push up the demand for food imports to almost 4 million tonnes in 1949–50. The state of the capital market also worried the new finance minister. The investment market in the country remained stagnant, with little money flowing into either government loans or industrial projects. This was a consequence of the mood of uncertainty that prevailed in the economy, which in turn adversely affected industrial development and its prospects.

The Challenge of Sterling Balances

What caused more concern to Matthai as he took charge of the government's finances was the rapidly declining sterling balances held by the Reserve Bank of India. They had risen to a peak level of Rs 1733 crore at the end of March 1946, only to fall to Rs 1612 crore by the end of March 1947, and further to Rs 1545 crore by the end of March 1948. The reduction was largely a result of an increase in imports of food and other goods. But the pace of the reduction had slowed in 1947–48 because of restrictions on imports.

In July 1948, India entered into an agreement with the United Kingdom whereby an estimated 80 million pound sterling was credited to India, which it could use to finance imports till June 1951. Consequently, Matthai could relax some of the import controls. Similarly, a currency agreement between India and Pakistan in July 1948 facilitated settlement of bilateral trade payments beyond a certain limit in pound sterling. These were developments that made Matthai's task as finance minister a little less onerous.

By October 1948, Matthai had introduced anti-inflationary measures which had a positive impact on the price situation. In a bid to prevent further creation of purchasing power in the hands of consumers, the newly appointed finance minister imposed higher import duties on articles of luxury, such as liquor, tobacco, motor cars, silk and art silk fabrics. In addition, an excise duty on superfine cloth was levied. The government assumed additional powers to make provisional assessment of income tax on the basis of returns submitted by assesses. Matthai also revived a scheme for interest-bearing deposits for income tax—a system that had been introduced in 1943. Refund of deposits of excess profits tax was postponed for a further period of three years, except for a few approved purposes. A temporary limit was imposed on the amount that could be distributed as dividend by public companies. All these measures were taken to clamp down on prices. Indeed, inflation came under control in the first few months of these measures. However, by the time Matthai was ready to present the Budget on 28 February 1949, inflation had begun to inch up once again.

While controlling inflation was a priority for Matthai, revival of the industrial investment climate in the country was no less a concern for him. The finance minister believed that as important as controlling inflation was the need to augment domestic supplies of goods, for which boosting production in the economy was necessary. Thus, there was a reduction in import duties on machinery and a few industrial raw materials. And import duty on cotton yarn was abolished. New industrial undertakings commencing production in the next three years were exempted from income tax for five years up to a limit of 6 per cent per annum on their capital, and depreciation allowance rules were liberalized. Expenditure schemes meant for the provinces and states were expedited so that they could help meet the demand for goods within the country.

Government finances during the year were also kept under a tight leash by Matthai. The relaxation in imports had meant a sharp jump in customs revenue. But this increase in revenues was set off by a rise in expenditure on both the defence and civil fronts. While defence expenditure rose because of the need for the Indian Army's presence and continued operations in Kashmir, civil expenditure went up as a result of the country having to meet its pre-Partition liabilities, for which no provision had been made earlier. The country had to spend more on relief and rehabilitation of refugees. In spite of that, the revised deficit for 1948–49 was only Rs 1.55 crore, lower than the earlier Budget estimate of Rs 2.14 crore.

Matthai's First Budget

It was against the backdrop of such an economic situation that Matthai presented his first Budget to the central legislative assembly on 28 February 1949. Quite ironically, Matthai devoted quite a few paragraphs of his Budget speech on the work undertaken by the Income Tax Investigation Commission, which had figured prominently in the controversial developments that led to the sudden resignation of Matthai's predecessor, Shanmukham Chetty. Matthai recalled that the Commission had the twin responsibilities of examining the income-tax laws and its effectiveness in preventing evasion, and of investigating specific cases of tax evasion referred to it by the government. The first responsibility, Matthai said, had been discharged by the Commission, whose report and recommendations were going to be the basis for further reforms in the income-tax legislation, a bill to which effect would be presented before the House at its next session. With regard to its responsibility of investigating specific cases of tax evasion, Matthai conceded that work in this area had got delayed a bit because of infrastructural constraints, including a shortage of officers who could be assigned such duties. The delay was also due to the realization of the Commission that sufficient care and advance preparatory work must precede investigations into alleged evasion of taxes. At the same time, Matthai made a proposal that favoured settling of tax evasion cases. 'In this connection I may add that the possibility of disposing of the referred cases by agreed settlement is being explored, and a bill will shortly be placed before the House for vesting the necessary powers for making such settlements in the hands of the Commission,' Matthai said. It was clear that Matthai was trying to resolve the problem that his predecessor, Shanmukham Chetty had created and as a result of which he had to quit as finance minister.

For 1949–50, Matthai proposed a Budget that envisaged a marginal cut in the government's total expenditure from what was spent in 1948–49. That move in itself was bold. In line with what his immediate predecessor had done, Matthai made sure that the allocation for defence was substantial. Indeed, defence accounted for almost half the government's total expenditure of Rs 322 crore in 1949–50. Over the years, the share of defence in the government's total expenditure would keep declining. A little over seven decades later, the total spending on defence by the government would account for just about 10 per cent of its total expenditure outlay.

But Matthai was, understandably, defensive about his defence outlay, which saw a small increase in 1949–50 and continued to be a very large 48 per cent of total government expenditure. He was defensive because there was a cease fire in the hostilities in Kashmir by that time. Anticipating adverse reactions from members of the House, Matthai justified the outlay on the ground that the operations in Kashmir were still going on and there was need for increasing the country's preparedness in defending its borders. In addition, he justified the large outlay and the increase on the ground that the government had approved a ten-year plan for the Indian Navy to improve its capabilities and training facilities for its personnel. In contrast, Matthai's outlay for the civil departments was mainly focused on continued provisions for relief and rehabilitation of refugees, loans to provincial governments and adequate allocation for food subsidy.

A key initiative unveiled by Matthai in his first Budget was the plan to set up a telephone factory and a shipping company in the government sector, for which budget allocations were made.

An Economist FM

As an economist finance minister, Matthai did not disappoint members of the House in sharing with them his wisdom on managing the economy in a crisis situation. On fiscal policy, Matthai outlined his broad principle in a succinct way: 'Fiscal policy is not an end in itself but has to subserve the ends of national policy and in a transitional period like this it is essential to keep the working of the taxation system under constant review and readjust it in the light of changing circumstances.' Matthai was also quite categorical about the role that savings and investment played in an economic revival. Without creating the conditions that incentivize savings and investment, the goals of industrial expansion and execution of development projects to raise the living standards of the people cannot be achieved, he said.

It was in that context that Matthai framed his taxation proposals, which provided a strong dose of reliefs in the form of three tax policy changes. His first big proposal was to abolish capital gains tax. He argued that the tax, when introduced, was expected to garner substantial revenues for the government. But the record of collections of capital gains tax was quite poor. So it was abolished in order to create a positive 'psychological effect on investment' and encourage free movement of stocks and shares, without which, he believed, a high level of industrial development could not be maintained. Two, he reduced the income-tax on the lowest and medium income-earning individuals as he argued that this class of taxpayers had been severely hit by inflation. Three, he reduced the super-tax rates on both earned income and unearned income by varying rates.

Matthai also modified two of the proposals that his immediate predecessor had introduced in his last Budget. He retained the tax concession that Shanmukham Chetty had provided to small companies, but he converted that into a rebate in the corporation tax, limiting it to public-controlled small companies that were not branches or subsidiaries of bigger companies. This was aimed at plugging a loophole in the earlier concession and at the same time sparing the states from any revenue loss arising out of the relief. The second Chetty proposal he modified was the taxing of foreign companies which were not distributing dividends to shareholders in India. In the modified form, privately controlled companies that did not distribute their profits in India would have to pay additional super-tax at the rate of 6.25 per cent. In order to simplify the taxation rules,

Matthai also changed the depreciation norms for claiming tax benefits. By way of relief on the indirect taxation front, Matthai withdrew the earlier export levies on oilseeds and vegetable oils and offered customs duty relief on several raw materials imported by industry.

What upset the common people of the country was Matthai's proposals to steeply increase the tariff on postal services. He came under severe attack from the government benches in Parliament. However, other indirect tax increases, like higher customs duties on liquor, fabrics containing silk, cutlery, metal furniture, motor spirit, and higher excise on petroleum products, tyres and cotton cloth, did not face any such opposition. With these proposals, Matthai projected a Budget for 1949–50 with a small surplus of Rs 45 lakh.

His final message to the country was one of optimism. He believed that the government's finances were sound, in spite of the challenges of inflation, food security and foreign exchange availability. Matthai said with an unconcealed sense of achievement and even pride:

> We have only a moderate public debt in relation to our national income and we have considerable external reserves with practically no external debt. We have weathered the storm and stress of the Partition and its terrible aftermath. In spite of the heavy demands on our resources for the relief and rehabilitation of refugees, the import of food on an unprecedented scale from overseas and the defence of Kashmir against aggression, we are in a position to balance our budget, without sacrificing any of our essential schemes of development.

India's First Big Currency Devaluation

Before he could present his second Budget, Matthai found himself in the middle of a major policy change with regard to the exchange rate of the rupee. The Indian rupee had to be devalued against the pound sterling. That took place on 16 September 1949. But discussions on the need for devaluation began about four months earlier, in May that year. Countries in the Sterling Area had been experiencing a heavy outgo of their dollar resources, and this led to a conference of Commonwealth finance ministers in London in July to discuss the steps to be taken to increase these countries' dollar resources and also reduce their dollar expenditure. The Sterling Area included the United Kingdom and about twenty countries that were part of the Commonwealth (except Canada). The countries belonging to the Sterling Area would keep their exchange reserves with the Bank of England, and by virtue of that would have access to the capital and money markets in London.[1] India was one of the Sterling Area countries. The London conference had prepared the basis for a discussion between the British Chancellor of the Exchequer and the US Treasury Secretary to discuss how dollar resources of Commonwealth countries could be increased. The agenda for the discussion, to be held in September, however, had no mention of devaluation. India's finance minister at that time, Shanmukham Chetty, did not attend the meeting, as no Commonwealth country's finance minister was required to be present. Instead of Chetty, the Washington meeting had an Indian representative— C.D. Deshmukh, who at that time was India's financial ambassador— taking part in the meeting. Deshmukh had completed his long tenure as Governor of the Reserve Bank of India at the end of June 1949. But soon thereafter, he was asked by Finance Minister John Matthai to become India's roving ambassador to help India deal with its financial negotiations with Western countries like the US and the UK.

Even while the World Bank and the International Monetary Fund were holding their annual meeting at Washington, Prime Minister Jawaharlal Nehru received a message from his British counterpart in the afternoon of 16 September 1949. That message was about the decision to devalue the pound sterling by about 30 per cent to $2.8 against one pound sterling. This would have an obvious impact on the Indian rupee, which was linked to the British currency. Nehru passed on the devaluation message to Matthai. Meanwhile, RBI Governor Benegal Rama Rau, who was in Washington attending the Fund-Bank annual meeting, cut short his stay there and left for New Delhi to explain to the Indian government the background of the devaluation. Nehru had convened a Cabinet meeting to discuss the decision that India must take to devalue the rupee in line with the sterling devaluation. The Cabinet meeting was scheduled to be held at 10 p.m. on 16 September so that Rama Rau, who was to land in New Delhi at 8 p.m., could brief the ministers about the developments in Washington. But his plane reached New Delhi late and the Cabinet discussed the matter without Rama Rau's briefing and decided to devalue the Indian rupee by a margin equivalent to the devaluation of the British pound.[2] Consequently, the Indian rupee was down to Rs 4.7 against the US dollar.

Finance Minister Matthai was aware of the international developments that preceded the devaluation of the pound sterling. Hence, he had got the entire issue examined in detail by technical advisers in the finance ministry as also in the Reserve Bank of India. Almost three-fourths of India's exports would be to markets falling under the Sterling Area. If the value of the rupee was not suitably adjusted following the devaluation of the pound sterling by a corresponding margin, India's exports to the Sterling Area countries would be severely hit as they would have become more expensive. India's foreign exchange situation would have become more vulnerable. For about two days, the issue of devaluing the Indian currency against the pound sterling was debated, and finally the decision was to go for it.[3] A comment reportedly made by Matthai on the question of devaluation captured the inevitability of what the Indian government did: 'I feel that in this matter I have had to act not on conviction born of logic necessarily, but so to speak, by the compulsion of events.'[4]

In Parliament, devaluation of the Indian rupee figured prominently. Matthai explained to the members the likely effects of the devaluation, although he cautioned that there were many uncertain factors and nothing definitive could be stated about the outcome of the currency adjustment. He also clarified that the bulk of India's exports to the US consisted of jute goods and tea, whose demand was inelastic to price changes. No sharp increase in exports of these products to the US was likely, even though Indian exports in general to dollar countries would become more competitive. The finance minister, however, told the Indian Parliament that in general terms the devaluation would encourage investment and provide protection to domestic industries as imports would become costlier. He also allayed fears of inflation rising during that year, since food imports from the US had already taken place. But there would be some adverse impact on prices of industrial raw materials that would still be imported from the US and whose landed costs would go up after the devaluation. Some members of Parliament criticized the devaluation move, but Matthai's explanation helped clear their doubts.

A couple of weeks after the devaluation, inflation did threaten to upset the government's economic planning. That was in October 1949. Matthai lost no time in unveiling a series of steps as a result of which inflation between October 1949 and January 1950 remained unchanged. Indeed, a benign level of inflation even weeks after the devaluation was a significant achievement for Matthai as India was among the very few countries where inflation remained under control in spite of the devaluation of its currency. The United Kingdom, for instance, saw a significant rise in prices in the same period. But this price situation in India did not last long. Inflation began rising again from February, largely because of an upward movement in the prices of industrial raw materials, triggered as it was by a global upturn in the commodity cycle. Not surprisingly, the finance minister had to refocus his energies once again to keep prices under check.

A politically tricky issue surfaced after Pakistan decided not to devalue its currency against the pound sterling, even though it was part of the Sterling Area. As a result, the Pakistani rupee became stronger than the Indian rupee. 'No one could politically stand this affront, not even an otherwise sensible person like Sardar Patel. He started, quite unnecessarily, an unprovoked economic attack on Pakistan by raising the price of coal,' S. Bhoothalingam, who was then a senior officer in the government, wrote in his memoirs.[5] Pakistan was deeply upset and retaliated against the Indian move. Pakistan was reported to have told India that even if it had to pay double the price, it would buy coal from Poland. How irrelevant and meaningless nationalistic jingoism can appear when economic policies are not framed on economic grounds became obvious in that scrap between India and Pakistan over the pricing of coal.

The question of Pakistan's approach to devaluation figured even in Matthai's Budget speech. The finance minister did not mince words when he remarked that Pakistan's decision to not devalue its currency in spite of remaining in the Sterling Area was an anomaly. His assessment of the situation made it clear that, whatever exchange rate the International Monetary Fund may fix for the Pakistani rupee, there were no early prospects of a revival in trade between India and Pakistan unless the latter's currency's exchange rate reflected the 'facts of the economic situation'.

Matthai's Second Budget

The unique feature of Matthai's second Budget was his speech, which was delivered extempore. There was no written speech he read out from. No other finance minister in independent India has ever delivered a

Budget speech that is not from a written text. Matthai's record remains unequalled even after more than seven decades of Budget-making at the Centre. Matthai's second Budget also stood out because it was the first Budget presented after the adoption of the Indian Constitution. And because the Budget was presented soon after India became a Republic, Matthai made some important announcements to provide a governance framework for evaluating the government's financial performance. He announced the government's intention to request the House to set up an Estimates Committee to 'scrutinize the expenditure of each department of government and of the government as a whole'. At the same time, Matthai also assured the House that the practice of having the Standing Finance Committee to evaluate the specific proposals of expenditure of each department of the government would continue. The proposed Estimates Committee would be focused mainly on undertaking a comprehensive examination of expenditures in relation to the resources available to the government.

Matthai's second Budget was presented on 28 February 1950. In the Budget's overall review of the economy, Matthai drew attention to the fact that the state of the Indian economy continued to pose many challenges. He conceded that the country still faced difficult problems, but he also exuded quiet optimism, adding that 'we have now been able to take the measure of these problems and, if there are problems in front of us, they are problems which would not be beyond the ability of Government to meet and to solve in due course'. His confidence was also evident when he explained the spectre of inflation haunting the Indian economy in the global context. He attributed the latest bout of price rise to international developments and even noted with concern how the world was a little apprehensive about the outbreak of another war, which could once again fuel a broad-based price rise.

Matthai argued before Parliament that the problem of inflation was attributable to the critical question of production. If production could be increased to augment availability of products, the pressure of inflation would be that much less. In this respect, he identified two industries— cotton and raw jute. 'In both these cases, the limiting factor in the matter of production is the supply of raw material, particularly as the result of the deadlock that has arisen in the trade between us and Pakistan,' he said. The government's response to this challenge was to arrange for higher imports of cotton and to initiate steps to augment domestic production of raw jute. On the food grain availability front as well, the finance minister sounded optimistic as he announced that the estimated production, higher than in the previous year, and the higher procurement still left a lot more to be desired, but there was no cause for concern either. While the railways had improved its performance in haulage of goods, the climate on the industrial relations front had become better with a sound relationship between labour and capital, Matthai said.

On the critical question of the country's balance of payments situation, the finance minister addressed the general concern about the recent relaxations in import norms that had also adversely affected the country's foreign exchange reserves, while justifying the need for keeping import options open to help meet the domestic demand for goods and articles. On consumption, Matthai also noted that imports also provided a source of customs revenue for the government, which it needed to finance its expenditure and reduce the deficit level. In any case, he told members of the House that the country's sterling balances had improved steadily in the last seven and a half months. But this was a temporary relief and there was an urgent need to encourage more exports to build on the existing situation. 'A healthy balance is the sort of balance that you attain at the highest possible level of imports as well as exports,' he said.

Reflecting on the financial sector, the finance minister presented a mixed picture. After a marked fall in bank deposits, as compared to advances, in the first half of 1949, the ratio improved in the second half, but Matthai did not draw comfort from this. But what gave him reasons to feel happy was the improvement in the industrial investment sentiment, which was buoyant for the first time since 1949. He used this opportunity to enunciate the government's policy approach to foreign capital. Both by way of foreign direct investment and foreign portfolio investment in the stock market, Matthai made it clear that India would be open to such flows. He underlined the need for creating reasonable conditions of security and fair treatment for those who were willing to risk their investments in India:

I would like to make just this brief proposition that any considerable assistance in the way of capital from foreign countries must hereafter be looked for not in the shape of fixed interest-bearing loans and bonds, but in the shape of equity capital on the basis of joint participation on strict business considerations without any political strings attached to it.

This was perhaps the first clarion call from a senior minister in the government inviting foreign investment to India after Independence. He referred to a statement that Jawaharlal Nehru had made a year ago inviting foreign investors to the country and said: 'The statement that the Prime Minister made last year still represents our policy in this matter and I believe that the terms and conditions outlined in that statement ought to provide reasonable security for foreign investors.'

The finance minister also provided further relief to Indian companies in a bid to improve the investment climate. Referring to the Dividend Limitation Act, which was to remain in force for an extended period up to March 1951, Matthai said there was no need to extend this law any more. The three reasons he cited in support of his decision were indicative of his approach to businesses that were creating wealth: One, the law had become practically ineffective because profits of companies had fallen significantly obviating the need for declaring dividends in many cases. Two, the law failed to make any impact as an anti-inflationary tool. Three, the provisions of the law had a 'disproportionately depressing effect on the investment market'.

With regard to fresh taxation in the second Budget, Matthai was in a truly generous mood. He had already slashed excise duty on cotton piece-goods, and now in the Budget he decided to undo some of the increases he had introduced a year ago in the postal rates, for which he had incurred the wrath of members of the House and the people in general. The rates for both postal and telephone services were reduced. In direct taxes as well, he abolished the business profits tax which was introduced three years ago and whose revenue was steadily falling. The maximum rate of income tax on individuals was cut from 31.25 per cent to 25 per cent and the rates on lower slabs too were reduced by almost similar margins. The tax exemption limit for an undivided family was further raised. The corporation tax was raised by a small margin, but its effect was neutralized by a reduction in the maximum income tax rate. The distinction between earned and unearned income for levy of the super-tax was abolished and the maximum super-tax rate too was reduced from the earlier range of 56.25–62.5 per cent to 53.12 per cent, to be levied only on annual income above Rs 1.21 lakh.

In spite of the munificent tax giveaways amounting to a revenue outgo of Rs 8 crore for the Centre alone, the Budget for 1950–51 had projected a surplus of Rs 1.31 crore. Indeed, Matthai conceded that he should have ideally gone in for a more fundamental reform in the taxation structure. But he chose to refrain from doing that because the Indian economy was going through a period of transition and the government did not have adequate data based on which such reforms could be initiated. Hence, he announced the government's decision to set up a committee to 'inquire into the whole question of national income and its distribution'. A six-member committee, including three distinguished economists and statisticians from India and three foreign advisers, was expected to give its report by the end of 1950, based on which the government could reform its taxation system. Matthai was not the finance minister when this committee submitted its report. Even the task of finalizing the details of the composition of the committee and of implementing its recommendations were left to the next finance minister, C.D. Deshmukh.

Setting up the Planning Commission

The biggest announcement Matthai made in his Budget by way of its impact on the country and also on his own future pertained to the government decision to set up the Planning Commission. Matthai referred to an announcement that President Rajendra Prasad had made to this effect earlier in 1950, in his address at the start of the Budget session of Parliament. Matthai expanded on that announcement and provided the rationale behind the decision to set up the Planning Commission. He said:

> It is necessary to undertake a review of our existing programme of development and our existing schemes of production. The geographical and economic facts on which the present programme is based no longer hold good, the estimate of financial resources on which the existing programme is based is no longer valid, and public opinion rightly demands a different kind of approach to the whole problem of development.

Significantly, it was Matthai who announced the composition of the Planning Commission. Prime Minister Jawaharlal Nehru was to be the chairman and Gulzari Lal Nanda, who was at that time the labour minister in the Bombay government, the deputy chairman. The other members of the proposed body were: C.D. Deshmukh, former RBI Governor and India's financial ambassador; Gaganvihari Lal Mehta, president of the Indian Tariff Board; R.K. Patel, Food Commissioner of the Indian government; and a fourth member yet to be named. Cabinet Secretary N.R. Pillai was to function as the Secretary of the Commission. The striking element in the composition of the Commission, announced by Matthai in his Budget speech, was that he himself was not a member of this body. Any apex body like the Planning Commission, which would review and chart out the course of economic development programmes for the country, could not function effectively without the finance minister as a member. Yet, Matthai chose not to have the finance minister as a member of the Planning Commission. This was a clear indication of Matthai's serious differences with the prime minister's idea of creating a Planning Commission for India; it was also a move that eventually led to his resignation within months of presentation of his second Budget.

Taking part in a debate in Parliament on the proposed Planning Commisssion less than a month after the Budget, Matthai highlighted the key goals that the new body was expected to achieve: Reappraisal of the economic factors behind planning, determination of the order of priority in which various plans under execution should be implemented, and assessment of the role the state should play in the country's economic development.

But the bone of contention related to the powers and jurisdiction the Planning Commission would have over the government's economic policies. These were Mathai's views on it:

> . . . the Planning Commission is to be primarily an advisory body. It would work in very close touch with the relevant ministries of the Government of India . . . But ultimately, when plans emerge from their discussions, those plans would be in the nature of recommendations to the Government of India. No Government, no Cabinet, could divest itself of its ultimate responsibility for putting proposals of this kind through; but I have not the slightest doubt that although their position technically is that of an advisory body, the Planning Commission would necessarily carry a great deal of weight with the Government of India.[6]

That is what Matthai had feared. He was of the view that policies should be framed or reviewed not by politicians or advisers but by experts and professionals on the basis of data and statistics-based studies. He was also opposed to the idea of the Commission because at that point in time, the country, in his view, needed to be focused on addressing the immediate economic difficulties instead of debating on what kind of planning should be undertaken for the future. 'He was also against the composition of the Planning Commission and was concerned with the authority given to it. He had the apprehension that the Commission might become the fifth wheel of the coach,' wrote his biographer V. Haridasan.[7] Matthai had wanted the Planning Commission as a body of experts whose advice the government would be free to reject. But the finance minister also knew that Nehru, keen as he was on industrial development in the state-owned sector, would be using the Planning Commission as an instrument with which to reduce the importance of the private-sector industry. 'Matthai was certain that the Planning Commission and the Cabinet Economic Committee (of which Nehru at that time was not a member) would be in conflict with the Finance Ministry,' wrote Sarvepalli Gopal, eminent historian and biographer of Nehru.[8]

Nehru, on the other hand, believed that the country's governance structure needed a coordinating body as different provinces were increasingly functioning in their own separate ways as far as the goal of economic development was concerned. Portions of a letter, cited by Nehru's biographer Sarvepalli Gopal in the second volume of *Jawaharlal Nehru: A Biography*, reveals a lot of about the prime minister's thinking in this context:

We may make mistakes and pay for them but surely the greatest mistake is not to view the whole scheme of things in its entirety, realistically and objectively, and to decide on clear objectives and plans. If once this is done, the next step of complete coordination follows much more easily and only by coordinated effort can real results be achieved.[9]

This created a rift between Prime Minister Nehru and Finance Minister Matthai. The differences between the two got wider and, according to Sarvepalli Gopal, they 'spread to other areas and even affected their personal relations'. In one of his letters, Nehru went as far as declaring that he 'was somewhat of a political missionary responsive to the masses and ready for action in their interest in contrast to men such as Matthai, who had spent their lives in offices irrespective of whether the Government was British or Indian'.[10] By early June 1950, less than four months after he had presented his second Budget, Matthai made public his decision to resign as the finance minister.

Matthai's letter of resignation was quite frank and forthright. He wrote:

> As regards working out the technical details of existing plans, it is obvious that a Commission like the present is not competent to handle the work involved. Our great need today is to decide in what order of priority the existing plans should be taken in hand and place them technically on a basis, which would enable them to be carried out. As I said, for neither of these purposes is the present Commission likely to be useful . . . I have objected not merely to the idea of a Planning Commission, but also to its methods of working. The main reason urged for setting up a Planning Commission was that the Government was pre-occupied with day-to-day administration and therefore had little leisure for thinking and planning ahead. But in the way things are working out today, the Planning Commission has been asking for a voice in the discussion of current economic problems and has, in fact, with the approval of the Prime Minister, been associated with the Cabinet in these discussions. The result is, first that the Commission tends to become a parallel Cabinet and secondly, it increases the area of argumentation and discussion inside the Government and makes for delay in arriving at decisions on immediate problems. In my opinion Cabinet responsibility has definitely weakened since the establishment of the Planning Commission. For these reasons I consider the Planning Commission not merely ill-timed, but in its working and general set-up ill-conceived.[11]

According to to S. Bhoothalingam, an ICS officer in the government at the time, Matthai's resignation letter lay with Nehru for about three or four months, pending action. Bhoothalingam wrote about it in his memoirs, *Reflections on An Era:*[12] .

> Nehru just ignored it and merely smiled it away at Cabinet meetings. Matthai himself told me that this was Nehru's method of ignoring the resignation. He was just becoming reconciled to continuing as Finance

Minister, having honourably made his protest, when to his surprise, he got a letter from Nehru accepting his resignation.'

Thus, there was an element of surprise and suddenness in the way Matthai's resignation was accepted at the end of May 1950.

That was how the short tenure of India's second finance minister ended. The tenure of the first finance minister was only about a year. The tenure of the second finance minister, John Matthai, was a little longer, at a little less than two years. The first three years of the Nehru government had already seen two finance ministers. Even as Nehru was zeroing in on C.D. Deshmukh as the next finance minister, the talk within the Congress and the government was on how long the tenure of his third finance minister would be.

C.D. Deshmukh (Finance Minister, 1950–1956)

A Former RBI Governor Steers the Economy

On 23 May 1946, Lord Wavell, Viceroy of British India, sent a brief note marked 'secret and personal' to Chintaman Dwarakanath Deshmukh, who at the time had already spent three years as the first Indian Governor of the Reserve Bank of India (RBI). The note explored the possibility of Deshmukh, an ICS officer, joining the interim government that the British wanted to establish before transferring power to the Indians. The letter said:

> Dear Sir Chintaman: I think there is a possibility that I may invite you to become Finance Member in the new Executive Council. The decision will of course depend to a considerable extent on the reactions of the parties, but I should like to know whether you yourself would be able to accept an invitation. I realise that it may entail some sacrifice on your part, but I am sure that India would benefit. Perhaps you would think this over and let me know as soon as possible.[1]

Deshmukh had enjoyed an illustrious career all through his working life as an ICS officer, having steered the finance department in the government of the Central Provinces and Berar under British India and then spending some time as the Deputy Governor in the RBI before being selected to head the central bank—a rare honour for an Indian in those days. Lord Wavell's offer now opened up a new opportunity for Deshmukh—to oversee the finances of the top political decision-making body in the run-up to the country's gaining independence from British rule. The Viceroy's executive council was to be the executive arm of the interim government that would facilitate governance in India before the country gained independence.

To be sure, the 'secret and personal' letter from Lord Wavell did not come to Deshmukh as a surprise. His name as one of the members of the interim government was doing the rounds and he was not unaware of this. More than ten months before Deshmukh received that short note from Wavell, he got to know of the government's deliberations to shift him from Bombay to New Delhi to be part of the executive council of the interim government.

A top-secret letter dated 3 July 1945 was dispatched by a Deputy Secretary in the finance ministry to Deshmukh. The broad message of that missive was that Deshmukh was one of those favoured to be the finance member (equivalent to the finance minister) in the interim government. V.P. Menon, who was then the Reforms Commissioner to Wavell, had endorsed the idea of getting Deshmukh as a finance member on a temporary assignment. Once a 'suitable non-official'[2] was identified, Deshmukh could go back to Bombay and resume his role as Governor of the RBI.

This plan, however, turned out to be stillborn. There were uncertainties over whether the plan would ever see the light of day. What's more, C. Rajagopalachari, a leading political figure, who would later join the interim government and also become independent India's first Governor-General, had by then shed his reluctance to move from Madras to New Delhi. Simultaneously, John Matthai a widely respected economist and economic administrator emerged as a consensus choice as the finance member. Hence, the Deputy Secretary had told Deshmukh that his services in New Delhi might not be necessary. Eventually, however, neither Rajagopalachari nor Matthai got the nod for the finance portfolio as political considerations of accommodating the Muslim League meant that one of its members, Liaquat Ali Khan, became the finance member. All this did not upset Deshmukh, who had never aspired to a career in politics. On the contrary, he felt relieved that he would no longer be required to play a role in such a political arrangement.

Thus, when he received the personal note from Wavell at the end of May 1946, Deshmukh did not think twice about writing back to the Viceroy with an unequivocal regret note. It was a longish reply and showed how tactful Deshmukh was in recusing himself from the job being offered. He wrote:

> I have given deep and anxious consideration to the question put to me and have come to the conclusion that I should not be in a position to accept should an invitation be extended to me. I am not thinking at all of the financial sacrifice that such acceptance will almost certainly involve and fully realise the far more important aspect of the matter, which is service to the country. There are two major reasons which have influenced my conclusion: One is that by temperament and training I am unsuited to the exigencies of what is bound to be, more than ever before, a political office, and that I feel that whatever service I am capable of, I could render in my present non-political, technical position more effectively and with possibly greater continuity. The other reason is that I have not been keeping good health for some time and while I have recovered sufficiently to keep my end up in my present job, I do not feel that I should be justified in entering on a new career to be pursued in the bustle and turmoil of politics. I assure Your Excellency that had I felt sufficient confidence on either score, nothing would have yielded me greater pride and pleasure than working under Excellency's illustrious and inspiring leadership in collaboration with distinguished and representative Indians.[3]

On 2 September 1946, Wavell announced the composition of the interim government of India. Members of the executive council were chosen from the Indian National Congress and the All-India Muslim League. Of the fifteen members, nine came from the Congress and five represented the Muslim League. Wavell was the head of this team as Viceroy and Governor-General, and Sir Claude Auchinleck was the Commander-in-Chief. Jawahar Lal Nehru was the vice-president of the executive council. As vice-president, Nehru played a role equivalent to that of prime minister. There were many other important leaders of the day on the executive council, including Vallabhbhai Patel, in charge of home affairs, Rajendra Prasad, heading the portfolios of agriculture and food, Baldev Singh, supervising defence, and Jagjivan Ram, looking after labour.

But two appointments were notable. C. Rajagopalachari was included in the executive council, but he was not in charge of finance and instead headed industries and supplies, in addition to education and arts. More significantly, the finance portfolio was handled by the Muslim League representative, Liaquat Ali Khan.[4]

If Deshmukh had acceded to Wavell's request in May 1946 to be considered for membership of the executive council, the history of the formation of the interim government of India before independence could have been a little different. One of the bones of contention between the Muslim League and the Congress during the early days of the interim government was a proposal by Liaquat Ali Khan to impose taxes on business groups. Patel deeply resented the proposal, and this led to the souring of relations between the Congress and the Muslim League. It is possible that if Deshmukh had become the finance member in the interim government, such a situation would not have arisen. But, to be fair, Deshmukh's appointment as a member in charge of finance would have been tripped up by many obstacles. Most likely, political forces at that time would have torpedoed Wavell's choice.

In retrospect, Deshmukh's regret note might have saved both Wavell and the ICS officer from an embarrassing situation. Destiny had willed otherwise, though. Deshmukh would be considered for the same job, as finance minister, after India became independent a few years later. But that happened after a tragic interlude in Deshmukh's personal life, which would impact his future decisions.

A Personal Loss but a New Career

The first meeting of finance ministers of the Commonwealth countries (a group consisting of former British colonies) was to be held in London[5] on 21 July 1949. The meeting was expected to review the economic position of the Sterling Area (consisting of countries that had pegged their currencies to the British pound sterling or used it as their own currency), in view of the recent fall in the level of gold and dollar reserves of the Commonwealth countries. India's finance minister, John Matthai, was leading a delegation to London to confer with his Commonwealth colleagues on the state of the economy in the Sterling Area. The delegation was also expected to discuss the critical question of settling India's not-so-insignificant sterling balances that Britain had accumulated at that time. One of the members of the Indian delegation was Deshmukh. However, only a month was left before Deshmukh was due to complete his extended tenure as RBI Governor in August 1949.

An idea had struck Deshmukh before he embarked on this trip to London. He had been married for many years to Rosina, who was staying at Leigh-on-Sea in Essex near London, where Deshmukh had built a small house and had named it Roha, after his home town in Kolaba, as Raigad district of current-day Maharashtra was known then. Their only daughter was also in the United Kingdom, but was estranged from them. Since he would be retiring from the RBI a month later, in August 1949, he decided to pack his bags, say farewell to his colleagues and use the official trip to London to return to his dear wife and lead a retired life there. But destiny had willed otherwise.

Just a week before his departure to London, Deshmukh received a telegram that brought to him the news of Rosina's passing away after she had suffered a stroke. Within hours of that attack, she had died. It was a tragic twist of fate for Deshmukh, who had planned to spend his retired life with Rosina, from whom he had to stay away for many years because of his busy work schedule. And just when he had decided to be with his wife, she had departed this world. With a heavy heart, Deshmukh did visit London and attended the meeting of the Commonwealth finance ministers. After attending to his official duties, he went over to Roha, the home that he had built in Essex and where Rosina had died. He wound up his affairs in Essex, sold the house and built a marble stone at Rosina's grave on Thundersley Hill overlooking Leigh-on-Sea. He also met his estranged daughter, Kiki, who had by now become a little penitent about her earlier rude behaviour towards her parents.

Deshmukh had already completed the formalities of retiring as RBI Governor and even attended a farewell function before leaving for London. The government had named his successor, Benegal Rama Rau, who was earlier Secretary in the finance department at the Centre. Deshmukh was still in London, when within days of his retirement, Finance Minister John Matthai approached him and explored if he would agree to become India's financial ambassador to look after the country's interests in the United States and Europe. Matthai's logic was that since

Deshmukh would no longer be rooted in London after Rosina's death, he could be useful to the country and play that role which would involve a lot of travel in the US, Europe and, of course, India. The most immediate task for Deshmukh, if he were to accept the assignment, was to negotiate a loan for the import of 2 million tonnes of wheat to meet the country's food requirements. Deshmukh did not take much time to accept the new job offer made to him.

It was during this stint that Deshmukh had his third interaction with Prime Minister Jawaharlal Nehru, a meeting that would eventually bring them closer to each other in the coming years and would get the country its second non-politician finance minister who had earlier steered the country's central bank. John Matthai, an economist and an economic administrator, was the first non-politician finance minister. Many years later, another non-politician who too had headed the RBI would become the country's finance minister. But that is a different story—one even more fascinating and with even more drama preceding his appointment.

Tryst with Nehru

Deshmukh's first meeting with Nehru took place at the end of February 1939, when he was with the government of the Central Provinces and Berar. In the course of his assignment there, he got involved in an intense debate over the formula for allocation of fresh expenditure between the two regions of the state. So contentious had that debate become that Deshmukh was asked to prepare a formula for expenditure allocation, which was finally accepted. A little before this, Deshmukh was presented to Mahatma Gandhi and Jawaharlal Nehru, both of whom had come to Wardha for a Congress Working Committee meeting to assess for themselves how the states would look at issues concerning their financial autonomy. That was Deshmukh's first meeting with Nehru, though he had also seen him from a distance at the Tripuri session of the Congress earlier, in 1939. That was also the occasion when his stock rose in the eyes of Vallabhbhai Patel, another tall leader of the Congress. It was at Patel's insistence that Deshmukh offered his formula to resolve the dispute. Patel remembered this incident. A few years later, Deshmukh would be his colleague in Nehru's Cabinet.

Deshmukh's second interaction with Nehru came in early August 1946, when he received a note from the latter asking him to donate generously towards meeting the expenses of an Inter-Asian Relations Conference, planned to be held in early 1947 in India. That letter from Nehru came in his capacity as the chairman of a committee appointed by the Indian Council of World Affairs. Deshmukh lost no time in sending a cheque for an amount that could be regarded as generous.[6]

As the newly appointed financial ambassador of India, Deshmukh got down to his job in earnest. But the highlight of his tenure was in the second half of 1949, when had held several meetings with important officials of the United States government to facilitate the supply of 2 million tonnes of wheat to India. Deshmukh was fairly confident that his efforts would bear fruit and that the US would supply the required wheat to India to meet its food shortage. But a tricky problem arose when Pakistan made it known that it had spare wheat which it could supply to India, although at the market price prevailing at that time. This offer could become a spoiler for India's getting wheat from the US on concessional terms. Deshmukh also learnt that the only way the US could be persuaded to ignore the Pakistan offer and go ahead with its wheat exports to India would be if Nehru were to make a request to President Harry Truman.

As it happened, Nehru was scheduled to visit the US in October–November 1949. Truman had sent his own plane to London, from where Nehru would be picked up and brought to Washington. Deshmukh joined Nehru in that plane, and the two were received by the US President in Washington D.C. with a warm welcome. The US ambassador to India, Loy Henderson, was present at the reception and took Deshmukh aside and told him that Truman would agree to ship the wheat only if Nehru asked for it. Henderson said to Deshmukh: 'Don't let Nehru lean backwards when he has anything to ask of the President.'

But wheat never figured in the interaction between Truman and Nehru. Nor did the Indian prime minister ask Truman to arrange for supplies of wheat to India. Of course, official-level discussion took place separately and the ground was laid for an agreement that would materialize later, after overcoming many a diplomatic and political hurdle.

That trip also saw a healthy equation build between Nehru and Deshmukh. The two interacted on many issues of governance and economic management as Nehru addressed several meetings of business leaders in the US. How healthy the rapport between Nehru and Deshmukh had become was evident from the way the prime minister would conclude his speeches at his meetings with business leaders. 'If you have any questions to ask, Mr Deshmukh here will answer them on my behalf as he knows much more about details than I do,' Nehru would say.[7] Of course, Deshmukh hardly had to step in to provide any clarification as business relations between the US and India were so lukewarm that there was no scope for such questions.

Deshmukh's relations with Nehru got stronger when, in late 1949, he was asked to return to New Delhi. Having settled down in the capital, Deshmukh got down to sorting out the knotty issues that were brought before him for resolution. Prominent among those were an assessment of the situation following the devaluation of the Indian rupee and the forging of an agreement on adjustment of budget allotments for the river valley projects in progress. There were many river valley development projects under construction at that time—at Bhakra-Nangal, Damodar Valley and Hirakud. The authorities of each of these projects were demanding increased allocation, and the head of the Damodar Valley project would often directly approach Nehru to secure financial allotment, which would lead to tension and unhappiness among the other project-executing agencies. Deshmukh suggested to Nehru that a proper channel of communication should be established for all project authorities, and the prime minister accepted the suggestion. Tensions had eased considerably after that mechanism was established.

By then it was becoming increasingly clear to Deshmukh that Nehru was only waiting for the right opportunity to induct him into the government and seek his services. At the end of 1949, Deshmukh's services were again sought by Nehru to help the government prepare a draft note for creation of a think tank under the direct supervision and leadership of the prime minister. It was ironical that while preparing that draft note, Deshmukh had even consulted John Matthai, who was then the finance minister. He found Matthai a little lukewarm to the idea, although he had not sensed any hostility in him to the idea of such a high-powered think tank, which would later be known as the Planning Commission. Weeks before the eventual constitution of the Planning Commission, on 1 April 1950, Nehru asked Deshmukh if he would agree to become a member of the think tank. Deshmukh accepted that offer without thinking twice. But within weeks of the setting up of the Planning Commission, Matthai quit as the finance minister, ostensibly in protest at the manner in which Nehru had set up a body that would effectively curtail the powers and role of the finance ministry in economic policymaking. The Planning Commission was set up with the help of a Cabinet resolution and had no statutory backing, a fact that, ironically, helped its abolition sixty-four and a half years later by another prime minister, Narendra Modi.

Matthai's departure also meant that Nehru had to look for a finance minister. And his choice fell on Deshmukh. Early in May 1950, Nehru made the offer to Deshmukh and, as expected, Deshmukh told him he had no desire to join politics and even suggested an alternative in Gopalaswami Ayyangar, who was at that time the minister for railways. Nehru liked the suggestion and told Deshmukh that he would offer the portfolio of finance to Ayyangar. But what happened after Deshmukh's refusal was quite dramatic.

This story is best told in Deshmukh's own words:

A few days later, he (Nehru) sent for me and said: 'You know, Deshmukh, we thought we had settled this matter that day, but nothing seems to get settled in this world. I have here a letter from Gopalswamy (at Ooty then) declining the post, as he is not familiar with international finance, and suggesting your name. I have also a letter from Vallabhbhai Patel strongly advising that you be appointed as Finance Minister. It is strange how everyone seems to trust you. Now will you accept?' I felt I had now no way of escaping, but asked for twenty-four hours to think over the matter to which Nehru agreed. When I put the issue to Pillai (N.R. Pillai, who was then the Cabinet Secretary), he said: 'You cannot let the Government down. You must accept.' I thought that was a telling argument and accepted and thus came to shoulder a heavy political responsibility which I had turned back from in 1946, but which now came to me under far more appealing and stable auspices.[8]

On 13 May 1950, the government notified the appointment of Deshmukh as finance minister, in addition to his continuing to hold his job as a member of the Planning Commission. That additional responsibility was divested a year later, when Deshmukh had to contest elections to become a member of the Lok Sabha. As an elected member of Parliament, he could not have enjoyed an office of profit as a Planning Commission member. The appointment of Deshmukh as the third finance minister of India after Independence took place under unique circumstances. Deshmukh had to fill in a vacancy created by the sudden resignation of the incumbent finance minister who was unhappy about the setting up of the Planning Commission, a proposal which he himself had helped draft. In the process, Deshmukh would become the first retired civil servant to don the finance minister's hat.

Not surprisingly, Deshmukh's appointment as finance minister was announced amidst considerable political opposition. This became evident from the many congratulatory messages that Deshmukh received from some of his friends and acquaintances. Two such messages provide a glimpse into the political resistance Nehru had to counter before ushering in a retired ICS officer as the country's finance minister. Vijayalakshmi Pandit, who was then India's Ambassador to the US and also Nehru's sister, wrote to Deshmukh to say:

> This is just to say how very glad I am that you have joined the Cabinet. I hope the petty pinpricks which our lesser politicians delight in giving will not get under your skin. We want men like you to preside over our national destiny. So, do become tough and stick to the job.[9]

Benegal Rama Rau, who succeeded him as Governor of the RBI, also wrote to Deshmukh:

> I must congratulate the country on your acceptance of the Finance Ministership. I am very glad that the Prime Minister had the courage to persuade you to accept the post in spite of strong party pressure. I do hope you will continue at least till the general elections next year.[10]

Rama Rau's fervent hope that Deshmukh would last till the next general elections that were to be held in 1957 was full of significance. Indeed, Deshmukh quit his job a year before the elections were held. What led to his departure is a different but equally fascinating story of the many turns and twists in India's politics.

Deshmukh's Priorities

The focus areas Deshmukh outlined for himself as the new finance minister showed that the Indian economy, still coming to terms with the pangs of Partition and Independence, was being steered by a competent pair of hands. The Budget had already been presented and Deshmukh was required to respond to the criticism that Opposition leaders had mounted against the President's address delivered a few days ago. President Rajendra Prasad had drawn the nation's attention to grave economic challenges that the country faced and Opposition leaders were keen on a response from the government on how it planned to face those economic challenges. In early August 1950, Deshmukh outlined before Parliament an eight-point plan of action that he would pursue as finance minister.

These were: Follow sound fiscal and monetary policy; no relaxation in the pursuit of economy; reduce the stress on the Indian economy arising out of its political and economic relations with its neighbouring countries; plan for attaining self-sufficiency in food, cotton and jute; take efforts aimed at maximizing industrial production; take steps to alleviate rural unemployment; maintain a close vigil on inflation to keep it under check and; utilize the country's resources in the 'most advantageous manner possible'.

Nehru was present in Parliament when Deshmukh laid bare his agenda for action. The initial anxiety of his expression, as Deshmukh began to speak, gave way to a look of satisfaction and comfort as he realized he had a competent man in charge of the exchequer.[11] Further proof of the positive and calming impact Deshmukh's debut speech made on the members of Parliament could be had from what Ramnath Goenka, media baron and a member at the time, said:

> I was not going to finish my remarks without paying the highest tribute to the present Finance Minister. The Honourable Finance Minister has taken up office at a time when the economic situation of the country is far from satisfactory and there I take him to be a very bold man and I particularly wish him good luck. What I say is only by way of guidance to the Honourable Finance Minister.

Building a team of experts

The appointment of Deshmukh as the finance minister coincided with the rise of Prasanta Chandra Mahalanobis in the Nehru government.

Deshmukh already had a great rapport with Mahalanobis, the physicist-turned-statistician who would later become one of Nehru's influential economic policy advisers. Mahalanobis had set up the Indian Statistical Institute in 1931 and had begun pioneering work on collection of data and strengthening of the statistical system in the country. In 1949, Mahalanobis had been appointed as Honorary Statistical Adviser to the government, and Deshmukh, on the other hand, had been appointed as president of the Indian Statistical Institute. As finance minister, Deshmukh recognized the need to strengthen the system of collecting and disseminating macro-level statistics within the country so that they could be used as a tool by the Planning Commission in planning for development. He had already been in consultation with Mahalanobis to build the country's statistics architecture. Soon, Deshmukh steered a proposal before the Union Cabinet for setting up a national sample survey, for entrusting the job of collecting and estimating the country's national income to the Indian Statistical Institute and for establishing the Central Statistical Organisation as a wing of the government. The idea was to ensure that the government, with the help of these new institutions and surveys, could collect household data and draw from it inferences on the state of the economy. These inputs would then help the government implement its plans for development and growth. A few years later, even as Deshmukh was at the helm of the finance ministry, the Indian Statistical Institute was entrusted with greater responsibilities. In September 1954, the Planning Commission asked it to jointly undertake with the CSO and the finance ministry two studies hugely critical for the Indian economy. One was to explore the possibility of solving the unemployment problem within a period of ten years, and the other was to find out what steps needed to be taken to achieve a rapid rise in the country's national income. As the following decades would show, both issues have continued to tease future governments and their finance ministers. But what remains noteworthy is that Deshmukh as the finance minister lost little time in identifying the two most critical economic policy challenges before the government—reduction in unemployment and achievement of higher growth.

No less important were Deshmukh's interventions in building the government's internal capacity for diagnosing the country's economic challenges and framing the needed policy options by putting in place a team of economic experts. By 1950, Dr J.J. Anjaria had already made a mark as one of India's bright young economists after having graduated from Bombay University. An alumnus of the London School of Economics, he began teaching at Pune before joining in quick succession the Reserve Bank of India and the newly created International Monetary Fund (IMF). Anjaria's stint at the RBI had brought him in touch with Deshmukh. As work on framing the First Five Year Plan had to begin under the auspices of the newly created Planning Commission, Deshmukh quickly drafted Anjaria in as its economic adviser, a post that had to be created specifically for the purpose. Assisting Anjaria was another well-known economist, Dr K.N. Raj, who was then just twenty-six years old, but who would later help set up one of India's best academic institutions—the Delhi School of Economics. While Anjaria was the economic adviser in the finance ministry in addition to heading the economic division in the Planning Commission, Raj was the deputy chief of that division. Anjaria would later return to the finance ministry as its first chief economic adviser, just after Deshmukh left North Block, the headquarters of the finance ministry. A few years later, Anjaria would be sent to the IMF as India's executive director before being appointed as deputy governor of the RBI. Raj's services were requisitioned so he could also assist Deshmukh when he visited the United States to attend the meetings of the World Bank and the IMF. Deshmukh's eye for talent was one of his major leadership qualities. He chose a band of officers very early in his stint as finance minister, many of whom would stand the country in good stead when it came to economic policymaking for the country much after Deshmukh's departure from the government.

The Jeep Controversy

Early in his innings as the finance minister, Deshmukh was witness to a tricky controversy over a financial scandal, perhaps the first such development in India after Independence. India's high commissioner in the United Kingdom at that time, V.K. Krishna Menon, came under attack for having entered into a controversial deal for the purchase of about 2,000 second-hand jeeps through an intermediary. It was in early 1951 that the government's audit report referred to the decision to purchase these jeeps under four contracts, leading to a loss of Rs 19 lakh—not a small amount those days! The audit report said:

> . . . the High Commissioner for India entered into four contracts for the supply of Jeeps and other military equipment with a group of associated private companies. No recorded information is available to audit how the group of associated companies were selected . . . All the contracts were signed by the same individual on behalf of the different companies concerned . . . It is difficult to resist the conclusion that the entire management of the first transaction has been unbusiness-like and has proved detrimental to the interests of Government.[12]

Nehru was at pains to convince Krishna Menon that there were traces of impropriety in the deal, but the Indian high commissioner was unwilling to accept it. Things became complicated when the British Prime Minister Clement Attlee raised another controversy over the alleged communist links of some of the staff at the Indian High Commission in London. Even though Krishna Menon put up a strong defence against these charges, he was clearly under such severe attack that Nehru even argued with him that there was hardly any alternative to accepting the British government's suggestion that high-level communication on intelligence matters would be communicated directly to the Indian government through the British High Commission in New Delhi, instead of being routed through the Indian High Commission in London. Nehru even suggested to Krishna Menon that the latter could take a longish break from work in view of his ill-health. Krishna Menon rejected all such suggestions.

The jeeps controversy blew over later, though it strained relations between Nehru and Krishna Menon, as subsequent developments showed that there might have been acts of indiscretion or cavalier decision-making in the deal, involving the payment of commissions, though there was no evidence of personal corruption.[13] Yet, the manner in which Deshmukh was involved in defusing the political crisis at home showed how Nehru was getting closer to his newly appointed finance minister. A rare and candid note Nehru sent to Deshmukh in July 1951 revealed the prime minister's confidence in his finance minister. Nehru described Krishna Menon as a man of 'high integrity', but who had at the same time 'a number of serious failings', and concluded that 'one has to balance his extraordinary capacity for good work with failings . . .'[14]

Deshmukh was not one of those who in any way was kindly disposed towards Krishna Menon. In his words, '. . . during my journeys to or through UK, I had taken the opportunity to call on him (Krishna Menon), but our relations have always been of uneasily peaceful coexistence'.[15] As finance minister, he had got the financial dealings at India House, the official headquarters of the Indian High Commission in London, examined, which worsened their relations. Once the audit report on the jeeps scandal became public, Nehru had to set up a sub-committee of the Cabinet to examine the charges. The deliberations of the sub-committee were stormy, as is evident from the fact that Deshmukh once even threatened to walk out of it. The differences were resolved on the understanding that Deshmukh would be authorized to make a statement in Parliament clarifying that an error of judgement had occurred, which had led to monetary loss for the government.

Dealing with a Difficult Prime Minister

Dealing with Nehru who was not only the tallest Indian political leader at the time but was also the head of the government was no easy task for a new entrant into politics like Deshmukh, even though he was the finance minister and one in whom the prime minister reposed enormous faith and trust. One such occasion arose when India was negotiating a wheat loan from the US to ward off a food shortage. The problem was that Deshmukh was not fully aware of Nehru's dislike of seeking financial assistance from abroad, a trait he must have imbibed from his deeply held belief in economic self-reliance and even autarchy. During Nehru's visit to the US and in his meetings with President Truman, when Deshmukh was present as India's financial ambassador, discussions on US financial assistance to help India tide over its food shortage had begun but had made little progress. As finance minister, Deshmukh believed that even though India had reasonably strong foreign exchange resources at the time, thanks to the sterling balances, the country could be needing dollars to import food grain in the event of a shortage. Grounds were laid for resuming talks with the US for securing US financial assistance for grain purchase, after of course obtaining the permission of the prime minister.

However, a delicate issue arose over the first draft of the Wheat to India Bill that landed in New Delhi for the Indian government's consideration. There were many features of the draft bill that Nehru was uncomfortable with—including the fact that the dispatch of wheat would be made as aid and that the money received by India against distribution of such food grain would be used to defray the US establishment's expenditure in India and, more worryingly, the condition that the wheat on its arrival in India had to be ceremonially transported so that the world would witness the generosity of Americans.

One morning, Deshmukh was summoned to Nehru's office. On his arrival, Deshmukh saw Nehru surrounded by his Cabinet colleagues—C. Rajagopalachari and Maulana Abdul Kalam Azad. They all seemed to be scowling. Nehru showed Deshmukh the wheat aid bill and blurted out to him his chief opposition to the provisions. Deshmukh was a veteran administrator, but not a veteran politician. He quickly understood the key reasons for the opposition to the bill and said: 'Instead of aid we should ask for a loan on concessional terms.' Half his battle was won with that statement, and the remaining part of the battle too was clinched when he said that defrayment of the US establishment's expenditure using the money received against distribution of the food in India could be subjected to a ceiling, and that the suggestion of ceremonial transportation of the wheat should be summarily rejected. The US bill was sent for redrafting, and after some tortuous rounds of negotiations, the deal was signed and India began receiving US food aid.

It soon became clear that in spite of the strong equation between Deshmukh and Nehru, there were many occasions when differences of opinion would arise, leading to moments of tension and uneasy relationship between the prime minister and his finance minister.

Debut in Politics

Deshmukh was a lateral entrant in Indian politics. He was reluctant to enter politics. It was the political leadership that chose him to play the role of finance minister because of his vast administrative experience. From the political leadership's point of view, the choice of Deshmukh as the government's finance minister was understandable. Here was a retired ICS officer who had become the governor of the RBI and had shown many admirable qualities as an economic administrator. India needed a finance minister who could steer the economy with a firm and sure pair of hands. But the idea of a finance minister who was not a politician raised many uncomfortable questions. Would he not have to be elected to the Lok Sabha, the lower house of Parliament? Or could he be nominated to the Rajya Sabha, the upper house? Could he even get elected to the upper house? Finally, there were many doubts as to how a retired civil servant would be able to mesh with the political leadership without any apparent disharmony.

But within the first few months of Deshmukh's joining the government as finance minister, Nehru and other top political leaders quickly recognized that they made no mistake in their choice. Deshmukh took little time adjusting to his new role. But a tricky question arose with regard to his political status: should he be sent to the Rajya Sabha or to the Lok Sabha? Eventually, Deshmukh decided to contest the Lok Sabha seat in Kolaba in 1952 and won by a handsome margin. This was significant, as in subsequent years a few of India's finance ministers would be allowed to function even while representing the Rajya Sabha as they could not be expected to win an election. Pranab Mukherjee in his first stint as finance minister, and Manmohan Singh through his entire political career, would represent only the Rajya Sabha.

The year 1952 was significant for Deshmukh for another reason. He became close to G. Durgabai, a member of Parliament with a formidable reputation as an acclaimed social worker. She was only forty-three years old at the time. They met for the first time when Deshmukh became the finance minister and they got closer to each other in spite of their cultural differences (Nehru's secretary M.O. Matthai exclaimed, when he learnt of their plans to get married, 'But how romantic! You with your westernized style and she with her simple freedom fighter habits.') It was at the behest of Deshmukh that Durgabai was inducted into the Planning Commission and was given the responsibility of looking after the social sector. It was for this reason that when the two decided to tie the nuptial knot, Deshmukh requested Nehru that Durgabai be allowed to step down from the Planning Commission. It was a request Nehru turned down without a moment's delay. 'What is the necessity for this?' Nehru asked, when Deshmukh made the suggestion, adding, 'Your suggestion was not made out of any private feeling.' It was apparent that Nehru believed that Deshmukh's recommendation that Durgabai be made a Planning

Commission member was made on merit and hence she need not step down just because she was to be married to Deshmukh.

The strong relationship between Nehru and Deshmukh was also in evidence in the manner in which the deputy chairman of the Planning Commission was changed. Deshmukh did not find Gulzarilal Nanda, the deputy chairman, as providing any clear direction or leadership to the planning exercise that was under way. Once Deshmukh brought this to Nehru's attention and suggested that veteran civil servant V.T. Krishnamachari was perhaps better suited for the role, Nehru took no time in bringing in Krishnamachari in place of Nanda because of the former's 'better economic credentials'. The First Five-Year Plan was being framed those days and Nehru recognized the need for a more focused leadership at the Planning Commission. Nanda may have been upset with Deshmukh as it became known soon enough that the change took place at the finance minister's intervention. Nanda was a senior Congress leader. But that Deshmukh could get Nanda removed from his job in spite of being a relatively new entrant into the Cabinet pointed to the finance minister's growing clout in the government.

A Union Cabinet Full of Stalwarts

The relationship between Deshmukh and Nehru was special in many ways. While Deshmukh himself had the reputation of having been an effective administrator as an ICS officer and a successful central banker on top of that, Nehru's aura as one of the tallest leaders in the country and as the first prime minister of India after Independence made him a far greater figure than Deshmukh, of course. Deshmukh's assessment of Nehru as the prime minister, therefore, sheds fresh light on how the prime minister ran his administration. Deshmukh believed that the only one to rival the towering personality of Nehru in his Cabinet of ministers was the redoubtable Congress leader and home minister, Sardar Vallabhbhai Patel.

Assessing and comparing them, Deshmukh wrote the following about the two leaders:

These two men (Nehru and Patel) were cast in different moulds, although both were patriots in the noblest sense of the term. Temperamentally, Patel was a realist, with the commonsense characteristics of the sturdy peasantry from Kaira district, Gujarat, from which stock he had sprung. Nehru on the other hand was an intellectual with a theoretical commitment to socialism dating back to the days of his early manhood, and traceable to his sojourns in Europe in the early 1930s. At the core of Vallabhbhai's realism was the recognition of the foibles of human nature and an awareness of its limitations, which stamped him as a conservative. Nehru, unsure as a judge of men, was inclined to overestimate the achievement potential of his fellow beings; he was in consequence only too ready to respond to the appeal of socialism. The Nehru-Patel balance in the Cabinet was therefore a case of unstable equilibrium, maintained only by a common effort on either side not to encroach on each other's assigned territory. How long this could have lasted was anybody's guess. However, after the commencement of the Constitution the equilibrium was destined not to be tested for long as Patel was a sick man in the latter half of 1950 and passed away in December of that year.[16]

Deshmukh did not have to contend with having to maintain a subtle balance in dealing with the two leaders as he joined the Cabinet only after Patel's death. But as far as any assessment of the two leaders and their relationship goes, Deshmukh's evaluation was not only perceptive but has stood the test of time as a yardstick for judging the two.

Deshmukh believed that the composition of Nehru's Cabinet in the early years after Independence reflected the prime minister's desire to put in place what could well be described as a national government. There were ministers in the Cabinet who were either close to Nehru or Patel, the two stalwarts in the government. If, for instance, Rafi Ahmed Kidwai was close to Nehru, N.V. Gadgil owed his allegiance to Patel. But there were many others who occupied key positions in the Cabinet not because of their political affiliation but because of their expertise in certain areas. These included Bhimrao Ramji Ambedkar with his expertise in law, and Gopalaswami Ayyangar. Deshmukh himself belonged in this category, having occupied the key portfolio of finance. What made Nehru's Cabinet truly national was perhaps the inclusion of some luminaries representing sectoral interests, like Shyama Prasad Mukherjee (Hindus of Bengal), Baldev Singh (Sikhs), Abul Kalam Azad (nationalist Muslims), Jagjivan Ram (scheduled castes) and Rajkumari Amrit Kaur (a woman and a confidante of Gandhi). Many of them occupied key positions in the Cabinet, and hence it was not that Nehru just paid lip service to the idea of giving sectoral interests representation in the Cabinet. Thus, Baldev Singh was in charge of defence, Jagjivan Ram headed the labour ministry and Rajkumari Amrit Kaur looked after health. Even before Deshmukh joined the Cabinet, the occupants of the finance ministry were Shanmukham Chetty and John Matthai, whose choice was driven not so much by their being representatives of the southern states as by the fact of their being noted experts in the field of finance.

Deshmukh also enjoyed a great degree of comfort from the manner in which Nehru ran his Cabinet and followed the decision-making process. Deshmukh found his prime minister to be 'gentle, considerate and democratic, never forcing a decision on his colleagues—some of them being distinguished men in their own right'. Consensus was the preferred mode of decision-making, and recourse to voting would be made on occasions where differences of opinion arose. For instance, Patel was not in favour of the Industries Development and Regulation Bill (a law that would reimpose state control on large areas of economic activities), but eventually gave his consent after some discussions. Similarly, Patel had expressed strong reservations about the government proposal to conduct investigations into private charities and trusts to plug any gaps in the taxation laws that allowed them to misuse the provisions. Patel's apprehensions were that these actions would discourage these entities from funding social and humanitarian initiatives. However, after some exchange of views—and many of Patel's differed from those of Deshmukh's—Patel let the matter be decided by the finance minister. Democratic traditions took precedence over seniority in the Cabinet. Patel was also opposed to the Income Tax Investigation Tribunal because the home minister believed it was an instrument for harassing honest and good people. He wanted the Tribunal to be wound up, but he agreed with Deshmukh's sensible suggestion that winding it up would be politically impossible. Instead, Patel helped Deshmukh secure the services of a Calcutta High Court Judge to head it. Patel was always in favour of free enterprise and was opposed to controls and restrictions. When Deshmukh proposed a ceiling on the skyrocketing prices of cotton, Patel had initially opposed the idea, but later consented to it in view of the larger interests of the cotton-using sectors.

With other Cabinet ministers, Deshmukh enjoyed a relationship of mutual trust and affection. Recognizing the seniority of Chakravarti Rajagoplachari, who was then the commerce minister, Nehru had proposed his name for the post of vice-president of the Economic Committee of the Cabinet. It could have been a tricky situation. In normal course, it would be the finance minister heading such a committee. Nehru asked Deshmukh if he would mind if Rajagopalachari were asked to head it. Deshmukh had no reservations in accepting Nehru's decision. But whenever meetings of the Economic Committee of the Cabinet were held, Rajagopalachari would show due deference to Deshmukh by starting the meeting and then saying: 'Now, Mr Deshmukh you may conduct the meeting.'[17]

As finance minister, Deshmukh also had a few trying times in dealing with some of his Cabinet colleagues. Though his relations with those ministers were cordial, Deshmukh would mince no words or flinch at no point in asserting his rights as the finance minister and vetoing any proposal from any of those ministers if he was not convinced of their merit. Thus, he would shoot down a proposal from Harekrushna Mahatab, the minister of industry and supply at that time, to allow Biju Patnaik, a budding businessman who would later join politics and become Odisha chief minister, to set up a steel plant with short-term money borrowed from French financiers. Later, Mahtab would succeed in getting permission for Patnaik to set up Kalinga Tubes,[18] but not before the risky steel plan proposal was thrown into the dustbin. Similarly, Rafi Ahmed Kidwai, a minister in the Nehru Cabinet in charge of the ministry of communications, had mooted the idea of nationalizing Himalayan Aviation, one of the handful of private airlines operating in the country at that time. It was ironical that even though Deshmukh rejected the idea, a few years later, in 1953, all domestic airlines, including Himalayan Aviation, were nationalized and a state-owned company by the name of Indian Airlines was created to run domestic air services. The other private airlines that were nationalized and merged with Indian Airlines included Deccan Airways, Airways India, Bharat Airways, Kalinga Airlines and Indian National Airways.[19] Deshmukh had another point of difference with Kidwai when the latter wanted the dismantling of food grain controls. The finance minister was opposed to that idea. It was clear that, like Patel, Kidwai was in favour of free enterprise and was opposed to controls. Deshmukh, in contrast, had a nuanced approach to controls as he believed in caution and in not allowing runaway prices to play havoc with the economy. As finance minister, Deshmukh had crossed swords with even Lal Bahadur Shastri, who was the railway minister then, on an issue of principle: Should the financial commissioner of the railways be answerable only to the railway minister? Or should he, as the nominee of the finance ministry on the Railway Board, keep the finance minister in the loop on all financial matters involving Indian Railways? Deshmukh was categorical that the financial commissioner must also remain in touch with the finance minister, while Shastri believed that the commissioner should report only to the railway minister. After some heated deliberations between the two, Shastri came around to Deshmukh's point of view and accepted the concept that the commissioner should not only report to the railway minister but also keep in touch with the finance minister. 'I am a newcomer and I consider it unwise to pick up a quarrel with you,' Shastri told Deshmukh.[20]

An interesting feature of the Nehru Cabinet during those days was the marked absence of any public airing of differences over what kind of economic ideology the government should pursue to bring about higher growth and eliminate poverty in the country. Whether in the newly created Planning Commission or in the Union Cabinet, differences over economic policies were primarily between Nehru and Patel, but these were not resolved. However, Patel's death in December 1950 paved the way for Nehru giving vent to his socialistic ideas on economic policymaking without much opposition within the government.

In Deshmukh's words,

> Nehru was theoretically a socialist, but was hemmed in by conservative modes of thinking especially as the Congress socialists led by Acharya Narendra Dev and Jayaprakash Narayan had already parted company with the ruling party. Pragmatism and mixed economy were the phrases that suited everybody and were heavily stressed by the Planning Commission.

But when it came to the framing of economic policies, Nehru gave sufficient freedom to his finance minister, who was also the minister for economic affairs. And yet, Nehru would push his socialistic policies.

Early Signs of Shift to Socialism

In the winter session of Parliament in 1954, there was a debate on the kind of economic policy the government should pursue. Bhagwat Jha Azad strongly pushed for pursuit of a socialistic pattern for the Indian economy. A suitable amendment to that effect had been moved in Parliament. At this point, Nehru asked Deshmukh if, as the finance minister, he had any objections to such a significant shift in India's economic policy. Deshmukh had none, since he had by then already begun to think of a similar focus for India's economic policy. With Parliament having already given its assent to pursuit of a socialistic pattern of economy, Nehru took the next move to get the proposal ratified by the Congress session held in January 1955 at Avadi. It was at this session of the party that the idea of nationalizing the insurance business was mooted and approved. Deshmukh had already begun preliminary consultations with the Reserve Bank of India on the imperatives that must kept in mind while nationalizing the country's insurance business. K.G. Ambegaonkar, who was then Secretary in the Economic Affairs Department, began taking the initial steps, and a final shape to the proposal was given by his successor, H.M. Patel.

A highlight of Deshmukh's tenure as finance minister was the finalization of the country's First Five-Year Plan in which the finance minister, who was also a member of the Planning Commission, played a key role. The term of the First Five-year Plan was to begin in 1951 and end by March 1956. But by the time it was approved, two years of the Plan period had already lapsed. In the shorter Plan period now available to the government, its priority became infrastructure creation. Three large multi-purpose irrigation projects, which had been chosen for implementation even before the Plan had begun, were taken up in earnest for completion. These were the irrigation-cum-hydroelectric projects at Bhakra-Nangal, the Damodar Valley project and the Hirakud dam.

Foundations of Federal Planning

But controversies did surface over the manner in which the Plan was finalized, giving early signs of how the federal character of the newly created country could come under stress if not handled maturely and with political sagacity. Once the report of the First Five-year Plan was ready, the

Planning Commission initiated a process to discuss it with the state chief ministers. Nehru convened a meeting of chief ministers at New Delhi for this purpose. The meeting saw a mild outburst from a few outspoken chief ministers who were not happy about their being involved at the last stage of the Plan, when almost everything had been finalized. Bombay Chief Minister Morarji Desai and Mysore Chief Minister Kengal Hanumanthaiah were quite resentful about the consultation process taking place at the eleventh hour. It was an odd and hugely embarrassing moment for Nehru just as he was going to release the First Five-year Plan.

Deshmukh made a significant intervention at this stage, which eventually led to an institutional reform that lasted many decades. To begin with, Deshmukh suggested to Nehru that he should constitute a Standing Committee consisting of a select group of chief ministers for periodic consultations on the Plan. This suggestion was accepted and a few meetings of the Committee were also held. But, expectedly, this arrangement gave rise to even more resentment among those chief ministers who were not part of the Standing Committee. At this point, Deshmukh suggested to Nehru the formation of a permanent body, to be called the National Development Council, which would review and discuss all developmental policy issues concerning the Centre and the states. The Council was to have all the state chief ministers as its members. This reform turned out to be one of the most effective interventions in creating a durable platform for resolving Centre–state issues over policies.

On 6 August 1952, the Council was established and entrusted with the following tasks: To secure the cooperation of the states in the execution of the Plan; to strengthen and mobilize the efforts and resources of the nation in support of the Plan; to promote common economic policies in all vital spheres; and to ensure the balanced and rapid development of all parts of the country. The planning process was abandoned by the Narendra Modi government and the Planning Commission was abolished by the end of 2014. A new body was created in its place, the National Institution for Transforming India or the NITI Aayog, but the National Development Council is yet to be formally abolished, although it has not met since 2012. The NITI Aayog has a Governing Council, whose membership largely replicates that of the National Development Council, but the body that Deshmukh helped create to address Centre-state issues over planning and development had a long life of over six decades before being given a quiet burial.

ICICI Is Born

By the time Deshmukh had taken charge of the finance ministry, the task of creating financial institutions to expedite industrial development across the country had already begun. In 1949, the first such institution, the Industrial Finance Corporation of India, was established. Its primary purpose was to provide long-term finances for infrastructure projects. Another financial institution that Deshmukh helped create was a national financial institution, the Industrial Credit and Investment Corporation of India, or ICICI, aimed at meeting the financial needs of small and medium industries in the private sector. However, controversy preceded its incorporation in 1955 as a company under the existing law. The Nehru government had reckoned that with more financial assistance coming into the country between 1952 and 1954, there was an accumulation of counterpart funds in the country—foreign aid received by the government which had to be converted into the local currency. While foreign aid that came into the country by way of commodities was distributed within the country, the funds created against such aid kept growing. Using a part of these counterpart funds, along with World Bank assistance and some equity contribution from the private sector, the government had mooted the creation of ICICI. The Cabinet too cleared the proposal.

But when Deshmukh was in New York in September–October 1954 to attend the meetings of the World Bank, the International Monetary Fund and the Commonwealth Consultative Committee, he learnt that the ICICI proposal had met with political resistance on the ground that one of the clauses of its incorporation had guaranteed a minimum 3–3.5 per cent dividend to the company's shareholders, which included big industrialists. Deshmukh argued against what he believed was nothing else but a reflection of a 'narrow point of view'.[21] There was a vital need for a financial institution for developing industries in the country at that time. Deshmukh finally won that battle, and ICICI came into being in January 1955, with an authorized capital of Rs 60 crore and a subscribed capital of Rs 22 crore. In the following decades, it played a key role in helping industrial growth in the country. And when economic reforms were ushered in in the early 1990s, ICICI converted itself into a universal bank and became a widely held listed company, offering a wide range of financial services across various segments. By 1999, it had earned the honour of becoming the first Indian company and the first financial institution from Asia (excluding Japan) to be listed on the New York Stock Exchange or NYSE.

Companies Law Revamp

A key initiative Deshmukh undertook as finance minister was in the realm of the legal framework that governed the Indian corporate sector. He pushed for a thorough revamp of the laws for companies and a new statute was put in place. Even though his role in this was limited, Deshmukh had a difficult time getting his Cabinet colleagues, like Commerce and Industry Minister T.T. Krishnamachari and Congress stalwarts like Feroze Gandhi, to accept his ideas on discontinuation of the management agencies system under the new companies law. But his efforts finally paid off.

It was at the end of 1950 that the Indian government set up an experts committee, headed by C.H. Bhabha, to examine the need for a comprehensive overhaul of the companies law to make it more modern and up-to-date. Bhabha was a Parsi businessman who was the first commerce minister of independent India and held that portfolio till April 1948. The terms of reference of the committee, formed by a resolution on 28 October 1950, outlined its objectives. It said:

> Having due regard to the conditions necessary for the healthy growth of joint stock enterprises and the desirability of adequately safeguarding the interests of investors and the public, to consider and report what amendments are necessary in the Indian Companies Act, 1913, as amended by Act XXII of 1936 with particular reference to- (a) the formation of companies and the day-to-day conduct of their business; (b) the powers of the management vis-a-vis shareholders and the relations between them; (c) the safeguards required against abuse of such company practices as the interlocking of directorates, voting control by majority interests in company ownership and management, etc., which may be prejudicial to the public interest; (d) the measures necessary to promote efficient and economic management of companies.

The Bhabha Committee began work in earnest and submitted its final recommendations to the government on 29 February 1952. The speed with which the Committee worked was exemplary, and the work it undertook was comprehensive.

But the speed of decision-making slowed considerably once the report of the Committee reached the government. In spite of Deshmukh's support to the initiative, it took almost four years before the Companies Act was passed by Parliament in 1956, barely months before Deshmukh himself quit the government. The changes introduced in the new law pertained to the promotion and formation of companies, their capital structure, meetings and procedures, presentation formats for company accounts, procedures for their audit, the power and duties of auditors, the process of inspecting and investigating the affairs of companies and the system of constituting boards of directors and the power and duties of the directors, managing director and managers.[22]

It was in the latter half of 1955 that Deshmukh piloted the companies bill, with as many as 650 sections containing various procedures. It is true that the companies bill that Deshmukh tabled in Parliament underwent various changes with the changing times, but the foundation of corporate law in India after Independence was laid with that bill. Two specific provisions in the law became controversial. One pertained to abolition of the managing agency system, and the other was the prohibition of donations to political parties by companies. T.T. Krishnamachari, industry minister at that time, made no secret of his unhappiness with the abolition of the managing agency system. Krishnamachari wanted that the existing managing agencies be allowed to continue while creation of new ones could be barred. The matter was referred to a select committee of Parliament, which, much to Krishnamachari's disappointment, turned down his suggestion.

On the question of prohibiting corporate donations to political parties, Deshmukh got a little isolated. Many members of the Nehru government were opposed to the idea of banning such donations. A compromise was worked out. Accordingly, companies could donate to political parties, but had to make such donations explicitly clear in their company accounts. This provision of the companies law has stood the test of time by and large, and has seen very little change. More than six decades after corporate donations to political parties were allowed, the specific provision of the Companies Act—Section 293A—continues to ensure that no company can donate to a political party in the first three years of its formation or donate more than 5 per cent of its annual profits or take such a decision without the approval of the board of directors and a declaration in the accounts.[23]

Nationalizing Imperial Bank of India

In 1955, Deshmukh steered another major change in India's economic landscape. The country's largest commercial bank, Imperial Bank of India, was nationalized in April 1955. The strange turn of events that led to this significant change in the bank's ownership brought out an aspect of Deshmukh's personality that showed his flexibility and refusal to be dogmatic. Nationalization of Imperial Bank of India was a proposal that Deshmukh had opposed just seven years ago as Governor of the Reserve Bank of India. But he batted for it when the political situation had changed somewhat.

Soon after India's independence, the demand for a government takeover of Imperial Bank of India figured during a debate in the Constituent Assembly, which was busy framing the contours of India's Constitution. In January 1948, India's first finance minister, R.K. Shanmukhan Chetty, had made a reference to that proposal. But it made no headway as Deshmukh, at that time Governor of the Reserve Bank of India, did not mince words and warned the government against biting off 'more than we can chew'. He had also argued, quite convincingly, that there was no 'pressing need to nationalise the banking system or any portion of it when business and commerce were to be left in the private sector'.[24] In the next two years, the government did its best to give the proposal a quiet burial. A study conducted by the Additional Secretary in the finance ministry, K.G. Ambegaokar (who would in 1957 become the RBI Governor), concurred with Deshmukh's line of thinking. John Matthai, who succeeded Chetty as the finance minister in 1948, declared that the state taking over Imperial Bank of India was not a feasible idea, although he did announce the government's intention to examine the provisions of the Imperial Bank of India Act so that some of the 'unsatisfactory' features of the bank's working could be removed.[25]

Not surprisingly, the debate over the ownership pattern of Imperial Bank of India reached India's Parliament in November 1950. The issue at stake was whether the state taking over the commercial bank would help channel more credit to agriculture and to cottage industries. Again Deshmukh, who had by now become the finance minister, rejected the idea. But things changed when later, in 1950, the report of the Rural Banking Enquiry Committee was released. The Committee did not recommend nationalization of the commercial bank but a reconstitution of its top management. Predictably, this idea too was strongly opposed by the management and owners of Imperial Bank of India. This gave rise to a stalemate, as the RBI and Imperial Bank of India could not resolve the issue of the latter's ownership. In early 1953, another group of experts, the Rural Credit Survey Committee, submitted its report. Among other things, it recommended that Imperial Bank of India needed to be brought under public ownership. This time, the RBI governor at the time, Benegal Rama Rau, endorsed the suggestion. The logic of this recommendation was that a change in its ownership would help the bank spread its facilities to remote regions of the country, which did not till then have access to such financial services. A new bank—State Bank of India—was proposed to be created by amalgamating Imperial Bank of India and all the ten banks associated with it. There were some hitches in implementing this idea as Rama Rau was opposed to amalgamation of all the associate banks in one go. Discussions with the bank's management ensued, and it was eventually agreed that a few of the associate banks of Imperial Bank of India would be amalgamated to create the State Bank of India. Nehru endorsed the idea as he found that this was in keeping with the political shift towards the Left that he was engineering in the government's economic policies. Deshmukh, who had opposed the idea twice in the past, changed his stance and supported nationalization of Imperial Bank of India. When, as RBI governor, he had opposed its nationalization, he had drawn support from Sardar Vallabhbhai Patel, who was a votary of free enterprise and was opposed to state control of economic activities. When he rejected the same idea for the second time, Deshmukh was the finance minister and was bold enough to take the stance he did as he had no regard for the logic in favour of the idea put forward by the then Commerce and Industry Minister T.T. Krishnamachari. But when the same proposal was revived again in 1955, Deshmukh accepted the change as he realized that Nehru had already moved towards building an economy along a socialistic pattern. Nationalization of Imperial Bank of India under those changed circumstances was necessary, Deshmukh had internally rationalized.[26]

Deshmukh released the report of the Rural Credit Survey Committee containing the recommendations for changes in the ownership of Imperial Bank of India in Parliament on 20 December 1954 and announced the government's decision to accept it. The die was cast as Deshmukh told Parliament that bringing the bank under public ownership was 'the first step towards establishing an integrated commercial banking institution catering to the entire country'.[27] An interesting feature of the government proposal was that the state would at no time hold less than 55 per cent of the shares of the newly created bank. A legislative bill containing these proposals was introduced in Parliament on 22 April 1955, and eight days later was passed. In the early days of State Bank of India, the RBI held as much as 92 per cent of its shares, but over the years it came down closer to the mandated minimum of 55 per cent before the bank was transferred to the Union government. Industry leaders were upset at the decision. The commentary in the financial media was highly critical. *Eastern Economist* wrote that the linking of the government decision on nationalizing Imperial Bank of India to the recommendations of the Rural Credit Survey Committee was to 'dramatize' the government's interest in the proposal, and *Capital* saw the move as part of the government's 'lurch to the Left', which had left businessmen 'confused and uncertain'.[28]

While announcing the decision on the bank's nationalization in Parliament, Deshmukh tried to assuage industry's ruffled feathers and address the media's concerns. He told Parliament that the government's intention was not to disturb other parts of the banking system, which would remain in private hands. Little did Deshmukh know then that just about fourteen years later, the Indian government under Indira Gandhi as prime minister would be taking over the ownership of fourteen private-sector banks as part of a larger nationalization drive.

Nationalization of the Life Insurance Industry

Deshmukh played a key role in two of India's early nationalization efforts. Nationalization of the life insurance industry and of the Imperial Bank and its renaming as State Bank of India were two such major developments that changed the economic landscape of the country within a decade of India gaining independence. Both developments also signified the gradual lurch of the Nehru government towards statism, wherein the state would gradually take over key economic enterprises in the name of speeding up development, achieving higher growth and reducing poverty.

The final trigger for nationalization of the life insurance industry came from the meeting of the All India Congress Committee (AICC) at Avadi, near erstwhile Madras, in January 1955. That meeting adopted a resolution that called for the state to take over the many life insurance companies in what was one of independent India's first big nationalization initiatives. But that was the political trigger. There was an economic trigger as well, which Deshmukh used quite effectively. Just as the Nehru government was giving the finishing touches to the contours of the new Companies Law that was to be introduced, a financial scandal broke out. There were allegations that Ramakrishna Dalmia, one of India's top industrialists, had used controversial methods in dealing with his companies and had enriched himself at the cost of the shareholders. These allegations were brought to the notice of Deshmukh, who lost no time in appointing an accounts officer in the government to investigate the charges. By 6 October 1955, the accounts officer submitted his report to the finance minister, substantiating the allegations made against Dalmia. The last paragraph of the report was a serious indictment: 'It is difficult to estimate the exact amount made by R. Dalmia by manipulating the transactions from one company to another, but the figures stated below will give a fair indication of the amount.'[29] The amount being referred to was Rs 4.74 crore. In addition, Dalmia was accused of having made illegal profits of over Rs 1 crore from the 'sale of disposal goods' held by one of his companies, Allen Berry & Company, which was not shown in the books.

Deshmukh consulted the Attorney General, Motilal Setalvad, and as the finance minister suggested that a commission of inquiry should be instituted to examine the allegations made in that report. According to Deshmukh, Setalvad was not initially convinced that such a commission needed to be set up to just probe an individual businessman's dealings. Setalvad's worry was that questions of propriety would be raised. But Deshmukh insisted that Dalmia's alleged acts of financial irregularities were not just about what an individual business leader was up to, but had wider ramifications. Deshmukh's arguments were solid. He argued in favour of an inquiry because the amount involved was huge at that time, and the number of companies whose shareholders were cheated as a result was about a dozen. Allowing such irregularities to go unexamined by a commission could encourage other private sector players to indulge in similar acts, and finally this could have an adverse impact on the entire private investment structure in the country. A reluctant Setalvad finally agreed to Deshmukh's suggestions after seeing merit in the finance minister's arguments. A judge of the Bombay High Court, S.R. Tendolkar, was appointed in December 1956 to head the commission. Two years later, Justice Tendolkar stepped down as its chairman, paving the way for the appointment of a retired justice of the Supreme Court, Vivian Bose, to complete the inquiry.

The political significance of establishing the commission of inquiry against Dalmia can hardly be ignored. Dalmia was not just one of the leading industrialists of the country, but had been deeply associated with the country's national political leaders before Partition as well as after Independence. He had relations with Mahatma Gandhi, Muhammad Ali Jinnah and Jawaharlal Nehru. However, he was seen to be closer to Jinnah, and that proximity is believed to have strained his relations with Nehru. According to Dalmia's daughter Neelima Dalmia Adhar, Nehru's ambition to become the prime minister came in the way of preventing India's Partition.[30] Remember that Dalmia had a few of his manufacturing units located in regions that would become part of Pakistan after Partition. Dalmia's sympathies for Jinnah also complicated his relations with Nehru, and naturally after Independence it became difficult for Dalmia to mend his relations with Nehru who was now the prime minister of the newly independent country. It is not clear if Deshmukh's moves on initiating the inquiry into Dalmia's business activities received any encouragement from Nehru. But that Nehru did not oppose his finance minister's action against Dalmia must have had its own unstated political resonance.

While the inquiry committee found the Dalmias guilty of having violated several economic laws and recommended actions against the group firms, it also made some recommendations for far-reaching changes in the conduct of business in India and many of them were incorporated in the Companies Law that was framed in 1956,[31] a far more sensational development took place involving the same industrialist, Ramakrishna Dalmia. Towards the end of 1955, Deshmukh received reports from his officers that Dalmia had removed Rs 2.25 crore of funds from Bharat Insurance Company, a firm he owned. Bharat Insurance Company was in the business of providing life insurance cover to people, and removal of money from any company, let alone one in the financial sector, was a major violation. Deshmukh got this probed, and once the investigations found proof of financial impropriety, set in motion the process for prosecuting Dalmia under the law. Members of the Dalmia family tried to make amends by making good the money that was removed from the company, but Deshmukh remained unmoved, even after the Dalmia family members tried to approach the finance minister's wife and lobby with her. The prosecution was instituted, leading to Dalmia's conviction.

The sixtieth session of the All India Congress Committee was held at Avadi, near Madras, in September 1955. Held under the presidentship of U.N. Dhebar, this meeting adopted a resolution that would signal a major shift in the government's economic policy by encouraging the state sector to lead all economic initiatives in the country. This also meant nationalization of key sectors of the economy, which until then were being run or led by private-sector companies. One of the many ideas ratified at the Avadi session was nationalization of the life insurance industry, which at that time was dominated by a host of private-sector companies. Deshmukh and his finance secretary H.M. Patel (who would later become the finance minister in the Janata Party government in 1977) had been evaluating various policy options to nationalize the life insurance industry. The scandal involving financial misappropriation by Dalmia from his own insurance company was an opportunity for Deshmukh to justify the nationalization move.

Already, in 1950, the Nehru government had abolished the system of principal agencies through the Insurance Amendment Act. The amendment to the law removed the restrictions in allowing new players to enter this sector. This also meant a larger number of Indian and foreign life insurers were now free to do insurance business in India. By the end of 1955, there were in all 245 Indian and foreign life insurers. Understandably, the level of competition was quite high. Such a high level of competition created a range of choice for the consumers. But it also led to rampant use of unfair means and business practices by many of these insurance firms to sell their schemes. Allegations of unfair trade practices committed by these insurance firms kept troubling the government. This, apart from the Nehru government's left-ward stance in economic policymaking, was also responsible for the move towards nationalization of the life insurance industry.[32]

On 19 January 1956, an ordinance was promulgated to nationalize the life insurance sector. The entire operation involving the policy change was conducted with utmost secrecy and quiet efficiency. A few days before the ordinance was to be issued, Deshmukh made sure that the relevant government officers were dispatched to the headquarters of the main insurance firms that were to be nationalized. Deshmukh sent Finance Secretary H.M. Patel to get the concurrence of T.T. Krishnamachari, who was then minister for commerce and industry. Once he obtained the prime minister's approval for the ordinance, Deshmukh informed the director-general of All India Radio that an announcement needed to be broadcast. Bypassing the convention that everything that is broadcast is usually vetted by the director-general of All India Radio, Deshmukh went straight to the broadcasting studio, and without showing anybody the script announced the government's momentous decision to nationalize the life insurance business in the country. Later that night, President Rajendra Prasad's approval to the ordinance was obtained, and the next morning Deshmukh's officers went over to the various insurance companies' offices to take over their assets under the new law. A new era in India's economic policymaking had begun. Less than four months later, on 30 April 1956, India's Parliament would approve the government's Industrial Policy Resolution, which would strive to achieve a socialistic pattern of society and accord a dominant role to the public sector in setting up industries and infrastructure to achieve higher growth and reduce disparities in income. (Thirteen years later, in another quiet and clandestine operation, the government would nationalize fourteen private-sector banks. The only difference was that in 1956, it was Nehru who was the prime minister, and in 1969 it was his daughter Indira Gandhi in the same role.)

The ordinance to nationalize the life insurance industry meant that the government would take over as many as 154 Indian private-sector insurance companies, many of them quite small, and sixteen foreign-owned life insurers. In addition, seventy-five provident societies were nationalized. All of them—the 245 Indian and foreign insurers—were merged and taken over by a new company created later that year, to be called Life Insurance Corporation of India (LIC). For well over three decades, LIC enjoyed the status of a monopoly life insurer in India, until in 1993 the P.V. Narasimha Rao government reopened the insurance sector to the private sector as part of its economic reforms programme.

How Nehru Defended Nationalization

Defending the move to nationalize the life insurance industry, Nehru told Parliament: 'The nationalisation of life insurance is an important step in our march towards a socialist society. Its objective will be to serve the individual as well as the state.'[33] On 29 February 1956, Deshmukh rose in Parliament to defend and explain the move with greater eloquence:

> Insurance is an essential social service which a welfare state must make available to its people and the State must assume responsibility for rendering this service once it cannot be provided in any other manner. So while it is the failure of the general run of insurance companies to live up to the high traditions demanded of them that has led the Government to take this step, I would like to emphasise that nationalisation in this field is in itself justifiable. With the profit motive eliminated, and the efficiency of service made the sole criterion under nationalisation, it will be possible to spread the message of insurance as far wide as possible, reaching out beyond the more advanced urban areas and into hitherto neglected, namely, rural areas.[34]

In his address, Deshmukh did not desist from pointing out the many instances of irregularities in the life insurance sector that were partially responsible for the nationalization move. He recounted how the government had begun investigations into the working of the private-sector life insurance companies from 1951, and how the government was convinced that the industry was not playing the role expected of it and was consistently failing to introduce the latest standards in service delivery. The industry's financial performance was nothing to write home about—there were wasteful expenses and the share of expenses of management in premium income was as high as 27 per cent. In spite of such high expenditure, however, the quality of service was poor, Deshmukh explained. Even statutory imposition of limits on expenses failed to yield any positive outcome. Mismanagement and financial irregularities, according to the finance minister, had pushed twenty-five insurance companies into liquidation between 1944 and 1954. This was a damning indictment of the private-sector insurance industry in India. As many as seventy-five insurance companies could not declare any bonus at their valuations. Settlement of claims was often delayed and the number of complaints of delayed settlements against the companies had risen to 1000 in 1954, Deshmukh told Parliament. Many of these complaints were referred to the Controller of Insurance under the law. Investigation into these complaints mostly highlighted the wrong practices followed by the insurance firms in their attempts to defraud the insured public. Rural penetration of the insurance industry was poor as the companies were mostly concentrated in cities and towns. Deshmukh's broad message was that the private-sector insurance companies had comprehensively failed to service the people of the country, and this was the justification for nationalizing the industry.

Deshmukh and His Budgets

From 1951 to 1956, Deshmukh presented as many as five full Budgets and one Interim Budget. His first Budget, for 1951–52, was presented soon after the setting up of the Planning Commission and the launch of the First Five-Year Plan. In his speech delivered while presenting the Budget, he did not reveal the government's decision to pursue a path of planned development, but said that the Planning Commission's report was expected by May 1951, after its consultations with the state governments and others. Deshmukh, though, left nobody in doubt about what the nature and pattern of economic development would be in the coming years. He said:

An underdeveloped economy like ours is inevitably one with a low volume of savings, which can be devoted to productive investment. Even this small margin has been affected as a result of the strains and stresses of the war and post-war years and the shifts in the distribution of income within the community. The resulting dearth of resources calls for a degree of national effort which makes planning and the fixation of priorities a vital necessity if even the meagre resources available are not to be frittered away. In recent years, there has perhaps been a tendency to identify planning with large-scale expenditure out of past savings. But the real problem is to increase the current flow of saving through a concerted effort by the present generation so as to make available, without a violent disturbance of the country's economy, which the unregulated release of accumulated savings will involve, resources for productive investment and for financing social services. Without in any way anticipating the findings of the Commission, it may be hoped that as a result of their examination of the problem they would advise Government of the lines on which national effort should be mobilised, the levels to which the Centre and the States should endeavour during the next few years to raise their financial resources and the targets which the country should try to achieve through intensive development.

The need to channel available savings to bolster national efforts was a clear hint towards how the First Five-year Plan would be formulated. As it turned out, the First Five-year Plan (1951–56) laid emphasis on increasing domestic savings and channelling them to finance investments in various basic infrastructure sectors of the economy.

Deshmukh's tenure as finance minister broadly coincided with the launch and completion of the First Five-Year Plan. He took considerable pride in the fact that the planning experiment had made significant contribution to the growth of the Indian economy under his watch. In the speech he delivered while presenting the 1955–56 Budget, Deshmukh said:

> The first Plan was formulated under difficult circumstances with inflation, shortages and the like clouding the economy. The formulation of a Plan was in itself a breaking of new ground, covering as it did a large part of the national life. The aim was to make a good enough beginning, and, looking back over the four years, I venture to suggest that this has been done with some success.

Indeed, Deshmukh was optimistic that more plans would be rolled out in the coming years to address the need for national development. He admitted to some failures too. He said:

> While there have been shortfalls in achieving the targets, considering the size of the Plan and the inevitable margin which is to be allowed for in any human planning, these have not been such as to discourage us. The country as a whole is becoming more and more plan-minded, and in the rural areas there is an awakening of interest in economic development, which is noticeable even to a casual observer. The achievements of the

first Plan in terms of irrigation and power, industrial development and the community and the national extension programmes have been by no means inconsiderable.

On the need for the next Plan, Deshmukh laid out its broad objectives that married the country's economic goals with its political objectives. He noted that the Second Plan must aim at accelerated development, 'consistent with the stability of our economy and our declared policy of adherence to democratic methods'. Dwelling on the factors that would be critical for the success of the Second Plan, Deshmukh focused on two imperatives: availability of finances and organizational effectiveness. The two have to be correlated to achieve the goal of fast economic development, he said. If Deshmukh's tenure as finance minister saw a major resource mobilization drive through higher taxes, it was because he was acutely conscious of the need for more funds to finance the Plan projects and achieve the goals of development.

Deshmukh's first Budget speech before Parliament, delivered on 28 February 1951, also provided a glimpse of the problems the Indian economy was going through at that time. Inflation had reared its ugly head and had become the main headache for the newly appointed finance minister. The devaluation of the Indian currency in 1949 had triggered inflationary pressures in the economy. The devaluation was quite steep, by about 30.5 per cent, effective from 19 September 1949. As a result, the exchange rate or the cost of the US dollar went up from Rs 3.23 to Rs 4.76. This triggered fears of imported inflation in the economy. A communique issued by the finance ministry stated:

> There will be no further imports of food grains from the dollar area during the year and food prices will not be affected by the devaluation of the rupee . . . The general price level or the cost of production should not increase and internal prices of commodities will not be affected.[35]

But the ministry's statement was only an expression of its fond hope that the inflation situation would remain benign in spite of the devaluation. Initially, those steps did help the government contain the price level, at least for some months. Indeed, by December 1949, the general price index had declined by 3 per cent from the level that obtained in October 1949. But the inflationary pressures were too strong to be contained by short-term supply-side measures. By June 1950, the general price index rose by close to 4 per cent, compared to the level six months ago. Unchecked, three months later, in September 1950, the index increased further, by over 4 per cent. On an annualized basis, this was a very steep rise in the inflation level.

Several natural calamities just before Deshmukh's first Budget had also made the new finance minister's task more complicated. There were floods in parts of Bihar and Uttar Pradesh and the monsoon had failed for the fifth year in succession. The earthquake in Assam on 15 August 1950 caused major devastation in the entire North-eastern region, and its impact was felt even in many of the eastern states. This was an earthquake with an intensity measured at 8.6 on the Richter scale and shook the region at 7.40 p.m., a few hours after Independence Day celebrations had ended. The United States Geological Survey (USGS), a scientific agency of the US government, noted that an estimated 536 people were killed and thousands of homes were in ruins.

The natural calamities that occurred in 1949 and 1950 had an expected adverse fallout as far as the country's food situation went. The overall food deficit widened, and India had to increase its food imports by as much as a third from the original figure of 1.5 million tonnes to 2 million tonnes. Worse, the government had even failed to build up the small, but necessary, level of food grain reserves of about 2,00,000 tonnes, as earlier planned. So serious was the food situation that Deshmukh had planned import of an additional 2 million tonnes of wheat from the US, a move that had caused some controversy in the country, incurring the wrath of even Prime Minister Nehru, the details of which have been narrated earlier. But over the next few years, Deshmukh's worries about prices, food availability and the balance of payments situation had become a thing of the past. The Indian economy had come out of its earlier weaknesses and was showing signs of new areas of strength.

A key initiative Deshmukh had rolled out in his first Budget was an action plan on the basis of the report of the Income-tax Investigation Commission that had been set up earlier to prevent tax evasion and to recommend the steps needed to remove the loopholes in the taxation laws. A legislative bill to implement the Commission's recommendations had been introduced in the Budget session of Parliament in 1951. That marked the beginning of a drive to prevent income-tax evasion, which continues even to the present day.

Reforms of Fiscal and Taxation Policies

By the time Deshmukh rose in Parliament to present his second but the first full Budget on 23 May 1952 (his Budget on 29 February 1952 had been an interim one, preceding the first general elections in India after Independence), the beast of inflation that had troubled him earlier had been considerably tamed. The annualized inflation rate had increased to about 16 per cent in April 1951. But since that time, the wholesale price index had begun its southward journey, and by January 1952, prices had actually fallen by about 6 per cent. The declining trajectory got steeper, and by the time Deshmukh had presented his Budget, the price index had fallen by a much higher 19 per cent over the level that prevailed three months earlier. The benign trajectory of wholesale prices continued for another year almost. In December 1952, wholesale prices fell by a whopping 13 per cent. The food availability situation in the country had also become better by the time Deshmukh presented his third Budget on 27 February 1953. An improvement in the country's balance of payments situation also contributed to a marked recovery in the macro-economic indicators. This period also saw the successful culmination of negotiations between the World Bank and the Indian government over the latter getting project aid. In 1952, the World Bank President, Eugene Robert Black, visited India. This was followed by visits by several senior officials of the Bank to discuss the terms of assistance for developmental projects being undertaken by the Indian government. The visiting World Bank missions had explored loans for steel projects and irrigation schemes in the country, which eventually led to approval of loans worth $31.5 million to Indian Iron & Steel Company and $19.5 million to Damodar Valley Corporation. Another World Bank loan to the newly created Industrial Finance Corporation was under consideration. In a bid to reform the way governments functioned in discharging their policy responsibilities, Deshmukh recognized the need for seeking assistance from international experts. In 1952, he invited Paul Appleby to study the Indian administration. Appleby at that time was a reputed theorist of public administration in democracies and was based in the United States. Appleby's recommendations led to the establishment of Indian Institute of Public Administration (IIPA) in 1954. IIPA played a key role in providing policy inputs for reforming the government's administration structure.

Deshmukh's Budgets were instrumental in the rollout of the fiscal devolution system that the Indian Constitution had mandated. In the process, he was the first finance minister who had to deal with the impact of the first set of recommendations on how Central taxes should be shared among the states as mandated under the Indian Constitution. The Indian Constitution had created an independent body to decide on the formula to be followed for distribution of taxes among the states. Article 280 of the Constitution mandated that the President shall set up a Finance Commission every fifth year, headed by a chairman and consisting of other members. The Commission was required to make recommendations to the President on the following:

> . . . the distribution between the Union and the States of the net proceeds of taxes which are to be, or may be, divided between them . . . and the allocation between the States of the respective shares of such proceeds . . . the principles which should govern the grants-in-aid of the revenues of the States out of the Consolidated Fund of India; the measures needed to augment the Consolidated Fund of a State to supplement the resources of the Panchayats in the State on the basis of the recommendations made by the Finance Commission of the State; the measures needed to augment the Consolidated Fund of a State to supplement the resources of the Municipalities in the State on the basis of the recommendations made by the Finance Commission of the State and; any other matter referred to the Commission by the President in the interests of sound finance.

On 22 November 1951, the first Finance Commission was set up through a Presidential notification. It was headed by K.C. Neogy, a former minister of finance in the Nehru government, though his tenure had lasted for just about thirty-five days, stepping in as he had to fill the void after the resignation of the first finance minister, Shanmukham Chetty. In less than a month, the Neogy-led Commission had submitted its report and the recommendations were implemented through the Budget presented in May 1952. The government's decision to accept all the recommendations of the Commission meant that a larger share of the income-tax collections had to be assigned to the states, and as much as 40 per cent of the net proceeds of the Union duties of excise on tobacco, matches and vegetable products had to be shared with the states. The net effect of these recommendations was an average annual increase of over 32 per cent in transfers to the state. Against an annual transfer of Rs 65 crore to the states, the transfer amount went up to Rs 86 crore with effect from 1952. About six decades later, the fourteenth Finance Commission would make waves by recommending an increase in the share of the states in the Central tax revenues by about 10 percentage points. Finance Minister Arun Jaitley earned plaudits from experts and commentators for accepting the sharp hike in devolution to the states without a murmur. Deshmukh had quietly accepted an even higher increase in allocations to the states, and this gesture laid the strong foundations of India's fiscal federal structure.

But Deshmukh had become increasingly uncomfortable with the growing burden of the Centre's expenditure and the increasing obligation on it to share its own tax revenue resources with the states. The government had set up the second Finance Commission on 1 June 1956. The final year for implementation of the recommendations made by the first Finance Commission was 1956–57. While presenting the Budget for that fiscal year on 29 February 1956, Deshmukh underlined some of the areas of concern that the government had to address in light of the growing demand from states for transfer of resources to them. The second Finance Commission, headed by K. Santhanam, a former minister in the Nehru Cabinet, had onerous responsibilities. Apart from addressing the increasing demand for more resources for the states, it was also expected to review how the need for financial resources for the newly reorganized states would be met. Indeed, the question of distributing the proceeds from the Estate Duty and raising the ratio of income tax revenues to be shared with the states would be among the important issues that the government would have to wrestle with in the following five years.

A key initiative in Deshmukh's Budget for 1953–54 came in the form of his announcement of the government's decision to set up a 'small compact Commission, with specialised knowledge, to conduct a comprehensive enquiry into taxation'. The background to the establishment of the first taxation committee of the Indian government after Independence was the demand of many years from members of Parliament and independent experts for a 'systematic enquiry into taxation'. The surprising element in that announcement was Deshmukh's choice of the chairman for the Commission. He chose his immediate predecessor, John Matthai, to head it, dispelling whatever rumours there were about the souring of their relationship. Matthai had quit the government in a huff over Nehru's decision to set up the Planning Commission, in whose formation Deshmukh had played a key role. But setting aside such concerns, Deshmukh got Matthai to accept chairmanship of the Commission. Earlier, when Matthai was the finance minister, Deshmukh had been persuaded to become India's financial ambassador, a job that brought him closer to Nehru and eventually to succeed Matthai as the finance minister. The other members of the Commission were V.L. Mehta, who was till recently a member of the first Finance Commission, V.K.R.V. Rao, an eminent economist and founder of the Delhi School of Economics, K.R.K. Menon, the finance secretary, B. Venkatappiah, a former finance secretary of the Bombay government, and B.K. Madan, economic adviser at the Reserve Bank of India. The composition of the Commission left nobody in doubt that Deshmukh had enlisted the services of the best minds available in the country to revamp the taxation system. The Commission, established on 1 April 1953, was given two years to submit its report.

The impact of the Taxation Enquiry Commission on government finances would be felt in the next couple of years and would figure in the budgets that Deshmukh presented in the subsequent years. The Commission had submitted its report to the government in December 1954, before the deadline it had been assigned. Deshmukh described the report in glowing terms. 'It is a massive and historic document covering the entire field of taxation – Central, State and Local – and the recommendations cover a very extensive field,' he told Parliament. While presenting the Budget for 1955–56 on 28 February 1955, Deshmukh conceded that the government had had very little time to examine the report in its entirety and its recommendations. After tabling the report in Parliament, the finance minister hoped that the states too would be able to access and study the many recommendations the Commission had made with regard to state and local taxation. The broad direction of the recommendations of independent India's first tax reforms committee was towards widening the tax base, for both direct and indirect taxation, and restructuring the prevailing rates. In spite of the short time at his disposal, Deshmukh made a series of changes in the taxation structure in his Budget for 1955–56. For instance, excise duty on sugar was raised quite steeply, in keeping with the recommendations of the Commission, and the rates for cotton cloth were rationalized. A host of new items was brought under the excise regime with an ad valorem rate of 10 per cent. These items included woollen fabrics, sewing machines, electric fans, electric lighting bulbs, electric dry and storage batteries, paper (excluding newsprint) and paperboard, paints and varnishes. On direct taxes, Deshmukh followed the spirit of the Commission's recommendations, raising the exemption slab for individual income tax and introducing the concept of progressivity in taxation by phasing out tax reliefs for higher income brackets. The era of increasing taxes on those earning high incomes had begun.

The process of implementing the recommendations of the Tax Enquiry Commission continued in Deshmukh's Budget for 1956–57. In what turned out to be his last Budget, which he presented in February 1956, Deshmukh went a step further to implement most of the remaining recommendations of the Commission. The Commission's recommendations came in extremely handy for Deshmukh in a different context too, and he made full use of them in his final Budget, which was for 1956–57. The Taxation on Income (Investigation Commission) Act of 1947 had empowered the government to set up an Investigation Commission to look into cases of income-tax evasion and take penal action against the guilty. One of the provisions authorized the Centre to refer to the Commission, before a specified date, any case in which it had prima facie reasons for believing that a person had evaded payment of tax on income. In the first half of 1954, the government faced a setback as the Supreme Court invalidated this provision as ultra vires the Constitution, as it was held to be discriminatory and violative of the Fundamental Rights guaranteed by the Constitution. Soon after this, in July 1954, Deshmukh got an ordinance issued to effectively nullify the Supreme Court order. The ordinance enabled the government to take over the cases which had been started under provisions that had been declared invalid by the apex court. The ordinance, which was subsequently passed by Parliament as a law, conferred on the government powers to reopen all cases of tax evasion of more than Rs 1 lakh during the war years. But there was a time bar on this as the government could exercise such powers only up to 31 March 1956. But the Supreme Court came out with a couple of more orders that invalidated the relevant provisions of the ordinance, which had become law from 17 July 1954, and even declared the law itself as retrospectively invalid from 26 January 1950, the day the Indian Constitution was adopted. The government too was in no mood to relent as it realized that without the powers of the Investigation Commission, the responsibility of carrying out investigation into tax evasion cases would have devolved on the income tax department, which would be overburdened with the additional workload.

In a bid to address the new situation, Deshmukh decided to redraft the existing provisions of the law to enable the government to reopen old cases. In this, he was emboldened by the report of the Taxation Enquiry Commission, which had recommended that, as in other countries, there should be no time limit for reopening of cases of fraudulent tax evasion. Welcoming this, Deshmukh told Parliament that this was a desirable reform, long overdue. He said:

> The power of reopening cases beyond eight years will not be exercised unless the amount of total tax evasion exceeds Rs 1 lakh and then only with the sanction of the Central Board of Revenue. This will ensure that the powers are exercised after proper scrutiny and only in cases of substantial evasion. It is also proposed to give the Department powers of search and seizure of accounts and documents, which the Investigation Commission had and which the Taxation Enquiry Commission have recommended the Department should have.

How the government should deal with tax evasion and conduct the procedures of investigation had become a bone of contention quite soon after India gained independence. In spite of several rounds of tax reforms and introduction of technology to detect and investigate tax evasion, this continued to be a matter of controversy for every finance minister that succeeded Deshmukh.

As early as in his Budget for 1953–54, Deshmukh had raised a Budget classification issue which, even after more than seven decades of India's independence, continues to be debated among economists and public finance experts. He underlined the importance of using discretion in determining how certain types of expenditure needed to be classified—whether as capital expenditure or revenue expenditure. He was conscious of the classical and accounting definitions of expenditure and had argued that 'every effort should be made to meet current expenditure, in the sense of administrative expenditure and expenditure that does not result in the creation of tangible assets, from current revenue'. But Deshmukh was of the view that exceptions could be made to this rule in the case of expenditure, 'which, in the broader national interest, is incurred at a faster pace than would be justified by the amount of revenue that can be raised'. He introduced another discretionary criterion for making an exception for all such expenditure that even while technically not creating tangible assets for the government would result in creation of assets for the community or for the state governments.

The reason Deshmukh raised the accounting classification issue was because he was trying to dilute a principle that he himself had introduced in the very first Budget he had presented in Parliament for 1951–52. In that annual statement of the government's account, he had transferred certain types of grants from capital expenditure to revenue expenditure, on the ground that those grants did not create any durable assets for the Union government. Two years later, Deshmukh was advocating for a more flexible approach to classifying expenditure under the heads of revenue and capital. His argument for diluting that principle was that there were many grants the Centre offered to the states, which if undertaken by itself, could have been met through borrowing (in other words, on the capital side). The logic until then used to be that revenue expenditure should ideally be borne through revenue receipts (taxation and non-taxation revenues) just as capital expenditure should be met through capital receipts (principally, borrowing). However, there had arisen practical difficulties in meeting all the revenue expenditure needs only through revenue receipts as the demands on the central exchequer were on the rise for launching a host of schemes that would not create any tangible capital assets. Thus, Deshmukh wanted to exclude specific types of revenue expenditure that could be met through capital receipts. That year, Deshmukh had succeeded in getting the classifications tweaked to suit his requirements. But the debate has continued, even decades later. Over the years, the narrow definition of meeting all revenue expenditure through revenue receipts has been discarded and the debate is now focused on how the classification of revenue and capital expenditure should be redefined.

Two years later, Deshmukh would complete yet another governance reform in the supervision of government finances. With effect from

April 1955, the functions of conducting audits and overseeing accounts began to be separated in some of the government departments. Over the years, more departments would see their audit and accounting functions separated and performed by different teams. What's more, Deshmukh propagated this idea for adoption by the state governments too. What he introduced in the 1950s laid the foundations of a strong and independent auditing culture in the government; auditing operates independently of the government and is completely segregated from the accounting function.

The need for speeding up the pace of industrialization became a concern by the time Deshmukh presented his Budget for 1955–56. He took credit for having granted 110 licences for new industrial undertakings in the previous year and another 226 licences to existing undertakings for expansion. The Industrial Policy Resolution of 1956 was yet to be announced, but the licensing regime was already in place. The Resolution would later accord greater primacy and importance to public-sector undertakings. Not surprisingly, therefore, Deshmukh announced the formation of a government-owned body by the name of National Industrial Development Corporation, with the goal of achieving rapid industrialization. A year ago, in 1955, Deshmukh had already facilitated the creation of a new undertaking, the National Small Industries Corporation (NSIC), which would be tasked to undertake promotion and development of small industries in the country. In his last Budget, Deshmukh told Parliament that several schemes for developing small industries in cooperation with the state governments had been approved and NSIC was at the forefront of making sure government purchase of goods from small units got a boost.

Deshmukh, the Person

What kind of a person was Chintaman Dwarakanath Deshmukh? When he entered the hallowed portals of North Block to become the finance minister, Deshmukh was a retired ICS officer, a former RBI governor, India's former financial ambassador and a member of the recently created Planning Commission. In his personal life he was a widower, having lost his wife Rosina to a heart attack in the United Kingdom in 1949, just before the end of his tenure as the first Indian governor of the RBI. His suave personality impressed everyone. When he became the finance minister, Deshmukh was often described as the 'most charming minister'[36] in Nehru's Cabinet. A believer in austerity, he would occasionally cycle from his office in North Block to his residence at Aurangzeb Road when his official car was not available.[37] Soon after he married Durgabai in 1953, Deshmukh had deposited with her the cheque books linked with his three bank accounts, requesting her to operate them and take care of his finances. What Durgabai discovered after looking into those accounts says a lot about Deshmukh and his spartan style of living. One account had a balance of Rs 2500, the other only Rs 4000 and the third, maintained with Grindlays Bank, a balance or $1000 or $2000. And his liabilities at that time included payment of Rs 10,000 to the contractor who was building his house in Pune. Considering that India's per capita income in 1953–54 was estimated at Rs 264, the deposits in Deshmukh's bank accounts were modest.

Deshmukh and Durgabai had a personal car each, and both were Austins. Deshmukh had bought his Austin when he was in England, and it was an old car. Soon enough, Deshmukh decided to sell his own car and decided to keep only one personal car for the family. The couple also took a decision that was quite rare. When both were working, only one would draw a salary so that the services of one of them was always given free. When Deshmukh was the finance minister, Durgabai would not draw any salary from her Planning Commission job. And when Durgabai was the chairperson of the Central Social Welfare Board, Deshmukh drew only a salary of Re 1 as chairman of the UGC, an assignment that he took up after having quit as the finance minister.

Deshmukh's Departure

Deshmukh's departure from the finance ministry was as abrupt and dramatic as his entry into the Nehru Cabinet. The sudden resignation of John Matthai as the finance minister soon after Nehru had mooted the idea of a Planning Commission for India had created a vacancy that had to be filled without any delay. The irony of it was that it was Deshmukh who had earlier prepared the draft note for establishment of the Planning Commission and had even joined the newly created think tank as a member on invitation from the prime minister.

Nehru had, by then, reckoned that Deshmukh, with his credentials as a former RBI governor and as India's financial ambassador, was an almost obvious choice who could step into Matthai's shoes quite perfectly.

Thus, in spite of many other political stalwarts around him, Nehru chose Deshmukh to become his fourth finance minister in less than three years of his government's tenure.

There was yet another irony in the manner in which Deshmukh left the finance ministry. For over six years, Deshmukh had held the reins of the Union finance ministry and had steered key economic policy changes. But the factor that led to Deshmukh's resignation was not any difference over economic policies, but the way the contentious issue of reorganization of states in the country was to be handled. That happened in the summer of 1956.

But even earlier in his tenure as finance minister, Deshmukh had run into a major problem with Nehru over a minor issue of procedure. That was in the first half of 1953. When Deshmukh was in Australia earlier that year, Nehru had asked A.C. Chanda, who had been named to succeed Narhari Rao as the next Comptroller and Auditor-General of India, to examine the system of budgeting and financial controls and prepare a report on it. Deshmukh took umbrage at Nehru's asking the CAG-designate to report to the prime minister directly on matters that strictly were within the ambit of the finance minister. When Chanda's report was scheduled to be discussed in the Cabinet, Deshmukh made his displeasure known and demanded that instead of that report, the finance ministry's report on the same issue should be considered and discussed. Nehru conceded his finance minister's point, but also made a statement that spun the situation out of control. Upon seeing Deshmukh upset about his decision to ask for a report from Chanda, Nehru exclaimed: 'But surely the prime minister is the boss.' Deshmukh was in no mood to take this lying down. Making no secret of his intention to resign over that issue, he shot back: 'Yes, but a minister has always the freedom to serve on his own terms or to resign.'[38]

Deshmukh's reply was enough to fuel speculation about his quitting Nehru's Cabinet. Many members of the Congress and Parliament were unhappy and worried about Deshmukh's intended resignation. Several Parliamentarians wrote to Deshmukh suggesting that he should not resign in a huff. Nehru also softened his stance a bit and made a conciliatory gesture, and the crisis blew over. Leading industrialist B.M. Birla advised Deshmukh against taking any hasty decision. Eventually, Deshmukh decided to stay on and the Nehru–Deshmukh pair brought about many significant shifts in India's economic policy in the following three years.

But just as it seemed that the dent in the relationship between Nehru and Deshmukh had been repaired as the latter began rolling out one after another economic policy initiative that pushed the government's shift towards statism and a socialistic pattern of development, Deshmukh decided to quit. And he quit not because of any differences over economic policies, but over a political decision that Nehru took in the reorganization of states. What led to Deshmukh's departure was the manner in which Nehru tried to settle the political question of how the state of Bombay should be reorganized. Needless to say, this issue acutely strained relations between the prime minister and his finance minister in the summer months of 1956 leading up to the latter's resignation from the Cabinet.

The seeds of this discord were sown, quite unknown to either Nehru or Deshmukh, when the report of the Linguistic Provinces Commission, headed by Justice S.K. Dar (a former judge of the Allahabad High Court) submitted its report to the Constituent Assembly in December 1948. The Commission was set up only in June 1948 by the president of the Constituent Assembly to advise it on the question of forming linguistic states. In its report, the Justice Dar Commission had made a strong case against reorganizing provinces in India purely on linguistic considerations, as that would be not in the larger interests of the Indian nation. The Commission, however, recognized that oneness of language should be one of the factors to be considered while reorganizing provinces. The Congress party decided to review and examine the recommendations made by the Justice Dar Commission and decided on it at its meeting in Jaipur in December 1948. A committee with three senior Congress leaders—Jawaharlal Nehru, Vallabhbhai Patel and Pattabhi Sitaramayya—was created to report to the government on whether the Dar Commission's recommendations against reorganization of states on linguistic considerations were still valid after India had gained independence. The findings of this group of Congress leaders—also known as the JVP Committee—stirred a hornet's nest. It agreed with the overall findings of the Justice Dar Commission but also opined that if public sentiment was overwhelmingly in support of creation of linguistic states, the practicality of satisfying such a demand should be examined. It went one step ahead by suggesting that a beginning could be made by experimenting with the demand for the creation of Andhra. This added fuel to the fire that was already raging in that region.

Even as the country-wide debate over the creation of linguistic states was going on, Home Minister Vallabhbhai Patel died suddenly, from a heart attack, on 15 December 1950. This was a major setback for the government, and Nehru felt considerably weakened in the absence of Patel, who was a strong leader and had built the reputation of taking firm decisions and implementing them, even when they were unpopular and faced resistance.

Not entirely unconnected with the passing of Patel was the lack of a clear direction in the Congress's approach to policies and governance in the run-up to the forthcoming general elections in 1951, the first to be held after India gained independence. Notable in particular was the ruling party's ambiguous stance on the creation of linguistic states in general and of the state of Andhra in particular. Deshmukh noted that the question of creating Andhra on linguistic considerations was never ever brought up before the Cabinet, as Nehru was firmly opposed to the idea.

But, after the elections, the public agitation for Andhra state gained momentum, and one of the agitation leaders, Potti Sriramulu, who went on an indefinite fast over the issue, died on 16 December 1952. Nehru was unnerved by his death. The die for the creation of Andhra as a separate state had almost been cast. Three days later, Nehru announced in Parliament that the government had decided to create a state consisting of the Telugu-speaking areas in the state of Madras, except for the city of Madras and other Tamil-speaking areas. It was only in the evening of 19 December 1952 that Nehru raised the issue of Andhra at the Cabinet meeting, which by then was already a fait accompli. Deshmukh as the finance minister did not object to the violation of a procedure but was disappointed that such a decision had been taken without keeping in mind the question of overall development of the region. Deshmukh was of the view that this decision could have been taken a few years later.[39]

Ironically, this decision of Nehru's triggered demands for creation of more states. The genie of demand for linguistic states was out of the bottle. A year later, on 22 December 1953, Nehru announced in Parliament that the government had decided to appoint a commission to examine 'objectively and dispassionately' the question of reorganization of the states of the Indian Union 'so that the welfare of the people of each constituent unit as well as the nation as a whole is promoted'.[40]

A week later, the government issued a notification for the setting up of the Commission, to be headed by S. Fazl Ali, a former judge of the Supreme Court. The Commission had two members—H.N. Kunzru, a member of Parliament, and K.M. Panikkar, a renowned diplomat and author.

The report of this Commission and the way Nehru dealt with its recommendations led to a serious rupture in his relations with Deshmukh. The States Reorganisation Commission (SRC), led by Fazl Ali, did not take long to finalize its recommendations and submitted a 267-page report to the government on 30 September 1955. The Commission recommended a balanced approach and held that the concept of linguistic homogeneity should not be considered as an exclusive and binding principle, overriding all other political, economic and administrative considerations, but that the concept should be recognized as an important factor conducive to administrative convenience and efficiency. It, therefore, rejected the theory of one-language-one-state, as it found the ground of linguistic homogeneity as a determinant for reorganization of states to be neither practicable nor justified. Coming to specific issues, the SRC did not recommend division of Bombay state into Maharashtra and Gujarat. Instead, it retained Bombay state, but wanted separate states of Vidarbha and Hyderabad.

The retention of Bombay city in the state of Bombay gave rise to fresh protests from non-Marathi speaking people. It was felt that the city of Bombay was cosmopolitan in character and that this could be diluted by making it part of Maharashtra. Several rounds of negotiations with leaders of Maharashtra and Gujarat regions were held, and eventually the Nehru Cabinet decided that instead of one state, as recommended by the SRC, there should be three states—Maharashtra, Gujarat and Bombay city. Deshmukh was given the responsibility of persuading the Vidarbha leaders to agree to become part of Maharashtra, even though the SRC had recommended a separate state for Vidarbha. Deshmukh was not fully convinced of the three-state formula adopted by the Cabinet because he believed that the economic viability of the new states would pose a big question mark. Indeed, he believed that not partitioning Bombay state would have been a better option. But he went along with the Cabinet decision and completed his discussions with the Vidarbha leaders, bringing them around to the Cabinet view of the three-state formula.

A shock, however, awaited him on 16 January 1956, when Nehru made an announcement at a public meeting in the city of Bombay overruling the Cabinet decision. Nehru declared that Bombay city would be a centrally administered territory under the three-way division of the state of Bombay. Deshmukh believed that Nehru did not have the Constitutional authority to make such an announcement, which ran against the decision taken in the Cabinet just a few days ago. Nehru's logic was that Bombay city, given its multicultural and multiethnic population, could be governed better if it was administered as a union territory. It would go neither to the Gujaratis nor to the Marathi people. But Nehru's logic had few takers among the people of Bombay city, among the political parties active in the region, and of course in Deshmukh, his finance minister.

The city of Bombay was ravaged by violent demonstrations and riots, leading to then Chief Minister Morarji Desai asking police to open fire, which led to over eighty deaths. The agitations continued for well over a week. Nehru tried to appease the crowds. The Marathi people felt betrayed, as instead of three states—Bombay state, Maharashtra and Gujarat—they were losing Bombay city to the Centre as it would become a union territory. The Gujarati business leaders were keen that Bombay become a union territory and found Desai and Nehru to be sympathetic to their views. But, under the banner of Samyukta Maharashtra Samiti, the agitation among the people spread and gained momentum.

A disheartened and betrayed Deshmukh decided it was time for him to quit the Nehru government. His colleagues in the Maharashtra Congress decided to resign their posts and Deshmukh decided to join them. But subsequently, many of these state Congress leaders developed cold feet and decided to rethink their move. Deshmukh did not. He sent in his resignation to the prime minister. Even as the rioting began affecting many parts of Bombay city, Deshmukh pressed for acceptance of his resignation. Nehru told Deshmukh that there was no hurry for his resignation to be accepted as he was optimistic of a resolution of the crisis at the forthcoming session of the Congress to be held in Amritsar. But Deshmukh remained unmoved. Finally, Nehru asked Deshmukh to wait till July as he would be away from the country for about a month and he would resolve the issue once he returned. Before he embarked on his foreign tour, Nehru made one more attempt at persuading the agitators in Bombay to accept his formula to have Bombay city as a centrally administered territory. He addressed a public meeting in Bombay on 3 June 1956 to reiterate his decision, but there was no way the people would accept that formula.

On his return, Nehru called for a meeting with Deshmukh. A few senior Congress leaders were also present at that meeting. Deshmukh's explanation as to why he felt the formula adopted by Nehru would not be in the national interest was met with silence. Finally, Nehru responded: 'I think there is something to be said for what Mr Deshmukh has to say.' That was all. No compromise formula was offered or suggested by either Nehru or any other members present at the meeting. Deshmukh got up and decided to leave the meeting. Even as he left the room, Govind Ballabh Pant, who was no friend of Deshmukh's, said: 'Don't go. We may find some solution.'[41] Deshmukh was still unmoved, pretty sure that no attempt would be made to break the deadlock, and made a public statement criticizing the move and explaining why he had resigned from the government and Parliament after having remained part of both for about six years.

All efforts to persuade Deshmukh to reconsider his decision failed. His private secretary did everything to delay the dispatch of his final resignation letter to the prime minister, hoping that Deshmukh would change his mind. One day, the secretary even approached his wife, Durgabai, to speak to Deshmukh asking him to not insist on resigning. Durgabai tried to convince her husband to change his mind. Deshmukh did not wish to retrace the steps he had decided to take and used an expression that appeared to tell off Durgabai, for which she remained upset for many days. 'Oh, you married me because I am the finance minister,' Deshmukh had remarked.[42] Durgabai was taken aback by that response as she felt her husband had misunderstood her. She went back to his private secretary and asked him to dispatch the resignation letter. Deshmukh was later quite penitent about having made that remark to Durgabai and also turned down her request.[43]

In the weeks following his resignation, Deshmukh made a series of pronouncements making his stance on Bombay state clear. In his public speeches, Deshmukh became highly critical of the police brutalities and the role of the administration of the time, headed by Chief Minister

Morarji Desai, in containing the agitation and violence that had rocked Bombay city. He began speaking openly about why he felt the move to make Bombay city a centrally administered territory would be inviting administrative and economic trouble as that region could not be separated from its hinterland. 'Whether this was a Marathi-speaking or Gujarati-speaking district was to me a matter of no consequence,' Deshmukh wrote in his biography.[44] Congress leaders like Feroze Gandhi and Deva Kant Barua made personal appeals to him to withdraw his resignation. But Deshmukh could not be persuaded.

However, as the agitation in Bombay spread and it became difficult for the administration to restore law and order, the pressure within the Congress began mounting to maintain the status quo as far as the proposed reorganization of Bombay state was concerned. The legislative bill for the reorganization of states was amended to keep the state of Bombay, including Bombay city, undivided. The bill was passed by Parliament and normality returned to Bombay. Deshmukh had already resigned as the finance minister, and this was accepted with effect from 25 July 1956. A little after the passage of the legislative bill, Deshmukh resigned from Parliament as well, ending his career in politics.

A disturbing question continued to linger—why did Nehru not persuade Deshmukh to stay on in the government as his finance minister or in politics as a Congress leader? The new legislative bill had addressed Deshmukh's concerns and the main reason that drove Deshmukh to resign no longer existed. This remains a puzzle. Independent India's fourth finance minister, who ushered in key economic policy changes at the behest of his prime minister, had to quit the government over political differences with his boss. But those differences had been sorted out. So, why did Deshmukh still have to go? Deshmukh's belief was that his relations with Nehru might have become a little strained in the last few years of his tenure, largely because of the presence of senior leaders like Govind Ballabh Pant, who would have been happy to see him go. And T.T. Krishnamachari, who was no friend of Deshmukh's, was waiting to take charge of the finance ministry, if there were to be a vacancy. And that is exactly what happened. Deshmukh's departure from North Block, headquarters of the finance ministry, was followed by the appointment of T.T. Krishnamachari as the next finance minister.

No Dent in the Nehru–Deshmukh Relationship

That Deshmukh had suffered no loss of Nehru's goodwill even after his open criticism of the government proposal for reorganization of Bombay state became evident soon after he quit the finance ministry. A few days before his departure from North Block, Humayun Kabir, education secretary at that time, visited Deshmukh at his residence and hesitatingly asked if he could explore an idea with the finance minister. Kabir had then just given up his additional responsibility as chairman of the University Grants Commission (UGC), an apex body set up in 1953 for regulating and maintaining standards in university education, granting recognition to universities and disbursing government funds to them. Reassured by Deshmukh that Kabir could go ahead and share his thoughts, the education secretary told him that he was actually an emissary of Education Minister Maulana Abul Kalam Azad, who wanted to find out if after his resignation Deshmukh would be ready to accept chairmanship of the UGC. Even though almost three years had passed after its formation, the Commission had not yet become a statutory body. In the absence of Kabir, long-standing parliamentarian and academic H.N. Kunzru had been asked to head the Commission till such time as a full-time chairman could be found. Deshmukh had always had a deep and abiding interest in education and academic matters. He expressed his apprehensions that Nehru and Azad might have second thoughts on his becoming the UGC chairman as they might be upset with him for the public speeches that he would deliver over the next few days criticizing the government for its policies on reorganization of states in general and Bombay state in particular. Kabir promptly replied that the proposal had been cleared by Nehru and Azad and that none of Deshmukh's speeches would alter their decision in the matter. Deshmukh gave his consent to the proposal.

But shortly after this, Deshmukh received a phone call from B.K. Nehru, joint secretary in the finance ministry at that time, asking if he would have any objection to his name being considered for the post of managing director of the International Monetary Fund. Deshmukh would have been a strong contender for the job, with an attractive annual salary of $30,000 and other perquisites. Once again, Deshmukh wondered if Prime Minister Nehru had cleared the proposal for his nomination as MD of the IMF. What B.K. Nehru said in reply dispelled all doubts about

Nehru's feelings towards Deshmukh: 'Oh, that is all right. In fact, it is he who has sent me to find out if you are willing. He says it will be a feather in India's cap if you were to be appointed managing director of the Fund.'

The ball was now in Deshmukh's court. After discussing the offers with his wife, Durgabai, Deshmukh decided against accepting the proposal for his nomination for the top job at the IMF. He wanted to be in India and devote more time to contribute meaningfully to the development of his motherland. He informed B.K. Nehru that he would not be interested in the IMF job. Azad learnt of Deshmukh's decision to opt for chairmanship of the UGC and sent a touching and gracious message:

> I am sorry to learn, Deshmukh, that you have expressed unwillingness to be considered for managing directorship of the IMF. If you think that the word you have given me to accept the chairmanship of the UGC stands in the way, I am prepared to absolve you of that promise.

Deshmukh was indeed touched and replied: 'No, Maulana Sahab, that is not the case. Durgabai and I do not wish to work abroad. We feel that the duty of each in the respective spheres lies here.'

Within a few days, Deshmukh joined the UGC as its fourth chairman and soon got the Commission the much-needed statutory backing through the enactment of a law. Nehru lost his finance minister because of his political miscalculations over reorganization of Bombay state. But, the tall leader that he was, Nehru did not get upset by Deshmukh's bold decision to quit the government and criticize the move publicly. Instead, Nehru got him back into the government system by having him as chairman of the UGC, a tenure that lasted for five long years.

Many years later, in March 1991, Manmohan Singh, who like Deshmukh was also the RBI governor, would become chairman of the UGC and just three months later move to North Block as the finance minister to usher in economic reforms to bail the Indian economy out of an unprecedented crisis. That is another story, but this connection between the RBI, the UGC and the finance ministry is unique and even uncanny.

T.T. Krishnamachari (Finance Minister, 1956–1958)

Singed by the Mundhra Scandal

When Tiruvallur Thattai Krishnamachari became India's finance minister in August 1956, he was not Prime Minister Nehru's first choice for that coveted position in the government. C.D. Deshmukh had quit as the finance minister soon after presenting the Budget for 1956–57 over the manner in which Nehru had proposed to reorganize the states, particularly those in the western part of the country. Nehru had zeroed in on Morarji Desai, the chief minister of Bombay, to succeed Deshmukh. Desai accepted the offer, but on the condition that he be allowed to wind up his responsibilities in Bombay, which he could do only by the end of October, allowing him to take charge of the finance ministry in November 1956. Nehru had even agreed to this arrangement and had decided that he would hold the additional responsibility of the finance ministry till Desai came to New Delhi to take charge at North Block, headquarters of the finance ministry.

However, the deteriorating condition of the Indian economy was worrying, and Nehru was advised by many of his senior colleagues that it needed urgent attention, particularly the rapidly deteriorating foreign exchange reserves, and that waiting for a finance minister for two more months would not be advisable.

An alternative had to be found soon, not just because Nehru could not hold the finance portfolio for two more months but because there were other powerful forces at work in New Delhi. There were many in the government who were not very comfortable with the idea of Morarji Desai as the next finance minister. Desai, after all, was a strict disciplinarian known for his no-nonsense approach and as a stickler for correctness to the point of being self-righteous. Krishnamachari, on the other hand, had already wormed his way closer to Nehru by professing his socialistic predilections as far as economic policies were concerned. In his heart of hearts, Nehru would have been more comfortable with Krishnamachari as his finance minister. Desai's condition that he would be able to join the finance ministry at the Centre only by November gave Nehru an opportunity to try out Krishnamachari as his man in North Block.

Deshmukh had quit the finance ministry by the end of July 1956. Nehru held temporary charge of the ministry for the whole of August before handing it over to Krishnamachari, who at that time was in the Union Cabinet looking after the ministry of commerce and industry with the additional responsibility of the ministry of iron and steel. From September 1956, Krishnamachari shifted to the finance ministry, taking charge of the government's economic management.

Krishnamachari was no greenhorn in Indian politics, quite unlike his predecessor C.D. Deshmukh, for whom becoming the minister for finance in 1950 had meant a direct plunge into the political arena after years in the civil services, including a stint as governor of the Reserve Bank of India for close to six years.

A graduate from Madras University, Krishnamachari was the only son of a High Court judge. He began his career as a government servant, but soon, at the age of twenty-eight, left that job to try his hand at business. The TTK Group was born, and the business flourished even as it became the representative of Lever Brothers in southern India, selling soaps and a variety of consumer items. With business growth came social prestige and equity, which Krishnamachari was keen to exploit in the world of politics. By 1937, the young business leader joined politics and the Congress-led movement for India's independence. He was focused on the goal of removal of poverty. He even began to wear homespun clothes as a mark of his empathy for this noble cause. In 1942, he was elected to the central legislative assembly. This plunged him into the centre of national politics—he became a member of the Constituent Assembly which had been tasked to draft the Indian Constitution.

Flaunting Socialistic Leanings

After India gained independence from British rule in 1947, Nehru formed his government, but Krishnamachari had to wait for about five years before he could make his debut in the Union council of ministers. He won the Lok Sabha seat, representing Madras in 1952, and became India's first minister for commerce and industry. Even in that position, Krishnamachari was quite open about his socialistic leanings. Soon after joining the government, he wrote to the finance minister, C.D. Deshmukh, about his views on the need for nationalizing Imperial Bank of India in a manner that was nothing short of calling a spade a shovel, if not a spade. His letter said:

> If I were in your position, I should have put up opposite my seat in the room on the wall a slogan *Delenda est Imperial Bank* (The Imperial Bank must be destroyed, after Cato the Elder), but luckily for the Imperial Bank it is not so, and a more sober person happened to occupy the chair.[1]

Eventually, Imperial Bank of India was indeed nationalized in 1955 and came to be known as State Bank of India. This was almost at around the same time that Krishnamachari's portfolio was expanded to include the ministry for iron and steel. And a year later, in 1956, he gave up the commerce and industry ministry to become the finance minister, while retaining charge of the iron and steel ministry for some more time.

The *New York Times* described Krishnamachari as a 'controversial politician [who] at the peak of his career in the 1950s and 1960s, helped Nehru implement the Congress party's socialist policies into legislative measures'.[2] There is no denying that Krishnamachari had a streak of Leftist economic thinking. The imposition of a wealth tax and estate duty were an outcome of his leadership as the finance minister in Nehru's Cabinet. But in 1959, he gave an interview to the *New York Times*, where he proclaimed he was an 'enemy of communism' and said in no uncertain terms that communist China was a danger. This created a major controversy and the minister had to retract his views.

But Krishnamachari continued to enjoy the confidence of Nehru. Even a scandal involving his dealings with a controversial businessman, Haridas Mundhra, caused no long-term damage to that confidence. Yes, under tremendous pressure, Nehru had to let go of Krishnamachari, who resigned as the finance minister in 1958, but Krishnamachari bounced back as a minister in Nehru's Cabinet by 1962, and a year later had regained the portfolio of finance.

Krishnamachari's dealings with businessmen, and indeed with his own business family, however, remained a cause for many a controversy. Krishnamachari did try to maintain a distance from the business he had set up and handed over to his sons. Once, when his family business was close to bagging a coveted deal for distributing milk products from Amul, a milk dairy cooperative in Anand, Gujarat, Krishnamachari intervened to make sure the deal did not go through.

But there would be occasions when he would become indirectly involved in the family business. The TTK Group had applied for a licence to produce products for Pond's, a multinational brand, but the then chief minister of Madras, C. Rajagopalachari, rejected the application, saying 'Sita never used cosmetics. I do not understand why Indian women need such products now.'[3] Krishnamachari was the minister for commerce and industry in New Delhi at that time. He did not wish to get involved and sent the file to Nehru, recusing himself as an interested party. Nehru, however, intervened and approved the project. Nehru is believed to have told H.V.R. Iengar (principal secretary in the industry ministry at that time) that 'Sita was a naturally beautiful woman and not many Indians are blessed like her, so they must have the help they feel they must need.'[4]

That was the kind of confidence Nehru had in Krishnamachari. This was also an indication of the strong relationship the two enjoyed. Even before he became the finance minister, Krishnamachari, as the commerce minister, played a critical role in policymaking in the government. B.K. Nehru, who enjoyed senior positions in the finance ministry from 1954 to 1961, summed up the relationship between the two and Krishnamachari's role in the government quite succinctly in the following words: 'T.T. Krishnamachari, a most dynamic Minister and a most powerful character, dominated the economic scene. He was the Commerce Minister but in practice it was he, not the Finance Minister who was in charge of economic policy.'[5] The finance minister at that time was C.D. Deshmukh.

B.K. Nehru believed that the prime minister's knowledge of financial and economic issues was very limited and therefore Krishnamachari had an almost free run in influencing economic policies at the time. What helped Krishnamachari grow his importance in policymaking was the fact that Deshmukh hardly had any political clout. 'TTK wanted the economy to develop and develop fast; for this purpose, he wanted to import and import here and now anything and everything that was not being produced in India,' wrote Nehru.[6] This eventually landed the Indian economy in a foreign exchange crisis, and the execution of the Second Plan, dependent as it was on a significant increase in imports, faced huge challenges. It was some sort of poetic justice that Krishnamachari, as finance minister from 1956 to 1958, had to pay the price for planning excessive imports as the commerce minister.

•

Backed by a Formidable Reputation

Krishnamachari was a towering personality in Nehru's Cabinet. His knowledge of finance, aided by his understanding of commerce from having run a business, was matched by few among his ministerial colleagues. Deshmukh was the other Cabinet minister who had a similar understanding of finance, but then his proximity to Nehru was far less than that of Krishnamachari. Remember that as the minister for commerce and industry, Krishnamachari had helped Nehru roll out the Industrial Policy Resolution of 1956 that ushered in greater control for the state over economic activities by introducing the licensing regime and by according a greater role to the public sector. One of the reasons why Krishnamachari became Nehru's favourite minister was the former's ability to articulate the government's economic policies in a format that was acceptable both politically and to industry.

For instance, in his introduction to the Industries (Development and Regulation) Amendment Bill, Krishnamachari's smooth use of words soothed the frayed tempers of industry which was threatened by the rise of statism and greater control of economic activities by the state. Camouflaging the actual intention of the bill, Krishnamachari said:

> The intention of the Government is not to work this measure from a punitive aspect but largely from the developmental aspect . . . I would assure them (industry leaders) that the Government would not needlessly interfere with the industrial process. The Government would not damage the climate that now exists in regard to the relationship between the Government and private enterprise . . . I would also say categorically that this Act is not to be used as a method for nationalization of industries . . . When we nationalize industries, we shall do it in a

very straight-forward manner. But this is intended to keep the industry moving, and our intention is merely to act as a trustee.[7]

Even before he took charge of the finance ministry, Krishnamachari had given ample evidence of his obsession with growing his jurisdictional power and expanding his turf of control within the government. Krishnamachari was not satisfied with just playing the role of a commerce and industry minister. In November 1954, he had argued within the government that he wanted control and direction of industrial policy unified under his charge. This implied that all iron and steel projects, those in the private sector as well as the public sector, had to come under the jurisdiction of the commerce and industry ministry under Krishnamachari. Prime Minister Nehru, on the other hand, was not agreeable to accepting such a demand and instead expressed his unhappiness at the relatively slow pace of progress of industrial projects in the country. But a change of heart took place, and by May 1955 Nehru agreed to create a ministry of iron and steel, and this was added to Krishnamachari's portfolio. Krishnamachari had asked for more. He wanted the heavy engineering projects too to be brought under his ministry, but that demand was not accepted. But the manner in which Krishnamachari asked for more and expanded his turf within the Cabinet was ample testimony to his growing importance in the government. His proximity to Nehru was certainly only one of the reasons he was chosen to succeed Deshmukh as the next finance minister in 1956, even though Morarji Desai was the first choice of the prime minister.

On an earlier occasion, Krishnamachari even went as far as rejecting the charge that his decision to liberalize imports in the early 1950s had dampened the sentiment in the domestic industry to produce more at home. In 1953, Jawaharlal Nehru wrote to him: 'The encouragement of Indian industry would only take place if there was the urge (to get our needs fulfilled from within) and a vacuum to be filled; if there is no vacuum, the urge to produce (in the spirit of the old philosophy of Swadeshi) grows less.'[8] In reply, Krishnamachari said:

The question, however, has to be viewed from a different perspective altogether. We in India have become an international trading community. We do want to export some of our manufactured goods, and some surplus raw materials. In adjusting a foreign trade of this nature, autarchic principles which we call in our language, Swadeshiism have only a limited application. If we do export, we must import, and what we import must be consumed in the country. We cannot import only what we consider to be good for the people.[9]

There can be little doubt that Krishnamachari's bond with and influence over Nehru grew also because the former was fully supportive of the latter's socialist policies. Not surprisingly, Krishnamachari also succeeded in making many enemies among those politicians like Morarji Desai, who subscribed to the idea of free enterprise, and among many industrialists. This was certainly one of the reasons why Krishnamachari had to quit the government soon after Nehru's death in 1964.

A Mini-Budget before the 1957 Elections

In just about three months after taking charge of the finance ministry, Krishnamachari had to present a detailed statement on the prevailing economic situation to Parliament and unveil an array of taxation proposals. The rationale for this was the steady deterioration in the state of the Indian economy. Inflation had reared its ugly head. The last two weeks of November alone had seen a rise of 10 points in the wholesale price index. The full year of 1956–57 would eventually end with an inflation rate (based on wholesale prices) of close to 14 per cent. Imports were growing at an uncomfortably high rate, widening the trade gap, turning the current account balance from a surplus to a deficit and depleting the foreign exchange reserves at a faster pace.

The full year's data on all these parameters would confirm the finance minister's worrying assessment: 1956–57 saw imports spurt by over 44 per cent to Rs 1,100 crore, the trade deficit widen to Rs 464 crore (up from Rs 121 crore in 1955–56), the current account balance turning into a deficit of Rs 312 crore from a surplus of Rs 12 crore in the previous year, and the country's foreign exchange reserves depleting by Rs 221 crore against an accretion of Rs 12 crore in 1955–56. As for national income, its real rate of growth was on a decelerating spree for the third year running— from 6 per cent in 1953–54 to 2.5 per cent in 1954–55 and further down to 1.9 per cent in 1955–56. There would be a recovery in national income growth in 1956–57 to about 5 per cent, only to give way to a bigger crisis in 1957–58, when the national income at constant prices would actually decline by around 1 per cent.

Aggravating the domestic economic situation was the pressure the Second Plan had begun putting on the government's resources. The two main objectives of the Second Five-year Plan, finalized in 1956 to run till March 1961, were an increase in national income and rapid industrialization, with the main focus being development of basic and heavy industries. The national income was targeted to grow by an average annual rate of 5 per cent in the five-year period, from Rs 10,800 crore in 1955–56 to Rs 13,480 crore in 1960–61 (calculated at 1952–53 prices). In order to achieve this ambitious goal, the rate of investment was slated to go up from 7 per cent of GDP in 1955–56 to 11 per cent in 1960–61.

An outlay of Rs 4800 crore for the public sector and Rs 3100 crore for the private sector constituted the total size of the Second Plan. All these targets were hugely ambitious. As feared, the execution of the Second Plan met with headwinds from many directions: a sharp decline in food output resulting in higher inflation, and increasing recourse to deficit financing for want of domestic government resources leading to further inflation. Moreover, the need for huge imports created a foreign exchange crisis.

Challenges before the New Finance Minister

As the finance minister, Krishnamachari was faced with the challenges of making both ends meet as far as the Second Plan was concerned. There was initial bravado on the part of the government that the Plan must remain ambitious and the hurdles overcome without scaling down its targets. Eventually, however, the Second Plan size had to be curtailed. The Plan was split in two parts—one part entailing an outlay of Rs 4,500 crore, including core projects, and the other part with an extra outlay of Rs 300 crore for projects if additional resources were available.[10] But till the Plan size was curtailed and resources found for its execution, Krishnamachari was a worried finance minister.

The international trade situation and international economic relations had also turned quite adverse. President Gamal Abdel Nasser of Egypt had decided in July 1956 to nationalize the Suez Canal, which was a key maritime trade route linking the Mediterranean Sea with the Red Sea, providing the shortest connection between the East and the West. This decision was frowned upon by many countries. Protesting the nationalization, the combined forces of England, France and Israel invaded Egypt in retaliation three months later, on 29 October 1956. The Canal remained closed for five months before it could reopen in March 1957, creating major difficulties on the imports front for countries like India on its eastern side.

In his statement before Parliament, Krishnamachari expressed concern about the adverse impact of the hostilities in that region and of the closure of the Suez Canal on the Indian economy:

> We are taking measures to ensure that the available shipping space is utilized for bringing in our priority imports. A certain lengthening of shipping schedules is, of course, unavoidable, and freight rates and insurance charges have already gone up . . . All I should like to say is that for the next few months we shall have to exercise the fullest vigil not only in regard to our internal situation but also in respect of developments abroad.

Both the domestic and international economic situation, including the resources and inflation challenges arising out of the Second Plan, were the main considerations that drove Krishnamachari's new taxation proposals announced by him that day. The Second Plan had envisaged additional taxation measures to net about Rs 850 crore over a period of five years, Krishnamachari reminded Parliament. But the challenges of raising taxes had dismayed the finance minister. Explaining the rationale for widening the tax base instead of just increasing the existing taxes, he said:

> If a development programme of the dimensions we have in hand is to be carried through successfully, the tax system has to be made more elastic. It is hardly possible to do this by stepping up any further the rates of direct taxation, which has now reached a stage when a straightforward increase in the rates would yield poor results. It is necessary now to increase the coverage of taxation by reaching a class of incomes, which has hitherto been kept out of the purview of the income taxation – I mean capital gains,

In India, capital gains tax was introduced in April 1946, but it remained in force for just about two years and was withdrawn in April 1948. In 1956, the Indian government had invited Nicholas Kaldor, a well-known British economist, to advise it on the kind of taxation reforms that needed to be introduced. One of the taxes whose introduction Kaldor had strongly advocated was capital gains tax, and Krishnamachari had accepted the idea.

Thus, on 30 November 1956, capital gains tax made its entry into the taxation system once again. It was a tax that from then onwards would permanently remain in the Indian taxation system. According to Krishnamachari's proposal, the broad concept of capital gains, as was prevalent between 1946 and 1948, remained unchanged, but some of the exemptions in the earlier scheme were removed to make the new taxation law tighter. As a result, capital gains on transfer of property on its compulsory acquisition, distribution of assets on dissolution of partnerships or on liquidation of companies and on the sale of residential property possessed by the taxpayer for at least seven years, were subjected to tax. The exemption limits were also lowered. Capital gains above Rs 5000 were now to be taxed, instead of the earlier exemption limit of Rs 15,000. Taxpayers with an annual income of less than Rs 10,000, however, were exempted from the new capital gains tax. While companies were made to pay the capital gains tax at their income tax rate, individuals were subjected to a higher rate. A leeway was given to taxpayers when it came to measuring the capital gains on which they were to pay the tax. They were free to have the gains measured either on the basis of the original cost of acquisition of the asset or on the basis of its value as on 1 January 1954. Nevertheless, Krishnamachari had given a clear indication of his keenness to tax the rich to make good the government's resources shortfall to finance the Second Plan so the country could withstand the adverse impact of the macroeconomic imbalances. Indeed, more taxation measures were to follow.

The second proposal related to an increase in the super-tax rates to be levied on companies that declared dividends in excess of 6 per cent of their paid-up capital. Once again, the principle of soaking up money from rich companies was in operation. From 1957–58, the new super-tax was to be 12.5 per cent for those companies that declared dividends of between 6 per cent and 10 per cent, 25 per cent on those giving dividends of between

10 per cent and 18 per cent, and a steep 37.5 per cent on companies that declared dividends in excess of 18 per cent. Before Krishnamachari's new super-tax imposts, the rates were 12.5 per cent on companies giving dividends between 6 per cent and 10 per cent, and 18.75 per cent on companies declaring dividends of more than 10 per cent.

Yet another change pertained to the norms governing depreciation allowances and development rebates for companies under the income-tax law. Companies have always been allowed to deduct the amount of money they earmark for depreciation allowances or development rebates from their taxable income. This is one of the instruments by which companies are encouraged to allocate more of their surplus income for renewing their assets or to make investment in new projects. These are tax-free reserves companies are allowed to maintain.

Short of resources to meet the government's investment outlay, Krishnamachari decided to tap into these reserves too, and made the following announcement:

In the interests of the industrial development of the country, it is necessary that these tax-free reserves are utilised for purposes conducive thereto and not frittered away in other ways. Once we accept the policy of discouraging the distribution of profits, it is essential simultaneously to ensure that the retained profits are put to uses which promote industrial development in accordance with the plan. I propose, therefore, that in the case of companies, depreciation allowances and development rebates due will be added back in the computation of the income, unless a certain amount is deposited with the Government or with the Reserve Bank of India, as the Government might determine, before the 30th June of the relevant assessment year.

This essentially meant that the tax benefits of depreciation allowance and development rebate would be withdrawn if a certain part of those reserves was not parked with the government or the central bank. There would be a ceiling on the amount to be so parked with the government and the RBI, and this ceiling was set by Krishnamachari at 50 per cent of the current profits after payment of taxes and dividends. Such impounding of corporate profits by the government shocked Indian companies and private capital, even though these deposits would have earned an interest and were refundable wholly or in part on request by the companies if the government was satisfied that the amount refunded would be used for furtherance of the investment objectives of the Plan.

Non-investment companies under Section 23A of the Companies Act also came under higher tax levy. The super-tax on companies that failed to declare a minimum dividend of 60 per cent of the share price was raised to 37.5 per cent on the whole of their undistributed profits, up from the existing rate of 25 per cent. However, in a bid to encourage investment companies to commit more to investing in new projects, Krishnamachari provided them an incentive. The 50 per cent super-tax on such investment companies would be levied only if they failed to make less than 50 per cent dividend distribution, compared to the earlier minimum requirement of 60 per cent.

Krishnamachari's new taxation proposals covered indirect taxation as well. He doubled the customs duty on wines and alcohol from 25 per cent to 50 per cent. Customs duty was raised for motorcycles, scooters, clocks and watches too. The logic was to tax more those items consumed by the 'more well-to-do sections of the population'. Another category of items that attracted higher customs duty included coal tar dyes, certain types of machinery and artificial silk yarn, on which it was felt that the existing duties were low and that indigenous manufacturing of those items had made decent progress. The influence of socialist policies on the Budget was evident as import duties were raised on items consumed by the rich or where domestic industry deserved some sort of protection. A similar approach informed Krishnamachari's excise duty changes. This led to a steep increase in the excise duty on more expensive types of motor cars, made in India, by Rs 3000. This duty was steep, considering that the price of Hindustan Ambassador, launched in 1957, was priced then at about Rs 14,000. It was no surprise that small cars and trucks were exempted from the higher excise duty. 'To the extent, it discourages the production of big cars, we will have diverted valuable foreign exchange to objects of greater utility,' Krishnamachari explained.

The logic of presenting what looked like a mini-Budget in the middle of the financial year was that the government needed to plug the deficit in the resources required for implementing the Second Plan. The full benefits of the measures announced in November 1956 would accrue to the government only from 1957–58, but the steps laid the foundation for securing an adequate flow of resources for the Plan. Krishnamachari also highlighted the need for raising the rate of savings in the country so that investment needs could be met from domestic resources. He was still confident that the Second Plan did not have to be pruned to overcome the shortage of resources, and ended his statement on a positive note:

> It is suggested in some quarters that we ought to revise our Plan in view of the increase in the outlays and particularly in view of the unfavourable turn in the international situation. I think suggestions of this kind are defeatist in themselves and are quite unjustified. We are only in the first year of the Plan and although the tasks we have taken upon ourselves are large and difficult, I see no reason to be pessimistic of our capacity to implement the Plan.

The irony of this optimism was that less than a year later, adjustments in the Second Plan were made.

Differences with RBI and Exit of Rama Rau

One of the taxation proposals Krishnamachari made in his November 1956 mini Budget pertained to the stamp duties levied on bills of exchange. That decision did not yield any revenues for the Centre, as the collections under this head had to be transferred to the states under the prevailing devolution formula. But the finance minister proposed to increase the statutory rate of stamp duties on such bills of exchange to Rs 10 per Rs 1000-denomination bills, with a proportionate reduction for bills of shorter tenures. This was a steep increase—up from the flat rate of two annas per Rs 1000, imposed in 1940. The effective rate, however, would be only half the proposed rate, which was to be a ceiling rate. 'This increase of duty is, it will be appreciated, a fiscal measure with a monetary intent,' Krishnamachari explained. As subsequent developments showed, it was the monetary intent of the proposal that provoked the Reserve Bank of India to oppose this move and that widened the differences between the RBI top brass at that time and the finance minister, eventually leading to the premature resignation of RBI Governor Sir Benegal Rama Rau.

Sir Benegal was an Indian Civil Service (ICS) officer, but he had spent several years abroad as India's ambassador to countries such as South Africa, Japan and the United States. On 1 July 1949, Sir Benegal joined the RBI as its second Indian governor, succeeding C.D. Deshmukh who had completed a stint of more than six years as the head of the country's central bank. When Krishnamachari became the finance minister in August 1956, Sir Benegal had already spent about seven years at the helm of the RBI. The experienced RBI governor, however, could not get his equations right with the new finance minister. Or perhaps it was the other way round. The entry in RBI History covering the period notes that 'Rama Rau's later years in office were ones of relative quiet, or of consolidation if one is disposed to take a more generous view, and he was a tired man by the time T.T. Krishnamachari forced him out of office in January 1957.' How the exit of an RBI governor, the first after India gained independence in 1947, took place is a story that also captures the deep tension implicit in the relationship between the finance minister, who is in charge of fiscal policy, and the governor of the RBI, who is in charge of monetary policy.

Strains in the relations between Sir Benegal and Krishnamachari became evident soon after the latter took charge of the finance ministry at the end of August 1956. The new finance minister did not take long to express publicly his differences with the RBI over the way the latter had framed its busy-season credit policy. In those days, the RBI would announce its credit policy to indicate its interest rate regime and the credit allocations twice a year—during the lean or slack season in April and during the busy season in October. Soon after the unveiling of the busy-season credit policy by Sir Benegal for 1956, Krishnamachari used the platform of a public meeting, where Sir Benegal was also present, to say that the central bank's policy stance was different from what it had indicated earlier.

The Reserve Bank of India had good reasons for adopting a cautious approach to an easier credit policy. With the end of the First Five-year Plan and the start of the Second Five-year Plan, the RBI was confronted with the dual challenges of acute financial stringency at one level and considerable inflationary potential at another. During its discussions with the government on the busy-season monetary policy for 1956–57, the RBI had made clear its preference for 'maintaining a complementary restrictive policy stance in both the fiscal and monetary spheres alongside making special efforts to meet clearly identified credit needs, which could be justified in the larger interest of the community'.[11] The government policy was different, and had favoured an easier credit policy to meet the requirements of the Second Plan's investment targets. The RBI adopted a policy of 'controlled expansion', since the finance minister had already held a series of meetings with bankers to release more credit into the economy. Thus, the RBI's busy-season policy-controlled credit flows after a phase of expansion. The credit extended by commercial banks to the private sector, as a result, rose by Rs 165 crore during 1956–57—a level of increase which was not exceeded until 1960–61. Yet, Krishnamachari was upset with the RBI for having regulated the credit flow with its overall policy stance. A few weeks after the announcement of the busy-season credit policy, relations between Krishnamachari and the RBI Governor saw a further deterioration.

What led to a major flare-up between the two was a proposal that Krishnamachari had announced in his November 1956 taxation proposals in Parliament. The relevant portion of the finance minister's speech ran as follows:

> I propose also to increase substantially the stamp duties on the Bills of Exchange. As the House is aware, there are certain slab rates prescribed in the Stamp Act which go up to 15 annas per Rs.1, 000 in the case of bills payable not more than a year after they are drawn. By a Notification issued in 1940, these slab rates were substituted by a flat rate of two annas per Rs.1,000. It is now proposed to increase the statutory rate to Rs.10 per Rs.1,000 for such bills with proportionate reduction for bills of shorter duration. These are intended to be ceiling rates and it is my present intention to operate on the basis of half these rates. This increase of duty is, it will be appreciated, a fiscal measure with a monetary intent. The additional revenue resulting from the increase will accrue to State Governments. There is thus no effect on Central revenues.

The decision to hike stamp duty was announced almost at the end of Krishnamachari's tax proposals, but it also revealed that the finance minister was conscious of the impact a fiscal proposal would have on the administration of the monetary policy. In effect, the controversial proposal would increase the stamp duty on bills of exchange from 0.006 per cent to 0.5 per cent immediately, with the provision for it being raised further, up to 1 per cent. This was a steep increase and had serious implications for the viability of the RBI's successful bill market scheme. The higher stamp duty effectively raised the lending rate under the bill market scheme by one percentage point. This also meant 'an implicit tax on the interest paid on accommodation against bills of nearly 29 per cent at the prevailing Bank rate of 3.5 per cent'.[12] How inexplicable the decision was could be gauged from the fact that even the immediate impact of the duty meant a 'tax of about 14.5 per cent on the interest charged or paid by banks on advances involving bills, at a time when the minister himself was in favour of easing financial stringency'.[13]

Was revenue mobilization the objective behind the increase in the stamp duty on bills of exchange? Not really. As the finance minister explained, the duty collected was to be shared with the states, and the Centre would not have gained from the duty. The government would have collected a total of only Rs 2 crore from raising the stamp duty, based on the total bill market transactions, valued at Rs 436 crore in 1956. So, why would the finance minister increase the stamp duty if not to needle the RBI governor? The RBI governor had taken pride in the working of the bill market scheme, and he treated this scheme as one of his key achievements. Krishnamachari's proposal, thus, threatened to damage the viability of that scheme. That the stamp duty was raised without any prior consultation with the RBI added fuel to the fire. The finance minister had merely sought the RBI's views on whether the new stamp duty should be forty times the prevailing rate or 10 times. The RBI governor was thus deeply upset by the proposal.

The increase in the stamp duty on bills of exchange met with stiff opposition from other quarters as well. With the tight credit policy announced for the busy season of 1956–57, there was a general rise in demand for easier credit and more liberal access to the bill market scheme launched by the RBI. The fact is that instead of relaxing norms for access to credit, the higher stamp duty on bills of exchange discouraged the use of these bills. The State Bank of India (SBI) also expressed its difficulties in borrowing under the bill market scheme, as it would have to undertake such operations at a loss to itself. Other banks too reduced their bill market limits with the RBI. The SBI chairman at that time was none other than

H.V.R. Iengar, who was earlier the Secretary in the ministry of commerce and industry when Krishnamachari was heading that ministry. Iengar told Sir Benegal and Krishnamachari in separate meetings about the problems created by the higher stamp duty. Krishnamachari took the financial sector's response to his decision in a different way. He apprehended that banks, perhaps under the influence of the RBI, were shunning the bill market scheme and creating a squeeze on credit availability to put indirect pressure on the government to rescind the stamp duty increase. When Sir Benegal approached the finance minister with a request to review the hike in stamp duty, Krishnamachari appeared to be further convinced that there was a concerted move against his stamp duty decision. After that, the finance minister was in no mood to even look at his decision afresh. Instead, he made a few public comments against banks in general and the SBI in particular, for creating roadblocks to smooth implementation of the duty hike decision. Needless to say, relations between Sir Bengal and Krishnamachari descended to a fresh low and resulted in the finance minister showing 'personal discourtesy'.

How discourteous Krishnamachari became was recounted quite graphically by B.K. Nehru, who was then the Joint Secretary in charge of external finance in the finance ministry. In his memoirs *Nice Guys Finish Second*, Nehru recalls that the stamp duty case had been escalated to Prime Minister Jawaharlal Nehru, who had placed it for discussion at a Cabinet meeting, which Sir Benegal was invited to attend. At that meeting, the RBI governor explained in detail his point of view on why the stamp duty on bills of exchange should not have been raised and how that move had added to the credit squeeze in the economy. Krishnamachari had taken serious objection to the RBI governor's suo motu explanation of the case since he was only an invitee to the meeting. He was only expected to answer questions asked of him.

Then there was an outburst from Krishnamachari, who talked in a raised and agitated voice against the RBI governor, and that too in the presence of others, including an industry leader. B.K. Nehru writes:

> The next thing I knew was that Sir Biren Mukherjee (Chairman of the Indian Iron and Steel Company) and I were waiting to see the Finance Minister in the ante room to his chamber, where his Private Secretary sat. TTK came into the room through one door, Rama Rau came in

through the other. TTK let fly in no uncertain terms, and in the loudest of voices, at the Governor of the Reserve Bank of India . . . Rama Rau, the mildest of men, did not know how to handle this unmeasured onslaught. Biren disappeared through the door leading to the verandah and after a moment I followed suit. It would not have been appropriate to witness this undignified brawl between the two highest-ranking officials of the financial establishment.[14]

It is ironical that RBI History has no clear account of this incident from the governor's point of view. All that RBI History has to offer on this matter is that, according to the references Sir Benegal made to this meeting or some other meeting with the finance minister, Krishnamachari 'spoke derogatorily to him of the Reserve Bank as a "department" or "section" of the Finance ministry'.[15]

After such a flare-up, Sir Benegal had no option but to resign as the RBI governor. But a few long meetings between Sir Benegal and Jawaharlal Nehru took place, where Home Minister Govind Ballabh Pant was also present. What actually transpired at these meetings was not made public, but the upshot was that Sir Benegal did not press for his resignation immediately thereafter. However, what the RBI governor did do created a bigger problem for Krishnamachari.

Sir Benegal decided to share these developments with the central board of the RBI, as he reckoned that it was a statutory duty to do so. A special meeting of the central board was convened on 12 December 1956, for which he circulated a memorandum titled 'Implications of certain provisions of the Finance Bill, 1956'. The memorandum noted that the government decision on increasing the stamp duty on bills of exchange was taken without consultation with the RBI governor or the board, 'on whom rests the statutory responsibility for altering the Bank rate'. Just six days before the introduction of the Finance Bill on 30 November 1956, the RBI governor and senior officers of the central bank were apprised of the decision, and the only point on which their views were sought was on the extent of the immediate increase.

The memorandum, placed before the meeting of the central board of RBI, was a frontal attack on the finance ministry and presented the entire sequence of events to show how the central bank's authority was being undermined by the finance minister. It noted that the RBI governor had approached the finance minister a few days after the introduction of the Finance Bill to discuss the implications of the decision on the stamp duty increase. But Krishnamachari had stated, without pulling any punches, that he took full responsibility for the decision and that the 'Bank was a "section" of the Finance Ministry of the Government of India'. Sir Benegal was also told that the RBI had to accept the finance ministry's decision on the matter, irrespective of whether it liked it or not.

The obvious question of the central bank's independence also figured in the memorandum. The government had the powers under Section 7 of the RBI Act to give directions to the central bank after consultation with the governor. The law said: 'The Central Government may from time to time give such directions to the Bank as it may, after consultation with the governor of the bank, consider necessary in the public interest.' But until this time, no occasion had arisen where the government had to give any direction to the RBI under this provision of the law. Citing this, the memorandum noted that while the relationship between the government and the RBI had so far been harmonious, treating the central bank as 'a department of the government of India' had serious consequences for its independence. The deleterious effects by way of such dual control over the Bank rate and the increase in the cost of credit for industry were also explained in the memorandum. In the end, it urged the central board of the RBI to consider explaining to the government the implications of the stamp duty hike and request its reconsideration.

Expectedly, the central board of the RBI resolved that it could not ignore that the finance minister had himself admitted that the stamp duty increase had monetary implications in spite of it being a fiscal matter. Since the stamp duty increased the incidence of the bank rate, which was the responsibility of the RBI, the government should have sought the views of the central bank. The resolution, which was sent to the finance minister, ended with a request to the government 'to consult the Reserve Bank in advance on all matters, which significantly affect . . . monetary structure and policy'.[16]

Nehru and the RBI

Whatever little chances there were of Krishnamachari cooling down after the initial flare-up simply evaporated after he received the resolution from the central board of the RBI. The finance minister duly forwarded the resolution to Jawaharlal Nehru, who took little time to write to the RBI governor a letter indicating that he was completely on the side of the finance minister and that his government had taken the first big step in dispelling the notion of RBI's independence. Nehru's letter to Sir Benegal expressed his 'great surprise' at the resolution, which the prime minister believed was 'improper' and 'agitational'. He took serious objection to the 'extraordinary' manner in which the RBI Governor had spoken to the directors of the central board about how the government move had undermined the central bank's autonomy. He also questioned the propriety of revealing in a memorandum the details of a private talk the RBI Governor had had with the finance minister. Going beyond the immediate issue of stamp duty, Nehru expressed his reservations about the manner in which he believed RBI's policies had gone against those of the government. The prime minister wrote: 'The Central Government . . . is directing its policy to attain certain objectives laid down in the Five-Year Plan. It would be completely absurd if the Reserve Bank followed a different policy because it did not agree with those objectives or with the methods of achieving them.'

The prime minister also made it clear to Sir Benegal that there was no attempt at undermining the RBI as the Governor had a flawed notion of the relationship between the central bank and the government. He wrote:

> You have laid stress on the autonomy of the Reserve Bank. Certainly it is autonomous, but it is also subject to the Central Government's directions. The question of fixing the bank rate is a matter for the Reserve Bank to consider. The stamp duty proposed by the Central Government is not the same thing as varying the bank rate, although it has certain effects upon it. That decision in regard to [the] stamp duty was taken by the Cabinet after full consideration and I cannot accept any plea that the Cabinet should not do so until the Reserve Bank approved.

The only concession Nehru made was to agree that it was perhaps desirable for the government to have sought the RBI's views, but on all other issues the prime minister unequivocally supported his finance minister. For instance, he said the finance minister had checked with the RBI Governor six days before the stamp duty issue came up in Parliament.

In any case, the RBI had no business to 'encourage and indirectly participate' in the criticism of the government by certain sections of industry, Nehru told Sir Benegal in his letter.

Even in his letter to Vaikunthlal Mehta, a leading Gandhian and one of the pioneers of the cooperative movement in the country, Nehru said the RBI board's memorandum was an indictment of the government's policy. He even defended Krishnamachari's public comments against the RBI as 'general remarks' made in response to the memorandum of the RBI's central board. However, he conceded to Mehta that the government could have handled the matter in a better way and the RBI Governor should have been consulted before the Union Cabinet approved the proposal to raise the stamp duty. But there was no such defensive or conciliatory gesture anywhere in the letter Nehru wrote to Sir Benegal.

Not surprisingly, Nehru's response came to the RBI Governor as a bolt from the blue. The earlier response from Nehru had encouraged Sir Benegal to believe that the prime minister would be more sympathetic to his concerns about erosion of the independence of the central bank. Soon after that letter, Nehru went off to an overseas tour. Emboldened by Nehru's defence of the government and his absence from the country, Krishnamachari stepped up his offensive against the RBI Governor. He addressed a few public meetings of industry representatives in southern India, where he accused the RBI of betraying a 'clerical mentality'. The finance minister also launched a broadside against the State Bank of India and other banks for having contributed to the credit squeeze that had resulted from the stamp duty increase, hardening the effective rate of interest. The SBI chairman, H.V.R. Iengar, and the SBI vice-chairman, Vaikunthlal Mehta, were upset by this criticism and even offered to be replaced if, as alleged by the finance minister, they had not outgrown a 'clerical mentality' or imperial outlook. In a bid to douse the fire, Krishnamachari spoke to Iengar to pacify him and Nehru managed to placate Mehta. But the bigger fire—an extremely hurt and upset RBI Governor—was not to be doused easily.

Jawaharlal Nehru's letter had deeply upset the RBI Governor. He did not take long to send an eleven-page reply, making no secret of his puzzlement and pain at the tone and contents of the prime minister's note to him. Rejecting the charge that he had adopted an agitational approach,

Sir Benegal drew comparisons between his actions, initiated with discretion, and the finance minister's actions of making private and public comments criticizing the RBI. He also recalled that the RBI Act had enshrined in it the idea of an autonomous organization, but said the finance minister clearly had other ideas. The finance minister's decision not to consult him sprang from his belief that the RBI was only a department of the government and not an autonomous organization deserving to be consulted before a decision with obvious monetary policy implications had to be taken. He also defended the RBI's track record in ensuring monetary stability and in supporting the government's development policies. In conclusion, he told the prime minister that he could not continue to remain in office in view of the finance minister's attitude and sought his permission to step down. Sir Benegal wrote:

> I assured you that I would not go against your wishes in regard to my resignation, but the public attacks of the Finance Minister on the Reserve Bank have created a new situation in which it will be absolutely impossible for me to continue in office. I hope you will appreciate my position and allow me to submit my formal resignation . . .

The correspondence between the prime minister and the RBI Governor did not end here. Nehru thought it was necessary to reply to Sir Benegal's long response, and in the process laid down the norms that in his view should determine the relationship between the RBI and the government. The prime minister maintained that the memorandum of the central board of the RBI was 'improperly worded' and urged Sir Benegal to treat the finance minister's comments about the RBI in a 'larger context'. He wrote: 'The Bank . . . was . . . obviously . . . a part of the various activities of the Government. Obviously also, it has a high status and responsibility. It has to advise the Government, but it has also to keep in line with the Government.'

In the first week of January 1957, the longest-serving Governor of the RBI sent in his resignation to the finance minister. Sir Benegal was frank and forthright in his letter as he protested the finance minister's 'unwarranted and insulting remarks' against the RBI, which according to him were 'unprecedented' and unfair in light of its creditable performance in managing the country's monetary policy. He recalled in the letter that he had overlooked the finance minister's 'personal rudeness in the past'. But now that the minister was making public attacks on the central bank, it was no longer possible for 'any self-respecting Governor to offer that wholehearted cooperation with the Finance Ministry, which is absolutely necessary in the interest of the country during the critical times ahead of us'. The resignation letter was drafted by B.K. Nehru, who wrote in his memoirs that Sir Benegal 'was naturally upset by the Finance Minister's intrusion into what was his legitimate domain but even more by the abuse showered on him'.[17] When that resignation letter reached the prime minister, Sir Benegal was asked who had drafted it. According to B.K. Nehru, Sir Benegal told the prime minister that the draft had been written by B.K. Nehru, but asked him to keep it a secret as he believed that Krishnamachari was a 'very vindictive man and he did not want me [B.K. Nehru] to be victimised'.

Sir Benegal wrote another letter to the prime minister conveying his decision not to issue any public statement after quitting the central bank, unless there was provocation. 'Any public controversy between the Reserve Bank and the Finance Ministry might have repercussions in the country and abroad,' he said, citing the reason for the need for no further public trading of charges on the issue.

The repercussions of such a major and politically significant resignation of the RBI governor before the end of his term were felt in different ways in different quarters. Sir Purshottamdas Thakurdas, a Gujarati cotton trader and a leading industrialist, had served on the central board of the RBI right from the central bank's inception in 1935. He was a Gandhian and an industrialist, and a signatory to the famous Bombay Plan that had just before Independence advocated greater involvement of the private sector in national economic development. But in 1957, watching the developments that saw the resignation of Sir Benegal Rama Rau under those controversial circumstances, Sir Purshottamdas decided to resign from the board of the RBI. On 8 January, a day after Sir Benegal had sent in his resignation to the finance minister, Sir Purshottamdas wrote to the RBI Governor:

The happenings in the last couple of weeks in the relation between the Board of the Reserve Bank and the Central Finance Ministry are

so extraordinary, one-sided and unprovoked that I feel it is not to the
interest of the country that any non-official should avoidably keep up
his connection with the Reserve Bank. I therefore hereby request you to
do the needful, so that I may not be re-nominated after what has been
happening lately.

Sir Bengal's resignation letter of 7 January 1957 was addressed
to the finance minister by name. There was, however, no reply from
Krishnamachari. Two days later, on 9 January, the finance secretary, H.M.
Patel, wrote to the RBI governor indicating the government's acceptance
of his resignation. Patel's letter had a short paragraph which was highly
significant, in as much as it showed how Krishnamachari viewed his
relationship with the RBI governor. It said:

> The Finance Minister does not wish to offer any comments on the
> reasons which have led you to take the decision to resign except to
> say that his views on the working of the Reserve Bank generally were
> explained by him to you when you last met him in Delhi.

K.G. Ambegaonkar, a member of the Indian Civil Service, had moved
to the RBI as a deputy governor in March 1955, after having served the
government as its finance secretary. The government decided to choose
Ambegaonkar to become the interim governor. Ambegaonkar acted as the
governor only till the end of February 1957, after which H.V.R. Iengar,
another member of the Indian Civil Service and at that time serving the
State Bank of India as its chairman, was appointed as the RBI governor.

On 12 January, a Saturday, Sir Benegal wrote a letter to his successor,
Ambegaonkar, reminding him that a meeting of the central board of
the RBI was scheduled to be held on 16 January. Since he would not be
present there and the members could raise the issue of his resignation, Sir
Benegal left a short note for Ambegaonkar to be laid before the meeting,
which explained in brief the circumstances under which he had quit. The
note stated:

> The members of the Board have, no doubt, seen the reports of the
> unwarranted and rather offensive remarks about the Reserve Bank
> in the recent public speeches of the Finance Minister at the South

Indian Chamber of Commerce in Madras and elsewhere. Such public attacks by the Finance Minister on the Central Bank of the country are without precedent and extremely unfair, especially as it would not be proper for the Reserve Bank to enter into a public controversy with the Government by replying publicly to these criticisms. While maintaining the independent status assigned to the Reserve Bank by statute, I have always considered it my duty to co-operate fully with the Government in the implementation of their national policies in the economic sphere. Throughout the period I have been Governor of the Bank, I have worked in complete harmony with the Finance Ministry. It will be realised that in view of these public attacks it would be difficult for the Finance Ministry and myself to maintain the harmonious co-operation that is absolutely necessary in the interest of the country. I, therefore, decided to submit my resignation, which has been accepted by the Government.

In what would probably be his last action before demitting office the following Monday, he also reiterated in that note that the members of the board must maintain utmost confidentiality about the reasons for his resignation as he himself would not make any public statement on the matter.

Sir Benegal Rama Rau vacated office on 14 January 1957, the first RBI governor after Independence to quit over differences of views with the the finance minister. The first RBI governor, Sir Osborne Smith, also had quit in 1937, two years after he joined, over his differences with the government policies on interest rates. After Sir Benegal as well, there would be a few RBI Governors who would either quit over differences with the government or whose terms would be cut short before their completion. But Sir Benegal's resignation would go down in history as one of the most controversial phases in the relationship between the finance minister and the RBI Governor. In spite of his resignation a few months before the end of his long term, Sir Benegal till today remains the RBI Governor who had the longest tenure, one of over seven and a half years.

B.K. Nehru, who watched these developments from his perch in the finance ministry from a distance, observed in his memoirs that the resignation of Sir Benegal marked an important turn in the history of India's financial institutions. He noted that the full support the prime

minister gave to his finance minister in his battle with the RBI Governor
was expected. Equally expected was the Union Cabinet's support to the
prime minister when the matter was discussed in that forum. But the
development had two major consequences, Nehru wrote:

> The first result was that from that day the Reserve Bank lost even
> such autonomy as it till then exercised and started becoming another
> subordinate office of the Government of India, taking orders even more
> than before from the Ministry of Finance. The second result was the
> resignation of Rama Rau.

Indeed, as it was noted in RBI History later, the resignation of Sir
Benegal proved that no Governor could any longer hope 'to defend the
autonomy of the Bank by unfurling banners announcing its independence'.
Not that differences between the RBI and the finance minister in the
coming years would disappear. But issues pertaining to the independence
or autonomy of the RBI would get debated even within the central bank
in a quiet manner. This only emboldened the government in the coming
years to assert its control over the central bank. It showed that it was
possible for a powerful finance minister to use the government's clout to
subjugate the RBI to fall in line with what the finance minister desired.
And those governors who chose to make their differences with the
government public had to quit, like Sir Benegal did.

Krishnamachari knew quite well how to wield power. Within months
of the resignation of Sir Benegal, he decided to divest the RBI of its
responsibilities in the arena of rural credit. Of course, he did it in the
name of strengthening the RBI's ability to conduct monetary policy
independently and without being held responsible for issues pertaining to
rural credit availability. But the actual intention could not have remained
a secret.

Interestingly, on his return to the finance ministry in 1963,
Krishnamachari tried to burnish his image, which had been considerably
bruised, being one of a finance minister who had unceremoniously clipped
the wings of an RBI Governor leading him to quit the job. This was when
he took part in a Lok Sabha debate in April 1964 after introduction of the
bill to set up the Industrial Development Bank of India as a subsidiary of
the RBI. A few left members of the Lok Sabha had demanded that the

proposed developmental financial institution should not be set up as a subsidiary of the RBI.

But Krishnamachari defended the RBI against criticism over its functioning by those parliamentarians. He said:

> The Reserve Bank is in the picture for everything today, and I am very happy that successive Governors of the Reserve Bank have been able to shoulder this increasing responsibility that is being cast on them, are able to take an independent view and do not completely subordinate their views to those of the party in power including the Minister. I have been very grateful during my two spells as Finance Minister for the independence shown by the Reserve Bank, and I want it to have that independence.

The supreme irony of what Krishnamachari said in the Lok Sabha was lost on nobody. A charitable view, perhaps, was that after having gone through politically trying times in the few years between 1957 and 1963, Krishnamachari was trying to repair his reputation that had certainly got sullied from his having driven an RBI Governor out of office in an open spat. Whatever may have been his motivation, the reality was that Krishnamachari's actions in the winter months of 1956–57 had given rise to a key governance challenge for the government. What should be the degree of autonomy that the RBI governor can be allowed to enjoy? That question continued to trouble many of Krishnamachari's successors.

Problem of Deficit Financing over the Second Plan

One of the challenges that Krishnamachari had to face immediately after taking charge of the finance ministry in August 1956 was to mobilize adequate resources to fund the ambitious Second Five-Year Plan, which was launched in April 1956. The challenge had already got complicated with the Reserve Bank of India having concluded by August 1957 that the borrowing targets for the five-year period were unrealistic. The loans floated in 1956 and 1957 failed to elicit positive response and raised questions about the feasibility of completing the borrowing plan. RBI Governor H.V.R. Iengar shared his concerns with Krishnamachari. But no solution was found and the government's continued reliance on the floatation of such loans essentially meant an increase in its deficit financing.

An associated problem in financing the Second Plan through increased borrowings arose from the existing legal framework of a proportional reserve system, which was adopted in 1934 under Section 33 of the RBI Act. This clause laid down a rather inflexible domestic currency system based on a proportional reserve, under which two-fifths of the assets of the RBI's Issue Department had to be held in the form of gold coins, gold bullion or foreign securities. Of these assets, a minimum of Rs 40 crore was to be in the form of gold coins and bullion. This arrangement—also known as the proportional reserve system—meant that the government could borrow more only if it had a surplus account. Borrowing more would have led to an increase in the money supply. And since a predominant portion of money supply in the country consisted of currency, the government's hands were tied as far as increasing borrowing or raising the money supply was concerned. Moreover, higher borrowings also posed a risk to monetary stability and, therefore, to price stability.

Not all countries followed a similar fixed and inflexible proportional reserve system. Also, a view had begun to gain ground that the policy of linking currency issue to the size of the country's foreign exchange reserves created needless complications. Worse, the idle foreign exchange reserves that remained locked up as a sort of guarantee entailed a cost for the economy in terms of foregone investment and growth. Thus, many countries by the early 1950s had begun suitably amending the norms for their proportional reserve system. In India, a move to relax these norms was initiated by B.K. Nehru, who was Joint Secretary in charge of external finance in the finance ministry. In 1955, Nehru wrote to the then RBI Governor Benegal Rama Rau expressing concern over how the existing proportional reserve system would impose severe curbs on the government's deficit financing needed to fund the Second Plan. Three alternatives were suggested to the Governor: a lowering of the proportional cover, a move towards a fiduciary system or doing away with the statutory requirement of a currency reserve. The government's suggestion was to settle for a simple fiduciary system. The urgency for a change arose from the need to find adequate resources for the Second Plan. The government's internal calculations showed that with the rapid pace of a drawdown in its foreign exchange reserves, the flexibility of the RBI to issue more currency against loans would be severely restricted and the Second Plan would have to take a big hit.

The RBI response was prompt. Sir Benegal suggested that instead of opting for a fiduciary system, it would be better to dispense with the entire statutory requirement for currency cover. The RBI's argument was that no statutory provisions concerning note issue could guard against the possibility of adverse inflationary movements, mainly because the commercial banks' deposit liabilities were the most 'dynamic component of money supply', and these were not affected by the statutory rules on currency cover. Nor did the RBI believe that the statutory currency cover system was a safeguard against any misuse of 'political power'. But what the RBI actually suggested to the Centre on this issue was far more conservative. It proposed that the government should prescribe a minimum currency reserve broadly equivalent to the amount of the note issue and use the opportunity to revalue the gold held by the Issue Department. That was in 1955–56 and the finance minister was C.D. Deshmukh, whose equation with a fellow ICS officer as his successor at the RBI, Benegal Rama Rau, was excellent. This was quite unlike the strains this relation would suffer when Krishnamachari would become the finance minister in August 1956.

Not surprisingly, the government accepted the RBI's main suggestions. But it added a rider that at least Rs 100 crore of the fixed currency reserve should be in gold, which would be revalued, another Rs 300 crore in foreign securities and, in addition, that the RBI should keep a foreign currency reserve of Rs 100 crore. If the RBI's gold and foreign assets fell below Rs 500 crore, it would discuss with the government the remedial course of action. The RBI accepted these changes, with minor modifications, and added an important provision in the proposed amendment to repeal a section that required the RBI to pay a tax to the government in the event of its gold and foreign exchange reserves falling below the prescribed minimum. This was a provision introduced when the RBI was not nationalized, and since all its surplus profits were transferred to the government, the provision on taxing the RBI had outlived its utility.

The government accepted the suggested changes. And the RBI Act was amended by October 1956, but not before a lively debate in Parliament showed how members of both Houses were worried about the prospects of the government gaining unbridled powers to expand currency and add to the inflationary pressures in the economy. Krishnamachari had become the finance minister by then and assured the members that Parliament must retain some control over the actions of the government on such monetary issues. But by the end of July 1957, in less than a year of these amendments, the finance ministry and the RBI recognized that the new currency cover requirements needed further changes as the foreign exchange reserves fell further, below the required level under the amended law, and this in spite of drawings from the International Monetary Fund. Since there was no realistic expectation of the foreign exchange reserves increasing in the following few months, the government and the RBI agreed on a fresh set of amendments pertaining to the currency cover provisions in the RBI Act.

The initial idea of abolishing the minimum foreign exchange reserve provisions for currency cover provisions was discarded in no time for fear of such a move eroding public confidence in the currency system and at the same time for keeping a check on the government's tendency to overspend. Thus, a realistic amendment to Section 33 of the RBI Act was mooted, and the new provision stated:

> The aggregate value of the gold coin, gold bullion and foreign securities held as assets and the aggregate value of the gold coin and gold bullion so held shall not at any time be less than two hundred crores of rupees and one hundred and fifteen crores of rupees, respectively.

The change was initially brought about through an ordinance on 31 October 1957, and later by obtaining the assent of Parliament. In the debate in Parliament, Krishnamachari defended the change by arguing that foreign exchange reserves were useful only if they could be drawn in times of a crisis. RBI History noted the following:

> Allaying fears that the latest changes were a recipe for inflation which the Bank now lacked the power to check, he (Krishnamachari) stressed that between the Parliament and the Reserve Bank, the system provided 'adequate machinery for exercising such vigilance as may become necessary from time to time in regard to the overall supply of monetary media in the economy'.

Such assurances, however, had no meaningful impact on actual developments in the coming months. While consultations between the

RBI and the finance ministry would take place periodically on the issue of currency, the absence of formal checks on the issue of ad hoc treasury bills diluted the RBI's powers to have an effective say on the extent of recourse the government could take to deficit financing. The net issue of ad hoc treasury bills during the five years of the First Five-Year Plan amounted to Rs 250 crore. But it spurted to Rs 945 crore during the Second Five-Year Plan that ran from 1956 to 1961.

The Budget for 1957–58

Krishnamachari presented his first full Budget for 1957–58 on 15 May 1957, after the general elections. There was no surprise that Nehru had retained him as the finance minister even as the Indian economy's key concerns had not changed very much from what they were in 1956—the level of foreign exchange reserves was low, imports had to be curtailed, and funding of the Second Plan was still proving to be a headache. At the outset in his Budget, therefore, Krishnamachari, announced that the government would soon unveil the import policy for the second half of 1957–58 'with the objective of securing a further sizeable saving on imports'. The tone of the Budget was summed up quite well when he set the context for the proposed squeeze on imports. 'It would . . . be idle to pretend that all hardship can be avoided. The exigencies of the situation require that a balance on external account must be restored as early as possible, and the necessary price has to be paid,' he said. He left nobody in doubt that more stringent measures to rein in imports were in the offing. 'The import programme for the first half of this year involved considerable cuts in imports, and the process will, I am afraid, have to be carried considerably farther in the import programme for the second half of the year,' he said. By the time Krishnamachari finished his Budget speech, the Indian economy had been subjected to a series of new taxation measures, from whose impact it would take many years to recover.

Before unveiling the taxation measures, Krishnamachari dealt with the crucial questions of the savings rate and the size of the Second Plan. In a bid to create incentives for people to save more so that the government could get more resources at its disposal for the investments it would like to make under the Second Plan, Krishnamachari decided to give a big push to a campaign for small savings. With effect from 1 June 1957, the rate of interest on Post Office Savings Bank accounts was raised by half a percentage point and new savings certificates with maturity of a longer period of twelve years and with higher interest rates were introduced.

On the prospects of the Second Plan, Krishnamachari presented a detailed analysis of why and how the outlay needed to be revised in light of the resource shortage. That was a kind of a retraction from his earlier enthusiasm in staying ambitious, virtually ruling out the need for scaling down the investment outlay. Krishnamachari noted that with the external assistance already promised and further support expected from the World Bank, the Second Plan's core projects in sectors such as steel, coal, transport and ancillary power could be funded and there would be no problem in implementing them. But there was some prudence as well. He explained:

> But, in regard to other projects, especially those for which no external resources are specifically forthcoming, and which are not otherwise of high priority, it would be prudent for us not to make fresh commitments for some time until the outlook becomes clearer and we have more assurance of our being able to find the foreign exchange resources needed for them. Some rephasing of the Plan is thus inevitable, but, if, as I hope, the balance of payments situation takes a turn for the better before long and if we succeed in securing adequate external resources, the achievement on the Plan should not fall much behind schedule.

This was a relatively small blow to the Second Plan. Projects valued at about Rs 300 crore faced the risk of being jettisoned on account of resource constraints. These projects accounted for only about 6 per cent of the total public-sector Plan outlay of Rs 4800 crore. The finance minister also had words of mild admonition for those who were critical of the government's ambitious Plan:

> To those who regard the Plan as too ambitious, I would respectfully submit that they should take a good look at the living conditions of the bulk of our people. If they would only do this, I am sure they will along with me, be able to see the several directions in which the Plan is inadequate. In the last few years, there has been some visible improvement in the standards of nutrition and probably of clothing.

The housing conditions and environmental hygiene in urban and rural areas of the low-income groups are deplorable; the slums in our cities are a disgrace to any society, which claims to be considered civilized. I am deeply anxious to see that the Plan is strengthened in this respect.

Krishnamachari's statement showed the deep commitment of the finance minister as also of the Nehru government to achieving economic development through planning. This left no scope for further debate for those who had a different view.

Major Taxation Changes Unveiled

By making a series of changes in the taxation policy, Krishnamachari made his 1957–58 Budget an event that would not be easily forgotten for years to come. On indirect taxes, he raised the customs duty by varying margins on about ninety items and rationalized the rates for a few hundred items more. Excise duties were also raised on a large number of goods, including petrol, diesel, kerosene, cement, steel ingots, sugar, vegetable non-essential oil, tea, coffee, unmanufactured tobacco, matches and paper. The additional annual revenue mobilization as a result of these increased imposts was Rs 6 crore on account of higher customs duties and Rs 61 crore on account of excise levies. This was a significantly high revenue collection effort as the additional amounts to be collected were over 3 per cent of the annual customs revenue and as much as 32 per cent of the annual excise collections. More than protectionism, Krishnamachari was taxing the domestic manufacturing and processing companies at higher rates to mobilize more resources—a development neither the Indian companies nor the stock markets welcomed.

The bigger taxation moves pertained to direct taxation. Krishnamachari made a fundamental change in the way personal income tax and super-tax rates were being imposed. Instead of using different methods of determining the permissible level of allowances for calculation of the tax burden, he proposed to enforce a standard schedule of rates for all earned incomes and a higher surcharge on unearned incomes. This was a major move as the finance minister, for purposes of tax treatment, wanted to differentiate earned income or income earned from employment (like salary or wages) from unearned income or income earned from instruments like bank deposits through interest, dividends from stock market investments or interest from bonds.

Krishnamachari's taxation philosophy acknowledged that the prevalence of high tax rates deprived the taxation structure of its flexibility and led to large-scale tax evasion. In other words, the high rates of taxation encouraged tax evasion, which also substantially reduced the tax base. He announced:

> I now propose a revised schedule of these rates and introduce a new scheme of surcharge levy, which will mean that the total of the income-tax, super-tax and surcharge for the highest slab will be brought down from the existing level of 91.8 per cent to 84 per cent for unearned income and 77 per cent for earned incomes.

These were still very high rates of taxation on individual incomes, but that the overall incidence was coming down provided some relief to taxpayers.

There was, however, no escape from the surcharges on top of these tax rates. A surcharge of 5 per cent on the tax computed at the standard schedule rates for earned incomes up to Rs 1 lakh and of 10 per cent on incomes higher than that sum was levied. For unearned incomes, a higher surcharge of 20 per cent was levied, but the middle classes with annual income below Rs 7500 were exempted from such a levy. Krishnamachari conceded a tax outgo of Rs 7.5 crore in the year as a result of these concessions. This was substantial, as it amounted to almost 9 per cent of the annual income tax collections in 1956–57. This loss, however, was partially made good by his subsequent proposal to widen the tax base. The exemption threshold for income tax was lowered from a minimum annual income of Rs 4200 to Rs 3000, which was expected to fetch additional revenue of Rs 5 crore in a year. A higher tax regime for the corporate sector was unveiled. He said:

> I propose to raise the income-tax payable by companies from the present level of 4 annas in the rupee (25 per cent) to 30 per cent and the corporation tax from the present level of 2 annas 9 pies in the rupee (a little more than 17 per cent) to 20 per cent.

In a bid to encourage savings by companies and to neutralize the impact of higher taxes, the finance minister reduced the tax on excess dividends paid by them. A few more minor changes in the tax rates for bonus share issues and undistributed profits were also made. But the two big new taxes that Krishnamachari announced in his first full-fledged Budget confirmed everyone's earlier apprehensions that here was a finance minister who was out to change the basic structure of taxation in the country.

Krishnamachari's first new levy proposed was a tax on wealth. The second was a tax on expenditure. The wealth tax was to be imposed on individuals, Hindu undivided families (HUF) and companies. Assets valued at up to Rs 2 lakh for individuals and up to Rs 3 lakh for HUFs were exempted from wealth tax. The rate of taxation was 0.5 per cent on the first Rs 10 lakh, 1 per cent on the next Rs 10 lakh and 1.5 per cent on the rest. The finance minister's justification for the wealth tax on individuals and HUFs was that this was a progressive tax, which together with the surcharges already levied on the income tax on unearned incomes would lead to 'a more effective taxation of the richer classes without diminishing incentives to earn in the process'.

The levy of wealth tax on companies had no such slabs. Assets of more than Rs 5 lakh in value were to be taxed at 0.5 per cent. Why was the wealth tax rate relatively low for companies and why were companies brought under its purview at all? Krishnamachari explained it thus:

> . . . the wealth tax is intended primarily as a measure of personal taxation but in the peculiar economic structure of India, I consider it advisable not to exclude companies from the purview of this tax. However, the rate of tax has to be low. This is why I have proposed a flat rate of only 0.5 per cent on assets above the exemption limit.

Not surprisingly, the newly introduced wealth tax regime had its usual quota of exempted categories. And there were no surprises. Categories exempted from wealth tax included agricultural properties, properties belonging to charitable or religious trusts, works of art, archaeological collections not intended for sale, balances in recognized provident funds and insurance policies, personal effects including furniture, jewellery, etc., up to a maximum value of Rs 25,000, and books and publications not intended for sale. The contentious question of valuing assets for levy of wealth tax was also tackled in a way that the government's revenues would get an added boost. While the various assets forming part of a business undertaking would be treated as a single unit for valuation, other assets would be taken at their market value. The finance minister was hoping to garner additional revenue of Rs 15 crore from the new tax.

Quite expectedly, the second new proposal—a tax on expenditure—created a mild storm. Krishnamachari was perhaps aware of the novelty of the idea. 'This is a form of taxation which has no backing as yet of historical experience,' Krishnamachari conceded, but nevertheless went ahead with its introduction: 'It is, however, a tax which, given effective administrative arrangements, can be a potent instrument for restraining ostentatious expenditure and for promoting savings.' The expenditure tax was thus levied only on individuals and HUFs whose income for tax purposes was not less than Rs 60,000 a year.

It was thus a tax patently on the rich. The expenditure tax was to be imposed on all expenditure incurred in excess of certain sums, depending on the size of the family. Accordingly, the expenditure amounts excluded from the purview of the tax would be a basic amount of Rs 24,000 for an assessee and his wife and Rs 5,000 for each dependent child. Explaining the details of his proposal, Krishnamachari said:

> The rate of tax will be based on a slab system, the rate for each slab increasing progressively with the increase in the level of expenditure. Thus, for excess expenditure up to Rs 10,000, the rate will be 10 per cent and for higher slabs, the rate will increase progressively. As in the case of wealth tax, the administrative set-up and the assessment and appellate procedure will be the same as for income-tax.

The only relief was that the expenditure tax was to become applicable from a year later, that is, from 1958–59.

In the end, Krishnamachari's direct tax efforts with regard to personal income-tax, super-tax and corporation taxes were expected to garner additional annual revenue of Rs 25 crore (about 19 per cent of what was collected by way of income tax from individuals and companies in 1956–57). An additional Rs 5 crore was expected to be raised through improved collections and administration to prevent tax evasion. The Budget, therefore, showed a revenue surplus, which, however, ran into a deficit after taking into account the transfer of revenues to the states. But the overall deficit amount had been reined in at Rs 275 crore. This was higher than the Rs 216 crore deficit in 1956–57. The relief, however, was that the gap could have been much wider but for Krishnamachari's massive tax mobilization efforts.

The fate of both these taxes in India, however, remained uncertain, and eventually both were scrapped. The expenditure tax was abolished in 1962 by Krishnamachari's successor, Morarji Desai. But it returned in 1964, when Krishnamachari made a comeback to the Cabinet as the finance minister. Two years later it was abolished again, but it returned in a different form as an expenditure tax on spending at expensive hotels and restaurants. The wealth tax remained on the statute book for several decades. In 2015, Finance Minister Arun Jaitley abolished it in the second year of the Narendra Modi government—almost fifty-eight years after it was first introduced. Instead, Jaitley raised the surcharge on income tax on taxpayers with annual taxable income of over Rs 1 crore. At the time it was abolished, the wealth tax rate was 1 per cent on assets above Rs 30 lakh. And the annual collection of wealth tax in 2014–15 was just Rs 1,086 crore, a tiny portion (0.087 per cent) of the gross tax collections of Rs 12.45 lakh crore that year. In 1957–58, when the wealth tax was mooted, the collection amount was expected to be only Rs 15 crore, just about 3 per cent of the gross tax collections.

The idea of a wealth tax and an expenditure tax came from Nicholas Kaldor, a British economist who had been invited by the Indian government to advise it on taxation reforms. Kaldor believed that in addition to the income tax, any government should also impose a capital gains tax, a wealth tax, an expenditure tax and a gift tax. The objective of levying so many taxes at the same time was to plug whatever loopholes there could be, allowing tax evasion. Kaldor, however, had made one important additional suggestion while recommending levy of all these taxes. The total incidence of all these various taxes on a taxpayer should not exceed 45 per cent of total income. In India at that time, the overall tax burden was much higher than it is today, and adoption of the Kaldor formula would have led to a higher incidence of taxes. B.K. Nehru, an ICS officer who had been made Secretary in the department of economic affairs in 1957, had been a contemporary of Kaldor at the London School of Economics, where the two had studied. When Kaldor made these proposals, Nehru told him 'he [Kaldor] did not understand the political environment in which he had made the proposals; all of these taxes would be added on to the then rate of income tax which had already reached fourteen annas as in the rupee or 87.5 per cent'.[18]

The final Budget for 1957–58, after the conclusion of the second general elections, was presented in Parliament on 15 May 1957. A few days before that, Krishnamachari had called a meeting of all the senior officials in the finance ministry. According to B.K. Nehru, the entire brass of the ministry was present at that meeting, along with a few others from the financial sector. Nehru, who was then the Economic Affairs Secretary, was present, along with Principal Secretary H.M. Patel, Central Board of Revenue Chairman A.K. Roy, Expenditure Secretary M.V. Rangachari, RBI Governor H.V.R. Iengar and State Bank of India Chairman P.C. Bhattacharya. At that meeting, Krishnamachari revealed his plan to accept the Kaldor proposal without any reduction in the rate of income tax. 'Every single one of us told him in no uncertain terms that these proposals would be disastrous for the economy, that confidence would be destroyed, that stock markets would collapse and that the economy would begin to flounder,' Nehru wrote in his memoirs, *Nice Guys Finish Second.*

Krishnamachari was upset with his senior officials and told them the next day that he was so disappointed that his taxation policy had no takers among them that he had not slept the whole of the previous night. But he was clear in his mind that his proposal showed the right way. Capital gains tax had already been introduced earlier, in November 1957. And in the Budget, the wealth tax and expenditure tax had also been introduced, and without any reduction in the income tax rates. The gift tax too would make its appearance in the Budget Krishnamachari had prepared for 1958–59. But he could not present the Budget himself as he had to leave the government in the wake of a financial scandal, after which the prime minister himself took charge of the finance ministry and presented the Budget that imposed gift tax on the nation.

Krishnamachari's biographer, R. Tirumalai, notes that the ideas for these taxes that the finance minister imposed in his first Budget originated not just from Nicholas Kaldor, but also from Kautilya, political and economic adviser to emperor Chandragupta of ancient India: 'But he (Krishnamachari) had not borrowed his ideas . . . entirely from Kaldor . . . TTK could . . . flaunt Kautilya's *Artha Shastra*, which had also envisaged an expenditure tax.'[19]

The reaction of Kaldor to Krishnamachari's taxation move showed how the internationally reputed fiscal policy expert was fully aware of the political opposition that the finance minister faced in imposing those taxes. Reacting to the Budget proposals of Krishnamachari, Kaldor had said:

> TTK made an honest and determined attempt in his May 1957 Budget to bring the tax system of India more in conformity with the socialist pattern of society so loudly proclaimed by the Congress Party as its major political objective. He faced severe opposition first in the Cabinet, and then in Parliament, and the Parliamentary battle can have few historical parallels apart from Lloyd George's famous fight following the 1909 Budget. But he (TTK) failed and only a truncated and emasculated form could be erected. The amendments made to the Wealth Tax Act exempting companies, and the withdrawal of the Expenditure Tax subsequent to TTK's resignation virtually made the 'package' a pale shadow of what its originator had in view.[20]

But the impact of the capital gains tax, the wealth tax and the expenditure tax on taxpayers in the space of a few months was unequivocally adverse. 'The first effect was a collapse of the stock markets. Even after the debate, in which the more sober members of Parliament pointed out the destructive effects of his taxation, he would not change. One of TTK's characteristics was his obstinacy,' B.K. Nehru recalled in his memoirs.[21] The stock markets were in a punishing mood. In *TTK: The Dynamic Innovator*, R. Tirumalai noted:

> The Budget of May 1957 had cast a gloom over the stock exchanges. Panic and nervousness followed. Many scrips touched levels which were never recorded in history. TTK had to take some corrective measures to restore confidence. The LIC lending support was one, and prices on the 29th of June, 1957 were a little above the levels obtaining on the Budget Day. Confidence was slowly revived.

But this was an ominous development. Stock market sentiment was revived, but the finance minister had in the process embroiled himself and his government in a major financial scandal. What was believed to have restored the stock market's confidence actually led to Krishnamachari's resignation less than nine months later. As Tirumalai recounted, June 1957 was a 'month of hazards' for Krishnamachari. Early that month, the plane he took on one of his travels, a Skymaster, suffered a major jolt because of an air pocket, injuring the finance minister. A bigger jolt awaited him in the third week of June. He would be involved in LIC's decision to invest in shares of companies owned by a controversial industrialist, Haridas Mundhra.

The Mundhra Scandal

A proper assessment of the Mundhra scandal is important to understand how the honchos of the Nehru government's economic establishment stood compromised before the wily moves of a dubious businessman, which led to the sudden resignation of its finance minister.

Haridas Mundhra, as the Chagla Commission that probed his business dealings had noted, was a 'financial adventurer' with a 'passion to swallow as many firms as possible'. And his business methods, according to the Commission, were 'dubious, to say the least'. Mundhra became adept at influencing government functionaries so that he could use public funds to bail himself out of difficult financial situations, just as he had built his business empire by means of takeovers with the help of bank and institutional loans procured against manipulated and overpriced stocks of his companies, and on occasion against fake or duplicate shares.

Gopalkrishna Gandhi, a diplomat and grandson of Mahatma Gandhi, had a lot more to say about Mundhra in 2013 in an article he wrote for *Hindustan Times*:

> A light-bulb salesman, Haridas Mundhra had by the mid-1950s grown by 'fast deals and stock juggling' into the author and king of a Rs 4-crore empire. 'Four crore?' one could ask with disbelief today. The amount sounds trifling. It was not, at that time. Mundhra's ethics may have gone unnoticed had he not been indicted, in 1956, by the Bombay Stock Exchange for selling forged shares. Though shaky on his wicket, in 1957, Mundhra got LIC (by then government-owned) to invest Rs 1.24 crore in the shares of six of his weak companies. The investment was done under pressure and LIC lost most of the money.[22]

Why it became a huge political and public controversy was also because LIC was dealing with ordinary insurance policyholders' money and its losses could adversely affect their returns. LIC was then a newly nationalized company and there were fears that public-sector money was being used to benefit a private enterprise. After all, LIC had purchased shares of Mundhra firms without obtaining approval from its investment committee on nineteen occasions over a period of six months in 1957, at prices higher than those prevailing in the market at that time. Indeed, the purchases were made when Mundhra company shares were on the decline.

How large was Mundhra as a business leader in 1957? Gopalkrishna Gandhi was not off the mark in suggesting that Mundhra had built a reasonably large empire by amassing business wealth of Rs 4 crore by the mid-1950s. An indication of how large his empire was can be had from the fact that as a share of India's gross domestic product in 1955, Mundhra's wealth was almost as much as that of India's hundredth richest business leader in 2020.

Mundhra's meteoric rise in the 1950s came to everyone's notice when he acquired F&C Osler (India) Limited, an Indian subsidiary of a reputed British lamp manufacturing company, and followed it up with the purchase of controlling shares in Richardson & Cruddas and Jessop & Company, two well-known foreign-owned engineering companies with their headquarters in Calcutta. Mundhra's acquisition appetite did not abate even after this. He set his eyes on a few tea companies, but he did not make much headway in that sector. In 1955, he succeeded in acquiring a controlling stake in British India Corporation, a managing agency, through which he acquired 49 per cent equity in Singapore-based investment company Turner Morrison. The game plan was that Mundhra would raise his stake in that company to 51 per cent a few months later.

Mundhra's strategy was to target cash-rich companies and managing agencies that had become vulnerable soon after India became independent and an economic policy shift was in the offing. Mundhra's modus operandi revealed how scheming he was. He relied on bank finance for his acquisitions, and he would meet the margin requirements for bank loans mainly through manipulation of the share prices of his companies. By the end of 1956, Mundhra had overreached to such an extent that his ambitions began to harm him. Increasingly, his attempts to buy his own companies' shares from the market to bolster their price had begun yielding less-than-optimum results. With the price of his shares falling,

Mundhra was getting into deeper trouble. His next misadventure was to raise bank finance against bogus or fake shares. Such a state of affairs was not a secret among industry and market circles, and by March 1957 Mundhra's financial dealings had begun to cast an adverse shadow of gloom on the Calcutta Stock Exchange.

Another disturbing signal emanating from Mundhra's business affairs at around the same time pertained to corporate governance. Since 1954, the government had been getting reports that Mundhra may not have complied with all the provisions of the company law. Simultaneously, Mundhra was booked for having entered into irregular foreign exchange transactions.

The irony was that in August 1955, none other than T.T. Krishnamachari, who was at that time the minister for commerce and industry, had written to then Finance Minister C.D. Deshmukh about Mundhra's questionable business dealings and had asked if the provisions under the Companies Act should be further strengthened.

The second volume of Reserve Bank of India's History (1951–1967) contains an account of the scandal:

> ... the Finance Ministry suspected even in December 1955 that Mundhra had defrauded Osler's (Osler Lamps, one of the Mundhra companies, whose share prices he would boost by rigging the market) shareholders to the tune of about Rs 6 lakhs, while in dismissing a petition he had filed against one Chimanram Motilal, a judge of the Bombay High Court remarked on Mundhra's 'thoroughly dishonest attitude . . . [and] conduct'.[23]

The assessment by then RBI Deputy Governor Ram Nath confirmed the general doubts about Mundhra's activities. According to Nath's report, written sometime in late 1956, Mundhra did not possess either the experience or the background to run an industrial empire. A fortnight after this report, the RBI Governor at the time, Benegal Rama Rau, acknowledged that he was disturbed by Mundhra's activities. RBI History notes: 'As Jawaharlal Nehru noted on a file in September 1957 well before the scandal broke, "the reputation of this gentleman [was] not good". It is instructive to note that rather than following it, Mundhra's poor reputation preceded the collapse of his industrial empire.'[24]

Genesis of the Mundhra Scam

By the middle of the 1950s, the RBI had begun receiving disturbing reports of how Mundhra was misusing banking facilities. The central bank conducted inspections of accounts of three Calcutta banks. The reports, made available at the end of March 1956, revealed several irregularities in their dealings with Mundhra. The irregularities included overvaluation of shares of Mundhra's companies while lending money to him. The inspection led to the resignation of the Calcutta managers of these banks and the RBI decided to increase the frequency of inspection of banks dealing with Mundhra. It was now decided to conduct the inspections every six months. RBI History goes on to describe what happened:

> . . . reacting to reports received from the government in December 1956 of Mundhra using finance from banks to corner shares of some Calcutta-based companies, the RBI initiated inquiries which showed that six banks, including one exchange bank, had sanctioned advances to share-brokers against the shares of these companies. Following this, the RBI issued instructions to all banks in April 1957 to desist from financing takeovers and speculation in shares. By May 1957 there were serious fears that Mundhra's financial difficulties would prevent banks from realizing their debts without unloading his shares on the market. Apprehensive that unregulated selling would lead to a collapse of the stock market besides eroding the realizable value of the banks' securities, the RBI mooted the possibility of Mundhra's creditors forming a consortium to coordinate the recovery of their advances to him. The banks refused to heed the suggestion following legal advice that they would be liable to civil action by Mundhra should he suffer any loss or adversity as a consequence of their action. Some creditor banks suggested instead that the Bank should itself convene a meeting for the purpose. But this suggestion too, was not pursued since it was felt to do little to improve the legal position.[25]

What helped the RBI zero in on Mundhra's irregular transactions were the several letters written by A. Raman, a research officer at the RBI office in Calcutta, to his superiors in Bombay. Raman's letters were shared with the Union finance ministry. Later, they also became a major source of information for the M.C. Chagla Commission that probed the Mundhra affair. These letters, according to a publication on RBI's activities during those years,

> . . . spoke at length about Mundhra's methods of operation, his manipulation of stock prices, the use he made of bank funds, and the drag his shares exercised on stock prices in Calcutta. Raman also faithfully reported to his employers rumours, which in the event were not without basis, of imminent LIC intervention to aid Mundhra, and the market's assessment of it.[26]

Even Mundhra's dealings with Life Insurance Corporation (LIC) were hinted at in Raman's letters. The letters he wrote in September 1957 spoke of the 'chronic nature of Mundhra's troubles, the transient impact of the LIC's support, and of the effects on the market of British India withholding dividend payments and of Jessop's inability to finalize its annual accounts'.[27] Raman was clear about what the government ought to be doing under such circumstances. According to him, the markets were expecting the government to order an inquiry into the affairs of Mundhra's companies. Not surprisingly, Raman's observations were duly conveyed to the finance minister, T.T. Krishnamachari, who only reacted with the bland comment that they did not 'make good reading'.

Things could not have got better after such a lukewarm response from the government. By September 1957, there were other reports from the market suggesting that Mundhra was now engaged in fraudulent transactions to sustain his empire and to rescue himself from his financial troubles. RBI History noted:

> Rumours abounded of shares in circulation of Richardson and Cruddas being in excess of the company's share capital. These rumours were confirmed in November 1957 when two banks reported to the Bank that they were in possession of duplicate shares of this company and of British India. Mundhra, one of these banks also discovered to its discomfiture, had pledged two sets of shares bearing the same serial numbers, neither of which was authentic, with two of its branches! The study the Bank conducted thereafter of banks' holdings of Mundhra shares showed that he and three of his concerns had pledged as security

to banks, shares amounting from 3.5 to 92 per cent of their paid-up capital. In five cases the shares pledged exceeded half of the respective firm's paid-up capital and in three cases, 75 per cent. The RBI's investigation also revealed the large-scale duplication, triplication, and in one case even quadruplication of his companies' shares.[28]

At around the same time, RBI Governor H.V.R. Iengar also began taking keen interest in the Mundhra affairs and how they were playing havoc with the banking system. Iengar began writing to the government more frequently about the danger of the Mundhra affairs becoming a major public scandal. The 'business of Haridas Mundhra is getting worse and worse', Iengar told Finance Minister T.T. Krishnamachari in November 1957. The Governor advised the government to undertake a comprehensive review of the Mundhra group's activities, and at the same time initiated legal proceedings against Mundhra.

RBI History notes in detail the various steps the central bank took to contain the adverse fallout of Mundhra's misadventures:

> One of the banks in possession of bogus shares was advised to lodge them with the State Bank of India, while following meetings with the chairmen of the latter institution and the Life Insurance Corporation, and Secretaries in the Finance Ministry, it was decided that the State Bank and the LIC should move the courts under the Companies Act to appoint suitable persons to manage Richardson & Cruddas and British India. At Iengar's instance, it was also decided to order, in the public interest, an investigation into the affairs of Mundhra's companies. Finally, upon the RBI's insistence, one of the banks in possession of bogus shares pledged by Mundhra agreed, though somewhat reluctantly, to lodge a complaint to that effect with the police in Delhi. Not long afterwards, the 'denouement' Iengar had been warning about for some weeks came about in circumstances which not only exploded Mundhra's flimsy industrial and financial empire, but also damaged the reputations and careers of a number of officials and public servants.[29]

The Heart of the Matter

What really cooked Mundhra's goose was his dealings with the Life Insurance Corporation of India (LIC). The decision to use LIC funds to rescue Mundhra was taken sometime between 22 and 25 June 1957. A few days earlier, on 18 June, Finance Minister Krishnamachari, accompanied by RBI Governor Iengar, Finance Secretary Patel and SBI Chairman Bhattacharya (who a few years later would become the RBI governor), addressed a group of business leaders and financiers in Calcutta. The meeting was held in the context of a slump in the Calcutta Stock Exchange, caused by many factors but no less by Mundhra's activities. In that meeting, Mundhra, a resident of Calcutta, and his adventurous deals figured, but Mundhra himself did not meet any one of them in Calcutta. There was, however, an important meeting between the president of the Calcutta Stock Exchange, B.N. Chaturvedi, Iengar, Patel and a member of the investment committee of the LIC.

The next important meeting took place in Bombay on 21 June at the headquarters of the RBI. This meeting was between Patel and Mundhra, who was accompanied by the same member of the LIC's investment committee who had been present at the Calcutta meeting. On the same day, Mundhra wrote a letter to Patel explaining his financial troubles and made a few suggestions on how he could be helped. One of them was for LIC to purchase shares worth Rs 80 lakh from Mundhra and buy some more shares of his companies, worth another Rs 30–40 lakh, from the market. This would stabilize the share prices of his companies and help him recover from the financial mess he was in. Mundhra's suggestions did not end there. He also requested that after such financial accommodation, LIC could give him a loan of Rs 1 crore on condition that the insurance behemoth would get equivalent value of business from Mundhra. By way of elaboration, the Mundhra note explained that LIC could buy fresh issues of preference shares of British India and Jessops to the extent of Rs 1.25 crore. In return, Mundhra would ensure that LIC got fire insurance business worth Rs 15 lakh. The suggestions were as blatantly shady as they could be and suggested a quid pro quo at every point. The letter from Mundhra also provided a broad outline of his financial status at that point in time. His total liabilities were estimated at about Rs 5.25 crore, of which Rs 3.93 crore was owed to banks and another Rs 1.55 crore being the value of unencumbered assets.

That almost the entire top echelon of India's financial establishment was somehow connected to the Mundhra episodes of financial impropriety became clear the following day, 22 June 1957. A gist of Mundhra's proposals was sent to the RBI Governor, who commented on that note three days later (25 June 1957) to say that LIC was looking into it in consultation with Patel. Indeed, Patel discussed Mundhra's proposal with LIC Chairman G.R. Kamat. At the end of the discussion, Kamat indicated that LIC could buy only Mundhra's shares and not of any of his companies. On the same day, Patel discussed the issue with the finance minister at the RBI headquarters in the presence of H.V.R. Iengar and P.C. Bhattacharya, chairman of SBI. Those days, the Finance Secretary had an office at the RBI headquarters on Mint Road in Bombay. Broadly confirming the trajectory of the developments, Braj Kumar Nehru, who was at that time the economic affairs secretary and who happened to be a nephew of the prime minister, recalled how 'TTK simply ordered Kamat to buy certain shares which included those of the Mundhra concerns'.[30]

The big drama took place on 23 June in Bombay. It was a Sunday. Present at that meeting were Mundhra, Patel, Kamat and Bhattacharya. Mundhra was asked to present definite proposals from his side, which were discussed at length the following day, on 24 June. At the Monday meeting, L.S. Vaidyanathan, managing director of LIC, was also present. The subsequent developments took place at a rapid pace. RBI History recounts it with great clarity:

> On 25 June the Life Insurance Corporation wrote to Mundhra communicating its willingness to buy from him an agreed list of shares of his companies at prices prevailing at close of trading the previous day. Not only were the various participants at the meetings clear about the prices, the LIC would pay for the Mundhra shares, the manner in which they were finalized allowed ample scope for the markets to be manipulated when they opened on Monday. The deal finalized by the LIC on 25 June was not the first investment by the corporation in shares of Mundhra's companies. In March and April 1957, in the course of three transactions of which the last two were conducted directly with Mundhra himself, the LIC bought substantial lots of his companies' shares. Nor was it the last, the LIC entering into four more purchase transactions in September 1957 through a firm of brokers. But the deal of 25 June 1957 was the biggest by far of any single investment the LIC had undertaken until then. Significantly, this transaction was conducted without any reference to the investment committee of the corporation.[31]

What could have been the compelling reasons for the government to bail out Mundhra by getting LIC to buy shares of his companies? In the early months of 1957, there were fears that the huge pricing pressure on shares of Mundhra firms could depress the overall sentiment in the Calcutta Stock Exchange. Contributing to the overall bearish sentiment in the market was the short-lived taxation proposal of an expenditure tax in Krishnamachari's first Budget. Bailing out Mundhra was perhaps a way of reviving the markets which had remained depressed for a variety of reasons, including the government's earlier proposals on the expenditure tax.

The Hand of TTK

What was the role of the finance minister in all these deals? Reconstructing the events that took place in June 1957 and later in the year, it transpired that T.T. Krishnamachari had his fingers in the till. Did the Finance Secretary ask the LIC chairman to buy Mundhra's shares on his own or after being advised to do so by the finance minister? There is no clinching evidence that allows one to come to any one conclusion. According to the finance minister, he had only told Patel, his Finance Secretary, to look into Mundhra's proposal for LIC to buy his shares. Patel, however, insisted that the minister had approved the proposal. The Chagla Commission sided with Patel in this matter. It had ruled that the minister could not escape 'the moral and constitutional responsibility for the dubious deal'.[32]

Complicating matters for Krishnamachari were his answers to questions posed to the government in Parliament. Thanks to a scoop in a newspaper, the Calcutta-based *Statesman*, the questionable deals pertaining to the purchase of shares of Mundhra companies by LIC came to light. The Delhi edition of the *Statesman* reported on 3 August 1957 that LIC had invested about Rs 1 crore in a private enterprise headquartered in Kanpur. The report did not reveal any more specific details about the deal. The connection to Mundhra's firms was not obvious as all his firms were listed on the stock exchange, and technically, therefore, were not private firms. But the government's reply, through its finance minister in Parliament, was equivocal, evasive and disingenuous. It merely stated that LIC had made no investment in any private firm in Kanpur. The government's response was technically correct as British India Corporation (BIC), whose shares were purchased by LIC, was not a private firm, but a public company.

That reply was on 4 September 1957, in response to a question from a Congress member of the Lok Sabha, Dr Ram Subhag Singh. The LIC-Mundhra deal figured again in the Lok Sabha on 29 November 1957, but it elicited a slightly different reply when Ram Subhag Singh's question was followed up by supplementary questions from another Congress member, Feroze Gandhi, who was also the prime minister's son-in-law. The government, represented by the deputy minister of finance, Bali Ram Bhagat, misled Parliament once again by claiming that the deals in question had been endorsed by the investment committee of the LIC. Bhagat's reply also indicated that the government had no hand in those purchases and that LIC's decision was prompted by considerations of returns and safety only. Favouring any individual or a business group was not one of the reasons, Bhagat clarified. LIC's decision was justified on the ground that it already owned shares in many companies owned by Mundhra and increasing its share in them could help it as these additional purchases were made at a lower price and could help it earn a profit when the share prices would go up. LIC, it was clarified, was not interested in the stock markets but in its own investments.[33]

But that these replies were disingenuous and misleading came out in the open when the Chagla Commission probed the matter. The records of all the answers that Krishnamachari had given to questions raised in Parliament on the Mundhra affair also revealed how the finance minister had indirectly implicated himself. The ministry's draft reply had stated that LIC had made no investment in any private firm in Kanpur or elsewhere. Subsequently, the reply added: '. . . but if the honourable member is referring to British India Corporation or the BIC and other firms, here are the details'.[34] BIC was one of the main Mundhra-owned companies. But as the records with the Commission showed, Krishnamachary had cut this statement on the investments made in BIC out of the reply and had substituted it with a comment that suggested that the newspaper report was without any basis.

The Chagla Commission got to know of this crucial piece of information in a dramatic fashion, after it had submitted its report to the government. Chagla writes in *Roses in December*, his autobiography:

I think it was on the very next day after I had sent it (the report) off, that Frank Moraes and Feroze Gandhi – Gandhi it may be recalled took up the matter in Parliament and fought the battle for probity in public administration with all the zest and persistence of which he was capable – came to see me at Chief Justice House, with news that they had discovered an important document which somehow could not be traced during the inquiry. As far as I remember, it was the pad, to use a parliamentary expression, which they said was given to the Finance Minister when he answered the original question in Parliament with regard to this matter, and which, as I saw, contained information which he did not then disclose.[35]

Chagla told them that he could not include their information in the report, which had already been submitted by him, and advised them to submit the documents in support of their contention to the government. Even though this information was not part of the Commission's report, the discovery must have built further evidence against Krishnamachari, the finance minister.

Krishnamachari's role became even more questionable after the revelations in the different accounts of his conversations with Patel, his Finance Secretary, and other stakeholders in the system. Crucial evidence was to have been furnished by RBI Governor H.V.R. Iengar, who was expected to reveal what actually transpired between the finance minister and the finance secretary on 22 June. It was Iengar who had received the proposals from Mundhra for a bailout by LIC. Mundhra had tried, unsuccessfully, to meet Iengar at his residence the next day. But, going by Iengar's account, Mundhra was thrown out of the RBI Governor's house. In his deposition before the Chagla Commission, Iengar offered no details of what transpired between the finance secretary and the finance minister during that conversation on 22 June. Iengar's version was accepted by the Chagla Commission but earned caustic comments from the Attorney General, M.C. Setalvad, who believed that the RBI Governor 'knew more than he was prepared to admit'.[36]

Braj Kumar Nehru at that time was the economic affairs secretary in the finance ministry, and his access to the happenings in the government was easier than for other bureaucrats as he also happened to be a nephew of the prime minister. B.K. Nehru's recollections of these conversations, recounted by RBI History, shed more light on the role of Krishnamachari and Patel in the entire Mundhra affair. The finance minister had sent

B.K. Nehru to Bombay to meet Iengar, Patel and Bhattacharya to brief them about not telling the Commission differing stories about the LIC-Mundhra transactions. Instead, they were all to defend the transaction on its merits. After that briefing, Patel, as also Iengar, had hoped that the finance minister too would defend the deal on its merits.

An unexpected drama unfolded when the finance minister presented himself before the Commission. RBI History notes:

> But once in the witness box, TTK, acting reportedly on G.B. Pant's (Home Minister at that time) advice, went back on the agreement he had deputed Nehru to Bombay to secure, and disclaimed all knowledge of the LIC's decision. An angry Patel reacted by placing the blame on the Finance Minister. Nor was Patel amused, it seems, by Iengar's claim of not having heard his conversation with the Finance Minister. While Setalvad drew pointed attention to it, Iengar's 'temporary loss of hearing' was, according to B.K. Nehru, an act of dissimulation which contributed to diminishing the 'prestige of the office of the Governor of the Reserve Bank of India'. The Bank's initiative to form a consortium of bankers to promote an orderly recovery of Mundhra's dues, Setalvad also suggested, was another reflection of its solicitude for the adventurer's interests. The Bank sought leave at this point to intervene in the proceedings, only to be told by the Commission that neither the Bank's conduct nor that of its Governor was under scrutiny.

In spite of this, however, the RBI and its governor H.V.R. Iengar faced a lot of flak for their failure to competently and maturely handle the developments following the controversial deal between LIC and Mundhra. Iengar had apparently testified that he had no knowledge of the conversation between the finance minister and the Finance Secretary because at that precise point in time he has 'too busy looking after the lunch arrangements'.[37] Such a statement from the RBI Governor further confirmed the view held by Attorney General M.C. Setalvad that Iengar 'knew more than he was prepared to admit'.

Uproar in Parliament

From September 1957 onwards, the LIC-Mundhra transactions began figuring in discussions in Parliament. Questions began to be asked about

LIC's investment in BIC after the Delhi edition of *Statesman* came out with its report on 3 August 1957, though it did not give any specific details but only pointed out that LIC had invested about Rs 1 crore in a private enterprise headquartered in Kanpur. Most of the answers were either misleading or disingenuous. This triggered more investigations by Congress member Feroze Gandhi into the deal, and he began to ask more questions in Parliament. All this led to the famous intervention Feroze Gandhi made in Parliament on 16 December, after which a heated debate took place among members of the legislature.

The son-in-law of the prime minister and a leading member of the ruling Congress party began his famous speech with these words: 'Parliament must exercise vigilance and control over the biggest and most powerful financial institution it has created, the Life Insurance Corporation of India, whose misapplication of public funds we shall scrutinise today.'[38] Gandhi had good reasons to be perturbed. At the time LIC was born in 1956 after nationalization of over 245 private insurance companies, he had played a major role in pushing the government to launch that nationalization drive. Now that he believed the nationalized company's resources were being misused for bailing out a discredited private businessman, he was deeply perturbed and launched a tirade against the government.

Gandhi's painstaking investigations to bring out damning details about the LIC-Mundhra transactions, the revelation of the findings made on the floor of Parliament in the subsequent days and the widespread support the investigations received, even from Congress members in the House, meant that the government was on the mat. About a month later, in January 1957, Nehru, stung by his son-in-law's devastating charges against his government and his finance minister, referred to the 'majesty of Parliament' and agreed to set up a judicial inquiry to probe the scandal. That was a different era in India's politics, when Congress politicians could engage in healthy debate and introspection to find out where their government had gone wrong. And such a debate could be initiated by a member from within the prime minister's family—by a son-in-law, who could point fingers at his wife's father!

Enter M.C. Chagla

In early January 1958, Mohammadali Carim Chagla was in New Delhi, staying with Attorney General M.C. Setalvad. All of a sudden, he received an invitation from Home Minister Govind Ballabh Pant to join him at dinner. As the Chief Justice of Bombay High Court, Chagla had very little to do with the home minister. But soon after reaching the venue, he understood why Pant had summoned him. There was nobody else at the meeting except Pant and Chagla. Pant said: 'Chaglaji, you have rendered many services for the country. We want you to render one more service to which the Prime Minister attaches the greatest importance.'[39]

Chagla told the home minister that he was always willing to be at the service of the nation, but expressed his curiosity as to the nature of the service that the prime minister wished him to render at that point in time. The home minister told him that he would be needed to head a one-man tribunal to inquire into the affairs of Life Insurance Corporation. Parliament had by then already witnessed a furore over the Mundhra affair, and this was not unknown to Chagla. There was some initial hesitation on the part of Chagla, who argued that he was already the chief justice of Bombay High Court and that was an onerous responsibility. But Pant was insistent and said Chagla should not decline the request to charge of this investigation.

Even as the two were talking, there was a visitor who walked into the room. The visitor, much to Chagla's surprise, was none other than Finance Minister T.T. Krishnamachari, the very person whose conduct in the LIC-Mundhra affair was proposed to be investigated by him. Pant told Krishnamachari that Chagla had agreed to head the tribunal that would inquire into the affairs of LIC. According to Chagla, Krishnamachari did not seem to take that news well. In his autobiography *Roses in December*, he writes: 'I could see from TTK's expression that he did not welcome the idea at all – either he did not like the inquiry, or did not like my being the person to conduct it.'[40]

Chagla was not a person who would take his new assignment lightly. He set two conditions before agreeing to accept the new responsibility. He insisted that Setalvad should appear for the government in the investigation. Setalvad would not appear for the government as though he was a party to a dispute, but as a representative of a government that was as keen as the tribunal to arrive at the facts of the entire LIC-Mundhra deal. His second condition, which too the government accepted, was that the inquiry should held in public, as he believed that the public was entitled to know what evidence any particular decision of the tribunal was based on. The notification appointing the Commission under the Commission of Inquiry Act was issued on 17 January 1958. The terms of reference included ascertaining whether the purchases of shares by the LIC in six Mundhra companies were in accordance with normal business principles, the propriety of the transactions, which persons were responsible for the purchases, and any other circumstances that may be found relevant by the Commission.

Once the decision to set up a commission of inquiry was announced, Krishnamachari met Nehru and expressed his desire to tender his resignation. However, Desai, who was then the commerce and industry ministry, argued that if Krishnamachari resigned before the inquiry got over, the finance minister would be presumed to be guilty by the public and this would not be either fair or proper. Desai's arguments were accepted and Krishnamachari was persuaded not to insist on his resignation at that time. But that turned out to be a reprieve of only one month for Krishnamachari, as subsequent developments would reveal.

Chagla had by then already reached the pinnacle of his legal career, having become the chief justice of the country's most influential high court in Bombay. He would later become India's ambassador to the US and the country's high commissioner in London, before holding ministerial positions in the Union Cabinet under Nehru, Lal Bahadur Shastri and Indira Gandhi, in charge of the ministries of education and external affairs. In line with the condition he had set before accepting the assignment of investigating the Mundhra affair, Chagla readied himself to hold an open and transparent inquiry. Writing in a special edition of *Economic Weekly* in 1959, Ashok H. Desai, eminent lawyer, had this to observe: 'The inquiry conducted by this Commission was held in public. In form, it resembled a preliminary investigation or a general inquisition (including loudspeakers and appropriate homilies from the chair) because there were no parties to the proceedings or charges in the formal manner.'[41]

During the Commission's hearings, Chagla noticed how there was great public interest in the inquiry, justifying his earlier decision to hold the investigations in public. Wherever he went, Chagla found that people were taking keen interest in the conduct of the probe by his Commission. The inquiry proceedings were covered in detail by all the newspapers. Chagla was also flooded with questions about the inquiry process. He noted in his biography:

I was proud of the fact that the public was taking so much interest in the inquiry . . . It also showed that democracy in our country was genuine and was functioning vigorously. The public also quickly recognised that no less a person than a Cabinet Minister was on public trial, showing thereby that even a Cabinet Minister was not above the law, nor beyond the scrutiny of a judicial inquiry.

Indeed, this was the first and the last occasion in India after Independence that a sitting Cabinet minister, and no less a person than on who headed the finance ministry, was put on public trial through a judicial inquiry, eventually leading to his resignation.

During the trial, Mundhra presented himself at the witness box as a man of 'colourful personality, extremely able and quick-witted and prepared to dodge any inconvenient question or give a plausible answer when dodging became difficult or impossible'.[42] Mundhra hardly looked repentant about having rocked India's financial establishment, and he seemed to enjoy the fact that he was getting all the attention in the country. Finance Minister T.T. Krishnamachari too came to the witness box to offer his evidence. Chagla had offered him the courtesy of providing a chair on which he could sit to give his deposition. But Krishnamachari declined the offer. But it was clear that Krishnamachari did not want to stand in the witness box. Well-known lawyer and former Advocate General of Bombay, Sir Jamshedji Behramji Kanga, had made an application so he could represent the finance minister. Chagla turned down that request, arguing that witnesses were not permited to be represented by a counsel at a hearing. Finance Secretary H.M. Patel also gave his evidence before the Commission. For Chagla, the evidence supplied by the finance minister and the Finance Secretary were at odds with each other and he found it difficult to reconcile what the two key witnesses said in the witness box.

Nehru Upset with Chagla Probe

There was little doubt that the manner in which Chagla held the inquiry had made the prime minister a little unhappy. The Commission's inquiry proceedings were being splashed on the front pages of Indian newspapers and Nehru saw that as adverse publicity for his government, which had just been formed after the Congress had registered another thumping victory for itself at the general elections in early 1957. The use of loudspeakers during one of the inquiry sessions even earned a caustic comment from the prime minister. In view of the crowds keen to hear the public inquiry being conducted by Chagla, the police commissioner on his own had arranged for loudspeakers to be installed outside his small office so that the people assembled outside could hear what was going on inside the inquiry room. Chagla objected to the use of the loudspeakers, which had been installed without his permission, but understood the circumstances under which the police took such an action.

Nehru did not take that incident lying down. A day or two later, Nehru referred to the use of loudspeakers at a public inquiry in a sarcastic manner. Chagla was not amused either at such a comment from the prime minister and wrote a letter explaining to him the circumstances under which those loudspeakers were installed by the police, and without his prior knowledge. Nehru got back and explained, rather lamely, that those sarcastic comments were not aimed at Chagla but at the audience at his public meeting at Chowpatty in Bombay.

That was not all. A few days later, Nehru chose to address a meeting of the Indian Merchants Chamber, where he 'went out of his way to pay a high compliment'[43] to the finance minister. Chagla found Nehru's praise for Krishnamachari in public improper, as a judicial inquiry into the finance minister's conduct, among other things, was going on at that time.

Chagla Probe Pins Responsibility on Krishnamachari

Chagla took less than a month to complete his inquiry. His appointment was notified on 17 January 1958 and his report was submitted to the government on 10 February 1958. This was the shortest time any commission of inquiry had taken to complete its task. Credit for this must go to Chagla's hard work and determination to complete the job at the earliest. During this period, Chagla would work for five hours every day, conduct the hearings and dictating the report. In all, it took about two and a half days of writing to complete the report. He requisitioned the services of a special messenger who was asked to carry the report and deliver it to the government in Delhi.

The report made the following conclusion about the LIC-Mundhra deal:

[that it was] suspicious, that proper formalities had not been observed, that the directive for the investment was given by the Finance Secretary, but the responsibility for it must be assumed by the Minister, and that the real purpose of the deal seemed to be rather to help Mundhra than to advance the interests of the Corporation.[44]

The Chagla Commission's report also concluded that the Mundhra deal with LIC had been undertaken at Finance Secretary H.M. Patel's instance. Moreover, LIC Chairman G.R. Kamat and its managing director, L.S. Vaidyanathan, were 'overborne' by Patel and failed to 'exercise responsibility'. The finance minister, in the Chagla Commission's view, had acquiesced in the transaction and even otherwise could not avoid responsibility for the decision.

Explaining the matter in greater detail, the Chagla Commission concluded that there was little basis to the argument that the LIC purchase of Mundhra shares was aimed at preventing a general meltdown in share prices on the Calcutta Stock Exchange. The logic that Patel's decision was influenced by the fear that the offloading of a large volume of shares of Mundhra firms in the stock markets at distress prices had to be averted was unsound. This was because Mundhra would not like his share prices to go down and would do his best to manipulate the market to secure favourable prices for his shares. The Chagla Commission concluded that the LIC undertook the deal not on advice but on direction from the Union government. The finance minister had accepted without any argument the role that Patel played in the transaction and had approved it.

Chagla also went out of his way to end the report with a detailed note on the principles that the government should follow in such financial deals in the future. These principles once again underlined how the Nehru government had failed to follow the best governance standards. The principles required that the government should not interfere with the working of autonomous statutory corporations and that if it wished to interfere, it should give directions only in writing. The head of a corporation such as LIC should always be chosen from among those who have business and financial experience and are conversant with the working of stock exchanges. If civil servants are appointed to head such a corporation, they must be told that their loyalty lay with the organization and not with the government, and if the government wanted to give them any directives, they should be made in writing. The funds of the LIC must be used for the benefit of the policyholders and not for any extraneous purpose. If at all such extraneous purposes are considered, these must be in the larger interests of the country. The minister must always take Parliament into confidence about all such matters pertaining to the government's dealings with a statutory corporation. And the minister must take full responsibility for the acts of his subordinates and cannot be permitted to say that his subordinates did not reflect his policy or acted contrary to his wishes or directions.

Nehru Unconvinced, but Accepts FM's Resignation

In spite of these categorical recommendations that brought out the failure of the finance minister, Nehru was not fully convinced of Krishnamachari's culpability. This could well be because Nehru had a great liking for Krishnamachari. In Chagla's view, Nehru always liked people 'who had high intellectual calibre, who had plenty of drive and had the capacity to get things done'.[45] Krishnamachari was gifted with all the three qualities. Since Nehru's weakness was to overlook major faults in people with those three qualities, Krishnamachari remained a favourite of his. Thus, even after the Chagla Commission's report indicting Krishnamachari was out, Nehru's response was that his finance minister's role in the whole affair was the smallest and that he was not fully aware of all that was being done.

Indeed, Nehru was not fully convinced that Krishnamachari should resign as the finance minister even after the Chagla Commission's unequivocal indictment of him. Krishnamachari had to quit because of the insistence of Maulana Abul Kalam Azad, who was at that time a tall Congress leader and was the education minister. Azad had told Nehru that not calling for the resignation of the finance minister after that report would cause a national scandal. Nehru could not ignore the advice of his senior Cabinet colleague, but made sure that Krishnamachari's exit was made as respectable as possible. Just eight days after the submission of the Chagla Commission's report, Finance Minister T.T. Krishnamachari tendered his resignation, on 18 February 1958.

All this happened in quick succession. The Chagla Commission was set up on 17 January 1958. The Commission completed its inquiry in twenty-four days and submitted its report on 10 February 1958. Soon after, the finance minister submitted his resignation. Within three days, the report was made public by its tabling in Parliament. The Union Cabinet considered the Commission's report on 18 and 19 February, accepted Krishnamachari's resignation and set up further inquiry processes to decide on the action to be initiated against the officials concerned. Parliament debated the Commission's report for three days, from 19 to 21 February. At around the same time, the entire issue was also discussed at the Congress Parliamentary Party meetings. The speed with which all this happened was remarkable and showed the importance the Nehru government accorded to both principles of financial probity and the need for quick action on reports and recommendations made by commissions of inquiry. In subsequent years, such standards became increasingly rare in governments at the Centre, as also in the states.

This was also no ordinary month in the Union government's calendar of events. Krishnamachari was to present his second Union Budget on 28 February 1958. But that was not to be. Nehru had to step in to shoulder the responsibility of holding additional charge of the finance ministry. It was largely Krishnamachari's Budget, but for the record it was Nehru who presented the Budget for 1958–59.

After his resignation, Krishnamachari drove to the airport to leave the city, but Nehru accompanied him personally to the airport to bid him farewell. Chagla described that gesture as 'unique in the annals of our parliamentary history'. Krishna Menon, who had joined Nehru's Cabinet as the defence minister a few months earlier, also visited Krishnamachari at his residence and accompanied him and Nehru to the airport. Menon was one of Nehru's favourite ministers. The idea behind all this was to publicly demonstrate that even though the Chagla Commission had indicted Krishnamachari for his role in the Mundhra scandal, Nehru continued to repose confidence in him. Ironically, instead of bolstering their image, this public display of solidarity with Krishnamachari did a lot of harm to the reputation of the government, as also of Nehru.

An Attempt at Minimizing Political Damage

The adverse impact of the LIC-Mundhra scandal on the reputation and credibility of the Reserve Bank of India was no less severe. During the debate in Parliament on this controversial transaction, many members of the Lok Sabha said the RBI governor, H.V.R. Iengar, and the SBI chairman, P.C. Bhattacharya, were at least partially responsible for the scandal. There was also the accusation that the prime minister was protecting the RBI governor because Iengar was earlier Nehru's Principal Secretary. Nehru did his best to come out in defence of Iengar and noted that there was 'nothing involving him at all' in the conclusions reached by the Chagla Commission. He added that it was 'unfortunate . . . not quite fair' that Iengar's name was 'brought in simply without any reason'.[46]

Just before the resignation of the finance minister, the government moved a resolution in Parliament to capture the broad points made in the Chagla Commission's report on the LIC-Mundhra transactions. The resolution was adopted in the second week of February 1958 and was followed up by the government's setting up of an inquiry in May 1958. This inquiry was headed by a judge of the Supreme Court, Justice Vivian Bose. Unlike in the case of the Chagla Commission, Justice Bose was not alone in steering the inquiry, but was assisted by two others—Sukumar Sen and W.R.S. Sathianadhan.[47] The three were entrusted with the task of investigating the charges brought against H.M. Patel and G.R. Kamat by the Chagla Commission. Though Patel was then the finance secretary and Kamat chairman of LIC, both were members of the Indian Civil Service and their conduct was being probed under the All India Service (Discipline and Appeal) Rules framed in 1955. The scope of the inquiry was widened to examine the charges against the LIC managing director, L.S. Vaidyanathan, too. As many as twenty-five more witnesses were examined, and this was done 'in camera', unlike the earlier public inquiry held by M.C. Chagla.

By September 1958, the Vivian Bose Board of Inquiry had submitted its report establishing some of the charges levelled against these officials. It recommended the removal of Patel from service and compulsory retirement for Kamat. It listed four important charges against the government and the LIC with respect to the share purchase deal.

One, it concluded that in June 1957, Patel had abused his authority by causing Kamat and Vaidyanathan to enter into a deal that was not only improper and contrary to business principles, but had also led to investments by LIC which it should not have made.

Two, it found Patel to be negligent in overseeing the entire transaction, in that he did not give clear directives to LIC about the price that it should pay for the shares of Mundhra firms under different tranches. This, the Board argued, caused losses to LIC. Three, the Board concluded that Patel's action was not covered by any ministerial approval or authority. The finance minister had given a vague approval to LIC's deal with Mundhra.

And four, it did not just agree with the Chagla Commission's views that the share deal was to benefit Mundhra and that it served no public interest, but went far beyond that by suggesting that there was a quid pro quo motive in the involved persons' entering into the share purchase deal. Mundhra had donated about Rs 2.5 lakh to the Congress election fund just before the 1957 general elections and had secured from the government some promise of help for his mills in Kanpur. The LIC-Mundhra share deal was a way of fulfilling those promises.

The most damning comment that the Vivian Bose Board made on the LIC-Mundhra deal came in its concluding observation after naming the several senior government officials it had met during its investigation. It noted: 'We regret that we have not been told the whole truth, and some of at least of what we have been told is demonstrably false.'[48]

The Nehru government referred these recommendations to the Union Public Service Commission (UPSC) for its advice on the charges levelled against the civil services officers and the penalty it proposed. The rehabilitation process of those indicted by the Chagla Commission had already begun taking shape by that time. The UPSC recommended that no charges could be levelled against Patel and, therefore, exonerated him. Kamat was held responsible for not exercising 'due care and caution' in fixing the prices of Mundhra's shares and for entering into an 'unbusinesslike' transaction. It, therefore, recommended censure for Kamat.

The manner in which the UPSC diluted almost all the charges levelled by the Chagla Commission and the Vivian Bose Board against the finance minister, the finance secretary and the LIC chairman seemed to almost suggest that no financial scandal had taken place at all. It argued that the charges of abuse of authority against Patel were baseless as he could not have forced Kamat or Vaidyanathan to enter into the transaction. The charge of negligence in not ensuring a proper price for the deal could not be proved either. On Kamat, the UPSC concluded that the charges of impropriety and the 'unbusinesslike' nature of the transaction were established only with regard to the prices fixed for the deal and the loss suffered by LIC. It upheld the allegation against Kamat that he had failed to discharge his duties as chairman of LIC by not taking adequate care in fixing the prices for the purchase of the shares. On why the deal took place, the UPSC concluded that Finance Minister T.T. Krishnamachari was aware of the controversial past of Mundhra and that was why Patel had apprised the finance minister about the transaction. And Patel honestly believed that the minister had indeed approved the transaction. Finally, the UPSC dismissed the Vivian Bose Board's charge that the LIC-Mundhra deal was a quid pro quo for Mundhra's donation of Rs 2.5 lakh to the Congress election fund and for his agreeing to defer the closure of Kanpur Cotton Mills, which could have created a political problem in the run-up to the general elections. It was pointed out that Patel had not mentioned this in his defence. Nor did the Vivian Bose Board put this proposition before the witnesses appearing before it. Hence, there was no ground for drawing such inferences.

The UPSC's recommendations, however, were not unanimous, with J. Sivashanmugham Pillai, one of its members examining the Bose Board's recommendations, deciding to make a dissenting note on the UPSC's overall course of action. But that did not deter the government from quickly accepting these recommendations, which diluted the nature of the penalties suggested by the Bose Board. The government also endorsed the UPSC's view that there was no clinching evidence to suggest a quid pro quo in the LIC-Mundhra deal, as suggested by the Vivian Bose Board. RBI Governor H.V.R. Iengar and SBI chairman P.C. Bhattacharya were not accused in the case and hence did not appear before the Vivian Bose inquiry committee. Nevertheless, the UPSC made some adverse observations against them, which the government termed as 'unfortunate'.[49] All these decisions were taken by the government on 27 May 1959, to bury the proverbial hatchet of the biggest financial scandal the Nehru government faced.

RBI's Reputation Takes a Hit

The Reserve Bank of India could not have been faulted for having taken an interest in LIC's dealings with the Mundhra firms. After all, many commercial banks had lent huge sums of money to Mundhra and many borrowers as well as depositors in these banks would have been impacted by what was happening at Mundhra and LIC. Even though the RBI had been keeping a watch on the stock market trends those days, it had no powers to intervene either in the stock markets or in the affairs of LIC, which was an autonomous but state-owned enterprise. There was a proposal that envisaged the RBI Governor heading the investment board of LIC, but it had not made any headway. Yet, because the discussion on the LIC-Mundhra transactions happened at the premises of the RBI in Bombay, the central bank and its Governor came in for adverse publicity and criticism. Iengar certainly had an idea of the extent of the crisis in Mundhra's finances, but he was certainly not responsible for LIC's controversial investment decisions. What hurt his reputation was his conduct during the Chagla Commission's inquiry, where he was seen as not divulging relevant information about the LIC-Mundhra transactions that he was in possession of.

Following the adverse comments of M.C. Setalvad and the Vivian Bose Board on his reliability as a witness, Iengar's image and even his self-esteem took a hit. The following excerpt from RBI History[50] says a lot about the anguish Iengar went through because of the Mundhra scandal:

> Writing in August 1958 to TTK (T.T. Krishnamachari) who had meanwhile taken up residence in the southern resort of Kodaikanal, Iengar remarked: 'You have asked about the boycott in Bombay. Quite frankly, I have ceased to be interested in it and I have ordered my life in such a way that I could not possibly care less. I do not think I have accepted a single invitation from any business magnate since January and it seems to be generally known that I am averse to accepting such invitations. I feel much happier because I am getting a great deal more time which I devote partly to reading economic literature and partly with my family; the latter is a pleasure which I have unfortunately denied myself for many many years.'

At the organizational level, the RBI did experience the impact of the Mundhra scandal. Its stance on the way it should deal with its relationship with the government and other financial intermediaries saw a significant change. Iengar initiated a drive to disengage the RBI from activities in areas for which it was not statutorily responsible. Soon after Setalvad's caustic comments on the RBI's interest in Mundhra's financial affairs, Iengar told Krishnamachari in February 1958 that he had asked a Calcutta-based manager of the RBI, D.D. Pai, who was on a Calcutta Stock Exchange committee, not to attend its meetings, lest some false conclusions should be drawn about the RBI's involvement in such matters by an inquiry committee in the future. The CSE committee was set up to evaluate some financial issues pertaining to Jessop. Krishnamachari, in the last few days before he quit the finance ministry, told Iengar that it would be difficult for the RBI not to be associated with such financial matters and the Governor should not be obsessed with what happened in the Mundhra case. Iengar referred the matter to a small group of Deputy Governors of the RBI to examine the future course of action. The Deputy Governors were of the view that the disadvantages of engagement by RBI officers in stock or commodity exchanges outweighed the advantages and instead recommended that the government should nominate its representatives on the exchanges. The government accepted the suggestion, though reluctantly, which is why it was not implemented. But a few years later the same proposal was revived. But for the present, the Mundhra scandal had made the RBI more cautious about how it should deal with other financial institutions or even the government.

Steps Towards TTK's Political Rehabilitation

Nehru's unhappiness at the investigations into the LIC-Mundhra transactions had begun manifesting soon after the Chagla Commission started its open hearings. The use of loud speakers in one of the hearings had irked Nehru, of which he made a mention with sarcasm at a public meeting. Even while the inquiry was going on, Nehru had given a certificate of integrity to his finance minister while addressing a business leaders' gathering in Calcutta. Nehru was also unhappy about the appearance of the government's chief and seniormost legal adviser, Attorney General M.C. Setalvad, before the Chagla Commission. It would appear that Setalvad's appearance took place without prior approval of the government. Chagla had requested Setalvad to appear not on behalf of the government, but to help the Commission unravel the facts of the case. This seemed to have irked Nehru.

The minutes of the Cabinet meeting that reviewed the Chagla Commission's report noted that in no uncertain terms:

> [The] Attorney General's line of argument struck the Cabinet as most extraordinary. He had not consulted government with regard to their point of view, although he was supposed to appear on behalf of government and, strangely enough, had proceeded to make insinuations of mala fides without adequate justification . . . The Cabinet decided that with regard to future inquiries of this kind, care should be taken not only for evolving a correct procedure but for proper briefing of the government counsel.[51]

The assumption that the Attorney General appeared before the Chagla Commission without the permission of the government was simply flawed. In the Rajya Sabha debate on the Chagla Commission's report, Nehru had stated that the government had neither appointed its counsel nor prepared a brief, but had left the entire process in the hands of Chagla. Bhupesh Gupta, member of the Rajya Sabha representing the Communist Party of India, had interjected: 'But you sent the Attorney General there.' Nehru replied: 'Quite so. Mr. Justice Chagla mentioned to Mr. Krishnamachari—remember, it was Mr. Krishnamachari who appointed Mr. Justice Chagla as the Commission—I think Mr. Chagla said that he would like the assistance of the Attorney General. Mr. Krishnamachari said, "gladly you can have him".' From Nehru's own statement, it becomes clear that the Attorney General appeared before the Commission after getting the green signal from the finance minister.

Even in his reply to a letter from RBI Governor Iengar on 5 February 1958, Nehru made no secret of his displeasure at the way the Chagla Commission had conducted its inquiry and framed its conclusions. Expectedly, Iengar had expressed to the prime minister his unhappiness at the conduct of the Attorney General during the inquiry. Nehru wrote:

> I quite agree with you that the way in which the Attorney General has handled the proceedings of the Chagla Commission has been extraordinary and has surprised us greatly. His references to you appear to me to be wholly unwarranted. Indeed, this could be said of some of his other references too about other people. He has put us in a difficult

position . . . We certainly did not expect all kinds of people to be put in the dock and not given an opportunity to defend themselves or even to explain their position properly. This has been a novel and painful experience not only for you, but for many of us also. I do not suppose we can do anything now about it, but statements will have to be made in Parliament, and I propose to refer to some of these matters.[52]

Nehru seemed to have had an inkling that he would have misgivings about the Chagla Commission's findings even before they were presented to the government. On 9 February, just a day before he received the report of the Commission, he had written to his sister, Vijayalakshmi Pandit, who was at that time India's high commissioner in the United Kingdom, saying:

This whole business has been a wretched affair. It is quite wrong, I think, to say that the Life Insurance Corporation has suffered any material loss by this investment. But the manner of carrying out this investment was improper . . . The way Setalvad conducted this case was rather extraordinary. He is a member of government and yet he functioned as a prosecuting counsel. Chagla appeared to encourage him . . .[53]

Far worse comments for the Chagla Commission were made by Nehru in a subsequent letter on 17 February 1958 to Vijayalakshmi Pandit, where he said that appointing a one-man commission of inquiry was not a happy decision. 'The one man is a good man, but rather hasty. The conditions created in Bombay at the time were so peculiar that this resembled in a sense somewhat the mass trials one hears of in Communist countries,' he wrote to his sister.[54]

So convinced was Nehru about his finance minister's innocence and lack of culpability that he did not hesitate in writing to Krishnamachari in a regretful tone that almost bordered on exonerating the man who had been indicted by a Commission appointed by his own government under the Commission of Inquiry Act:

As the enquiry proceeded, it struck me, as it struck many others, that this manner of approach to a complicated problem was hardly satisfactory . . . It was neither judicial nor capable otherwise of eliciting all the facts . . . In effect, there was rather a one-sided presentation of facts. This was unfortunate in such a matter in which the public was rightly interested. I am not mentioning this by way of complaint but merely to point out that such an approach did not appear to me to be satisfactory. I have still a feeling that all the relevant facts connected with this unhappy matter have not been brought out . . . So far as you are concerned, I am myself convinced that your part in this matter was of the smallest and that you did not even know much that was done.[55]

Nehru's letter had caused him to face some embarrassing moments in Parliament. The Prime Minister's letter had become public and its content figured in a discussion in the Rajya Sabha. An independent member of the Rajya Sabha, H.N. Kunzru, who had also been a member of the Constituent Assembly, took exception to some of the observations in Nehru's letter and said in a discussion in Parliament:

It is not for the first time that the Prime Minister has allowed his feelings to get better of him but it is a matter of great regret that the Prime Minister should, in this manner, reflect on the report of a Commission presided over by one of the most eminent judges in the country. The Prime Minister has a right to differ from the Commission . . . but then, it is his duty to state the reasons that make him differ from the Commission's view.

Nehru was not at peace with himself over the manner in which he had to let go of his favourite finance minister. Soon after he received the Chagla Commission report, Nehru took a decision to conduct a secret inquiry into the role of his finance minister and other senior government officials in the LIC-Mundhra transactions. This was despite the government having accepted the Chagla Commission's report and the Union Cabinet having approved a course of action and Parliament having debated the issues raised in the Commission's report. Nehru asked Bhola Nath Mullik, director of the Intelligence Bureau at that time, to find out what had actually happened and to what extent Krishnamachari was involved in these transactions. The reason he asked Mullik to do this was that though Krishnamachari had resigned on a matter of principle, Nehru was not convinced that his finance minister had received a proper hearing from the Chagla Commission. Mullik was told that he would be given a free hand in deciding his mode of inquiry and was assured that the report would remain a secret document, to be seen only by the prime minister and the home minister.

Interestingly, Mullik was not very keen on undertaking the inquiry and he did try to wriggle out of the assignment. He argued with the home minister, Govind Ballabh Pant, that such a job should be entrusted with the Special Police Establishment or SPE (which would be later rechristened the Central Bureau of Investigation or CBI). Pant's explanation to Mullik as to why the inquiry suggested by Nehru should be conducted by the IB was an eye-opener. Pant said that since a political decision had to be taken on Krishnamachari, the inquiry was within the scope of the IB. Pant agreed to allow Mullik to associate the inspector general of the SPE in the inquiry. As Madhav Godbole, a civil servant, would write in his book on Nehru (*The God Who Failed – An Assessment of Jawaharlal Nehru's Leadership*), Pant's argument was disingenuous. The IB's charter did not include holding inquiries into political matters, Godbole, who occupied senior positions in the government as an IAS officer, noted. The political ground was already being cleared for the eventual rehabilitation of Krishnamachari. Hence the plan for an inquiry by the IB.

Mullik's report helped Nehru secure Krishnamachari's political rehabilitation a few years later. It confirmed that Mundhra had paid Rs 1 lakh to the Uttar Pradesh Congress and another Rs 1 lakh to Bengal Congress as donation for the general elections in 1957. The fact of the donation was known to Krishnamachari, and it must have created in the finance minister's mind a favourable impression of Mundhra. Krishnamachari, the report by Mullik observed, was not directly involved in the transaction, but did not oppose it when the proposal was put up before him twice. This could be because Krishnamachari was aware of the political necessity of not allowing the Mundhra-owned British India Company's Kanpur-based factory to shut down before the elections. The task of keeping the factory operational could be achieved by helping Mundhra financially. In contrast, Mullik's report held Finance Secretary H.M. Patel to be mainly responsible for the transaction, though there was no suspicion of any dishonesty on his part.

Mullik took about three months to complete his secret investigations. Recounting these developments in *My Years with Nehru 1948–1964*, Mullik wrote:

I presented my report to the Prime Minister sometime towards the end of May 1958, and he agreed with my conclusions and was relieved to hear that neither T.T. Krishnamachari nor any other Minister was directly involved in this deal. He told me to show this report to the Home Minister, which I did. The latter also accepted the report and advised me to keep it in my custody. Both were happy to know that there was no dishonest motive in this transaction.[56]

Perhaps emboldened by the findings in Mullik's report, Home Minister Pant addressed a public meeting in Madras, where he declared that Krishnamachari was not at fault and he had to resign in keeping with the highest traditions of democracy. In effect, the seat of the finance minister in North Block was being kept warm for Krishnamachari to return—at an appropriate time!

Morarji Desai (Finance Minister, 1958–1963)

Presiding over Aid India Club and
Bank Failures

It is quite ironical that the elevation of Morarji Desai as the finance minister in March 1958 followed a financial scandal that singed the Jawaharlal Nehru government and damaged its clean reputation. Ironical, because Desai had by then acquired the halo of an austere Gandhian with the principles of an ascetic and a marked predilection towards displaying public morality in every action he would undertake. The scandal that shook the Nehru government involved virtually everybody in the government's economic establishment at that time.

The finance minister at that time, T.T. Krishnamachari, was not spared. Nor were the Principal Finance Secretary, H.M. Patel, and G.R. Kamat, the chairman of the recently set-up Life Insurance Corporation, which had taken over as many as 245 foreign and Indian private-sector companies as part of the government's decision to nationalize the life insurance industry in 1956.

Called the Mundhra scandal, its chief perpetrator was Haridas Mundhra, a businessman with a dubious reputation who had used the government system to get loans from LIC to help prop up the value of his companies' shares and had unlawfully benefited himself and his businesses.

Punitive action had followed quickly. A one-man commission of inquiry was set up under the chairmanship of the chief justice of the Bombay High Court, M.C. Chagla, whose report indicted the finance minister. Mundhra was found guilty of having abused the system. He was sent to jail. Patel and Kamat, both Indian Civil Service officers, were accused of having facilitated the questionable deals with Mundhra, but were eventually exonerated. While the civil servants got away, Krishnamachari had to resign as the finance minister. It was against this backdrop that Desai was invited to step into North Block and steer the government's finances.

Desai Approached Again to Become FM

For Desai, Nehru's invitation came as no surprise. Nor was it the first time that Nehru had made an offer to him to become the finance minister at the Centre. Almost two years ago, in 1956, Nehru had made that first offer, but the manner in which developments took place subsequently had upset Desai, who carried with him unpleasant memories of why and how he was not made the finance minister in spite of having reached a broad understanding with Nehru about it. That development must have hurt Desai, although temperamentally he was not someone who would make a big issue out of it.

In 1956, Desai was no greenhorn in Indian politics. He had already spent about four years as chief minister of Bombay, one of India's most important provinces and the country's financial hub. Desai's experience in public administration had also been varied and rich. Born in 1896 in present-day Valsad district of Gujarat, Desai had graduated in 1918 from Wilson College, Bombay, and immediately thereafter had joined the British government to work as a deputy collector for about twelve years. His last posting was in Godhra, where he had to handle the communal riots that affected the town in 1927–28.

It was the same place where an Indian Railways train carrying some Hindu pilgrims returning from Ayodhya would be set on fire by miscreants some sixty-four years later, triggering communal violence against Muslims in Gujarat. Narendra Modi, the chief minister of Gujarat in 2002, would weather the political storm and charges of abetment in that violence against his government, and continue to rule that state till 2014—a reign that would eventually catapult him on the national scene as India's prime minister that year.

For Desai, the outcome of his travails in Godhra in 1927–28 was quite different. In *The Story of My Life,* he writes:

> I had received a notice from the Commissioner saying that the Collector of Panchmahals (of which Godhra was the district headquarters) had asked for an inquiry into my part in the riots. The burden of the issue framed by the Commissioner was that I was a communalist and that I supported the Hindus against the Muslims.

Desai gave a detailed reply to all the questions put to him during the inquiry, but in April 1930 he was found by the British government to be 'guilty of acting in a partisan way on account of communal bias'. The only action taken against Desai resulted in his relegation in the seniority list of government officers by four notches. Desai believed this was an arbitrary and unjust action, essentially aimed at maintaining 'the prestige of the white officer'.

At around the same time, he had been attracted to the movement for liberating the country from British rule, led by Mahatma Gandhi. Once he quit the government in protest, he decided to join the national movement for freedom and joined the Congress in 1931. His rise in the freedom movement led by the Congress in Gujarat and Maharashtra was phenomenal. Desai became an important leader of the freedom movement. He was sent to jail by the British government not once, or twice, but thrice. He also became part of the provincial government that was formed in the Bombay province and played an important role as a minister for revenue, agriculture, forests and cooperatives. A few years after Independence, in 1952, he became chief minister of the province of Bombay, which included present-day Maharashtra and Gujarat.

The outbreak of violence and riots in Bombay in the wake of the Centre's flip-flop on the proposed reorganization of Bombay took a political toll on Desai, whose administrative skills as chief minister were put to the test. Desai brought the rapidly deteriorating law and order situation under control with an iron fist, but his handling of the crisis had earned the displeasure of a few influential sections in the Congress. Initially, Bombay was to have become a centrally administered territory while the remaining areas under Bombay state were to be carved out into Maharashtra and Gujarat. However, this triggered a spate of protests leading to violence, and the Nehru government went back on this decision. As a way out, it retained the entire Bombay province as a bilingual state.

The Centre's handling of the reorganization proposal for Bombay had another casualty. Finance Minister C.D. Deshmukh, who hailed from Maharashtra and did not agree with the idea of carving out Bombay city as a separate, centrally administered territory, had sent his resignation in protest. Even though Nehru changed his decision on the reorganization of states later, he did not ask Deshmukh to change his mind. He only requested Deshmukh to continue in the job for a few months until he could find a replacement.

Bidding Goodbye to Bombay

Coinciding with Deshmukh's resignation and the politically unstable situation in riot-torn Bombay was a decision that Desai had taken about his own future. In one of his meetings, Desai told Nehru about his plan to quit as the chief minister of Bombay and instead devote himself to undertaking 'constructive work'. Nehru's reply took Desai by surprise. The prime minister suggested to Desai that he would be needed in the Union Cabinet. After that fateful meeting of the Congress Working Committee in July 1956, which decided to formalize the creation of a bigger state of Bombay, including the city of Bombay, Vidarbha, Marathwada and Gujarat, Nehru invited Desai to his residence at Teen Murti. The conversation the two had was significant and reflective of the character and personality of Desai, as also of Nehru.

According to Desai, as recounted in his autobiography, the conversation went as follows:

> Nehru: 'As you have decided to relinquish the chief ministership of Bombay State, you should join the Central Cabinet and take up the responsibility of the Finance Ministry as Shri C.D. Deshmukh has resigned.'
> Desai: 'I have already completed sixty years of my life and it is my view that it would be better for me not to remain in any position of power. I have, therefore, no desire to take up any position of authority. I shall continue to serve the people as a non-official through the Congress.'
> Nehru: 'You can be the President of the Congress also, but it will be better if you come to the Centre.'

Desai: 'The presidentship of the Congress is also a position of authority and I have no desire to take it.'

When Nehru insisted once again, Desai came out with yet another reason for why he did not wish to be the finance minister, and he was pretty confident that Nehru would not insist on his coming to the Centre after that. He had said: 'It will be difficult for me to take up the administration of the finance ministry as I have not studied economics and have never prepared my own budget. I have no attraction for money and it is, therefore, difficult for me to look after the finance ministry.'

Nehru was not going to give up easily. He reminded Desai of a conversation they had just a couple of months ago about who an ideal finance person should be and what kind of character attributes he should have. That was when Deshmukh had just sent in his resignation to the prime minister. Nehru wanted to seek Desai's views on Deshmukh's resignation and what the government should do in such matters.

Desai had minced no words in telling Nehru at that time that if a minister offered to resign, it should be accepted immediately, lest that resignation should be used as a threat by some people, setting an unhealthy precedent. Desai's view was perhaps one of the reasons why Nehru did not ask Deshmukh to reconsider his decision to resign, even though the latter's grievance that had triggered the resignation had been effectively redressed.

Nehru listened to what Desai had to say, but in a crucial revelation let him into the ongoing internal Congress debate on whom to appoint as finance minister. Nehru told Desai that many members of the Congress were of the view that a member of the Congress party should be made the finance minister to fill the vacancy caused by Deshmukh's resignation. Many members argued that having a finance minister who is not a member of the party created many difficulties.

In choosing his finance ministers, Nehru had until then shown a marked preference for those who did not belong to the Congress party. Barring Kshitish Chandra Neogy, who was the finance minister for just about thirty-five days, none of the other finance ministers till then had been from the Congress. R.K. Shanmukham Chetty, the first finance minister of India after Independence, was a member of the nationalist

Swaraj Party and also the Justice Party. Indeed, even when Chetty was named as the finance minister, Nehru earned the wrath of many Congress leaders, who believed the new minister for finance had explicit leanings towards the British. After Neogy's short stint, John Matthai became the finance minister, but he too was not from the Congress. Matthai was a well-regarded economist. Following Matthai was C.D. Deshmukh, who was a retired civil servant and a former Governor of the Reserve Bank of India, who later fought elections but only as an independent candidate with the support of the Congress.

There was a clear pattern in Nehru's choice of finance ministers. The preference was for a professional expert, an economist or a retired civil servant. It so happened that none of these professionals and experts belonged to the Congress. Why was this so? Nehru explained to Desai that his choices were driven by his assessment that there was nobody within the Congress party who was an expert in financial issues and, therefore, capable of handing the finance portfolio.

Desai had differed with Nehru's belief that only an expert in financial matters should be considered fit to become the finance minister. Instead, the more important attribute of a finance minister, according to Desai, was that he must be a member of the Congress party. That was necessary in view of the criticality of the functions of the finance minister. Nehru became curious. He wanted to know what Desai thought were the key attributes necessary for a finance minister. Desai lost no time in listing out four conditions that a finance minister must fulfil.

One, the person chosen as the finance minister must enjoy the prime minister's full confidence. And, just as the prime minister must be confident that the person chosen to be the finance minister would be able to discharge his responsibilities competently, the finance minister should also have complete confidence in his own abilities. Two, the finance minister must be a 'full-fledged party man, believing in the ideals and programmes of the party and also in implementing them'. Three, the entire country must have full faith in the integrity of the person chosen as the finance minister. And four, the person chosen to be the finance minister should have the required intelligence and common sense to seek the help of experts and benefit from their advice to arrive at proper decisions and implement them. Nehru had concurred with Desai's analysis.

The Offer That Was Not Honoured

After reminding Desai about this conversation that had happened just a few weeks ago, Nehru decided to once again insist on his request. In a dramatic manner, recalling the four attributes that Desai saw necessary in a finance minister, Nehru said:

> You satisfy all these conditions and should therefore accept my suggestion. There is none at present in my Cabinet whom I could select for the finance ministry for more than three or four months as none would be able to carry it on longer. You should therefore accept the finance ministership at the Centre.[1]

Desai realized that Nehru was keen to have him as his finance minister. He accepted the offer, but added a rider. He told the prime minister that it would take him some time to disengage from his responsibilities as the chief minister of Bombay. Nehru told Desai that he would keep the finance minister's portfolio under his own charge till 1 November, by which time he expected Desai to join the Cabinet. Desai thought the matter was settled and had even shared this information with then Congress President U.N. Dhebar, who, however, expressed some reservations about the development.

Desai was a little puzzled by Dhebar's reaction. The puzzle got resolved a few days later when Nehru called him late in the evening at about 9.30 p.m. Nehru told him on the phone:

> I had told you that I would keep the finance ministry with me and look after it until you come to Delhi, but difficulties have arisen here in relation to foreign exchange and also internal resources and it is not possible for me to look after the work. I have, therefore, decided to entrust this responsibility to T.T. Krishnamachari, though this arrangement is temporary. I have also to consider the commerce and industry ministry which is at present with Krishnamachari. When you come to Delhi we shall think of this and make permanent arrangements.[2]

It took a while before the significance of what Nehru had said on the phone dawned on Desai. The prime minister had decided to change his mind on his choice of finance minister made just a few days ago. Desai would not be the finance minister. Instead, T.T. Krishnamachari, who was then the minister for commerce and industry, would become the finance minister. The vacancy caused by Krishnamachari's elevation as the finance minister was proposed to be filled by Desai. Nehru also seemed to suggest that the arrangement was not permanent and there was scope for adjustment and changes after discussions, when Desai came to Delhi.

To be fair, Nehru was indeed under pressure to appoint a full-time finance minister without any delay as the Indian economy was going through an acute resource crisis. The Second Five-year Plan had been launched two years ago and had run into major financial hurdles as the government was finding it difficult to mobilize adequate internal and external resources to keep the Plan investments on track. The country, the Second Plan and the Nehru government could not afford to wait for a full-time finance minister for another two months.

Nevertheless, that phone call had, quite understandably, upset Desai. A commitment made a few days ago at a physical meeting was being withdrawn over a conversation on the phone. In a firm but polite tone, Desai told Nehru over the phone: 'I had no particular desire in this matter then, nor have I any now. You can, therefore, make permanent arrangements even now.'

Deshmukh quit the government by the end of July 1956. Nehru had assumed temporary responsibility of the finance ministry for about a month in August. On 30 August, Krishnamachari was appointed the finance minister. This meant that the portfolio of the ministry of commerce and industry, which Krishnamachari was earlier heading, fell vacant.

Meanwhile, Desai was preparing for his exit from the chief ministership of Bombay and exploring various options to play a 'constructive' role in public affairs. But Nehru had not given up on his plans to get Desai to join his Cabinet. The two met at Ahmedabad in October 1956 and the discussion once again veered around to the portfolio that Desai should take up after coming to Delhi. Nehru told Desai in no uncertain terms that he would like to announce his joining the Centre as a Cabinet minister by the end of October. Desai was a little amused to note that the prime minister had completely forgotten about his earlier decision of offering the post of the finance minister to him. Desai took it as a clear signal that Krishnamachari's elevation as the finance minister was a permanent appointment, contrary to the earlier impression he was given that this was an interim or temporary arrangement.

Nehru presented an interesting option to Desai. He could either take the ministry for commerce and industry or the ministry for defence. Desai made it clear to Nehru that he had no problem in accepting whatever job he would be entrusted with. But, as always, Desai set an important rider. He made it clear that if he were asked to take charge of the defence ministry, then he could not be expected to take active part in day-to-day party politics. Desai's arguments were reflective of his personality and character. As the head of the armed forces, he believed that the defence minister must keep out of politics. Nehru sympathized with Desai's logic. At the same time, he was not willing let go of Desai's services as a member of the Congress Working Committee, which were necessary for the party. The second general elections in India were due to be held less than a year later and the Congress party needed all the support it could garner in the following months. Desai was also the Congress party treasurer at that time. Thus, in the forenoon of 14 November 1956 (coincidentally, also Nehru's birthday as he turned sixty-seven), Desai joined the Nehru Cabinet as the minister for commerce and industry. Desai was sixty.

For the next few months, Desai was deeply immersed in Congress party work. Nehru had desired that Desai should take upon himself the responsibility of collecting funds for the Congress party for the forthcoming general elections. That was understandable as Desai, after all, was also the Congress treasurer. Desai was relatively new to the idea of collecting funds for the party. Only once did he do so during the 1952 elections, when he was the chief minister of Bombay.

He wanted to be absolutely sure that Nehru did desire him to collect election funds. He checked with Nehru directly and told the prime minister that all the money collected for the party would have to be deposited in a bank account, to be operated jointly by him and Nehru.

With the compliance of those formalities, Desai reached out to an array of industrialists and business leaders to consider donating to the Congress to help it fund its election costs. Those were the early days of electoral funding in India after Independence. Desai would be upfront and frank about his mission while meeting a small group of business leaders in Bombay. He told them about the transparent manner in which the collected funds would be deposited in a bank account. 'If you honestly feel that the country's government would be run properly and with stability if the Congress gets a majority, you should contribute to this fund and make arrangements for collection from others,' Desai would tell his interlocutors during this mission.[3]

Did the business leaders Desai met during this exercise, have the option of not contributing to the Congress fund? It would seem so, going by Desai's account. He says he told the business leaders:

> If you do not have that confidence in the Congress, I cannot ask for any contributions from you. My dealings will be the same with all, whether they contribute to the fund or not. I shall not be able to help more the person who contributes nor will I do injustice to a person who does not contribute to the fund. You can rest assured that everyone will be treated fairly and properly.

Not every industry leader was convinced of the need to contribute to the Congress fund. Many of them were encouraged by the fact that Desai did not put any pressure on them to do so. J.R.D. Tata, along with a few other industry leaders, told Desai that they would need to seek permission from the high court before contributing to such a fund, as their articles of association had no such provision. They did obtain the permission of the court and made contributions to the Congress election fund. Whether the raising of such questions on the legal feasibility of providing funds to a political party had an adverse impact on the fortunes of these businesses was not immediately clear. Even several decades later, the jury is still out on whether industries that did not spontaneously contribute to the Congress election fund were singled out in any way or were out of favour with the government.

But there was no doubt about the success of the Congress drive to collect election funds. In about two years, Desai managed to collect Rs 1.2 crore, which was more than adequate to meet the election expenses of the Congress during the 1957 elections. About Rs 25–30 lakh out of the amount collected was saved, and this was used for other elections in the coming years.

The 1957 general elections, held over a span of three and a half months from the last week of February to the first week of June, returned the Congress to power at the Centre. The Congress under Nehru won a second five-year term at the Centre, winning 371 of the 494 seats that were contested. The Congress increased its tally by seven seats, and its vote share also increased from 45 per cent to 47.8 per cent. In the new Union Cabinet formed after the elections, Desai was retained as the commerce and industry minister. T.T. Krishnamachari too was retained as the minister for finance.

In less than a year of that thumping victory notched by the Congress at the hustings, its government faced its worst crisis caused by a financial scandal, leading to the resignation of Krishnamachari just a couple of weeks before he was due to present his second Union Budget. Nehru stepped in to take charge of the finance ministry. Budget work had already been finalized. Nehru faced a few difficulties in presenting the Budget on 28 February 1958. That was also the first time in independent India when the prime minister had to present a Union Budget in his additional capacity as the finance minister.

But Nehru needed a full-time finance minister, as he recognized that his taking over the ministry was only a stop-gap arrangement. In Nehru's calculations, Desai was a clear choice as someone who could easily step into the void created by a resignation made under a cloud of suspicion. A few days after the presentation of the Budget, Nehru called Desai and Govind Ballabh Pant for a meeting. Pant was then the home minister in the Nehru government and had just begun to resolve the knotty problem of reorganization of states on linguistic lines. Nehru's suggestion to Desai to accept the portfolio of the finance ministry met with a negative response. Desai argued that if he were to be the finance minister, the prejudices of his predecessor, T.T. Krishnamachari, against Desai would get stronger. Krishnamachari might get the impression that it was Desai who had masterminded the inquiry against him and was behind his eventual removal from the finance ministry. Nehru dismissed such suggestions from Desai, arguing that everyone in the government knew he had no hand in the way Krishnamachari had got himself embroiled in the Mundhra scandal. Desai asked Nehru why he had not thought of Pant for the post. Nehru was clear in his mind that he needed Pant in the home ministry to resolve the many remaining knotty issues with regard to the reorganization of states.

That left Desai with no option other than to accept the new ministerial assignment. Less than a month after Nehru had presented the Union Budget for 1958–59, Desai took charge of the finance ministry at the end of March 1958 and began preparations to defend a Budget that his prime minister had presented to Parliament.

Even as Desai shifted from the commerce and industry ministry to the manifestly higher office of the finance minister, a few troubling questions continued to be asked. If Desai had agreed to join the finance ministry immediately after Nehru had made him the first offer in July 1956 (when C.D. Deshmukh had quit), would he have handled the Mundhra scandal in a different way from Krishnamachari? Would the Nehru government have been saved from the ignominy of the Mundhra scandal consuming its finance minister? Would Desai have allowed Haridas Mundhra to misuse Life Insurance Corporation's funds the way he did for the benefit of his own companies? And finally, if Desai had become the finance minister in 1956, would the story of business houses funding Congress's electoral campaigns in 1957 have been written differently? Would Desai, as the finance minister, have ensured that no business leader, let alone Haridas Mundhra, was allowed to donate to the Congress to help it fight the general elections? Quite clearly, there are no easy answers to these questions.

Nehru's Budget and Its Implications for Desai

Nehru's Budget made no secret of the strains in the economy under which he was presenting the Budget for 1958–59. 'By an unexpected and unhappy chain of circumstances, the Finance Minister, who would normally have made this statement this afternoon, is no longer with us. This heavy duty has fallen upon me almost at the last moment,' Nehru said at the start of his Budget address. A heavy duty no doubt it was because of the circumstances under which Nehru had to assume additional charge as the finance minister and present the Budget. The only relief was that the state of the Indian economy was not a cause of concern.

Indeed, the economy had improved somewhat in the preceding few months. Inflation had become stable and the balance of payments situation had got slightly better with a deceleration in the pace of depletion in the country's foreign exchange reserves. The flow of foreign assistance had also improved, with India signing new agreements for project aid with the World Bank and with friendly foreign countries, including the Soviet Union, the UK, Japan and France.

Gift Tax Makes Its Debut

Nehru's Budget stood out for its several messages and initiatives. An important one among them was the introduction of the concept of gift tax in India. This idea, endorsed and promoted by T.T. Krishnamachary before stepping down as finance minister, was mooted in an attempt to crack down on tax evasion and avoidance. Simultaneously, the logic of the gift tax, as explained by Nehru in his Budget speech, was to spread the direct taxes burden more equitably. But more importantly, the gift tax was seen by the government as an instrument for discouraging and preventing the common practice of people making gifts to avoid the burden of estate duty (levied on inheritance following the death of the holder of property and other assets being inherited) and even of income tax, wealth tax and expenditure tax. A couple of years earlier, the Taxation Enquiry Commission had recommended the levy of gift tax. Nehru also pointed out that many other countries like the US, Canada, Japan and Australia was already levying gift tax on their people.

Over the following years, the concept of the gift tax would evolve and undergo interesting turns and twists. Nehru's gift tax was initially levied on all amounts in excess of Rs 10,000 in any one year and the tax was to be paid at the same rate as was levied for the estate duty. Thus, the gift tax rate ranged from 4 per cent on the first slab (up to Rs 50,000) to a steep rate of 40 per cent on gifts of over Rs 50 lakh.

However, the basic exemption limit of Rs 10,000 was to be reduced to Rs 5000, if gifts to any one individual during a year exceeded Rs 3000. There were other exemptions as well. These included gifts to central and state governments, local authorities and charitable institutions; gifts to female dependents on the occasion of marriage up to Rs 10,000 in each case; gifts to one's wife up to a total limit of Rs 1 lakh; and gifts to dependents of policies of insurance up to Rs 10,000 for each.

In 1987, the tax rate was raised to 30 per cent and the exemption limit for gifts was raised to Rs 20,000. And in 1998, the gift tax as it existed was simply abolished, but it was simultaneously mandated that gifts, other than those from non-resident Indians through banking channels, would be taxed in the hands of the recipients at the prevailing income tax rates. A further amendment was made in 2004, by which gifts from unrelated persons above a value of Rs 25,000 were to be taxed at the prevailing rates.

Three finance ministers who tinkered with the gift tax regime used broadly the same arguments, though couched in different words, to amend Nehru's decision on the gift tax 1958. Finance Minister Vishwanath Pratap Singh raised the gift tax rate to 30 per cent, raised the exemption limit to Rs 20,000 and justified the changes on the ground that these were in conformity with the long-term fiscal policy he had announced earlier.

Yashwant Sinha, in his Budget for 1998–99, was more direct when he abolished the gift tax. He said:

> Gift-tax has been levied in India since 1958. The revenue yield from this tax has been insignificant. Last year we collected barely Rs. 9 crore. The Gift-tax Act has also not been successful as an instrument to curb tax evasion and avoidance. I, therefore, propose to discontinue the levy of gift- tax on gifts made after 30th September, 1998. At the same time, to ensure that there are no leakages of income-tax revenue through the mechanism of gifts, I propose to tax the gifts under the Income-tax Act itself in the hands of the recipients. However, the gifts from non-residents including NRIs through banking channels will continue to enjoy exemption as at present.

Palaniappan Chidambaram justified the change in the law to tax gifts made by unrelated persons with an important rider in his Budget speech for 2004–05: 'Gifts received from blood relations, lineal ascendants and lineal descendants, and gifts received on certain occasions like marriage will continue to be totally exempt.'

Estate Duty and Other Tax Initiatives

Nehru's second taxation proposal pertained to a few amendments to the Estate Duty Act to plug what he believed were many loopholes in the law. The many concessions and exemptions provided under the Estate Duty Act had contributed to insignificant growth in its actual collections. Nehru, therefore, reduced the exemption limit for the estate duty from Rs 1 lakh to Rs 50,000, allowed only one-half of the probate duty or court fees paid on succession certification as a deduction from estate duty instead of the full amount, enforced the estate duty on gifts (other than those for charitable purposes) made within five years prior to death, instead of the earlier limit of two years prior to death and taxed the value of coparcenary interest in Hindu Undivided Families at the rate applicable to the value of the estate of the branch of the family concerned. Nehru justified these changes purely as a revenue mobilization exercise.

Companies under Section 23A of the Income-tax Act got a relief from Nehru. Such companies were required to distribute the whole or a large share of their profits to the shareholders. Since these by their very nature were shareholder-friendly companies, Nehru decided to reduce the incidence of the excess dividend super-tax rates on such companies. The normal excess dividend super-tax rates for all companies were 10 per cent, 20 per cent and 30 per cent on the slabs of dividends over 6 per cent of capital, 10 per cent of capital and 18 per cent of capital, respectively. For Section 23A companies, he reduced the excess dividend tax rates to only two slabs—10 per cent on dividends of over 6 per cent of capital and 20 per cent on dividends of over 10 per cent of capital. Three other concessions announced by Nehru were to increase the development rebate allowed at 25 per cent of the cost of ships to 40 per cent and on the investment in ships, new machinery or plant by companies, withdraw the cumbersome rules for employees for availing tax exemptions on the leave passages granted to them and exempt a foreign citizen from the payment of wealth on his foreign wealth even while being a resident or ordinarily resident in India.

On excise, Nehru increased the duty on cement by 20 per cent from Rs 20 per tonne to Rs 24 per tonne, withdrew the concessions allowed to power looms producing cotton textiles and lowered the duty on vegetable products up to a limit. There were minor changes in the customs duties, whose financial effect, Nehru believed, would be negligible.

The Second Plan and Financing Woes

More significant than the introduction of the gift tax was Nehru's articulation of the serious macroeconomic challenges the Indian economy was facing at the time and the urgency for remedial steps to address them. Early in his Budget speech, Nehru made a candid admission of the government's concern about the growing imports, including those of consumer and capital goods. Non-government private imports had spurted by 31 per cent in 1956–57 to Rs 796 crore, riding on a 37 per cent increase in imports of capital goods and another 21 per cent rise in imports of consumer goods. Nehru underlined the need for exercising vigilance on the import front and apprised the Lok Sabha of the government's recent initiatives to enforce 'drastic cuts' in the import of consumer goods, exercise vigilance in respect of licensing of imports including those of capital goods and secure external assistance as well as deferred payment terms for project imports. External loans were negotiated with the World Bank, the United States Export Import Bank and the President's Development Loan Fund, the Export Import Bank of Japan and the governments of the Union of Soviet Socialist Republics or the USSR, the United Kingdom and France.

Undoubtedly, the concern about the burgeoning imports was inextricably linked to Nehru's continued focus on capital expenditure. Even in this Budget, he announced a hefty capital outlay, presumably because of the need to make a success of the Second Five-year Plan that was to enter the third year of its term. An estimated capital outlay of Rs 412 crore for the Plan was more than half of the government's total expenditure projected for 1958–59. Over the subsequent years, as the private share in investments in capital expenditure would rise, the government's contribution to capital outlay would decline. Several decades later, by 2020, capital expenditure by the Union government had shrunk to as low as 14–15 per cent of total government expenditure.

But in February 1958, Nehru had good reasons to justify the increase in capital outlays. He reminded the people of the need to make the Second Five-year Plan a success and to make the necessary sacrifices. In his Budget speech, he said:

> The coming year, which will be the third year of the Plan, is bound to be one of difficulty calling for a considerable measure of sacrifice on the part of everyone. It is unnecessary to reiterate that the plan of development the country has set before itself has to be implemented whatever the sacrifice that may be called for because without economic development we cannot bring relief and prosperity to the millions of our countrymen who have suffered for so long from the curse of poverty. The crisis through which we are passing is a crisis of development, a

crisis of resources. We must try to produce more, export more and save more to find the resources for implementing the Plan. In the budget for the coming year we have set ourselves high targets for both taxation and borrowing. I have no doubt in my mind that these targets are not beyond our capacity provided there is a sense of discipline and a sense of urgency in the country. I am sure the effort to realise the resources planned for the coming year will be forthcoming.[4]

The Tasks Ahead of Desai

For Desai, therefore, the task ahead of him was clearly laid out by Nehru's Budget. There was a twin-deficit challenge facing him as the finance minister. The government's own revenues were becoming inadequate to meet the growing demand for resources to finance an ambitious Second Five-year Plan. At the same time, the demand for more imports was on the rise and the country's foreign exchange reserves were not proving to be sufficient to meet the foreign currency needs for financing such imports. Desai recognized early enough that the Second Five-year Plan's biggest hurdle was domestic as well as foreign exchange resources.

Already, imports had to be curtailed because of the scarcity of foreign exchange. More rupee resources had to be provided to meet the massive capital required for projects envisaged under the Plan, which had just entered its third year in 1958. But the more worrying part of the resources crisis was the shortage of foreign exchange. Ways had to be found to augment foreign exchange resources to meet the shortfall or risk curtailment of the ambitious investment targets set by the Nehru government for the Second Five-year Plan.

Making a success of the Second Five-year Plan was also a matter of keeping the government's reputation intact. Desai noted in his autobiography that the efficient and successful execution of the First Plan by the end of March 1956 had been noted globally:

> India had earned a good reputation internationally. A very favourable world opinion was created as regards the administrative efficiency of the Indian Government and those in charge of it. International institutions and experts were therefore recommending the example of India to other undeveloped countries as worth emulating.[5]

Quite ironically, therefore, it was the success of the First Five-year Plan that contributed to the implementation challenges for the Second Five-year Plan. The absence of adequate ideas for rustling up the required resources to implement the Second Five-year Plan had begun to pinch the government. When Desai took charge of the finance ministry at the end of March 1958, his biggest headache was to provide resources for the Second Plan. He wrote in his autobiography:

> Great difficulties were experienced in husbanding internal financial resources and even greater difficulties were encountered in providing external resources in the form of foreign exchange. Our foreign exchange reserves were depleted by 200 million dollars in the very first two years. We had besides spent the loan which we had taken from the International Monetary Fund.'[6]

The task of mobilizing more foreign exchange resources brooked no further delay. One of Desai's earliest decisions in this direction was to reorganize his team in North Block, headquarters of the finance ministry, and make some important appointments to assist him. These changes were made both in his ministerial team as also in the Secretariat of the finance ministry.

Setting North Block in Order

Given his vast administrative experience of having been a chief minister of a state, Desai also laid a lot of stress on reorganizing the finance ministry, keeping it lean. There was a minor hitch when Nehru suggested to Desai that B. Gopala Reddy, who was already a minister of state in the finance ministry, be given independent charge of a specific department. This was an unusual suggestion as it would have meant that a part of the finance ministry would not be under Desai. Quite understandably, Desai expressed his reservations about Nehru's proposal. Once Nehru got to know of Desai's reservations, the proposal was dropped and Reddy continued to function as a minister of state in charge of revenue and civil expenditure in the finance ministry. While B.R. Bhagat was retained as a deputy minister, Nehru discussed with Desai the induction of yet another deputy minister—Tarakeshwari Sinha. Nehru was not too sure if Desai would agree to having Sinha, a 'young, brave and uninhibited' Congress Parliamentarian who would harry ministers with all kinds of questions, in the ministry. Desai, much to Nehru's surprise, agreed to have Sinha as his colleague. Thus, Desai had a team of three ministers under him—Reddy as a minister of state and Bhagat and Sinha as deputy ministers.

Having revamped the ministerial team, Desai focused on the secretaries of the different departments in the finance ministry. Already he had a capable team in place, with B.K. Nehru as the economic affairs secretary, N.N. Wanchoo as the expenditure secretary and A.K. Roy as the revenue secretary. H.M. Patel, who was the finance secretary, had left the ministry in the wake of the Mundhra scandal, and Desai did not fill that vacancy. In addition, he had the services of Prof J.J. Anjaria as the economic adviser and I.G. Patel as the deputy economic adviser.

A key change Desai made was to shift B.K. Nehru out of the Economic Affairs Department and assign him the responsibility of heading the special office of commissioner general in Washington. His specific task was to hold talks with foreign countries to help India meet its foreign exchange requirements for implementing projects earmarked for the Second Five-year Plan. Desai had immense faith in B.K. Nehru's ability as a person who could think independently and suggest new schemes in that difficult situation of resources constraint. Since B.K. Nehru had to leave for Washington, Desai decided not to hire a new secretary but entrusted A.K. Roy with the additional responsibility of looking after the Economic Affairs Department. Instead of five secretaries, Desai was now working with three.

Having already built a healthy relationship with the World Bank president, Eugene Black, during his visit to Montreal to attend the Conference of Commonwealth Finance Ministers, Desai now impressed upon him the need to use the Bank's clout and goodwill to request a few developed countries to provide financial aid to India to help it overcome its foreign funds crisis. The presence of B.K. Nehru in Washington was of immense help in this mission. Black agreed to convene a meeting of countries that could be requested to provide financial aid to India when it direly needed foreign exchange to meet its import needs to fund the Second Plan. A meeting was convened in Washington in August 1958 where, apart from the World Bank president, representatives from the US, the United Kingdom, Germany and a few other countries participated. Thus was born the Aid India Consortium, also known as Aid India Club, which continued to provide aid to India every year after an annual meeting, until the economic reforms of 1991, when the arrangement was disbanded.

What Led to the Aid India Club

In many ways, the setting up of the Aid India Consortium in 1958 was the culmination of a series of developments concerning India's external financing problems that began manifesting in the previous two years. The success of the First Five-year Plan, ironically, was also the genesis of the problem for India's external crisis. A successful Plan with growth rates higher than what were targeted, low rates of inflation and a reasonably comfortable external payments position had given rise to a sense of optimism about India's economic prospects. In 1953, the International Monetary Fund (IMF) sent a mission to India, led by its research director, Edward M. Bernstein. The mission submitted a report that declared India to be creditworthy. More importantly, it dispelled concerns expressed by the World Bank as to whether there were risks associated with lending to India. Among Bernstein's recommendations was the suggestion that India should get untied aid to help it finance imports to rein in inflation caused by a spike in investments. The message was not lost on the Indian government. Bernstein's recommendations meant that India, with its relatively small debt-servicing burden, should go in for overseas borrowings to finance its domestic investments.

There is little doubt that such soothing and reassuring messages from global institutions like the IMF were a major factor behind the doubling of the total investment outlay for the Second Five-year Plan to Rs 4800 crore from the Rs 2400 crore in the First Five-year Plan. Coupled with that were the prevailing stable economic conditions and a comfortable foreign exchange reserves situation. Quite surprisingly, however, no specific arrangements for meeting the huge increase in the investment requirement were tied up before the launch of the Second Plan in 1956. The Planning Commission had expected that the country would have a current account deficit of Rs 1120 crore because of the demand for foreign exchange resources, of which a tiny portion of Rs 200 crore was to be financed out of the reserves. The remaining amount was to have come from a host of unconventional sources, including the tapping of unused credits, floatation of public issues in foreign markets, private foreign investments, suppliers' credit, and borrowings from multilateral institutions and friendly foreign governments.

The rollout of the Second Plan coincided with a sudden spike in India's imports, draining its foreign exchange reserves. Imports increased to Rs 1100 crore in 1956–57, up 40 per cent from Rs 775 crore in 1955–56. Contributing to the country's foreign exchange woes was the fall in exports, widening the trade deficit from Rs 130 crore to Rs 465 crore in this period. Stringent exchange controls were imposed to discourage imports. The Foreign Exchange Regulation Act of 1947 had a life of only ten years, but it was made permanent in 1957 to enable the government to restrict imports by regulating the release of foreign exchange. This led to a decline in private imports by 14 per cent in 1957–58. But there was no respite from overall imports rising, which had burgeoned to Rs 1235 crore in 1957–58, the second year of the Second Plan, and from the trade deficit widening further, to Rs 565 crore. India's foreign exchange reserves saw a significant decline—from $1.9 billion in 1955–56, the last year of the First Plan, to $1.4 billion in 1956–57 and further down to $0.9 billion in 1957–58. The fall would have been more but for two drawings from the International Monetary Fund amounting to a total inflow of $200 million.

The sudden surge in imports causing a balance of payments problem for India during those years had triggered a political controversy. An analysis by the Reserve Bank of India had shown that one of the reasons for the surge in imports was the decision to relax import licensing taken by the then commerce and industry minister, T.T. Krishnamachari, in 1955–56. The lag effect of this was a sudden increase in consumer goods imports in the subsequent two years.

In January 1958, C.D. Deshmukh, who was the finance minister till 1956 and had subsequently been made the chairman of the University Grants Commission, drew Nehru's attention to the RBI's analysis of the reasons for the surge in imports, which was made public later in a journal. Deshmukh's grievance was that the decision on relaxing import licensing was taken by Krishnamachari without keeping the finance minister in the loop. This issue figured even in Parliament. Krishnamachari, who had by then become the finance minister, was upset by Deshmukh's charges and told Nehru that the crisis was due to the Planning Commission's careless resource planning and Deshmukh's failure to spot that weakness. Nehru was in a dilemma. His former finance minister had levelled charges against his successor, Krishnamachari, and had asked for an inquiry to find out the genesis of the crisis. Nehru turned down that request from Deshmukh. The Planning Commission, meanwhile, explained away the crisis as attributable to deterioration in India's external environment resulting from increased demand for defence and food imports, in addition to the 'impact of the Suez crisis on prices and freight rates'.[7]

Quite apart from such controversies over what led to the sharp rise in imports, the more immediate cause for alarm in the government was the deterioration in its external account. India's current account deficit was huge, as it rose to 4 per cent of gross domestic product. Such a high level of deficit would be reached later only twice in its entire history to date after Independence. The current account deficit would breach the 4 per cent mark only in 2011–12 and 2012–13.

The Reserve Bank of India had found the Nehru government's assumptions behind the huge investments needed for the Second Five-year Plan to be over-optimistic. Just two months before the Second Plan was launched, the RBI Governor Benegal Rama Rau shared his apprehensions about the feasibility of the Plan numbers at a meeting of its central board of governors. Rama Rau, who succeeded C.D. Deshmukh and till today has had the longest tenure in that position at the RBI, drew the government's attention to the fact that the Second Plan had projected a foreign assistance requirement of Rs 800 crore, four times more than what obtained in the First Plan. In addition, the Second Plan had assumed that it would be able to secure foreign private investment to the tune of Rs 100 crore, a goal that the RBI found would be difficult to achieve. However, such warnings had fallen on deaf ears in the government.[8]

According to P.S. Narayan Prasad, India's executive director at the International Monetary Fund, the estimated requirement of external assistance for the Second Plan would not be less than $300 million. The Union finance ministry's assessment, on the other hand, was that in order to finance the Second Plan, it would have to draw its reserves down by about Rs 200 crore (about $420 million) and look for $1400 million of additional loans from abroad. But the big challenge was that the Indian government till then had made virtually no preparations for tying up such a huge quantum of development assistance from abroad. The government's initial response was to go in for long-term suppliers' credit to finance imports, little realizing that such arrangements implied tied loans, which could lead to compromise of the Plan priorities. Globally also, there was a drying up of suppliers' credit. Hence, India had to perforce explore loans and assistance without being tied to either their use or application. The option that had not been explored till then was development assistance for financing India's development plans.

The first such initiative was taken by the Reserve Bank of India after Finance Minister T.T. Krishnamachari visited Germany in October 1957, where he got the impression that the German central bank might consider extending development assistance. RBI Governor H.V.R. Iengar held consultations with the finance ministry, and the consensus was that only long-term financial assistance would be of help and not short-term credit. With this brief, Iengar visited Germany and met his counterparts in Bonn. But those meetings drew a blank. The German government was initially willing to explore offering some assistance, but soon even that offer fizzled out. Iengar's visit to Switzerland, France and Italy also met with failure, with these countries sending out clear signals that they would not be able to offer any long-term financial assistance for India's development needs.

Iengar's assessment, based on his visits to these European countries and his other such meetings with British and US government representatives, was that the Indian government should try to impress upon multilateral institutions like the World Bank the need for providing development assistance to India. He even suggested that the government should work hard towards persuading the World Bank to change its terms and conditions to facilitate grant of financial assistance to India. Simultaneously, Iengar suggested that India should explore changing its economic policies to attract private capital flows from the US and other Western countries. These suggestions were ignored by the government, which chose to explore development assistance from Western countries with the help of the World Bank to meet its requirements of long-term financial assistance for implementing the Second Five-year Plan.

In opting for this approach, the Indian government was also guided by its assessment that while the US was willing to help it meet its financing needs and the World Bank was favourably disposed towards it, a more sensible and sustainable approach would be to not rely on only one source. Instead, it would be better to use the World Bank as its international banker and use its good offices to organize a group of foreign countries to provide development assistance to meet its needs. The United Kingdom was already a little concerned at the rapid decline of India's sterling balances and was willing to help organize alternative assistance for India to prevent its foreign exchange problem from snowballing into a major crisis. RBI History notes:

> Once Jawaharlal Nehru and the Home Minister, G.B. Pant, overcame their reluctance and the former gave him the signal which he sought to proceed, B.K. Nehru got in touch with Eugene Black at the World Bank to mobilize funds for India. According to B.K. Nehru, India did not wish to go to 'individual creditors and ask them for money' since this would be 'most undignified and politically impossible'.[9]

The Aid India Club in Action

It was in this background that the first meeting of the Aid India Consortium was held in Washington on 25 August 1958. The US, Britain, Canada, Germany and Japan, along with the World Bank, participated in the meeting. The International Monetary Fund was invited, but its managing director, Per Jacobsson, was not in favour of participating in the jamboree. Jacobsson, a Swedish economist, had a kind of a love-hate relationship with India. He was of the view that solving India's external account problems was the IMF's responsibility. At the same time, he had serious differences with the development model that the Nehru government had adopted for the Second Plan, advised and guided as it was by Prasanta Chandra Mahalanobis, member of the Planning Commission and close adviser to Nehru. Jacobsson was reported to have told Mahalanobis in February 1958 that there were 'very few countries that he (Mahalanobis) could not succeed in ruining'.[10] Jacobsson had also reasoned that the IMF, by participating in a meeting convened by the World Bank, would lose some of its standing in putting the necessary pressure on India to bring about the necessary policy changes in return for its financial bail-out.

In the end, the IMF sent only an observer to the Aid India Consortium meeting. The participating countries were in two minds. France was invited but did not attend the meeting. Canada attended the meeting but showed little interest in the deliberations and eventually reduced its role in the meeting to that of observer. The initial response from Germany, Japan and even the US was quite tentative. Difficult questions were also raised about the factors that could have led to India's financial problems. One of the difficult questions pertained to whether the situation had worsened because of increased defence imports.

In spite of these doubts and troubling questions, the meeting in Washington was a success in securing for India a decent amount of foreign assistance. The immediate target was to obtain an assistance of $350 million, but a higher amount of $580 million was needed for the next two years. The immediate target was obtained at the August 1958 meeting, but no commitment for assistance for the coming two years was available. It was significant that when there was a danger of a shortfall in meeting the immediate target of $350 million, it was the World Bank President Eugene Black's intervention that helped. He suggested that if the commitment amount was not raised, then India would be forced to impose more curbs on imports. The spectre of India imposing import restrictions helped increase the commitment amount. The United Kingdom emerged as the biggest donor at $108 million, followed by the World Bank at $100 million, the US at $75 million, Germany at $40 million, Canada at $17 million and Japan at $10 million.

No conditionality of policy reform was attached to the assistance, except that India was expected to implement the Second Plan as envisaged and shared with the donor countries and the World Bank. A bone of contention was that Britain wanted this condition of Plan implementation to be linked to announcement of the commitment of assistance. The Indian government expressed its reservations about such an announcement for its obvious political implications. In his visit to London later, Finance Minister Morarji Desai clinched the issue during his meetings there, and announcement of aid commitment was made without any linkage of it to any Plan implementation commitment by India.

The World Bank and Rupee Trade

What helped India cement its ties with the World Bank was the holding of the latter's annual meeting of its board of governors in New Delhi in October 1958. Two years earlier, in 1956, the government had begun building the Vigyan Bhavan and Ashok Hotel. Both buildings, constructed in a relatively short time of eight to nine months, proved to be very useful in 1958 when India had to host the annual meeting of the World Bank in New Delhi. Desai as the finance minister was a key member of the Indian government who played host to the meeting. Desai recalls that the foreign guests who came for the meeting were happy with the arrangements and even recorded their appreciation through public comments.

The annual meeting of the board of Governors of the World Bank was held between October 4 and 10, 1958. Prime Minister Nehru delivered his welcome address, which was widely praised. In his speech, he focused on how the world was divided between countries that were developed and those that were undeveloped. Therefore, he underlined the need for removing the imbalances in the development pattern in the world. World Bank President Eugene Black noted how India was making economic progress with massive plans for development and said the world was looking forward to India's economic march in the twentieth century.

Even as India was building strong ties with the World Bank and with Western countries, it simultaneously left no stone unturned to exploit the new economic and financial arrangements that had been established with the Soviet Union in 1953. The special arrangement with the Soviet Union envisaged trade with it in Indian currency. This is how the system of rupee trade had begun with the Soviet Union. Now, Desai not only expanded the scope of rupee trade with the Soviet Union but also extended it to cover some of its allies in the socialist bloc. Essentially, this meant that India would be paying for its imports from these countries in rupees, while they would pay for their imports from India in rupees too. In such an arrangement, there was an automatic mechanism for maintaining a balance in India's bilateral trade with these countries.

Rupee trade expanded rapidly in the subsequent years, although problems also cropped up. India's exports to many of these countries were less than its imports from them. But the rupee trade arrangement meant that their imports from India by these countries had to increase so that they could use the rupees they had accumulated as a result of their exports to India. This meant that they often had to re-export some of the goods they imported from India to markets that would pay them in hard currency. But with the Soviet Union, rupee trade grew without such problems as trade between the two countries saw a rise both ways.

The Axe on the Second Plan

That was not all. Desai pressed the button for a massive economy drive to save resources and channel them to meet the resources gap for the Second Plan. For Desai, charity began at home. The Staff Inspection Unit of the government was instructed to look into the possibility of saving the government's own expenditure on the running of various schemes of the finance ministry. There was a lot of resistance in the finance ministry and Desai had to step in to secure the concurrence of his own colleagues in North Block. Once he achieved that, it became relatively easy to implement similar economy drives in other Central ministries.

A bigger move was to review the feasibility of the outlay for the Second Plan. It's true that additional foreign financial assistance had been secured, but there was still a gap in the finances. And equally worrying was the gap in domestic resources. Desai believed that instead of failing to meet the targets set in the Second Plan at the end of its term in 1961, it would be wiser to accept the resource constraints and reset the targets appropriately. He presented before Nehru the stark reality of the resources gap. The Planning Commission also met to discuss the points on financial constraints that Desai had raised. There was general agreement that it was more important to implement the core of the Second Plan instead of trying to achieve everything that was set earlier, disregarding the limited resources the government had. The targets for the Second Plan were thus reset.

As the Second Five-year Plan was to end by 1961, the overall investment outlay was revised down from the earlier target of Rs 4800 crore to Rs 4600 crore. While the amount of foreign assistance used for the Plan had gone up from Rs 800 crore to Rs 1090 crore, the government succeeded in raising the contribution from additional taxation measures and surpluses from public sector enterprises, from the originally planned Rs 450 crore to Rs 1052 crore by 1961. This helped the government to reduce its deficit financing during this period, from the earlier high level of Rs 1200 crore to Rs 948 crore.[11] The Second Plan achieved an annual growth rate of 4.3 per cent against the target of 4.5 per cent. The government described the performance of the Second Plan as 'moderately successful'.[12]

Ghosts of the Second Plan Haunt the Third Plan

Desai faced a bigger challenge with the planning exercise while framing the Third Five-year Plan, which was to begin from 1961. The experience of the Second Plan was useful in ensuring commitment of assistance from the Aid India Consortium before the finalization of the Third Plan. The Soviet Union had given an assurance of providing an estimated $1600 million. When the Indian government made a request to the Soviet Union to increase the allocation, the initial response was a flat refusal. It was only after Desai's visit to Moscow in 1960 that the Soviet Union agreed to increase the amount by a small margin.

The manner in which the increase of about $530 million was granted once again showed how Desai would deal with such matters in his own way. During his visit to Moscow, the vice-premier of the Soviet Union, Anastas Ivanovich Mikoyan, was asked by Indian journalists whether he was extending more financial assistance to India. Mikoyan had given a cryptic reply: 'Your finance minister has not made any request in this connection.' Immediately after this comment, Desai had met Mikoyan and explained to him that India understood the reasons why the Soviet Union had agreed to grant only $1600 million in assistance in view of its own financial constraints. India was comfortable with these reasons. But Desai said he would make a request for a larger loan amount if economic conditions in the Soviet Union should improve, enabling it to offer more aid, and if the vice-premier desired that the Indian finance minister should make such a request. Desai's ploy worked. Mikoyan smiled and said he understood what Desai was suggesting and assured him that the Soviet Union would consider his request and let him know of its decision. A few days later, the Soviet Union had raised its financial assistance to India from the original amount of $1600 million to $2130 million.

The goodwill built with the World Bank also came in handy. It, along with the Aid India Consortium, sent a team of three experts to New Delhi in 1960 to assess the state of the Indian economy and its financial needs. They were Sir Oliver Franks, Dr Hermann Joseph Abs and Allan Sproul. All held important positions in the financial sector, holding key positions in some of the best banks of the world and with vast experience of governance behind them. Franks was the chairman of Lloyds Bank and a former ambassador of the United Kingdom to the United States. He also had a good equation with Prime Minister Nehru. Abs played a key role in the distribution of Marshall Plan resources for the rebuilding of West Germany after the Second World War, and at the time of his visit to New Delhi had just joined the board of governors at Deutsche Bank. Later, in 1967, Abs became the bank's chairman. Sproul was an American banker and had headed the Federal Reserve Bank of New York for about fifteen years till 1956, after which he joined Wells Fargo Bank as its director.

The high-powered delegation of bankers had several rounds of discussion with Desai and his team of finance ministry officials. In the end, they were convinced about the inherent strength of the Indian economy and sent a favourable report to the World Bank and the Consortium, endorsing India's need and claims for increased financial assistance to implement its ambitious development plans. This went a long way in positively influencing the multilateral financial institutions and the member countries of the Aid India Consortium to relax their purse strings and release more assistance for the Third Five-year Plan. In sharp contrast to the serious financing problems in which the Second Five-Year Plan had got embroiled, preparations for the Third Five-year Plan began smoothly and with great promise.

Ironically, however, this led to another tricky problem for the planners. The political establishment in the government, led by none else than Nehru himself, started putting more pressure on making the Third Plan more ambitious by projecting a much higher investment outlay than had been planned by the economists in the finance ministry and the Planning Commission. Desai put his foot down when it came to suggestions for raising the outlay. J.J. Anjaria, the economic adviser to both the finance ministry and the Planning Commission, had presented a detailed account of how and why the Third Plan outlay should be finalized, linking it tightly to the financing sources that could be tapped from both external and internal sources. Once those pushing for a higher outlay got access to these calculations, they asked the planners to look for ways of raising more resources. The challenge before Desai and his team was now to prevent the finalization of a Plan that in their view could spell trouble by making the targets for resource mobilization over-ambitious.

Desai took upon himself the responsibility of dissuading Nehru from insisting on a further increase in the Third Plan outlay, whose feasibility would depend on an increase in domestic resource mobilization. Desai's argument was simple. The country should plan what it can achieve. There was no point in setting targets that were not realistic. The Third Plan, therefore, should have realistic targets so that international agencies, foreign governments and the people of the country have greater confidence in the planners. On the other hand, unrealistic and highly ambitious targets could undermine that confidence. Politically also, failure to achieve the targets set in the Third Plan could be counterproductive as the parties in the Opposition would find an opportunity to embarrass the government, Desai argued. In short, India could not afford another mistake of the kind that had hobbled its Second Five-year Plan.

Nehru gave Desai and his arguments a patient hearing. But the prime minister seemed hardly convinced. He remained ambivalent towards Desai's reasoning and seemed to be swaying in favour of many of his other ministerial colleagues who wanted the Third Plan to be bigger and more ambitious. The National Development Council, where the prime minister, Central ministers and chief ministers of the states were represented, held its meeting in this context to resolve the dilemma over the size of the Third Plan. At the Council meeting, Nehru's address was a big surprise for Desai. The prime minister underlined the need for setting ambitious targets for the Third Plan and even urged his colleagues to think big in this respect. And then, Nehru made a gentle suggestion that Desai, who as the finance minister would have spoken immediately after the prime minister did, should respond to the Plan size issues after hearing what others had to say on the matter.

Explaining why Nehru behaved the way he did, Desai wrote in *The Story of My Life*:

He (Nehru) thought, I felt, that he might succeed in getting the targets raised if other members of the Council pressurized me for expanding the provision of resources before I spoke. I myself did not want to speak immediately as I felt that if I replied to the arguments advanced and the questions raised by other members after they had spoken, it would be easier for me to check their pressure. I therefore decided to speak after all had spoken. This suited Jawaharlalji.[13]

It became clear that Nehru wanted to neutralize his finance minister's reservations about a bigger Third Plan. Even before convening the meeting of the National Development Council, Nehru had set up a small group of eminent Congress leaders from the Centre and the states to examine the outlay proposals for the Third Plan and present their findings to the Council. The members of this committee included Maharashtra Chief Minister Yashwantrao B. Chavan, Rajasthan Chief Minister Mohan Lal Sukhadia and Madras finance minister Chidambaram Subramaniam. Desai stayed away from the deliberations of this committee so that he was not bound by its recommendations. As expected, the trio of Chavan, Sukhadia and Subramaniam suggested that the Third Plan should think big, explore ways to mobilize more resources and revise its outlay substantially upwards from the Rs 7500 crore proposed by the Planning Commission and the finance ministry.

After having managed to dissuade Desai from speaking immediately after he did at the National Development Council meeting, Nehru asked Chavan to present before everyone the findings of the committee that had been set up to examine the proposed Third Plan outlay. Chavan presented the key findings of the committee, and then came the turn of Subramaniam, who gave an emotionally surcharged speech that called for raising the outlay by showing courage and by ensuring that additional resources needed to meet the higher target came from higher profits from public sector enterprises. Subramaniam's call of 'we must dare and do' pleased Nehru no end, and the prime minister made no secret of his satisfaction at the manner in which the finance minister of Madras made his intervention. Seeing how enthusiastically Nehru had endorsed the demand for higher outlay, most of the other members present at the Council meeting also supported the idea of a bigger Third Plan.

It was now Desai's turn to pour cold water on Nehru's plans and Subramaniam's arguments. Desai's response to the calls for higher outlay was firm and categorical. He recalled in no uncertain terms the travails the government had gone through while implementing the Second Plan because of under-provisioning of resources to meet its investment targets. He also said it was possible that more profits could be generated from a few public sector enterprises, but there was also a strong possibility of rising losses at many other public sector enterprises. He stressed the need for planning resources on the basis of facts instead of on speculation. It was important to plan big, but also to be wary of the pitfalls. The finance ministry could not adopt the methods of the Stock and Share Brokers Association, and doing so could bring ruin to the country, Desai said without mincing words. Desai also launched a personal attack against Subramaniam and said that before asking the finance ministry to 'dare and do', he should have walked the talk by presenting a Budget for the Madras government to raise resources through additional taxation. But Subramaniam made no such attempt to raise taxes through his own state budget. In contrast, Desai had presented a Union budget that had contained a good dose of additional taxation to raise resources.

Such a candid and forthright response from Desai settled the debate on the need for a higher outlay for the Third Five-year Plan. Other members of the National Development Council saw the force of reason in Desai's response and the need to be realistic in setting investment targets. Desai was relieved, and so were his colleagues in the finance ministry and, most importantly, the economic adviser, J.J. Anjaria, who was a strong believer in fiscal discipline and economic reform. The investment outlay for the Third Five-year Plan was finalized at Rs 7500 crore, which was still 63 per cent higher than what was eventually spent during the Second Plan. The reliance on external assistance had increased significantly, to Rs 2200 crore, almost 29 per cent of the total outlay, marginally up from 24 per cent in the Second Plan.

Desai as an Economic Diplomat

The finance minister in India is not just responsible for overseeing the government's finances but also has to play the role of an economic diplomat. The role of the finance minister as an economic diplomat became more important and even critical during the 1950s, when India was facing an acute shortage of foreign exchange resources to meet its development expenditure. Morarji Desai was known for his spartan lifestyle and his strict Gandhian regimen. The big question that arose when India was facing the resources crisis was whether Desai would be able to engage with global leaders in appropriate economic diplomacy and secure for the country the much-needed financial assistance from foreign governments and multilateral institutions.

One of the first hurdles Desai had to overcome in his role as an economic diplomat was his own reluctance to visit foreign countries. Indeed, even though Desai had held many public offices (before becoming the finance minister, he was the commerce and industry minister and the chief minister of Bombay), he had avoided overseas tours. Until he became the finance minister, it was not clear what the reasons for this were. But what became clear to the Nehru government in March 1958 was that Desai's reluctance to go abroad could be traced to the requirement of vaccination for anyone undertaking foreign travel those days. Desai was staunchly opposed to the idea of vaccination as he believed that 'one should not take another life to save one's own', and he believed in nature cure instead of vaccination.

When India's high commissioner to the UK, Vijaya Lakshmi Pandit, asked Desai to visit the UK as the British prime minister Harold Macmillan was keen on meeting him, the question of vaccination cropped up. Desai insisted that he was willing to travel to the UK, but only if he was exempted from the mandatory requirement of vaccination. It needed a special exemption order from the British prime minister to facilitate Desai's first foreign tour of any country, but not before he had a difficult time outside London airport, where he was accosted by British media persons who asked him why he had sought exemption from vaccination and whether that would be a health risk for those he would be meeting in the UK during his stay. Desai's answer to those embarrassingly blunt questions was straightforward:

I believe in nature cure and also consider vaccination harmful. I also consider that it is wrong morally. I have read the opinions of several people in England who have the same belief. A healthy person has no need of vaccination. It is only the unhealthy who require it. It is, therefore, not I who am exposing you to danger, but if there is any infection prevailing here, I would be put to danger. Your fear therefore has no basis.[14]

That put an end to the questioning of Desai on why he had declined vaccination before entering the United Kingdom.

During his stay in London, Desai had quite a few rounds of discussions with his UK counterpart, Derick Heathcoat-Amory, the chancellor of the exchequer. One of the contentious issues that arose during these talks was Heathcoat-Amory's suggestion that the British loans to India for its development projects would carry a higher rate of interest, in addition to a 0.75 per cent additional levy by way of reimbursement of the administrative expenditure Britain would incur on them. Desai was quick to respond to what he saw as an irrational and unreasonable suggestion. Invoking the principle of reciprocity, he said that he did not find Heathcoat-Amory's suggestion proper. He reminded him that when Britain was in some sort of financial trouble, it was not paying interest to India on its sterling balances of £750 million. As recounted in *The Story of My Life*, Desai recalled what he had said:

> When we proposed to transfer the balances elsewhere so that we could get proper interest, you refused to release them and later on decided to give us interest at only 2.5 per cent. We accepted all this, considering your difficult circumstances and did not quarrel about it. It is not therefore proper that you today put this larger burden on us in the name of administrative expenditure.

The direct manner in which Desai spoke to Heathcoat-Amory was no example of polite diplomacy. Instead, it was a classic case of direct talk, calling a spade not just a spade but a shovel. However, that settled the issue for Desai and the UK chancellor of the exchequer agreed to not impose the higher rate of interest.

Desai used the opportunity of his meetings with British leaders and the media to dispel many of the flawed impressions about India's financial problems. An obvious question that arose was on how India had rapidly used up its sterling balances with the UK and was now seeking loans to tide over its foreign exchange problems. Desai set the entire issue of sterling balances in their historical context. He explained to the British media that the huge sterling balances had accumulated with the British as its dues on the large imports of raw materials it got from India during the Second World War. But now that India was undertaking economic development on a massive scale, it needed to use those sterling balances and even needed more than what was available through that channel. Hence, it needed loans from the UK to meet the financing needs of its development projects. If Britain wanted that India should develop economically, it must also consider it its moral duty to extend the loans sought by India. At the same time, Desai made it clear that if Britain did not wish to offer the loans, nothing would be held against it. But on India's part, it would not agree to receiving loans that were tied to any condition. Instead, the Indian government was committed to repaying the loans as this was in keeping with the Indian tradition of thousands of years. In the process, he made a strong and convincing case for more assistance to India.

In the coming weeks, Desai would visit the US and Canada. He would meet the leaders of those governments as also those of the World Bank and the International Monetary Fund. His pitch for foreign assistance would remain the same. It sounded genuine, though it was not the usual kind of request a developing economy leader beseeching assistance from a position of weakness made. Desai was seeking financial aid, but on India's own terms and without compromising its honour. The nature of that articulation was unique, and yet it made the necessary impact on the donor countries.

Widening Differences with Nehru

Desai's relations with Nehru were never without any stress or strain from either side. Desai was firm and often inflexible in his views. Nehru, on the other hand, was quite flexible, opportunistic, and would often expect his finance minister to be politically more understanding and accommodating. Early signs of tension in the relationship between Nehru and Desai were noticeable in the way Nehru went about the reorganization of states, particularly Bombay. Nehru's sudden decision to make Bombay a centrally administered territory, separated from Maharashtra, ignited a bout of unrest and violence that Desai as the chief minister of Bombay had to control and prevent from spreading further. Desai had also been upset about the manner in which the prime minister made an offer to him to become the finance minister, only to withdraw it a few days later citing reasons of a national economic crisis. After Desai became the finance minister, Nehru made a suggestion for one of the ministers of state for finance to be given independent charge of a function, a suggestion that Desai rejected outright and Nehru did not persist with. On the question of raising the outlay for the Third Plan, Nehru wanted to be more ambitious, but Desai injected a dose of realism and succeeded in reining in the size of the outlay within the confines of feasibility.

A similar difference of opinion had arisen in 1961 after Home Minister Govind Ballabh Pant fell ill after suffering a cerebral stroke. A year earlier, Pant had suffered a heart attack and had recovered after medical assistance from well-known physician Dr Bidhan Chandra Roy, who was also at that time chief minister of West Bengal and a close friend of Nehru's. Pant was an important member of the Congress, as also a key player in the government. He was the home minister and the deputy leader of the Congress party in Parliament. For about two weeks, Pant remained in a coma and finally died on 7 March 1961. The question of who should step into the shoes of Pant as the deputy leader of the Congress in Parliament arose, and Desai, as the seniormost leader in the party after Pant, considered himself a strong contender for that job. Pant had succeeded Maulana Abul Kalam Azad to that post after the latter's death in 1958. Desai had good reasons to believe that he was next in line to become the Congress deputy leader in Parliament.

But Nehru had other ideas. The candidature of a relatively junior leader in the Congress, Jagjivan Ram, as the next deputy leader was mooted and an election was planned to finalize the choice. Desai, as frank and forthright as always, approached Nehru and told him that traditionally the second in command in the party always became the deputy leader in Parliament and hence he deserved the post. Nehru countered that by saying that if Desai was keen on becoming the deputy leader, he could contest in the proposed election. Desai's principled response was that given the past convention of the number-two person in the government becoming the deputy leader, any contest at that stage would suggest a lack of confidence in the finance minister, and in such an eventuality he would like to quit the government. That ruled out any contest to be held to elect the deputy leader. But Nehru came up with an alternative idea: Why not have two deputy leaders—one from the Lok Sabha and the other from the Rajya Sabha? Nehru even suggested that such an idea had been mooted when Sardar Vallabhbhai Patel was alive. Desai pooh-poohed that idea too, saying bluntly that if such an idea had indeed been mooted, then Patel would have quit the government that very day. Nehru was not going to give up easily and was keen on finding Pant's successor through a process that looked democratic but would at the same time allow him to find a deputy leader of his choice. He renewed his request to Desai to agree to take part in the contest for the post of deputy leader. So persuasive was Nehru that Desai even agreed to take part in the contest, but he maintained that if he were to lose the election, he would have no option other than to leave the Cabinet.

But even before the election could be held, Nehru changed his mind. He asked Desai if he would agree to a new arrangement where two non-ministers could become deputy leaders, representing the two Houses of Parliament. By now Desai had been completely browned off by Nehru's flip-flopping on who should be the deputy leader. Desai told the prime minister he was not desperate about becoming the deputy leader and Nehru could decide on a candidate the way he deemed most appropriate. Nehru went ahead with his plans and got the Congress party's constitution amended suitably to facilitate the appointment of two deputy leaders. In the process, Desai's desire to become the deputy leader remained unfulfilled. To be fair, it had not been just Nehru's plan to foil Desai's attempts to succeed Pant as the deputy leader, but a host of Congress leaders at that time had backed Nehru's plans in this regard. Those who supported Nehru in this minor battle included T.T. Krishnamachari, C. Subramaniam, Gulzarilal Nanda, Jagjivan Ram, Lal Bahadur Shastri and Indira Gandhi. The idea of two non-ministerial deputy leaders was actually mooted by Shastri, and Nehru lapped it up to thwart Desai's ambitions.[15] Significantly, Shastri was rewarded soon thereafter with the portfolio of the home ministry, to succeed Pant.

Yet, Desai did not fail to notice the many fine leadership traits in Nehru's personality. Nehru, according to Desai, would not keep the same person as his adviser for more than three years, in order to make sure that nobody stayed in the same job for a sufficiently long time to create difficulties for him. That was a pretty harsh judgement of Nehru. At the same time, however, Desai would be generous in his praise for Nehru as a leader who would encourage his colleagues in the Cabinet to argue independently and offer their views without any hesitation. Nehru would also try hard to convince his ministers about his point of view if they disagreed with him. But with Desai the approach was a little different. Nehru recognized that Desai was frank in his views and did not mince words in airing his differences with him in private conversations as well as at Cabinet meetings. Desai would express his differing views. But if Nehru as the prime minister took a certain decision he would abide by it even if he had earlier opposed it.

Not surprisingly, therefore, speculation was rife over Desai's exclusion from the Union Cabinet that got formed after the general elections of 1962. The Congress, under Nehru, won the general elections for the third consecutive time, winning 361 out of the 494 Lok Sabha seats. In the second general elections, the Congress had won 371 seats. Compared to the 364 seats the Congress had won out of the 489 Lok Sabha seats in the fray, its performance in the 1962 general elections was certainly not as impressive as in the previous two polls. But forming the government with a majority of more than two thirds posed no difficulty for Nehru. Nor was there any opposition to Nehru within the Congress. Desai, therefore, was not expecting to be included in the Cabinet that Nehru would form in 1962. He avoided calling on Nehru after the elections. But it was Nehru who asked him to meet him at his residence. Nehru was not keeping well. A proposal for bifurcating the ministry of finance was doing the rounds. Desai viewed this proposal as the handiwork of his political opponents who wanted his clout as the finance minister to be curtailed, by advancing an idea that was completely impractical and unfeasible. Nehru raised the issue of bifurcation of the finance ministry with Desai when the two met at Teen Murti a few days after the election results were out. Desai made no bones about his disapproval of the proposal and Nehru too did not persist with the subject. That was how Desai became the finance minister in the new Congress government after the general elections of 1962. Nehru's relations with Desai were never strained, but neither were they smooth or stress-free. Nevertheless, Nehru could hardly ignore the rich experience of Desai in public administration and in handling of governments.

Desai's Dilemmas on Second and Third Plan

The Reserve Bank of India had realized early on that it was important for the government to rein in the size of the Second Five-year Plan to a level that not only remained sustainable but also did not trigger a rise in its deficit financing and, therefore, kept a check on inflation. The central bank was of the firm view that there was no alternative to financing investments except through higher savings or through mobilization of additional resources. In the summer of 1957, the RBI, led by its Governor H.V.R. Iengar, had begun meeting the government to impress upon it the need to cut the Second Plan size. When Morarji Desai presented his first Budget for 1959–60 and proposed a higher deficit of Rs 245 crore, Iengar could not keep quiet and lodged the central bank's protests at the deficit level, which he feared would trigger an inflationary cycle which monetary policy interventions may not be fully able to control. After these protestations, the deficit financing was brought down by Rs 100 crore as the year ended.

In the calculations for the Third Five-year Plan, the RBI's inputs supported Desai's conservative disposition and neutralized the force exerted by Nehru and a few other Congress leaders who wanted a much larger and ambitious Plan. Two factors worried the central bank no end. One pertained to the feasibility of ensuring adequate supply of wage goods (mainly food grain), and the other was the extent of monetary expansion as a result of the increase in RBI's credit to the government to help it finance the Plan. Thus, the RBI was of the firm view that the Third Plan should be financed primarily through 'realizable revenue and public borrowings' so that there is no pressure on the government or the central bank to accept a higher level of deficit financing.

In determining the share of public borrowings in the Third Plan, the Reserve Bank of India was engaged in a heated debate with the finance ministry. As a consequence, public borrowing was scaled down to Rs 850 crore for the Third Plan, a little lower than the estimate originally proposed by the Planning Commission. Desai sat down with Iengar initially, and later with Bhattacharya after 1962, when the latter succeeded Iengar as the head of the RBI, to decide on the various loans and schemes of different maturities to meet the public borrowing requirements of the government during the period of the Third Plan. The success of the different schemes varied. For instance, the National Plan Bonds, launched in May 1961, managed to secure about Rs 93.5 crore, making the issue a success, though a little below the expectations of the RBI and the government. Desai preferred another, larger issue of bonds to meet the government's annual borrowing requirement of Rs 225 crore. Eventually, the next issue of bonds raised Rs 109 crore. The total borrowings for 1961–62 thus amounted to Rs 203 crore, a little short of the annual target. More such bonds were floated to meet the Centre's borrowing needs for the rest of the years of the Third Plan period, which became a bit more challenging after the border conflict with China flared up in the middle of 1962. Indeed, soon after the Chinese aggression in September that year, the National Development Council decided in 1963 to combine the market borrowings of the Union and state governments to mobilize more resources to meet the emergency situation. In spite of Desai's intervention in the form of a request to all the state chief ministers to subscribe to the loans, the response and, therefore, the total resources mobilized, estimated at about Rs 365 crore, fell short of expectations.

In spite of the lukewarm response to the combined loan-raising operations of the Centre, the idea of combined loan-raising was not dropped altogether. Chief Economic Adviser I.G. Patel advised Desai that a permanent arrangement for combined loans for the Centre and the states could be created. RBI History notes:

> A background note prepared by I.G. Patel, the Chief Economic Adviser to the Government of India, for a conference of finance ministers of states held in November 1963 argued for a permanent arrangement in which the Centre undertook all general-purpose market borrowings, while the states borrowed for specific purposes on behalf of institutions under their control. In return, the Centre would share the loans it raised with the states and give them a higher share of collections of small savings. This arrangement, Patel argued, would make for better management of the public debt and monetary control, besides more clearly defining the responsibilities of institutional investors such as the Life Insurance Corporation in relation to the government's borrowing programme.

The proposal did not make any headway as the RBI opposed the ideas as being inconsistent with the Constitutional provisions governing the borrowing rights of the states. Desai did not join issue with the RBI in this matter and reverted to separate floatation of papers by the Centre and the states to meet their individual borrowing requirements.

Defining Powers to Fix Government Borrowing Limits

It was during Desai's tenure as the finance minister that the contentious issue of determining the protocol between Parliament and the government over borrowing was settled. The debate arose from the interpretation of Article 292 of the Indian Constitution, which stated:

> . . . the executive power of the Union extends to borrowing upon the security of the Consolidated Fund of India within such limits, if any, as

may from time to time be fixed by Parliament by law and to the giving
of guarantees, within such limits, if any, as may be so fixed.

The question of fixing a limit on the Centre's borrowing thus
figured in debates in Parliament, and this was even raised in the reports
of Parliament's Estimates Committee as also of the Public Accounts
Committee. The government was categorical in its view that Article 292,
while allowing Parliament to frame specific laws to limit the government's
borrowings, did not in itself impose such a limit. Further, it pointed out
that the government in any case would seek Parliament's approval for
Budgets and the Five-Year Plans, which would contain the government's
borrowing programme. Hence, the question of imposing a specific limit
on borrowings did not arise.

The issue got escalated when Parliament's Estimates Committee
submitted a report in 1958 recommending that the government should
submit to Parliament details of its borrowing programme both before
and after it approached the market each year. The finance minister was
opposed to the idea, on the ground that such advance information would
be prejudicial to its interest in securing the best rates for the loans it
would raise to meet its borrowing requirements. Moreover, borrowing
was an executive function and should not be subjected to legislative
clearance. Instead, the ministry suggested that it would present reports
before Parliament containing the details of the loans raised by the
government. The issue was thus resolved, even though the RBI expressed
its reservations about the long-term sustainability of the position taken
by the government. The central bank argued that the possibility of a
Parliamentary committee imposing legislative limits on government
borrowing could not be ruled out in the future. However, RBI's fears on
this count were exaggerated. Even more than six decades later, there has
been no demand by any Parliamentary committee to impose legislative
limits on government borrowings.

Small Cooperatives Are Beautiful

The Desai tenure was also witness to the finance ministry differing with
the Reserve Bank of India on the crucial question of managing cooperative
credit in the country. The disagreement was over the model to be followed

for cooperative organizations as also the broad principles that should govern agricultural lending. The differences between the Centre and the RBI did not go away easily, and even after they were ironed out the RBI was not fully satisfied with the resolution. Often, some long-standing policies would be reversed and what was accepted would not be implemented even after the RBI had given the government its full concurrence. In the end, as RBI History noted, the casualty of these differences was the cooperative movement, which suffered 'confusion and uncertainty'.

The finance ministry's renewed focus on the cooperative movement and agricultural credit was a relatively new phenomenon. Not until the mid-1950s did the cooperative movement become an article of faith for the Indian government. The finance ministry's interest in the cooperative movement grew largely as a result of its recognition of the need for a robust food policy that paralleled the stress being laid on development of heavy industry. Food prices had risen in the Second Plan period and the government had cracked down on the flow of agricultural credit, in the belief that it was higher lending to the farming sector that was responsible for the rising prices of food. Farmers and traders were believed to be using their loans to hold back their produce from reaching the markets in the hope of prices going further up, fetching them better realizations. But the sixty-fourth session of the All-India Congress Committee in June 1959 in Nagpur brought about a change in approach. It passed a resolution promoting the village as the basic unit of economic development and identified cooperatives and panchayats as the principal agents for ensuring agricultural development. The Nagpur session also showed a preference for small village-level service cooperatives instead of credit cooperatives. This shift was also endorsed by the Planning Commission, as it had been dissatisfied with the large cooperative societies, which often had the government participating in their share capital. The Commission argued that large-sized cooperative societies negated the basic principle of cooperation, which was facilitated by intimate and mutual knowledge among members. Thus, it called for a one-village-one society policy.

Shift in Lending Policy for Agriculture

That policy shift soon became another major area of difference between the RBI and the finance ministry. The government wanted smaller village-

level societies, but the RBI was categorical in its view that achievement of
the social objectives of the cooperative movement was critically dependent
on the financial viability and size of cooperative societies. In March 1957,
when such a policy shift was being engineered by the Planning Commission,
RBI Governor H.V.R. Iengar sought a meeting with T.T. Krishnamachari,
who was at that time the finance minister. At the meeting, Iengar thought
he had made a positive impression on the finance minister, only to be
disappointed later that the Commission had begun moving towards
promoting smaller cooperatives. Worse, the Commission had mooted a
proposal to reduce credit flows to existing large cooperatives in pursuance
of the policy shift. In complete panic, Iengar sought the intervention of
Prime Minister Nehru in a letter that he wrote in August 1957, pointing
out that discontinuing credit to large cooperatives would amount to
dishonouring a joint commitment that both the government and the RBI
had made to them. Iengar's pleadings made no impact on the government,
and in September 1958 the Planning Commission recommended curbs on
creation of new large cooperative societies and expansion of existing ones,
and introduced a specific condition that the existing ones should remain
confined to the backward areas. By then Morarji Desai was in the saddle
at the finance ministry. But RBI's requests for a review of the government
shift in policy in favour of small cooperative societies fell on deaf ears
again. Iengar was deeply disappointed and wrote on the relevant official
file in his own hand:

> I am afraid he [Morarji Desai] is wholly unsympathetic to our views.
> He is quite prepared for us to stop further expansion of Reserve Bank
> credit for agricultural production till what he calls the basic objective
> is achieved, viz. of setting up cooperatives which can move on their
> own (people's) momentum, without official support or patronage. He
> thinks that the decisions taken on the basis of the Rural Credit Survey
> Committee Report were completely misconceived and that the sooner
> they are reversed the better. All he is prepared to do is not to break up
> the large-sized societies that have (unfortunately) already been set up. In
> view of [the] Finance Minister's attitude we must assume that Cabinet
> will approve . . . [the] Planning Commission's views. I think we must
> now reconsider the entire problem of [the] Reserve Bank's policy and
> administrative arrangements.[16]

A major shift in the government's policy on cooperative societies had taken place, ushering in a new preference for development institutions that were small. A meeting of the National Development Council in November 1958 recommended radical reforms in the organization of societies at the village level. The Council suggested that organization of individual village communities and vesting the village cooperatives and panchayats with the responsibility of undertaking initiatives for social and economic development would go a long way in developing cooperatives as a people's movement. Such a world view was also fully endorsed by the Planning Commission, which saw such cooperatives as playing a key role in facilitating state trading in food grains. The focus was now on small village-level cooperatives and away from large cooperatives, and suitable credit arrangements were being favoured to achieve the new goals. This obviously left the RBI completely crestfallen and even rudderless as far as its policy thrust on agricultural credit flows was concerned. There were serious questions within the RBI as to whether there was any future role for its agricultural credit department.

Worse, the RBI's relations with the finance ministry in the matter of lending to the agriculture sector became a bone of contention. The Planning Commission expressed its dissatisfaction at the RBI's lending activities in the agriculture and cooperative sectors. There was a suggestion that the central bank should increase its lending to new cooperative societies and that the lending should not be linked only to their share capital and reserves. Iengar once again took up cudgels on behalf of the RBI and spoke to Desai to explain that 'it would be a complete disaster to the financial reputation of India which at present is very high, if the Reserve Bank had to show in its books sums as overdues from cooperative institutions'.[17] Iengar further argued that in such a situation the RBI would have to adopt a tough line on grant of credit to institutions beyond their limits of creditworthiness, as defined by its prudential norms. The RBI governor's solution to the problem was for the government to consider creating another institution that would handle agricultural credit. Eventually the money would come from the RBI, but a separate corporation would permit the bad debts, if any, to be shown in the books of that new entity, and not in RBI's.

That was the beginning of the inception of a separate apex agricultural credit institution. Iengar's idea in October 1958 took many years to result in the creation of an apex institute for development financing for the agricultural and rural sectors. On 12 July 1982, almost twenty-four years after Iengar's suggestion, the National Bank for Agricultural and Rural Development, or NABARD, was set up, with its headquarters in Bombay.

SBI Gets Bigger with More Mergers

Even as Imperial Bank of India had been taken over by the government and rechristened State Bank of India in July 1955, no decision had been taken about the ownership pattern of about half a dozen banks promoted by the erstwhile princely states, like those of Indore, Mysore and Rajasthan. This issue came up before Desai sometime in 1958. It was originally suggested that the State Bank of India would be asked to acquire majority shares in these six banks. However, this was found to be impractical as there was virtually no market for the shares of these banks. Also, such large-scale purchase of their shares would drive up the market price of those few banks which still had some floating stock in the market. An associated problem was that provisions in the Banking Companies Act would come in the way of SBI's purchase of majority shares in these banks, unless some exemptions were made through some legislative changes.

In view of these considerations, RBI Governor H.V.R. Iengar sent a detailed note to Desai in June 1958, who had just taken charge of the finance ministry. Iengar's note made two points: One, the RBI was broadly in favour of the SBI taking over these six banks because they could be used to effectively reach cooperative credit to different parts of the country and in many areas where other banks had no penetration. Two, a preferred way to achieve that goal would be for the SBI to acquire a controlling interest in the share capital of these banks in a manner that made for smooth acquisition that did not provoke any adverse reactions. The finance minister agreed with that approach. Accordingly, the government began exploring the possibility of persuading the shareholders of these state-associated banks to pass resolutions consenting to those institutions being taken over by the SBI and operated as its subsidiaries. The State Bank of India was a bit lukewarm to the proposal for tagging these state-associated banks along as its subsidiaries. Its management, which had just begun to function after its nationalization in July 1955, was apprehensive as to whether these takeovers would be challenged in a court of law by some shareholders and would run into legal hurdles.

As an alternative, the SBI management suggested that all the state-associated banks be asked to get shareholders' resolutions passed to the effect that they are willing to be taken over as subsidiaries of the SBI. This, it was argued, would give all the subsidiary banks a statutory character and uniform constitutions without their takeover becoming vulnerable to legal challenge. Desai accepted this proposal, and P.C. Bhattacharya, who was then a secretary in the finance ministry (before becoming chairman of the SBI and later succeeding Iengar as the RBI governor) wrote to all the six state-associated banks that they must secure their shareholders' approval for such a takeover. The requisite shareholders' resolutions were obtained without much difficulty for most of the banks. The Bank of Rajasthan, whose majority shares were owned by a few members of one family, resisted the move. In the case of the Bank of Mysore, there was a minor hiccup as a few shareholders, after having agreed to the takeover, had second thoughts about it. But their reluctance was overcome after some persuasion and consultation.

On 4 March 1959, Desai introduced in Parliament the State Bank of India (Subsidiary Banks) Bill, which was immediately referred to the Select Committee for scrutiny. Later in the year, on 12 August, the Lok Sabha passed the bill without much debate and the Rajya Sabha gave its approval in the following week. With President Rajendra Prasad giving his assent to the bill, a major banking reorganization exercise was completed with the vesting of ownership of half a dozen state-associated banks with the SBI and their reconstitution as SBI subsidiaries. RBI History documents the end result of this exercise:

> Having already come under the Bank's ownership, the State Bank of Hyderabad presented the least complications. It was the first state-associated bank to be reconstituted as a subsidiary of the State Bank of India, commencing business in that capacity on 1 October 1959. The State Banks of Bikaner, Indore, and Jaipur came into existence on 1 January 1960, and the other subsidiary banks were established during the course of the next few months. The State Bank of India's holdings of the shares of the new institutions ranged from 100 per cent in the State Banks of Hyderabad, Patiala, and Saurashtra, to just over 81 per cent and 75.5 per cent respectively in the State Banks of Indore and Travancore, and about 58.5 per cent in the State Bank of Mysore.

Desai's Banking Woes

The Indian banking sector kept Desai busy on many fronts. While on the one hand he supervised the merger of six banks run by princely states with the State Bank of India, on the other he was also witness to the Indian banking system's biggest crisis period after Independence. Arguably, the most difficult and trying time Desai faced with regard to the banking sector was when Palai Central Bank and Laxmi Bank had to be closed down in August 1960 after they ran into financial trouble. Palai Central Bank was a commercial bank headquartered in Kerala. It was set up in 1927 in Palai, a remote town 28km east of Kottayam. Over the years, it grew to become the biggest bank in Kerala and was the seventeenth largest among the ninety-four scheduled banks in India before financial trouble engulfed it in 1960.

The first alarm bell had rung by the end of May 1960, when the Reserve Bank of India got to learn of misappropriation of funds by the top management of Laxmi Bank, a scheduled bank headquartered in Akola of Maharashtra. Soon there was a run on the bank, which had deposits of over Rs 3 crore. The RBI lost no time in filing an application in the Bombay High Court for winding up the bank. The failure of Laxmi Bank did not get much publicity. Nor did it become a big political issue. But when a similar problem engulfed Palai Central Bank and the RBI had to move the Kerala High Court on 8 August for winding it up, there was a big furore not only in the state but also in the entire country over the safety of bank deposits, which as a consequence saw a decline that year. The collapse of Palai Central Bank, the largest bank to fail in India after Independence, also became a major political controversy Desai had to deal with in the months following RBI's moving the Kerala High Court on 8 August 1960. At the time of its collapse, Palai Central Bank was the largest in Kerala and among the top twenty-five banks in the country, with deposits of over Rs 9 crore and a network of twenty offices, many of them outside the state of Kerala.

Bank failure in India was not unusual those days. The first big bank that failed was the Travancore National and Quilon Bank, in 1938, just three years after the RBI began its operations. This was a merged entity. Only a year earlier, in 1937, had the Travancore National Bank (set up in 1912) and the Quilon Bank (set up in 1919) merged and became the

Travancore National and Quilon Bank. The bank was a victim of politics, mismanagement, unstable finances and unsustainable expansion. The dewan of Travancore—Sir C.P. Ramaswami Iyer—was once a supporter of the merged entity, but later turned against it for its involvement in religious and political campaigns. Its logo resembled that of the princely state of Travancore, and that was also one of the irritants for the dewan. Iyer's campaign against the bank, its unstable finances and rapid expansion plans led to a run on its deposits. By the third week of June 1938, the bank had suspended payments and by August the same year, it was liquidated. At the time of its liquidation, the bank had a branch network of seventy-five offices and deposits of over Rs 3.5 crore.

The TNQ Bank management did reach out to the RBI for assistance, but the RBI declined to step in as it found the books of the bank were not clean and questionable loans had been made to its own directors. And there were other financial irregularities. The RBI, with James Taylor as its Governor, was criticized for its inaction, but its powers to intervene were also limited given the absence of any legislative framework under which such assistance could be extended. As a consequence of what happened with the TNQ Bank, therefore, Taylor proposed legislation of the Banking Regulation Act in 1939, which was approved and became a law, but only in 1949. The new law gave the RBI the requisite powers to regulate banks.

The frequency of bank failures increased after India gained independence. By one estimate,[18] as many as 183 banks failed in India between 1947 and 1950 alone. Bengal saw the largest number of bank failures, at an alarmingly high number of seventy. The incidence of bank failure was huge, considering that there were 850 to 900 small banks in the Bengal region alone at that time. In *Mahanagar*, a film made by Satyajit Ray in 1963, based on a story written by Narendranath Mitra in 1949, a key turning point in the story is the failure of a bank. Clearly, fiction and films in Bengal then were reflecting the reality of the banking sector at that time.

While many banks were rescued after the enactment of the Banking Regulation Act in 1949, there was no end to the incidence of bank failures even after the legislative change, and the RBI both strengthened its inspection system as well as acquired powers to liquidate banks with deposits of above Rs 5 crore. Between 1951 and 1960, 315 more banks failed in the country. The failure of Palai Central Bank in 1960 was the most significant of them all.

The run on Palai Central Bank began in late June 1960, even as the Reserve Bank of India became worried that, given its size and influence in the region, the contagion could spread to other banks in Kerala. But much before that, as early as in 1951, an inspection of Palai Central Bank brought out glaring irregularities and mismanagement of depositors' money, including loans to directors and their families and declaration of dividends aimed at benefiting the shareholders and hardly reflecting the bank's financial performance. The Reserve Bank of India issued a warning to the bank but failed to take adequate measures to prevent recurrence of similar errant behaviour on the part of the bank management. The performance of the bank kept deteriorating over the next ten years as it kept losing capital as well as deposits. A point was reached when the RBI suggested that the bank must remove its head, K. Joseph Augusti, but this was ignored, as it argued that any such step would undermine people's trust in the top management. Even an idea mooted to revoke the banking licence granted to Palai Central Bank was not enforced by the RBI. A stand-off between the RBI and the Kerala bank was one of the unsavoury moments in this crisis, where the bank management kept ignoring the central bank's directives on the false assurance that its financial situation had improved. The bank had even opposed the RBI's order that it should not be declaring dividends in 1958. A year later, the RBI allowed the bank to launch a new deposit scheme but imposed curbs on it, disallowing it to advertise or open new branches.

The bank management in December 1959 appeared to have realized that its functioning had landed it in the soup, but this realization came too late. An RBI inspection conducted in 1960 revealed that the crisis at the Kerala bank had actually worsened. Of the total advances of Rs 5.28 crore, advances to the tune of Rs 2.21 crore were to be treated as 'definitely irrecoverable'. Worse, the bulk of the remainder of the advances were either sticky or their recovery doubtful. The inspection officers concluded that Palai Central Bank would at that stage have to show a loss of at least Rs 13.73 lakh in 1958 and Rs 15 lakh for the following year. When the bank's account showing a loss became known to people, there was a rush among its customers to withdraw their deposits. By June 1960, there was a run on the bank.

As Finance Minister Morarji Desai told Parliament later, deposits withdrawal at Palai Central Bank picked up at an alarming pace from July

1960. The withdrawals increased from Rs 12 lakh in the week ended July 1 to Rs 17 lakh in the following week and to Rs 20 lakh in the week ended July 15. In the following three weeks, ended 22 July, 29 July and 5 August, the withdrawals amounted to over Rs 23 lakh, Rs 29 lakh and Rs 35 lakh, respectively. In other words, the bank's deposits fell by a sixth in the space of just six weeks between 24 June and 8 August.

On 30 July, the board of Palai Central Bank met to consider an action plan to repair the damage already inflicted to its finances. Already the bank had been directed to appoint an independent chief executive officer as an immediate step. T.R. Sivaraman, the agent of the Cochin branch of State Bank of India, had stepped in to take charge of Palai Central Bank as its general manager in July 1960. At the board meeting of the bank, a decision was taken to send Sivaraman to the RBI headquarters in Bombay to apprise it of the situation at the bank and to find out whether it could open a couple of branches as part of a confidence-building exercise. The RBI sent out a stern message to the bank's management through Sivaraman. It told the new GM that the bank had only a month's time to explain the irregularities and a year's time to remedy the weaknesses in the system. Less than a week later, Sivaraman returned to the RBI to inform it that the situation was far worse than earlier assessments might have suggested. He told the Governor and his top team that Palai Central Bank could no longer be saved and should be liquidated as early as possible, since it was left with a cash balance of only Rs 50 lakh and had reserve borrowings of Rs 1 crore against government securities. That was the proverbial nail in the coffin for Palai Central Bank.

RBI Governor H.V.R. Iengar telephoned Finance Minister Morarji Desai on 8 August to inform him that the central bank had decided on liquidating Palai Central Bank. Soon afterwards, the RBI moved an application before a judge of the Kerala High Court at Ernakulam to seek the winding up of the bank. Its liquidation was sought under Section 38 of the Banking Companies Act. The high court admitted the application and passed an interim order appointing a provisional liquidator. At around the same time, Sivaraman convened a meeting of the board of the Palai Central Bank to inform it of the developments. There were unproven charges against Sivaraman that he had delayed the meeting deliberately so that the court order on liquidation was passed before the board met. Expectedly, the RBI decision was widely discussed, often with acrimony and criticism that the central bank took such an extreme step causing untold misery to thousands of the bank's depositors and without having taken earlier remedial action to prevent such a crisis. Such criticism was made both in the media and in Parliament.

In Parliament, the liquidation of Palai Central Bank was discussed for many days in the following weeks. The tenor of the discussion was how the RBI had allowed the problems at the bank to fester for a long period and had failed to take corrective action before it was too late and liquidation became inevitable. Desai defended the RBI against those charges. Desai argued that there had been no delay in taking action. On the contrary, if early action had been taken, the criticism would have been that the RBI did not give the bank adequate time to recover from its difficult situation. And if any further delay in closing the bank had taken place, then that would have endangered the credit system. 'One has to balance nicely the various conflicting considerations and with full knowledge of all the factors involved, I have little doubt that the action taken by the Bank and the timing were appropriate,' Desai told Parliament, while showering generous praise on the RBI for the admirable manner in which it was discharging its responsibilities.

Desai's defence of the RBI in Parliament, however, was in sharp contrast to the internal discussion he had with the RBI Governor. Just two days after the liquidation of Palai Central Bank, Desai wrote to Iengar drawing his attention to the criticism the government had to face in Parliament and asking him why the RBI had allowed the Kerala bank to drift to such an extent that it had to be eventually closed. Desai also advised the RBI to consider more effectively some of the powers it had under law. Iengar responded to the finance minister by saying that his decisions were the result of a considered review of the developments in these banks and that he believed any earlier action would have invited the criticism that the RBI had acted in haste. The RBI's official response to the wide range of criticism about its action against Palai Central Bank was limited to a press release it issued on 9 August explaining the reasons for its decision. Subsequently, Iengar would make some public speeches, where he would repeat what he had told Desai, that if the RBI had acted earlier it would have been accused of taking a premature decision.

The process of liquidation of Palai Central Bank in the courts of law was rather long. The Constitutional validity of invoking Section 38 of the Banking Companies Act was upheld by the Kerala High Court in December 1960. An appeal was heard in the Supreme Court, which by a majority judgment dismissed it in March 1962.

That brought the case back to the Kerala High Court. But the main proceedings for liquidation of Palai Central Bank dragged on for more than twenty-seven years as the final orders dissolving the bank were passed only in December 1987. RBI History noted: 'The real losers, both due to the bank failure and the prolonged liquidation proceedings, were the unfortunate depositors of the Palai Central Bank, who managed in all to recover some two-thirds of their 1960 deposits. In real terms, of course, depositors' losses were much greater.' In effect, the liquidator failed to recover the Rs 2.88 crore of liability towards the directors and auditors of the bank.

Fears that public suspicion about the safety of bank deposits spreading to other banks in Kerala, after how the RBI had dealt with Palai Central Bank, were not exaggerated. RBI Governor H.V.R. Iengar did explore the option of invoking Section 18 of the RBI Act to offer emergency assistance to banks in Kerala. The press note the RBI issued a day after the liquidation did refer to its commitment to grant assistance 'with utmost expedition' to any bank whose affairs were 'satisfactory'. There was no immediate need for extending such assistance. But by the middle of August, two scheduled and two non-scheduled banks in Kerala applied to the RBI for emergency help. The top management at the RBI did not fear any run on deposits held by these Kerala banks, though they were uncomfortable with the nature of media reports and politicians' statements on the issue. Nevertheless, on 18 August, the RBI invoked Section 18 of the RBI Act and emergency assistance was made available to the Kerala banks that had asked for assistance.

The impact of the liquidation of Palai Central Bank was felt on many other banks, even outside the state of Kerala. As many as five banks in Delhi (Punjab National Bank, Oriental Bank of Commerce, New Bank of India, Lakshmi Commercial Bank and National Bank of Lahore) saw an unusual rise in withdrawal of deposits in the remaining months of the year. The Madras-based Indian Bank also suffered withdrawal of deposits. But the bigger and longer-lasting impact of what happened at Palai Central Bank was witnessed in the banking scene in Kerala, particularly in the Travancore region, where moratoria had to be imposed on several small banks, leading to the amalgamation and consolidation of many of them.

The reverberations of the closure of Palai Central Bank were felt even on the political firmament in New Delhi. A high-level discussion among Prime Minister Nehru, Finance Minister Desai and RBI Governor Iengar took place. The emphasis was on how well the RBI could make more effective use of its powers after it carried out inspection of banks. An immediate fallout of the discussion was that the RBI acquired in September 1960 new powers under the existing laws to enforce amalgamations and delicensing of banks. Both these powers were aimed at making inspection of banks more effective. Indeed, in 1961, the RBI hired D.R. Joshi, who was then secretary and treasurer of the Bengal circle of the State Bank of India, to work as an executive director entrusted with the specific responsibility of reorganizing, expanding and strengthening the central bank's inspection regime.

Among the many policy consequences of the failure of Palai Central Bank was the enactment of a law that could guarantee a part of bank deposits through an insurance mechanism. The idea of insuring bank deposits was first mooted after the Bengal bank failures in the late 1940s, but it was kept in abeyance till the Reserve Bank of India strengthened the bank inspection system. The Rural Banking Enquiry Committee had also recommended introduction of deposit insurance in its report in 1950. But no action had followed. It was only after the failure of Palai Central Bank and Laxmi Bank in 1960 that the government swung into action to provide legal cover for providing insurance to bank depositors. On 21 August 1961, Desai introduced the Deposit Insurance Corporation Bill, which was passed by Parliament without any delay. With the President giving his assent to the bill on 7 December 1961, the legislative regime of providing bank deposit insurance came into force from 1 January 1962.

Palai Central Bank was the last major bank that failed in India. The RBI strengthened its inspection system in the following years. Liquidation of any bank in trouble was no longer the preferred route for the central bank. Instead, the RBI opted for merger of the stressed bank with a healthy bank. A bank in trouble would initially be placed under moratorium, followed by its merger with another bank.

An unintended but obvious consequence of the liquidation of Palai Central Bank was the spate of mergers and consolidation that the Indian banking space witnessed in the following decade. With the Reserve Bank of India becoming more alert and encouraging mergers or amalgamations to help troubled banks, as many as 204 banks were either merged or saw their assets and liabilities transferred to other banks over a period of seven years, between 1960 and 1967. Of these 204 banks, as many as twenty banks had volunteered to be amalgamated instead of facing the trauma and stigma of moratorium and compulsory merger. But forty-five of those 204 banks had to be compulsorily amalgamated (thirty of them in 1961 alone) under the new powers of the RBI in the wake of the Palai Central Bank crisis. In addition to the 204 bank mergers, there were fifty-seven banks that were placed under moratorium in this period.

The spate of bank amalgamations during this period soon became a bone of contention between the RBI and the finance ministry, and the eventual winner in that battle was the latter. Desai convened a meeting with Iengar in July 1961 to discuss this issue in particular. Desai suggested to Iengar that the RBI should go slow with the amalgamation of banks whose finances had not deteriorated and were capable of improving their financial condition with their own efforts. The RBI disagreed with the government's point of view, but deferred to its line of thinking. Thus, reflecting the relations that the central bank used to enjoy even in that era, it told the government that from then on compulsory amalgamation would remain confined only to banks that were grossly mismanaged, had failed to follow RBI directives or had lost a part of their deposits. To further assuage the government, the RBI told it that the central bank would be willing to do a hand-holding operation with commercial banks, unless they themselves opted for the moratorium route if a run on their deposits was inevitable. More importantly, the RBI gave what appeared almost an undertaking that it would not frame new proposals for amalgamation of banks until the government had taken a policy decision on the matter. Not surprisingly, the number of compulsory amalgamations dropped dramatically to only one each in 1962 and 1963, nine in 1964, four in 1965 and none in the following two years. The threat of compulsory amalgamation, however, continued to work on the banking system. As many as 122 banks went for voluntary amalgamation and transferred their assets and liabilities to other banks under Section 293 (1) (a) of the Companies Act in the seven years after the liquidation of Palai Central Bank. In 1964 alone, as many as sixty-two banks went in for voluntary amalgamation. Interestingly, forty-six of these banks were in Kerala and most of them were gold-loan banks that were hit hard by the Gold Control Order of 1962. The State Bank of

India was also in the amalgamation game, having merged seventeen banks into itself. It was not that the liquidation route was completely abandoned. In these seven years, forty-five banks went into voluntary liquidation and twenty more were compulsorily liquidated.

The liquidation of Palai Central Bank had ramifications for the banking regulation space in a variety of ways. It not just triggered a spate of amalgamations—voluntary as well as compulsory—but it also led to a revamp of the RBI's bank licensing policy. Reviewing the banking industry immediately after liquidating Palai Central Bank, RBI Governor H.V.R. Iengar found that there were as many as 250 unlicensed banks operating in the country. This was a bit of a scandal—the regulator getting to know through a crisis that there were entities that had been functioning without any specific licensing approval from it. An RBI note revealed that about fifty of these unlicensed banks were good enough to qualify for a licence in two to three years, about 170 banks might need five to ten years to graduate to a level where they could be licensed, and the remaining forty-odd banks were not likely to ever get licences in accordance with the regulator's licensing criteria. The objective was to reach a stage where all banks met the licensing conditions and the distinction between scheduled and non-scheduled banks disappeared.

Even in the area of bank licensing, the government had a slightly different and more nuanced approach. The finance ministry told the RBI that it should give banks as much flexibility as possible in conforming to the licensing regimen. Thus, the RBI laid down a more nuanced licensing regime: As long as the interests of depositors were not compromised, the banks could be given time to improve their performance and become eligible for a licence. And the banks that failed to adhere to this course correction could be pushed into entering into schemes of arrangements or mergers. In spite of this nuanced approach, in deference to the finance ministry's wishes, RBI supervision of the banking sector between 1962 and 1967 resulted in as many as 139 banks being denied licences. Taken together with the banks that had lost licences since 1951, the total casualties among banks deprived of licensing in the entire period of seventeen years (1951–67) was 278. In contrast, only fifteen banks were granted licences between 1961 and 1967. Along with tighter licensing supervision, the RBI also began using its other powers more regularly, appointing chief executives for banks more freely and regulating the banks' dividends more frequently.

Dilemmas over Securing Loans from the IMF

Seeking recourse to loans from the International Monetary Fund has often been a political controversy in India. This was so in spite of India having been a founding member of the IMF. Even when the Congress party had a clear majority in Parliament, it would hesitate to seek loans from the IMF. In light of the falling foreign exchange reserves as a result of an increase in imports, the Nehru government had drawn Rs 34.5 crore (about $72 million) from the IMF in 1957–58, even as its foreign exchange reserves depleted by Rs 260 crore (about $544 million). But the pressure of repaying the IMF loan kept mounting, and India repaid it Rs 24 crore (about $50 million) in 1959–60 and another Rs 11 crore (about $23 million) in the following year. The lag between aid commitments and disbursements added to the pressure on foreign exchange reserves. The net outcome was that in July 1961, Desai had moved the IMF with a request for drawing $250 million from it.

This was a big amount, considering that it was more than India's Gold Tranche and the First Credit Tranche, facilities that the country could access if it felt there was need for funds. What complicated the request was that the facility was also being sought as part of a roll-over of the earlier drawings of 1957. But India had the support of some sympathetic ears among the top leaders at the IMF, and it went ahead with its application. The going was not easy this time. The IMF asked India to submit a statement of intent, since the loan sought was higher than its eligibility amount under the First Credit Tranche, and an assurance that the accommodation sought was for development needs and not assistance for meeting its payment liabilities. I.G. Patel, who had just moved from the finance ministry as an economic adviser to the IMF as India's executive director, made a strong case for the facility on the ground that India's foreign exchange reserves were unsatisfactory and that this was needed to prevent any further depletion in the reserves. Patel also suggested that the IMF could not wash its hands of the problems of a member country just because the money sought was for meeting its development needs. IMF chief Per Jacobsson supported India's application as he saw the loan extension as a way of influencing the Indian government to bring about reforms and liberalize the economy at a faster pace. By August 1961, the IMF board sanctioned a loan facility of $250 million for India. As expected, a little more than half of the loan amount, an estimated $127 million, was used to repay the outstandings against the earlier loan taken in 1957. This also helped prevent further depletion of India's foreign exchange reserves. But India's external account problems were not fully over and a recourse to the IMF became necessary again a year later.

Sometime in June 1962, the RBI Governor P.C. Bhattacharya met the top team of secretaries in the finance ministry to apprise them of the deteriorating external account. He informed them that the RBI's foreign currency assets were declining rapidly, and since the problem did not look to be of a short duration, there was no alternative but to curtail imports as part of a long-term policy. He also mentioned the rise in instances of Indians travelling abroad and accessing foreign exchange through unauthorized channels in Malaya or West Asia, which had an indirect, adverse impact on India's remittances. The group of secretaries, at the instance of the RBI Governor, recommended that unauthorized foreign travels should be stopped and that import licences should be issued in all cases, except where imports were financed through foreign aid money. A proposal to suspend the requirement of providing a minimum foreign currency fee for obtaining sterling pound or dollar from banks was also mooted to reduce the demand for foreign exchange. The British High Commissioner in New Delhi was to have been informed of the proposed step. But Nehru intervened and decided against the move. Even the idea of devaluing the Indian currency was discussed, but this too found no favour at that time.

By the time Finance Minister Desai rose in Parliament to make a statement on the steps the government planned to bolster India's external account, it became clear that the original ideas discussed by the RBI Governor with the group of secretaries had been substantially diluted. Only foreign travel for business and education was to be regulated and imports were to be curbed, even though Desai's statement in the Lok Sabha on 8 June 1962 referred to how colossal the challenge facing the nation was and noted that it was one of those situations where the country must demonstrate that it was prepared to take whatever action was necessary.

With the depletion in foreign exchange reserves showing no signs of slowing, Desai saw no option left to him other than to knock at the doors of the IMF once again. The government was reluctant to go for another IMF loan, for obvious reasons. There was also a perception that India had perhaps over-borrowed from the IMF, and Jacobsson was reportedly insisting on a statement of intent from India on the policy changes it would bring to make better use of the next tranche of loans it was hoping to receive. India had a strong case for a financial accommodation from the IMF. This was because India's problems arose in no small measure due to the slow pace at which Western donor countries were fulfilling their aid commitments. The US, Britain, Germany and other members of the Aid India Consortium would have no option but to support India's application. Measures to restrict imports and plug leaks in its invisible receipts had already been taken, and some more discussion on the steps to be taken on the monetary policy front was under way. Armed with these steps, India applied for a one-year standby loan of $100 million from the IMF in July 1962. The IMF took little time in sanctioning the loan to India, which quickly drew the first instalment of $25 million, giving its foreign exchange reserves the much-needed boost. This obviated the need for the kind of drastic measures on economy and import curtailment that were discussed earlier in June that year.

The War with China and Its Impact on Desai

The Chinese aggression in September 1962 was a major setback, both for the country and for the Nehru government's finances. There was a political demand from within the Congress to present a supplementary Budget aimed at helping the government raise the required additional resources to meet the extra expenditure on account of the border conflict and provide more as defence outlay to improve the country's preparedness for another war and prevent any expenditure cutback on the Third Plan that had just been launched.

Desai opposed the idea of a supplementary Budget. His argument that a supplementary Budget would not be able to raise resources for the government on a permanent basis. Also, any supplementary resource-raising exercise could create complications and unnecessary challenges for the government in preparing the Budget due to be presented in February 1963. Increasing the taxes in the middle of the year would also create difficulties for the tax-paying public. Already, Indians had responded favourably to the government's call for contributing to the exchequer to help it fight the Chinese. So, why tax them again now? Desai had a meeting with Nehru to explain his arguments against a supplementary Budget. Nehru saw reason in Desai's point of view. The idea of a supplementary Budget was dropped, but not before Desai agreed to increasing the defence outlay for the year. There were no new taxes, but in November 1962 Desai announced an additional financial provision for defence expenditure of Rs 95 crore, over and above the Rs 376 crore that had already been provided in the Budget for 1962–63. But only a small part of the additional outlay was spent before the year ended, reflecting the poor absorptive capacity of the defence establishment in India. In addition, Desai also launched the National Defence Bonds scheme, as well as another scheme for accepting contributions from people for the National Defence Fund. The total collections under the two schemes were estimated at Rs 65–70 crore.

That was not all. The national emergency in the wake of the Chinese aggression had led to a few more initiatives. Already, the Customs Act had been amended to strengthen the customs administration in preventing the smuggling of gold. Given the national emergency, Desai gave the green signal for the launch of a public education campaign to reduce the demand for gold. On 4 November 1962, the government announced the issue of gold bonds, a scheme launched to encourage Indians to deposit their gold with the government against assurance of an interest payout at a fixed rate. Less than ten days later, on 13 November, the government banned forward trading in gold to make disposal of smuggled gold more difficult.

Using the Yellow Metal in Different Ways

More measures on gold were in the offing. This was the Gold Control Order, which was promulgated through an ordinance on 9 January 1963. In a national radio broadcast that day, Desai effectively banned the manufacture of gold ornaments of more than 14 carats purity. Along with that ban were enforced various other provisions, including those that introduced a licensing regime for trading in gold and refining of gold. Gold traders and refineries had to declare their gold stocks, other than gold ornaments, beyond a specified limit. A Gold Control Board had been set up to keep under constant review the question of discouraging the use and consumption of gold and to suggest methods for reducing the demand for gold within the country. Gold smuggling had become rampant as the domestic price of the yellow metal was much higher than its international price. There was a huge mismatch between the domestic production of gold and the demand for gold as well as gold ornaments. By Desai's account, annual gold smuggling those years was as large as Rs 50 crore, while the combined value of all other smuggled goods was just Rs 5–7 crore.

The Union Cabinet had met on 9 January for just about an hour or two before Desai announced the promulgation of the Gold Control Order. Desai recalls that many of his colleagues had asked for more stringent steps under the new dispensation to extend the controls to even possession of gold ornaments. Desai opposed the suggestion, on the ground that such draconian measures could be considered only after successful implementation of the steps that had already been proposed under the Gold Control Order. The fear was that this could trigger a public protest, which could be difficult to manage. Eventually, controls on gold ornaments were not imposed, and the irony was that those Cabinet colleagues who were keen on more stringent regulation were the first to indirectly and discreetly support the opposition to the Gold Control Order by remaining silent and not defending the new policy, Desai recalls.

Desai's Gold Control Order went through a fairly long gestation period. Desai believed that Nehru and V.K. Krishna Menon, the defence minister, were in favour of such an order to crack down on gold smuggling. But Desai's view was that without a proper scheme a crackdown on gold smuggling could be counterproductive. By July 1962, he had prepared the draft of a scheme and had presented it to Nehru. Once the prime minister gave his stamp of approval to it, Desai went ahead to plan its implementation, which took almost six months. Desai's logic was that gold smuggling had to be prevented and that it would be difficult to stop smuggling as long as there were no checks on the demand and attraction for the yellow metal. There were no legal imports of gold. And since the smuggled gold was refined in illegal refineries across the country, the demand for gold as well as the refining of gold in the country needed to be controlled.

The Economic Survey presented in February 1963 explained the logic of the government's initiatives on gold, including the Gold Control Order, in the following words:

> The government has initiated a major and determined effort to stamp out a significant source of drain on India's national exchange resources. The generally high demand for gold in the country for traditional and other reasons has led to smuggling of gold on a considerable scale in recent years and the financing of this illegal traffic has led to malpractices in violation of exchange control regulations and to clandestine transactions at unofficial rates of exchange. In the wake of the emergency, a campaign to educate public opinion was launched and the Gold Bonds were issued as a first step towards weaning people away from gold. The forward market in gold was closed to reduce the ease with which smuggled gold could be disposed of in the country. Later, Gold Control Rules were promulgated in order to regulate internal transactions in gold in such a way as to bring about a progressive reduction in demand so as to provide a series of checks on smuggling. The new gold policy marks an important departure in the social and economic history of the country, and it is an index of the seriousness with which the balance of payments position of the country at present has to be viewed.

What this, however, meant for the February 1963 Budget was that a record level of additional taxation measures was introduced by Desai. Additional customs levies were raised and some other adjustments were made to mobilize additional revenue of over Rs 87 crore in the full year. The higher customs duties were not only aimed at mobilizing more revenue, but also at applying the brakes on the pace of imports so that the government could save its foreign exchange resources. Excise duties were raised, yielding a net additional revenue of Rs 107 crore. A progressive surcharge on personal incomes after tax was levied, and a super-profits tax was imposed on corporations. As a result of all this, additional direct tax revenue would go up by Rs 110 crore, of which Rs 40 crore would come from compulsory savings by income tax payers, Rs 33 crore from the new surcharge on personal income tax, Rs 25 crore from the super-profits tax and Rs 12 crore by way of measures to rationalize, reduce or eliminate exemptions. On a total Budget size of Rs 1852 crore, the additional revenue mobilization effort was high, at about 14 per cent.

Bolstered by such additional revenue measures, Desai was in a position to make higher allocations for the defence sector. From Rs 395 crore spent on defence in 1962–63, the 1963–64 Budget saw a near trebling of outlay, at Rs 868 crore. This increase was unprecedented but a sad reminder of the past neglect in meeting the requirements of India's armed forces. The Third Plan allocation for 1963–64 also was raised to Rs 1750 crore, up from Rs 1500 crore earmarked for the previous year.

Marking the government focus on raising more resources, Desai's 1963–64 Budget launched the Compulsory Deposit Scheme. Under this scheme, specified classes of income taxpayers, property taxpayers, land rent receivers, employees of Central and state governments and taxpayers on sale of goods would be required to deposit specified amounts of money with the government, on which they would earn a simple interest of 4 per cent per annum till they were repaid after the expiry of five years. The objective of the scheme was to raise resources in the interest of 'national economic development'. Before introducing the scheme, Desai had consulted the state chief ministers, and all of them had supported the move. Effectively, the amount of deposit the government employees were required to make was about 3 per cent of their annual salary. Income tax payers could get relief from the surcharges on their tax to the extent of their deposits under the scheme. Desai's argument was that while on the one hand the scheme helped the government raise resources, on the other it encouraged people to cultivate the habit of saving.

The Compulsory Deposit Scheme and the Gold Control Order were an instant hit among the left leaders, who welcomed them but did not say so in public or make any statement supporting them. Not surprisingly, the schemes became controversial as they met with stiff opposition from many members of Parliament. So incensed were they with the provisions of these schemes, which they claimed were violative of the Indian Constitution, that they demanded that the Attorney General be called to Parliament and explain their legality. C.K. Daphtary had joined as Attorney General on 2 March 1963, succeeding M.C. Setalvad, who had a long stint in that position from 1950 to 1963. Desai resisted such a demand on the ground that the Opposition leaders could not force a summoning of the Attorney General in Parliament. But once a whisper campaign that the finance minister was apprehensive about calling the Attorney General for fear of the two schemes being declared ultra vires of the Constitution started doing the rounds, Desai consulted the prime minister and conceded to the demand. Much to Desai's and the government's relief, C.K. Daphtary came to Parliament and gave the two schemes a clean chit.

But there was no respite in the political opposition to the two schemes. Agriculturists argued that they should be exempted from the Compulsory Deposit Scheme and goldsmiths formed powerful lobbies to put pressure on the government to rescind the Gold Control Order. The protests gained momentum when a few goldsmiths were reported to have committed suicide. But Desai did not relent as long as he was the finance minister. Once, however, Desai quit the ministry by the end of August 1963 under the Kamaraj Plan, Nehru got the necessary changes made in the Compulsory Deposit Scheme by replacing it with the Annuity Scheme. The Gold Control Order continued to remain in force and would be repealed only twenty-seven years later, in 1990, by another finance minister from Maharashtra, Madhu Dandavate.

Desai's Five Budgets in a Nutshell

Morarji Desai's first Budget was presented in the context of an improvement in agricultural output and industrial growth, even as some industries were handicapped by restrictions that had been imposed on imports on account of a shortage of foreign exchange in the country. At the end of March 1959, India's foreign exchange reserves fell to $795 million, compared to $884 million a year ago. Not surprisingly, the current account deficit had also risen to Rs 451 crore at the end of March 1958, up from Rs 307 crore at the end of March 1957. And in the first half of 1958–59, the deficit had already widened to Rs 211 crore. This was one of the factors why India's dependence on foreign assistance in the form of loans and aid from the World Bank and other friendly countries was on the rise.

Not without reason did Desai agree to increase India's contribution to the International Monetary Fund by raising its quota from $400 million to $500 million in 1958–59. Similarly, India had decided the same year to increase its subscription to the World Bank's capital stock from

$400 million to $800 million. At around the same time India signed two agreements with the Unites States under Public Law 480, commonly known as PL 480, for the import of food grain at a concessional price valued at about Rs 140 crore.

On the domestic front, the demand for industrial imports had been on the rise even as India began setting up new capacities to manufacture industrial goods. In 1958, Heavy Engineering Corporation was set up in Ranchi to produce capital equipment for steel, mining, railways, power, defence, space research, nuclear and strategic sectors. Although money supply was under control, inflation based on the wholesale price index was on the rise. At the end of February 1959, inflation was 5.66 per cent.

In the Budget on 28 February 1959, Desai introduced a major change in its coverage and scope. For the first time, the Budget for 1959-60 brought together the expenditure estimates of each ministry in one comprehensive document. Earlier, such estimates of different ministries would be announced separately. Additionally, Desai presented the estimates relating to Plan expenditure separately from the estimates for non-Plan items. This classification was also introduced in the Budget for the first time.

Taxation Proposals for 1959–60

Desai announced no change in the existing rates and structure of personal income tax but raised the wealth tax rates by half a per cent at each slab. Thus, the wealth tax payable by individuals and Hindu Undivided Families went up from 0.5 per cent to 1 per cent on wealth valued at between Rs 2 lakh and Rs 12 lakh. The wealth tax rates were 1.5 per cent on wealth between Rs 12 lakh and Rs 22 lakh and 2 per cent on wealth higher than Rs 22 lakh. There was no wealth tax on wealth less than Rs 2 lakh. He expressed his reservations about the expenditure tax that was introduced by T.T. Krishnamachari, but since revenue from the new tax was negligible, he decided to withdraw some of the exemptions so that collections under the tax could be improved. He also simplified the way companies could adjust the tax they paid on the dividends they distributed to the shareholders. Another simplification was to combine in the income tax and super tax rates of companies the net incidence of the present taxes on income, excess dividends, and wealth. Thus, the total tax on companies was levied at 45 per cent, after subsuming in the overall tax the levies under the wealth tax and excess dividend tax on companies.

On the indirect taxes front, Desai made no changes in the customs duty. However, he increased the excise duty on a large number of items including diesel, art silk fabrics, rayon yarn, staple fibre, motor vehicle tyres, vegetable products, vegetable oils and khandsari sugar. The additional resource mobilization from the new taxes was estimated at about Rs 23 crore (on a total budget size of Rs 1157 crore). When the final figures for 1959–60 were available, it became clear that Desai had managed the finances competently as the deficit had been brought down as tax collections were higher and expenditure had been reined in.

Budget for 1960–61

Desai's second Budget had to bear the burden of the recommendations of the Second Central Pay Commission to increase pay and allowances of central government employees. Set up in August 1957 under the chairmanship of Justice Jagannath Das, the Commission submitted its report two years later in November 1959, and Desai had to implement the recommendations, which meant an additional annual expenditure burden of about Rs 44 crore in 1960–61.

The other development that impacted the Budget was the government's assessment that the situation on India's borders was tense with the threat of an attack from its neighbours looming large. Desai, raised the allocation for defence by 12 per cent to Rs 272 crore in 1960–61. About a year later in October–November 1962, India was indeed engaged in a war with China over a disputed border.

A new scheme the finance minister introduced was the launch of prize bonds. The scheme was launched from 1 March 1960 and their sale began a month later. These prize bonds were in the form bearer bonds in two denominations of Rs 100 and Rs 5. While the bonds would not carry interest and would be repaid after five years, but the holders would participate in quarterly draws of prizes, which would be free of income tax. The prizes ranged between Rs 500 and Rs 25,000. This was a scheme to mobilize resources so that the government could use them for development projects. Prize bonds yielded a sum of Rs 12.5 crore by the end of 1961, which was a decent amount those days.

As far as direct taxes were concerned, Desai continued with the 45 per cent tax on companies but decided to provide relief to companies with a total income of less than Rs 25,000. Accordingly, the tax on such small companies was to be levied at 40 per cent. In another concession, the finance minister applied a uniform rate of 30 per cent for deduction of tax from both individuals and companies.

Desai raised excise duty on many items to raise revenues to bridge the government's deficit. Items, whose duties went up as a result of his proposals, included tin plates and tinned sheets, pig iron, aluminium sheets and circles, internal combustion engines, essential cycle parts, electric motors and parts, silk fabrics, diesel oil, parts of footwear, electric fans, bulbs and batteries.

The total additional resource mobilized through new taxes was estimated at over Rs 23 crore, but it left a deficit of about Rs 153 crore to be met through borrowing. For the second year running, Desai succeeded in ending the year with higher collections of revenues and the expenditure was restricted to a figure lower than what was budgeted for.

Budget for 1961–62

Desai's third Budget for 1961–62 was presented on 28 February 1961 and it had recognized the resources constraints encountered by the planning process. The Second Five-year Plan that was to end in March 1961 had to overcome difficulties with regard to domestic as well as external resources. Some adjustments in the outlays had to be made, resulting in the reduction in the public sector Plan outlay from Rs 4800 crore to Rs 4500 crore. Learning from the experience of the Second Plan, Desai had made sure that the Third Plan made adequate arrangements for securing adequate resources to execute the projects envisaged under it. The Third Plan from April 1961 to March 1966 was to rely a lot on the surpluses of various public enterprises including the Indian Railways. The Third Plan was also prepared in a way that dependence on foreign exchange was reduced considerably.

In Desai's assessment, the economy had not done too well in 1960. Agricultural output did not come up to the government's expectations owing to adverse climatic conditions, with food output at about 72 million tonnes declining by about five per cent over the previous year. Industrial output did well and several new industrial projects were under execution. Three public sector steel plants were under constructions and had made progress with all of them expected to see the commissioning of their blast furnaces, steel melting shops and rolling mills in 1960–61, while the expansion programme of the two steel plants in the private sector had been completed.

On the energy front, coal production had increased, the Oil and Natural Gas Commission had continued its search for oil in Jwalamukhi and Hoshiarpur areas of Punjab, in the Cambay and Ankleshwar regions of Gujarat and in Rudrasagar areas in Assam. Early signs of success were noticeable in Gujarat, Desai noted in his Budget speech. Inflation maintained its stickiness with wholesale prices rising by about 6.5 per cent in 1960–61 and the balance of payments situation turning for the worse, with a further decline in the country's foreign exchange reserves from $762 million at the end of March 1960 to $637 million a year later.

External assistance continued to help the Indian economy. The World Bank sanctioned two new loans for the development of the Indian Railways and for the Industrial Credit and Investment Corporation of India. Other agencies that came forward with assistance packages included the US Development Loan Fund for a fertilizer plant at Trombay, the US Export-Import Bank, the United Kingdom government to finance capital goods imports from England, West Germany, the Aid India Consortium, the Soviet Union, the Public Law 480 agreement with the US for import of 18 million tonnes of wheat and the Colombo Plan countries (largely belonging to the Commonwealth).

Desai oversaw a significant change in the tenure of the Third Finance Commission. Since the Second Finance Commissions had faced difficulties in assessing the requirements of the state governments and the Centre as the period covered by its recommendations extended over both the Second and the Third Five-year Plan periods. The period covered by the Second Finance Commission was from April 1957 to March 1962, but the Second Plan ended in March 1961 and the Third Plan began in April 1961. Thus, there was an overlap. The Third Finance Commission, therefore, was set up in December 1960, but its recommendations were to be enforced only for four years from April 1962 to March 1966.

This allowed the Fourth Plan period of April 1966 to March 1971 to coincide and become coterminous with the period when the fourth Finance Commission's recommendations would be implemented.

Taxation Initiatives

With respect to direct taxes, Desai sought to bring near-parity for the tax incidence on earned income and unearned income. He argued that earned incomes (wages and salaries earned from work) of over Rs 1 lakh in a year should be subjected to tax at a rate near to that at which unearned income (retirement benefits, annuities, dividend, interest, etc.) was taxed. The prevailing tax rates stipulated that earned income above Rs 1 lakh would attract a surcharge of 5 per cent and unearned income would attract a surcharge of 15 per cent of the basic income tax and super tax. This meant that the maximum slab rate of tax including surcharge on unearned income was 84 per cent, while that on earned income was 77 per cent. Desai decided to increase the rate of special surcharge of 5 per cent on earned income above Rs 1 lakh to 10 per cent of the basic tax.

Desai reduced the tax on new bonus issues of shares by companies from 30 per cent to 12 per cent. This he believed was desirable both from the revenue point of view and with a view to widening the equity base, in particular after he had abolished the tax on excess dividends. The tax rate was raised also because Desai found that companies must be encouraged to capitalize their reserves instead of dissipate them through higher dividends. With a view to discouraging the formation of subsidiaries, he decided that the rate of super tax on dividends paid on inter-corporate investments should be fixed at 20 per cent, a little lower than the prevailing rate. The lower rate was to be levied irrespective of whether the inter-corporate investment was made in an Indian or foreign company or whether it was made on a majority or minority basis.

There was relief by way of lower taxation on royalties received by foreign companies from Indian enterprises. The existing rate of 63 per cent inclusive of income tax and super tax, one of the highest rates among countries, was reduced to 50 per cent subject to the condition that such royalties were paid on agreements approved by the government after March 31, 1961. Curbs on the tendency among companies to spend money on entertainment while claiming tax deduction on it were also placed by Desai as he imposed stringent conditions on how and when such concessions could be enjoyed.

Turning Protectionist to Raise Revenue

In what was clearly a major drive towards raising the customs duty to discourage imports, whose rising trend had adversely impacted the country's foreign exchange reserves, Desai decided to raises the customs duty on as many as 41 items. These included betel nuts, unmanufactured tobacco, specified textile manufactures, machinery and components, electrical and other instruments, certain apparatus and appliances and newsprint. Total mobilization of additional resources through the customs duty change was estimated at Rs 16.95 crore.

Desai also increased the excise duty on more fourteen commodities and imposed a fresh levy on eighteen new items. These items included loose tea, tobacco, kerosene, diesel oil, yarn, staple fibre, vegetable products, paints, varnishes, paper, cotton fabrics, glass and glassware, wireless receiving sets, air-conditioning machinery and refrigerators. Excise duty changes were expected to fetch him an additional revenue of about Rs 31 crore in a full year.

Since the increase in the excise duty also meant a corresponding rise in the countervailing duty on such imported products, the government expected additional revenue of Rs 12 crore on this account as well.

The Fiscal Outcome

In his Budget for 1961–62, Desai used new taxes and higher tax rates to mobilize a good amount of additional revenue. His proposals on customs duty were to fetch him about Rs 29 crore, excise duty were to get him an additional Rs 29 crore and direct tax policy changes were to garner a relatively small amount of Rs 3 crore. The additional revenue of about Rs 61 crore was to wipe out the Budget's revenue deficit and result in a nominal surplus. The overall deficit was thus expected to come down from Rs 125 crore before taxes to Rs 64 crore after taking into account the revenue raising proposals. When the year ended, Desai could proudly claim that the revenue mobilization efforts had yielded unexpectedly good results. Tax revenues exceeded the estimates and the revenue deficit was converted into a surplus of Rs 34 crore. The overall deficit still remained, but was only about Rs 30 crore.

The Budget after the Elections

General elections for the Third Lok Sabha were held between February 19 and 25 in 1962, returning the Congress under Nehru to power for the third time running. The formation of the Nehru government saw the return of Desai as the finance minister again, although the prime minister did show some signs of looking for a replacement. But eventually Desai returned to North Block. He presented an interim Budget on March 14 and returned to Parliament again on April 23 to present what would be his fourth Union Budget.

The Third Five-year Plan had been launched in April 1961. The goals set in that Plan were ambitious, targeting an average annual growth rate of 6 per cent. Relying on an outlay of Rs 7500 crore in the public sector, almost 66 per cent more than what was spent in the Second Plan, Desai hoped that such emphasis on public sector outlay and an average growth rate of 6 per cent would help the country develop at a healthy rate without external assistance. However, that hope was not fulfilled. India's foreign exchange reserves fell to $624 million by the end of March 1962. Reliance on assistance from friendly countries, an increase in exports and seeking recourse to more small savings by the people were three of the measures that Desai believed would become necessary. That was one of the reasons why he reduced export duties on some exportable items and allowed contributions made by people to 10–15 year Post Office deposit schemes to enjoy a rebate of income tax as was available for the payment of life insurance premia and contributions to provident funds.

A Heavy Dose of Taxation

Recognizing the need for raising resources to meet higher investment outlays for the Third Plan, Desai went in for significant increases in tax rates. The corporation tax on Indian companies was raised from 45 per cent to 50 per cent, while that on foreign companies remained unchanged at 63 per cent. Export earnings, however, were exempted from the increased taxation to provide an incentive for more exports. Since the corporation tax was going up, Desai reduced the tax on inter-corporate dividends received from an Indian subsidiary company.

Desai was not too happy about the fact that in a country of 443 million people, just about a million people were subjected to any taxation. Since the base of income tax was narrow, the finance minister realized that the tax burden on those who were under the tax net would be steep. In the new income tax structure for individuals Desai announced, the tax at the highest slab of income was fixed at 72.5 per cent excluding the surcharge, while the rate for the lowest income slab remained unchanged and the intermediate slabs saw minor adjustments. By way of relief, the surcharge on income tax for salaried taxpayers was reduced from 5 per cent to 2.5 per cent. Similarly, capital gains tax norms were relaxed by levying a 25 per cent tax on gains on assets held by individuals and a 30 per cent tax on companies, if the assets were held for more than a year.

In a major decision, Desai abolished the expenditure tax, which was introduced in 1957 as he found the collections under the tax were small and the levy was cumbersome and creating procedural complications. But the wealth tax rates were raised by 0.25 per cent and 0.5 per cent on the two highest slabs and the exemption on shares held in new companies during the first five years was discontinued.

With regard to indirect taxes, excise duty was raised on a wide range of goods including unmanufactured tobacco, cigarettes, yarn, coarse yarn, processed cloth, match boxes, jute manufactures, specified iron and steel products, electric cables and wires, specific acids and gases, plywood, asbestos cement, tread rubber, latex foam sponge, gramophones, gramophone parts and their accessories. The excise duty was reduced on unprocessed woolens, rayon, art silk fabrics and specified drugs.

Customs duty also was raised on a wide range of items. These included iron and steel items, art silk yarn, tin plates, stainless steel plates, sheets, rods, bars, copra, certain types of tools (excluding machine tools and agricultural implements) and on cars (up from 100 per cent to 150 per cent). The export duty on tea was reduced to encourage its exports.

Of the total Rs 72 crore of additional resources to be mobilized in 1962–63, as much as Rs 45 crore was to come from excise and customs, while Rs 27 crore was to come from direct taxes. Not surprisingly, Desai was conscious that the bulk of the revenue mobilization drive was fuelled by indirect taxes, which were considered by many as regressive, since their incidence fell more heavily on the poor than on the rich. But he countered that belief by arguing that the indirect taxes that he raised on products were used by the rich and, therefore, would not have hit the poor. However, economists would still disagree with that argument of the finance minister. Unlike in the previous couple of years, Desai's 1962–63 taxation initiatives did not yield the kind of the revenues that he had hoped to collect. His expenditure, particularly on defence as a result of the war with China in October–November 1962, exceeded his estimates. Taken together with a shortfall in revenues, Desai's Budget for 1962–63 showed that the actual deficit had widened.

Desai's Budget for 1963–64

The country's foreign exchange reserves had deteriorated further by the end of March 1963, when they were down to $619 million only. The pressure on expenditure was also on the rise as the government needed to spend more on defence after its war with China showed that a lack of preparedness in defending the borders had been embarrassing for the country. The challenge for Desai was to bridge a larger deficit through a mix of taxation and other revenue raising measures.

Desai introduced a comprehensive scheme for compulsory savings, whose proceeds were to be shared between the Centre and the states. He introduced a legislative bill to provide for compulsory saving by different levels of income earners. The rates were 3 per cent of the annual rental value of property for property-owners in urban areas, 3 per cent of salary for employees earning more than Rs 1500 per annum but were not subjected to income-tax. Such deposits could not be withdrawn for a period of five years and were to carry a simple interest rate at 4 per cent a year.

More importantly, the finance minister levied an additional surcharge of 4 to 10 per cent on the post-tax income of individuals, Hindu Undivided Families, unregistered firms and associations of persons. He withdrew the existing exemption up to Rs 25,000 allowed for jewellery for computing the net wealth for the payment of the wealth tax. He also imposed on Indian companies a super-profits tax when their post-tax income exceeded 6 per cent of their capital and reserves.

On the indirect taxes front, Desai increased the Customs duty on several goods including mineral oils, machinery, iron and steel products, raw cotton, rubber, palm oil, cinema films, tobacco, dyes, hardware, electrical and other instruments, motor vehicle parts, petroleum products, iron and steel products and raw cotton. A general surcharge of 10 pe cent was also levied on all import duties.

On the excise front, the increases in rates impacted the following items: petrol, diesel, kerosene, vaporizing oil, vegetable products, paints, varnishes, soap, cigarettes, unmanufactured tobacco, strawboard, synthetic dyes, printing and writing paper, jute manufactures, glass, chinaware, porcelainware, tinplate, internal combustion engines, electric storage batteries, electric bulbs, tea and coffee.

The additional resource mobilization effort from Desai's fifth Budget was substantial, estimated at Rs 306 crore. The total gap between the government's expenditure and receipts was estimated at Rs 454 crore. Hence, the additional revenues helped in reducing the deficit, but could not wipe it out entirely.

Desai's Exit from the Cabinet

The manner in which Morarji Desai exited the Union Cabinet in 1963 was quite similar to the manner of his joining the Nehru government in 1958. Both were preceded by a controversy and drama of no small magnitude. Desai was invited to join the Union Cabinet after the then finance minister T.T. Krishnamachari had to quit in the wake of a financial scandal that shook the Nehru government. Five years later, Desai had to quit the same Union Cabinet because the prime minister wished to shift some of his Union ministers and state chief ministers to work for the Congress party in a bid to strengthen the organization. Desai was a victim of what is popularly known as the Kamaraj Plan.

Kumaraswamy Kamaraj was no ordinary leader of the Congress party. Belonging to a socially under-privileged Nadar family in the southern province of Madras, Kamaraj lost his father early in life, dropped out of school when he was just twelve to work in a cloth shop and plunged into the Independence movement under Mahatma Gandhi's leadership when he was just seventeen years of age. He became a member of the Constituent Assembly which drafted India's Constitution. He won his first Lok Sabha elections in 1951 before he became the chief minister of Madras in 1954. He held that post for three consecutive terms, leaving his mark on the state's governance. Kamaraj took a series of steps that advanced education in Madras by building new schools, introducing compulsory education and providing meals and free uniforms to students. The state's economy too benefited from Kamaraj's leadership, as he helped construct several irrigation projects and enacted laws to protect small farmers against exploitation by landlords. Any other state leader with a national profile would have remained content with the role he was playing in his own state. But not Kamaraj!

At the national level, the Nehru government was going through an existential crisis in the early 1960s. Having won three consecutive general elections, the Congress under Jawaharlal Nehru was still the ruling party with a clean single-party majority, though its seat strength in the Lok Sabha had seen a decline in the third general elections in 1962. Having won 369 out of 489 Lok Sabha seats in 1952 and 371 out of 494 Lok Sabha seats in 1957, the Congress tally in the 1962 elections came down to 361 seats. The total number of seats to be fought in the third general elections was 494. But what was more significant than the decline in the number of Congress seats was the rise in the number of seats won by a clutch of influential and powerful Opposition political parties with leaders with country-wide following challenging both the Congress and Nehru. Thus, the Communist Party of India had won twenty-nine seats, the Swatantra Party eighteen and the Bharatiya Jana Sangh fourteen.

That was not all. Soon after the elections of 1962, the border conflict with China in Ladakh resulted in an embarrassing loss of territory. Nehru agreed to drop his favourite defence minister Krishna Menon from the Union Cabinet. Nehru replaced Menon with Yashwantrao Chavan, but with a heavy heart and great reluctance. He took that decision after being advised by many of his colleagues that he should take such a step without further delay. Lal Bahadur Shastri, the home minister, had reportedly told the prime minister: '*Panditji jab chhoti ahuti nahin di jaati, tab badi ahuti deni par jaati hai . . .*' (When a small sacrifice is withheld, a bigger one gets to be demanded).[19]

On the economic policy front too, the Nehru government was facing a rough time. Finance Minister Morarji Desai had presented a Budget in 1963 that imposed higher taxation, introduced the Gold Control Order that had turned the traditional gold trading system upside down and launched the Compulsory Deposit Scheme requiring most taxpayers to deposit a part of their income with the government at a nominal rate of interest.

There was considerable disenchantment over the Budget initiatives and criticism of many of its proposals. The proverbial last straw on the camel's back was perhaps the outcome of three Lok Sabha by-elections held that year and three stalwarts from the Opposition camp defeating Congress candidates in each of them. The three stalwarts were Acharya Kripalani, Rammanohar Lohia and Minoo Masani.

It was at that point that Kamaraj made his historic proposal to Nehru. He suggested that too many senior leaders of the Congress party had been occupied with government responsibilities for many years and had as a result lost touch with the people and their concerns. It was time, therefore, to re-energize the Congress organization. And his suggestion was that Central ministers and chief ministers belonging to the Congress party should submit their resignations so that they could devote themselves to strengthening the party organization, while those who were working for the party could be inducted into the governments at the Centre and in the states.

Morarji Desai had a different understanding of who was the true proposer of the plan to strengthen the Congress party by this swapping of roles between party functionaries and those in government as Central ministers and chief ministers. According to Desai,[20] it was Biju Patnaik who germinated the idea in Nehru's mind when the two met in June 1963 in Kashmir. Patnaik was the chief minister of Orissa at that time and also enjoyed close friendly relations with Nehru. A few days later, in early July, Kamaraj broached the same idea with Nehru, who promptly accepted the need for such a plan in principle and indeed suggested that he himself should step down and refocus his energies towards rebuilding the party organization. This was vehemently opposed by Kamaraj and the few senior Congress leaders with whom this idea was discussed. Kamaraj was reported to have said: 'No, Panditji, you are unique, you must remain Prime Minister.'[21] Nehru did not insist on his own resignation after that and the Kamaraj Plan was focused on the resignation of only Central ministers and state chief ministers.

In his discussions with Nehru on the Kamaraj Plan, Desai suggested an alternative approach. The finance minister argued that if Nehru decided to choose the people who would be asked to give up their ministerial assignments and work for the party, the prime minister would face a lot of criticism for having randomly decided to deprive some of their ministerial privileges. Instead, Nehru should be framing a set of criteria based on performance, integrity, need and utility to decide which ministers could be assigned the responsibility of strengthening the Congress party. The rationale for this alternative approach, according to Desai, was that the Central ministry as well as ministries in many state governments could do with fewer ministers, which would also go a long way in reducing the size of the government and which would conform to the austerity measures needed to be adopted at that time. Desai told the prime minister that if he were to draw up a list of ministers who, based on these criteria, could be asked to strengthen the party, there would be no such charges of favouritism or any allegation against him. Nehru and a few of the senior colleagues in the government did not agree with Desai's suggestion. Soon after that, Nehru visited Hyderabad and held another round of consultations with Kamaraj and Chidambaram Subramaniam, who was then the Union minister for steel and mines. By the third week of August, Nehru convened a special meeting of the All-India Congress Committee where the Kamaraj Plan was approved and a working committee was set up to give effect to it. Desai remained aloof and was not included in the deliberations that the working committee would hold. According to Desai, the working committee consisted of the prime minister and senior Congress leaders, including Subramaniam, Lal Bahadur Shastri, Gulzarilal Nanda, Indira Gandhi and Kamaraj. Desai wrote to Nehru making it clear that he would abide by the Kamaraj Plan and accept whatever decision the working committee made. He would also send in his resignation as and when directed to.

A series of developments that took place in the course of the next few days convinced Desai that one of the many objectives of the Kamaraj Plan was to side-line him at the Centre and dilute his chances of staking a claim to succeed Nehru as and when that situation would arise. Nehru was not keeping well; he was seventy-three, and there was speculation as to who would succeed him at the helm of the government. Desai was a clear contender for the top job, but if he were side-lined now he would no longer be in the reckoning.

Just two days before the crucial working committee meeting that was to discuss the Kamaraj Plan, Shastri met Desai in the Lok Sabha lobby and volunteered a piece of advice that surprised Desai no end. Shastri said he had decided to resign from the Union Cabinet but that Desai need not quit the government. Desai was intrigued; he suspected that some political game was being played. He told Shastri that he had not yet spoken to Nehru and he would like to check it out for himself. The next day, Desai met Nehru. The meeting was short and quite abrupt. Nehru told Desai that they (Nehru and Desai) were the only senior leaders in the government who had not yet decided to send in their resignations and that one of the two would have to give up office. Since everyone at the AICC session had suggested that he (Nehru) should not quit as part of the plan, there was no option but for Desai to be relieved of his ministerial responsibility, Nehru said. The prime minister also informed the finance minister that, along with him, three other ministers would be dropped. They were Jagjivan Ram, Lal Bahadur Shastri and Bezawada Gopala Reddy. Desai suggested that asking Gopala Reddy to quit would not serve any purpose because he was no good as an organization person.

The meeting between Nehru and Desai was significant for another reason. Desai said he had no problems in giving up his office, but made the request that his successor should not tinker with or scrap any of the major policy decisions that he as the finance minister had taken after due consultation with Nehru. He also raised the sensitive issue of how Nehru's style of operation had not led to a relationship of trust between him and the prime minister. Desai even asked Nehru if he had any prejudice against him. Nehru was obviously upset to hear all this. He denied that he harboured any such prejudice against Desai. At this point, Desai asked Nehru how his letter to him on Krishna Menon's work as the defence minister had reached the former defence minister, but that he (Desai) would never get to know what Menon had told the prime minister about him. Before he left that tense meeting, Desai argued that Nehru's operational style had created groupism within the Cabinet and that he should abandon that kind of functioning. With those words, he told the prime minister that he was quitting the government.

A day later, the working committee met and took the decision to drop half a dozen Cabinet ministers. Desai's suggestion to Nehru on excluding Gopala Reddy from the Kamaraj Plan was ignored. The six ministers to be dropped were: Morarji Desai (finance minister), Lal Bahadur Shastri (home minister), Jagjivan Ram (transport & communications minister), S.K. Patil (food & agriculture minister), K.L. Shrimali (education minister) and Bezawada Gopala Reddy (information & broadcasting minister). Several chief ministers had also resigned as part of the Kamaraj Plan. They included Kumaraswamy Kamaraj (Madras), Bhagwantrao Mandloi (Madhya Pradesh), Binodanand Jha (Bihar), Chandra Bhanu Gupta (Uttar Pradesh) and Biju Patnaik (Orissa).

A minor tussle took place over the choice of Desai's successor. Chidambaram Subramaniam was keen on stepping into Desai's shoes. But Nehru preferred T.T. Krishnamachari, who had to leave the finance ministry in the wake of the Mundhra scandal in February 1958. Krishnamachari had been rehabilitated a few months earlier, in November 1962, with his induction as a minister without portfolio, initially, and later as a minister for economic and defence coordination, a ministry created primarily for him and which was wound up after he returned to the finance ministry following the Kamaraj Plan. Krishnamachari had made a request that since his earlier stint had begun in August and had ended in a controversy, he would prefer to take charge of the ministry in September 1963. Desai, therefore, stepped down as the finance minister in the afternoon of the last day of August and Krishnamachari took charge on the first day of September.

Lal Bahadur Shastri was brought back into the Cabinet in January 1964, paving the way for his nomination as the next prime minister after Nehru's death in May 1964. Desai also lost the battle for gaining a key position in the Congress party. Soon after the implementation of the Kamaraj Plan, the Madras leader was made the president of the Congress, with the support of Nehru and other regional leaders of the party like Atulya Ghosh and S.K. Patil.

Desai's exit, however, did not completely snap his links with the finance ministry. Just about four years later, Desai would enter North Block once again as the finance minister, but under a different prime minister and more trying circumstances.

T.T. Krishnamachari (Finance Minister, 1963–1965)

Clouded by Differences with Shastri

Krishnamachari's political banishment after he had to resign as the finance minister in the wake of the Mundhra scandal in 1958 did not last long. General elections were held in February 1962. In the new government Nehru formed, T.T. Krishnamachari regained his place in the Union Cabinet, first as a minister without portfolio and later as a minister for economic co-ordination. In 1963, Krishnamachari was back again as India's finance minister. Why it took so long for Nehru to offer Krishnamachari the finance ministry immediately after the general elections of 1962 shows how even for a powerful prime minister with a complete single-party majority in the Lok Sabha, choosing his own finance minister was not as easy a task as many might believe. The first hurdle for Nehru was the fact that Morarji Desai, a senior and powerful Congress leader, had been the finance minister before the general elections. To replace Desai as the finance minister would have required a strong reason—charges of either of some financial impropriety or of poor performance on his part. Neither of these charges could be levelled against Desai. Thus, Nehru broached the idea of splitting the finance ministry, expecting Desai and Krishnamachari to handle the two different sections of the finance ministry. When Nehru mooted this idea with Desai, the latter flatly rejected the suggestion, adding that if the prime minister wished to split the finance ministry he would not be interested in handling any section of the bifurcated ministry.

Thus on 19 March 1962, Nehru wrote to Krishnamachari saying that it would not be possible for him to offer him the finance portfolio, but that he would like him in the Union Cabinet 'in charge of an important portfolio, and for . . . general advice and help in the Cabinet'.[1] A few letters were exchanged between Krishnamachari and Nehru on this matter, which once again underlined the deep bond and affection between the two. When Krishnamachari told Nehru that he was not interested in being rehabilitated with a ministerial portfolio, the prime minister was a little upset. He wrote back to say that Krishnamachari did not 'require rehabilitation' so far as the prime minister was concerned. A few months later, in June 1962, Krishnamachari was inducted into the Union Cabinet as a minister without portfolio. By November the same year, Nehru created a new ministry for Krishnamachari—the ministry for economic and defence coordination. The ministry under Krishnamachari would be responsible for coordinating policy responses in a vast range of sectors like the railways, mines, energy, including power, irrigation and transportation. What's more, Krishnamachari was made head of the Cabinet Committee on Economic Affairs (CCEA), a post which was earlier held by the finance minister. Thus, Desai as the finance minister would be part of the CCEA, but its chairman would be Krishnamachari.

In his fourteen-month tenure, first as a minister without portfolio for about five months and then as the minister for economic and defence coordination for the rest of the time, Krishnamachari was responsible for many decisions, including creation of a central authority for ensuring effective distribution of coal, a more efficient system of railway transportation, greater stress on energy planning, including better use of natural gas, and increase in production at ordnance factories. But there was also no doubt that the ministry for economic and defence coordination was created primarily to accommodate Krishnamachari. This became evident when Desai stepped down as the finance minister under the Kamaraj Plan. The Kamaraj Plan was rolled out in an apparent bid to use the services of veteran Congress leaders in charge of different ministries for strengthening the party organization, requiring these senior ministers to quit their ministerial jobs. Desai was one of the senior leaders who lost their ministership under the Kamaraj Plan. The man who succeeded Desai in the finance ministry was T.T. Krishnamachari. That happened on 1 September 1963, the same day the newly created ministry for economic and defence coordination was abolished.

TTK's Second Term as FM

The Indian economy posed many challenges when Krishnamachari assumed charge as the finance minister in his second term. The gap between the end of his first term in August 1958 and the beginning of his second term in September 1963 was just five years. But a lot had happened during this period—the launch of a less ambitious Third Plan after the downsizing of the previous one because of the obvious constraints of resources, the Chinese aggression shattering the confidence of a young nation in managing its foreign policy and neighbours, and a decline in the fortunes of the Indian economy. Growth had been fluctuating—from a high of 7.6 per cent in 1958–59 to 2.2 per cent in the following year, before recovering to 7.1 per cent in 1960–61 and then clocking a relatively low 3.1 per cent and 2.1 per cent in 1961–62 and 1962–63, respectively. The finance minister in this period, Morarji Desai, had steered the economy competently, but a few of his proposals like the gold control rules and the compulsory deposit schemes had left their scars on the economy.

On taking charge of the finance ministry in September 1963, just about six months after Morarji Desai had presented the Budget for 1963–64, Krishnamachari had to contend with the many deficiencies in the way the Third Plan had been implemented. These deficiencies had already been brought out into the open during the just-concluded mid-term appraisal of the Third Plan (1961–66). The demand on the Union government for providing more financial allocations for development as also for defence was on the rise, for understandable reasons. A marked decline in the performance of private industries was no less worrying than the growing constraints on account of a shortage of resources and foreign exchange.

Politically also, the situation was hardly inspiring. Nehru's health was on the decline. Opposition parties like the Swatantra Party were growing in strength. At a personal level, Krishnamachari had become acutely conscious of the fact that just a few years ago his name had figured in the Mundhra scandal, as a result of which he had to tender his resignation from the finance ministry. Indeed, in one of his speeches in Parliament, Krishnamachari spoke like a man who was conscious of his past. In a debate in May 1965, he said:

I think that Parliamentary democracy can be worked without personal mudslinging . . . If we disagree, I do not think there is any need for me to question another's bona fides, or for any other to question mine. I do not want to claim that I am a paragon of virtue. But I believe that I have lived a life of which I need not be ashamed. There is nothing that I have done – the House will forgive me for saying – in my past ever since I became an adolescent and adult, of which I should be ashamed; I have not taken any man's money.

Even before Krishnamachari could present his first Budget as the finance minister in his second term, he had to deal with at least four important issues. One pertained to a non-official motion moved in Parliament on nationalization of banks. In spite of the Nehru government's support for a socialistic pattern of development, Krishnamachari rejected that idea quite comprehensively. Pointing out that already the nationalized banks in the country had accounted for about a third of the working funds of the entire banking system, Krishnamachari said that the need was to extend the operations and reach of the public-sector banks to more areas and improve their service quality. The finance minister made it clear that the additional benefits from further nationalization of banks would not be significant. In any case, the provisions in the existing laws on banking already allowed the government to guide bank lending to the desired segments, and any lending to sectors which the government believed was undesirable could be kept under check, the finance minister had argued. Little could he then anticipate the rapid developments that would take place in the coming years. In less than six years, the government would embark on a massive bank nationalization drive, leading to the takeover of fourteen privately run banks in the country.

The second policy issue Krishnamachari tackled without any delay was the controversial Gold Control Order that Morarji Desai had introduced in his Budget a year earlier. In the wake of the foreign exchange crisis, accentuated by the border war with China in 1962, Desai had got the Gold Control Act legislated in 1962. The new law led to the recall of all gold loans issued by banks and banned forward trading in gold as well as production of gold jewellery above 14 carat. The objective was to check gold smuggling and use of the yellow metal for unproductive purposes. However, the new regime had dealt a big blow to the livelihood of thousands of goldsmiths and jewellers. There was an urgent need for policy correctives. While acknowledging the need for such a gold control regime, Krishnamachari had announced a set of policy changes that would address the financial woes of the goldsmiths and jewellers. Thus, the government decided to issue licences to self-employed goldsmiths, subject to conditions and on payment of a nominal fee. These licences also would allow them to convert the existing gold ornaments in excess of 14-carat purity into ornaments below the permissible level. It was also decided to make available a limited stock of primary gold of up to 14 carat to goldsmiths and jewellers.

Krishnamachari's third policy intervention was with regard to a major change he brought about in the Compulsory Deposit Scheme that Morarji Desai had introduced through a law in May 1963. The provisions of this law required a compulsory deposit to be made with the government by the following categories of individuals and entities: persons paying land revenue, income tax payers, holders of immovable properties in urban areas assessed for tax but not paying income tax, employees of central and state governments, local authorities, companies in the private and public sectors and non-government companies and dealers. The rates at which such deposits were to be made were specified under the rules of the scheme, and income tax payers could avail of tax adjustments against such deposits. The objective of the scheme was unexceptionable, as it was aimed at helping the government to raise resources to fund its development plans. But there was widespread criticism of the scheme. Krishnamachari made a significant change by restricting its scope only to income tax payers, which meant that all other categories earlier included under the scheme got a big relief.

Krishnamachari became quite popular with these two interventions. His earlier speech in Parliament to reject the non-official motion for nationalizing more banks must have also pleased Indian industry. But his amendment of the Gold Control Order and reduction of the scope of the Compulsory Deposit Scheme came in for praise from top industrialists. Industry leader Ghanshyamdas Birla said: 'Both actions taken by you have brought sunshine in the hearts of people. It is creating a new psychology and a new hope . . . Lots of loose ends have still to be tied up, and plenty of garbage to be cleared up. But hope is inspired that it will be done.' Nani

Palkhivala, eminent lawyer and a sharp observer of government Budgets, said 'there was a blast of fresh air' in the fiscal policies.[2]

The Unit Trust of India

Krishnamachari's fourth big move was launch of the Unit Trust of India. Just before that, in November 1963, he had deepened the general insurance market by asking the Life Insurance Corporation to enter into the general insurance business. Life insurance had been nationalized in 1956, but general insurance was not. The entry of LIC into general insurance paved the way for the nationalization of general insurance, which eventually took place in 1972, under a different finance minister.

But the launch of UTI was a major move of Krishnamachari's. The idea of an investment trust that could channel people's savings into investments in the stock market had been endorsed long ago, by the A.D. Shroff Committee on Finance for the Private Sector, which submitted its report in 1954. Shroff was a widely respected industrialist, banker and economist, whose report helped clinch the issue for the government to go ahead with the formation of an investment trust. Even though it took ten years before the idea fructified, the fact is that the news that Pakistan had almost completed the formalities to set up a unit trust had helped speed up the process of seeking the necessary approvals from the government to set up what later came to be known as the Unit Trust of India.

What did the Shroff Committee recommend? The objective behind the setting up of investment trusts, according to the Committee, was to promote industrial investments in the country. Sir Benegal Rama Rau, the RBI Governor at that time, was not greatly enthused by the idea, although he acknowledged that investment in stocks through units would help small investors, who had little knowledge and understanding of how the stock market behaved. But there was no endorsement from the RBI of the idea of setting up an investment trust with the support of the government. When Krishnamachari had become the finance minister in his first stint in 1956, he had explored the idea but could not pursue it after his involvement in the Mundhra scandal and eventual resignation in February 1958. At that time, only two investment companies were in operation in the private sector—the Industrial Investment Trust, associated with the stock-broking firm of Premchand Roychand, and the Investment Corporation of India, which was controlled by the Tatas. These two entities had large and diversified portfolios of securities at that time. However, in the early 1960s, the idea of a state-sector investment trust gained traction as the government began recognizing the need for stepping up private investments by industry to supplement the initiatives on public investment and industrialization under the Second Plan. What aided the move on this front was also the fact that the controversy over the Mundhra scandal had died down and the government did not fear any adverse political reaction to any such move.

The man behind the move was none other than T.T. Krishnamachari. He had joined the Nehru Cabinet, initially as a minister without portfolio in June 1962 and later, from November 1962, as the minister for economic and defence coordination. He put his entire weight behind the proposal and sent it to Nehru, who in turn forwarded it to Morarji Desai, who was then the finance minister. The first time the government made public its intention to set up an investment trust in the state sector was during the Roy Chand debate in Parliament after the presentation of the Union Budget for 1963–64. That was Desai's last Budget before he would resign under the Kamaraj Plan. Desai told the Lok Sabha that the government would set up an investment trust, which should provide the 'common man a means to acquire a share in the widening prosperity based on steady industrial growth'. The proposed trust, Desai, assured the members of the Lok Sabha, would also have the twin virtues of providing security to investors and ensuring reasonable returns.

At around the same time, the Reserve Bank of India was also working on what could be the contours of a state-owned investment trust. By July 1963, the RBI sent to the government a draft bill called the Unit Investment Trust of India Bill. The proposed trust was to have an initial capital base of Rs 5 crore, half of which was to be subscribed to by the RBI and the remaining half by the Life Insurance Corporation, the State Bank of India and its subsidiaries, the Industrial Finance Corporation, the Industrial Credit and Investment Corporation and scheduled banks. To be headed by a chairman, the proposed trust was to have a six-member board of trustees. The draft bill also envisaged tax concessions to be granted by the government to improve the attractiveness of the units as a form of investment.

Krishnamachari took charge of the finance ministry in September 1963. Within a month, the government got the RBI plan discussed internally with the help of a committee of secretaries set up for that purpose. The World Bank too had agreed to depute an expert on unit trusts to hold discussions with the government. The Secretaries Committee accepted the broad contours of the structure of the unit trust, as proposed by the RBI. Industry chambers' suggestion that similar unit trusts also be allowed in the private sector was summarily rejected by the Secretaries Committee, on the ground that privately owned unit trusts could be owned or taken over by managing agency houses or business groups. Two other reasons were cited for the rejection—that more such entities would require creation of a regulatory body for their supervision and that they would create competition for the government-owned trust for a small chunk of business, thereby undermining the business prospects of all such trusts.

The Committee of Secretaries was opposed to the idea also because it would mean extension of tax concessions for the proposed trust to the private-sector bodies too—which it was not comfortable with at all since this would mean special tax benefits for investments by entities that would not come under the supervision of Parliament. This essentially meant the creation of a public-sector monopoly in the business of channelling retail investments into the stock markets through units—a monopoly that would be broken after almost three decades, coinciding with the launch of economic reforms in the 1990s. The World Bank too was unhappy with the idea of a unit trust only in the public sector, but the government went ahead with it even though the bill provided that it would be run along business lines, like a company, and should not function like a department or like a statutory corporation.

On 26 November 1963, Krishnamachari introduced the bill to set up the Unit Trust of India. During the debate on the bill in Parliament, members did express fears that investments by the new company might benefit only large business houses or state-owned companies. But those fears were addressed by the finance minister. In response to the members' observations that the UTI bill would pave the way for a monopoly company in the public sector, Krishnamachari said the government would stay away from the investment policies of the Trust and it would not limit the holding of units by individuals. The bill was passed by the Lok Sabha

on 5 December and by the Rajya Sabha on 12 December. The President
gave his assent to the bill on 30 December and the Unit Trust of India
was formed on 1 February 1964 as an outfit of the RBI, under whose
regulatory and administrative control it would function.

Krishnamachari played a crucial role in appointing U.S. Bhatt as the
first chairman of the Unit Trust of India. Bhatt was apparently asked
by P.C. Bhattacharya, who was the RBI Governor at that time, who the
best candidates would be to head the proposed investment trust. Bhatt,
who was at that time the executive director of the Indian Investment
Centre, confessed to Bhattacharya that there were only two persons fit
for the role—Bhatt himself and H.T. Parekh, who at that time was the
general manager of ICICI. Bhattacharya told Bhatt that he too had the
same names in mind to head the new investment trust. But there was
a problem. G.L. Mehta, who headed both the India Investment Centre
and ICICI, was unwilling to relieve Bhatt. Krishnamachari stepped in and
persuaded Mehta to spare his services. UTI eventually had Bhatt as its first
chairman for about eight years—from its inception in 1964 to 1972.[3] The
first scheme of the UTI, US-64, was launched in July 1964 and Finance
Minister Krishnamachari inaugurated it.

Among the many contributions of Krishnamachari's in those early
years of the nation after Independence were the initiatives he took to build
institutions. He was somewhat like his prime minister, Jawaharlal Nehru,
in this area, with the difference being that his contributions were mostly
notable in the economic policy sphere. Even as a minister for commerce
and industry, Krishnamachari had proposed the setting up of an industrial
development corporation. In October 1954, thanks to Krishnamachari's
initiatives aimed at creating an institution to provide finance to industries
undertaking development activities in the areas of manufacture of capital
goods, machinery and equipment, the government had set up the National
Industrial Development Corporation, or NIDC. The new company in the
public sector, with an authorized capital of Rs 1 crore and a paid-up capital
of Rs 10 lakh, was also expected to set up new 'projects involving ancillary
linkages with the private sector'.[4] Less than a year later the government had
set up another financial institution—the Industrial Credit and Investment
Corporation of India or ICICI. This was an initiative of the then finance
minister, C.D. Deshmukh.

Birth of IDBI

As commerce and industry minister, Krishnamachari had also mooted the idea of an industrial development bank. That was in August 1953, but no follow-up action was taken once he left that ministry, and even after he joined the finance ministry in 1956, the idea remained dormant. Krishnamachari's logic for suggesting such an institution reflected the deep thinking that had gone behind the proposal. He was of the view that the task of industrial development must go beyond merely setting up a few public-sector companies or providing financial assistance to help the private sector to set up enterprises. The way forward, according to him, was to create a financial institution that could help private enterprises set up more industries in different sectors of the economy. In some cases, such an institution could even set up industries jointly with the private sector. The proposed institution was also expected to reduce the pressure on the government to extend finances for development projects. Since the government was already facing criticism for the rise in deficit financing, a practice that was being increasingly frowned upon, the new institution was seen as an instrument by which the financing pressures on the government would be relieved.

Keeping this in mind, Krishnamachari had proposed the setting up of the Industrial Development Bank of India, or IDBI, to provide help to private-sector projects by way of expertise and financial assistance. By the time Krishnamachari had returned to the finance ministry on his second stint, the idea of IDBI was converted into reality. In his Budget for 1964–65, he said:

> The House will . . . be considering the Bill for the establishment of a Development Bank, which is intended to make an additional contribution to the resources for the development of our industrial economy. Important and significant as these measures are, basically the resources for development are generated not entirely by the setting up of institutions such as these, but in the community through the savings that are made. One of the prime objectives of our economic and fiscal policy, therefore, must be to generate savings both in the hands of individuals and in the hands of corporate bodies.

India's Finance Ministers

This was the economic philosophy underpinning the creation of IDBI, which after the passage of the legislative bill came into being as a statutory body as a development financial institution on 1 July 1964. Inaugurating the IDBI on 3 July 1964, Krishnamachari gave an indication of the kind of role the government wanted it to play:

> The Development Bank will not only give fresh strength to the existing institutions – subscribing and purchasing their stocks, shares, bonds or debentures, and guaranteeing underwriting obligations assumed by them – but it will also enter new fields and set up new standards of constructive and imaginative endeavour . . . I hope the Development Bank will build up its working traditions in such a way that the very fact that the Development Bank is financing a project will inspire public confidence in its soundness, reliability and perfectibility.[5]

IDBI continued to be regarded as a public financial institution under the provisions of Section 4A of the Companies Act. That arrangement continued till 2004, when IDBI was converted into a bank.

Krishnamachari Presents Last Budget under Nehru

By the time Krishnamachari rose in the Lok Sabha on 29 February 1964 to present the Budget for 1964–65, the state of the Indian economy had stabilized significantly. Early indications available to the finance minister showed that India's gross domestic product (GDP) would clock a growth rate of a little over 5 per cent in 1963–64, the current account deficit would be lower at 2 per cent of GDP, down from 2.25 per cent in the previous year, and the country's foreign exchange reserves would make a marginal recovery, from $620 million in 1962–63 to $642 million by the end of 1963–64. The big worry would be inflation, which would rise disconcertingly to 9 per cent by the end of the financial year of 1964, after having been tamed to below 4 per cent as at end March 1963.

A key policy initiative Krishnamachari took in his Budget was on the kind of control or supervision the government should exercise over concentration of economic power and monopolies. This was a mindset that would be fully reflected a few years later with the legislation of the Monopolies and Restrictive Trade Practices Act in 1969. But the seeds of such controls were sown by Krishnamachari in his Budget for 1964–65. He told Parliament:

> I should like to say a word about the equally important point that we must not, in the process, allow concentration of economic power and growth of monopolies. The question, which we have to consider is, how we are to achieve this objective consistently with our concern to see that genuine and desirable development is not stifled. For a proper formulation of our policies and attitudes in this respect, Government feels that there is need for an impartial and objective enquiry so as to bring the relevant data out in the open.

Laying out this logic of the government thinking, he announced the setting up of a commission under the Commission of Enquiries Act, to examine monopolies and concentration of economic power in the Indian economy. What happened in the next five years, under a different dispensation, is a matter of history.

The Budget for 1964–65 contained only a few major taxation proposals. On the indirect taxes front, several items of common consumption were exempted from excise duty, and the customs duty changes were marginal. On the direct taxes front, some adjustments were made in the manner in which the super-profits tax was to be levied on companies. Some minor changes in the norms for levy of wealth tax, estate duty and gift tax were also announced by the finance minister in the Budget.

In keeping with his tradition of introducing new taxes, as he did in his previous Budgets, Krishnamachari introduced yet another new tax, to be levied on amounts distributed by companies on their capital. He argued that the government needed to discourage 'dissipation' of resources in the form of higher dividends and, therefore, proposed a tax of 7.5 per cent on the 'amounts distributed as dividend on capital other than preference capital'. Companies which had to distribute dividends compulsorily were exempted from this tax. Similarly, new companies, which had to wait for some years before declaring dividends, were also exempted from the dividend tax for five years from the year of their first declaration of dividend, as long as the dividend amount was not more than 10 per cent of capital. What Krishnamachari began with that Budget became a widely practised instrument of tax collection by finance ministers in the years to come. The idea of taxing dividends continued to be embraced by all of them, although the manner in which the tax would be collected underwent changes from time to time. While for some years, the dividends were collected from the shareholders, relieving the companies from paying the tax, on other occasions the tax was to be paid by the companies, making the task of dividend tax collection relatively easy.

Krishnamachari was not content with his earlier move of restricting coverage of the Compulsory Deposit Scheme only to income tax payers. His Budget for 1964–65 retained that relief, but like the proverbial sting in the tail, he introduced an Annuity Deposit Scheme to replace the Compulsory Deposit Scheme, which would operate at the income level of above Rs 15,000 per annum. In its nature, the new scheme was somewhat similar to the Compulsory Deposit Scheme that it purportedly sought to replace. The few changes meant some relief, but those hardly endeared the finance minister to income tax payers in the country. The compliments that Ghanshyam Das Birla and Nani Palkhivala had showered on Krishnamachari earlier in the year had come a bit too soon and it would be not be unreasonable to conclude that they might have wondered if they had praised the finance minister a bit prematurely.

The Last Budget from Krishnamachari

Less than three months after Krishnamachari's Budget for 1964–65, Prime Minister Jawaharlal Nehru breathed his last on 27 May 1964. Lal Bahadur Shastri succeeded Nehru.

Not surprisingly, Krishnamachari, in his Budget for 1965–66 began with paying tributes to the departed leader, who for seventeen long years 'dominated the Indian scene, giving meaning and substance to our aspirations as a nation'. Krishnamachari's next focus was the Plan. He reminded his colleagues in Parliament that the 1965–66 Budget was the last such exercise for the Third Five-year Plan, which would end by March 1966. He also announced that the Fourth Five-year Plan, due to begin from 1966, would 'involve large investments in the public and the private sector'. He underlined the need for maintaining an environment of financial and monetary stability, without which the necessary resources to finance the required investments could not be mobilized. The irony of these statements would dawn on the nation a few months later when, because of a series of adverse developments, the roll-out of the Fourth Plan would be deferred by three years and the interim period would have to make do with annual plans.

Indications of an economic crisis were already visible when Krishnamachari rose to present the 1965–66 Budget on 27 February 1965. While economic growth would be maintained at 7.6 per cent for the full year of 1964–65, inflation, based on the movement of the wholesale price index, would still remain high at 8.7 per cent, the current account deficit at Rs 656 crore would rise to 2.5 per cent of GDP, and with the widening trade deficit the country's foreign exchange reserves would decline to $524 million, a drop of over 18 per cent from the level at the end of March 1964.

In his Budget speech, Krishnamachari made no secret of the government's concern over the declining foreign exchange reserves. Referring to his earlier statement made on this issue on 17 February, Krishnamachari said: 'I would only underline the fact that our foreign exchange reserves have been depleted to such an extent that we are unable at present to withstand any small pressure on these reserves, without running into a critical situation.' The policy prescription the finance minister outlined to address these forex challenges is worth recounting here. At one level, he advocated the need for strengthening the foreign exchange reserves by a mix of measures to reduce the country's reliance on imports in many areas and roll out 'vigorous' export promotion measures to both bolster the reserves situation and to meet the import needs.

Indeed, the Budget for 1965–66 expanded the benefits extended to exporters. Already, duty drawback benefits were given to exporters by way of refund of customs and excise duties paid on export production. But Krishnamachari wanted the cost disadvantages arising out of railway freight and profit taxation too to be neutralized by expanding the scope of such benefits. In addition, he announced the launch of a scheme under which the Centre would issue tax credit certificates to exporters up to 15 per cent of the value of their exports. These tax credit certificates could be used for payment of taxes or even for refunds in cash 'to the extent that their value exceed(ed) tax liability'. There were also increases in the customs duty on a wide range of goods, and once again the stated objective was to promote domestic industry and conserve foreign exchange. Ironically, the policy had shifted towards promoting exports, but the instruments chosen were still not effective enough in improving the competitiveness of Indian exporters. Not surprisingly, these measures made little impact on India's trade deficit or on the foreign exchange reserves situation. In the next two to three years, India's trade deficit continued to hover between 2.2 and 2.5 per cent of GDP; its foreign exchange reserves stabilized at the prevailing levels but saw no significant improvement.

On the direct taxes front, Krishnamachari made small procedural changes for taxes to be paid by companies and broadly maintained the overall tax incidence on India Inc. at the prevailing rates. India's corporation tax rates had begun moving northwards from the 1960s—a trend that began hardening in the following years. A basic corporation tax rate of 40 per cent, prevailing in 1960, went up to 55 per cent in 1966. But in 1963–64, the principle of progression was introduced by levying a super-profits tax, which was later converted into a sur-tax on corporate income. Thus, moving past the 55 per cent basic rate of tax, the total burden on companies because of the sur-tax was as high as 71 per cent. There were, of course, many rebates and allowances that finance ministers introduced. But, going by a calculation made by G. Narayanan in an article published in *Economic & Political Weekly* in May 1967, the effective rate of tax on corporations was 38 per cent in 1960–61, 63 per cent in 1962–63 and 50.5 per cent in 1964–65.[6] In his Budget for 1965–66, Krishnamachari did not make any further changes in the corporation tax regime, apart from some minor adjustments to make the process of claiming rebates and allowances a little more easy.

For individual taxpayers, Krishnamachari had a special package of incentives and schemes. He restored the exemption from wealth tax for five years for equity investments in new industrial companies that would issue capital for the first time after 28 February 1965. He went in for a massive streamlining and simplification of the income tax structure for individuals. Even after these measures, the tax rates on individual incomes were quite high, but the reduction was significant. As a result, the highest marginal rate of tax on unearned incomes (mainly from investments and other sources like bank deposits, dividends, etc., unrelated to employment) came down from 88.12 per cent to 81.25 per cent. Similarly, the highest marginal rate on earned incomes (mainly salary or earnings from employment) dropped from 82.5 per cent to 74.75 per cent. This rate of taxation was still very high, though the finance minister assured Parliament by saying 'the peak taxation will be reached in respect of income above Rs 3 lakh of earned income and above Rs 70,000 of unearned income'. The suggestion was that the higher rates of taxation would be levied only on high-income earners. The existing concessions for estate duty and gift tax were also enlarged to remove hardships to the taxpayers.

Two other big announcements marked Krishnamachari's Budget for 1965–66 which, as subsequent events would unveil, turned out to be his last for the Union government. Both announcements were aimed at tackling the growth in unaccounted income and wealth in the economy. The finance minister was keen that after he had simplified the tax structure and reduced the rates, the taxpayers should be given an opportunity to disclose their concealed income and make a clean breast of their past evasions.

The first announcement pertained to the floatation of gold bonds. This was the second time in recent years that gold bonds were being issued. The first scheme had not evoked a good response. Thus, the new scheme was modified in one respect. 'In view of the increase in interest rates since the last issue was made, the new bonds will carry interest at 7 per cent per annum,' Krishnamachari said. Those who had subscribed to the earlier scheme were also entitled to the higher rate of interest from 1 April 1965. The modified gold bond scheme was to remain open for subscription only for three months, till the end of 31 May 1965. 'I would appeal to everyone who holds gold, either under declaration or otherwise, to subscribe to the new bonds to the maximum possible extent,' the finance minister exhorted the people, thereby betraying his eagerness to ensure that the modified scheme became a success.

The second announcement by Krishnamachari pertained to the launch of a scheme allowing voluntary disclosure of concealed income on payment of a penal rate of tax, but without attracting any prosecution for having flouted the tax laws earlier. The rationale for the scheme was the government's desire to attack and eliminate unaccounted incomes and wealth. Outlining the objectives and background of the proposed scheme, Krishnamachari said:

We have already taken a number of measures, apart from intensification of searches and the like, to encourage voluntary disclosures. Amounts so disclosed are being exempted from penalty. These measures have had some success in encouraging voluntary disclosures particularly from people who have comparatively small and medium incomes to disclose. Various suggestions have been made from time to time to encourage disclosures on a larger scale and to give an opportunity to those, who wish to turn a new leaf to do so without undue harassment. I have every hope that with the reduction in tax rates that I have already proposed the scope and incentive for tax evasion in future would be reduced.

Under the scheme, persons having undisclosed income could declare it with the relevant particulars and make a payment equivalent to 60 per cent of the amount declared to the Reserve Bank of India. The remaining 40 per cent of the declared income could be included in the taxpayer's accounts after intimating the income tax authorities of it. 'No further question of assessment in regard to the income so disclosed by this process will arise and the identity of the persons will not be revealed,' Krishnamachari explained. The scheme was kept open only for three months and was to end on 31 May 1965. To incentivize those who had concealed incomes to declare them under the scheme, the finance minister provided more rebates. A rebate of 5 per cent of the tax on all incomes declared—on which the penal tax was paid in the month of March itself— would be available, thus making the effective rate of taxation on such cases 57 per cent, instead of 60 per cent.

The finance minister was conscious of the moral hazard the scheme would cause for honest taxpayers. He said:

> I recognise that it is not at all an easy matter to devise a solution, which would at the same time be fair to people who have paid taxes honestly in the past and reasonable enough to encourage voluntary disclosures on an adequate scale on the part of those who wish now to be relieved of their past evasion . . . I can only hope that honest tax-payers will not be aggrieved by what I propose to do and that those who have been misled in the past would find in it reason enough to return to the path of civic responsibility.

Krishnamachari was completely mistaken in his faith. The scheme failed to elicit a decent response. The tax rate of 60 per cent was considered to be a deterrent even though immunity against legal action for having evaded taxes and full confidentiality were promised. Only about Rs 52 crore of undisclosed income or black money was declared, entailing for the government a tax revenue of Rs 29 crore, which was not small compared to the total annual income-tax collections that year. Encouraged by this, Krishnamachari came out with an amended income disclosure scheme to make it more attractive for tax evaders. On 9 August 1965, the finance minister unveiled before Parliament the contours of the amended scheme. The amended scheme was to be operational for a longer period—from 9 August to 31 March 1966. The tax was to be charged on the entire amount of disclosed income, to be treated as a single block, at the same rates that were prescribed for personal income tax at that time. The tax evaders were also permitted to pay the tax in instalments over a longer period of time, of about four years, subject to a down payment of 10 per cent of the tax due and the furnishing of a security for paying off the remaining tax dues. The promise of immunity and confidentiality was retained.

The amended scheme came in for a lot of criticism for giving tax evaders a sweet deal. Those who would declare their concealed income would not only pay tax at the prevailing rate on the entire amount, but the entire concealed income would be treated as a single block of income of one year and attract the duty prevailing that year. There was also the added attraction of the longer period of time within which the tax could be paid. Not surprisingly, the scheme was a success as it saw declarations at Rs 145 crore. But the tax collected was only Rs 20 crore as the tax evaders had gamed the system. Most of the disclosures were made in the names of spouses and children to take advantage of the lower slab rates. The amount of black money unearthed through the amended scheme was still small compared to the estimate of Rs 1000 crore of black money made by the Wanchoo Committee Report of 1971.[7] In spite of the failure of the voluntary income disclosure schemes of 1965 to unearth black money, many more finance ministers would fall prey to the lure of such schemes in subsequent years, only to meet a similar fate.

A Worsening Indian Economy

In the weeks that followed the presentation of Krishnamachari's Budget, the external account of the Indian economy got worse. India's foreign exchange reached a level of just Rs 100 crore, which was not even adequate to meet the seasonal fluctuations in the country's trade and foreign exchange payments, let alone provide a cushion against sudden adverse developments in the external account. Two factors principally contributed to India's foreign exchange woes—growing imports to meet commitments towards sustained industrial development and a marked deceleration in exports in the last two years. Exports in 1964–65 had remained stagnant at around Rs 800 crore, the level obtained in the previous year. Worse, exports in the first three months of 1965–66 fell by almost 6 per cent to Rs 185 crore. Predictably, the government had cracked down on imports, staggered payments against imports, continued the export incentive scheme to promote exports and announced a tax credit scheme for a number of export items. These measures had some positive effects on the country's balance of payments situation, but the government was equally conscious that it could not allow complacency to set in.

Krishnamachari was also aware that the continuance of the restrictive measures he had introduced in the wake of the foreign exchange crisis would have an adverse impact on growth. What became critical, therefore, was to quickly take the necessary steps by which imports could be liberalized soon and the support of friendly countries could be secured for financial assistance. The long-term goals were to increase exports so that a liberal import policy could be sustained and the country's debt repayment burden met. Sufficient attention also needed to be paid to the inflationary situation in the country. All these factors—increased exports, easier flow of financial support from abroad, a liberal import policy and a moderate inflation rate—were critical to help the government mobilize the necessary resources for sustaining a higher level of investment and for improving the level of productivity.

With the end of the Third Five-year Plan in March 1966, Krishnamachari also recognized the need for taking preparatory steps for launching the Fourth Plan from April 1966. The government was unhappy with its own performance in implementing the Third Plan. After a reasonable performance in terms of growth during the Second Plan period (1956–1961), when the economy staged an annual growth rate of 4.3 per cent against the targeted 4.5 per cent, execution of the Third Plan (1961–1966) had run into several headwinds. The war with China in 1962 had imposed extra pressure on the planners to allocate more for defence and the Indian Army. And closer to the end of Third Plan period, India would be engaged in another war—this time with Pakistan in September 1965. Within months of the presentation of the Budget for 1965–66, the monsoon failed in India and all of Krishnamachari's rosy forecasts on agricultural output were coming to naught. A drought followed. Food grain output that year would decline by 19 per cent to 72 million tonnes only. The country's gross domestic product or GDP would contract by 3.7 per cent. Wholesale prices would rise by 7.6 per cent.

Not surprisingly, the outcome of the Third Plan was rather unflattering. The annual growth rate achieved in the Third Plan period was just 2.4 per cent, while its ambitious target was 5.6 per cent. By August 1965, although border tensions had begun to build up, the war with Pakistan was yet to begin. But the economy had started showing signs of strain. Perhaps sensing the imminent decline in India's economic fortunes, Krishnamachari went before Parliament on 9 August 1965 and referred to the need for more steps to address the concerns arising out of falling foreign exchange reserves. At the same time, he outlined the challenges of raising more resources for implementation of the Fourth Plan from next April, without of course revealing the extent of the poor performance of the ongoing Third Five-Year Plan.

Indeed, the Planning Commission had by then made a tentative recommendation for aiming at a total outlay of Rs 21,500 crore for the Fourth Plan, out of which Rs 19,000 crore would be for investments and the remaining amount for meeting current revenue needs. This was a hugely ambitious target, representing a 90 per cent increase over the outlay for the Third Plan. Just how ambitious it was could be gauged from the fact that the Third Plan outlay saw a much lower increase of 46 per cent over the outlay of the Second Plan. The Fourth Plan projections were significant for another reason. The proposed share of the public sector in the Fourth Plan outlay projections increased substantially from its share in the Third Plan. Yet, Prime Minister Lal Bahadur Shastri had underlined the need for meeting this huge increase in investment outlay after ensuring that inflationary financing was completely avoided. This also meant that adequate steps would have to be taken to generate adequate internal resources to finance the higher outlay for the next Plan. A continued focus on agriculture, as also on industrial projects, was advocated in the proposed Fourth Plan. But for meeting the huge outlay for creating such capacities, resources were needed. Since almost 88 per cent of the proposed outlay for the Fourth Plan was for the public sector, the government had to examine ways in which it could mobilize those resources.

A Package Bigger than the Budget

The spectre of widening deficit financing also loomed large before the government. The Reserve Bank of India had hardened its views on the permissible deficit financing level that the Centre could be allowed. The RBI Governor, P.C. Bhattacharya, sent a note to the prime minister in June 1965, underlining the need for eliminating or at least reducing the deficit financing, even if that meant a slowing down of economic activities like the setting up of new projects in the state sector. The Governor warned that without a check on deficit financing, the alternative would be deflation later—a development with serious repercussions for the economy. Indeed, the actual deficit in 1964–65 was wider than what was projected earlier. This became known when the 1965–66 Budget was presented by Krishnamachari in February 1965. Recognizing these developments, Prime Minister Shastri wrote a letter to his finance minister in June asking him to take early steps to revise downwards the outlay for some major items of expenditure, which could offset the likely shortfall in revenues during the year.

It was in this context that Krishnamachari outlined his revenue-raising plan before Parliament on 9 August 1965. He said:

> The additional efforts at resource mobilisation that we might adopt therefore at this stage have to serve a number of objectives. Apart from contributing to the objective of raising resources for growth without inflation, these measures must be consistent with the broad objectives and priorities of the Plan. They must, in other words, take into account the emphasis we wish to place on agriculture and on higher productivity all round. They must also subserve the paramount objective of giving

the maximum possible encouragement to the domestic production of machinery and materials. The measures that I propose to announce today have been designed in keeping with all these considerations.

What he announced that day was bigger than even the annual Budgets would usually propose. A hike in customs duty on a wide range of items, including machinery, industrial raw materials like prime steel and non-ferrous metals, and consumer goods was to fetch Krishnamachari additional revenue of about Rs 119 crore in the full year. The apparent objective of the increase in import duties was to give a boost to domestic industry, resulting in import substitution and reduction in the demand for foreign exchange for imports. Those were the years of promotion of import substitution. In a bid to encourage domestic industry, development rebates for investments were also enhanced. An increase in excise duty on petroleum products followed, raising the retail prices of petrol and diesel. Excise duty on steel and pig iron too was raised. The total additional excise mop-up was estimated at Rs 54 crore.

Measured by the fiscal impact of Krishnamachari's announcements, this was like a mini-Budget. The finance minister himself confessed his 'proposals represent(ed) a formidable fare for a supplementary Budget'. The annual additional revenues to be raised by Krishnamachari were estimated at over Rs 170 crore, after adjustments. This was huge, compared with the 1965–66 Budget Krishnamachari had unveiled a few months ago, entailing a revenue loss of about Rs 30 crore due to concessions on the indirect taxes front and a revenue concession of Rs 43 crore on account of direct tax reliefs.

A month later, India was involved in a war with Pakistan on its Western borders. The Indian economy began going downhill, not just because of the impact of the war but also due to the series of new taxes levied in Krishnamachari's mini-Budget of August.

End of the TTK Era

Quite apart from the deteriorating economic conditions in the country, another deterioration taking place at the same time was far more worrying. Krishnamachari's relations with the new prime minister, Lal Bahadur Shastri, were showing early signs of stress. They began to be evident initially from the manner in which differences between the finance ministry and other key economic ministries began cropping up with fair regularity. Unlike in the past, Krishnamachari was often at pains to explain his stance to the new prime minister and secure his support in resolving those differences. The commerce ministry had insisted on grant of advance licences to permit exporters freer access to imports. The food and agriculture ministry had made a plea for increased allocation of foreign exchange to help it import fertilizers and set up factories to produce them at home. Krishnamachari recognized the need for higher imports, as also for increased allocation of foreign exchange for fertilizer imports or for setting up fertilizer plants. But his hands were tied as the country was going through an acute foreign exchange crisis, and he could not accept those requests. Complicating the finance minister's position was the growing demand from states asking for more resources to help them tide over their financial constraints. In the good old days, when Nehru was the prime minister, Krishnamachari would go across to Teen Murti House and sort out such issues through a candid discussion. Not that Krishnamachari would clinch the issues in his favour all the time, but he had the satisfaction of having poured his heart out and that Nehru had given him a patient hearing. Krishnamachari ceased to enjoy this comfort of access and consultation over critical economic issues after Shastri became the prime minister. Instead, each and every issue would be escalated to the Union Cabinet for discussion. Krishnamachari had few friends in the Cabinet and he had to often agree to allocate resources to certain ministries even though in terms of priority and urgency they figured quite low on the list.

Krishnamachari's differences with Shastri also arose because of the proposal to devalue the Indian currency. While Shastri had been convinced by his officers on the need to devalue the Indian rupee and undertake trade policy reforms, including reduction in import duties and other discretionary controls, Krishnamachari had serious reservations about such a policy approach. S. Bhoothalingam, who was a senior Secretary in the government at that time, wrote in his memoirs:

It was at this time I began to think seriously of the possibility of a devaluation. And strange as it may seem, the dual personality of TTK stood in the way. He was I can say even today intellectually quite convinced, but because of the political side of his personality he would not agree to it. He would go along with me 90 per cent of the way and after that he would quickly turn round and say, 'You can call it what you like, but for heaven's sake, don't use the word devaluation.'[8]

What added to Krishnamachari's political discomfiture was his past. Krishnamachari knew the requirements of business and industry, as he had himself run a successful business before giving that up and taking up politics as his vocation. But once he was in politics, and particularly after he began holding political offices, he severed all his connections with the businesses he had run. But his extended family was in business. In October 1964, the Shastri government had initiated a move to prepare a code of conduct for ministers. Krishnamachari had not hesitated to offer his views, which were a little different from those of many of his ministerial colleagues. Like all ministers, he had declared all his assets as part of that code of conduct. But he raised a relevant question: How could any minister compel any adult member of his family, over whom he had no control, to furnish details of his or her businesses and assets? Krishnamachari was saying that as a minister he would not be taking any decisions on businesses with which he was connected through family. But a tricky situation would arise with regard to the question of how a minister should deal with his past connections with industry or about friends and family members who would be engaged in businesses. Krishnamachari's family had close relations with the family of T.V. Sundaram Iyengar, who ran a successful business group. At one point, Krishnamachari said: 'If a minister has to be put in a Procrustean bed, either you compel him to leave the job if he is truthful, or, in the alternative, make him tell lies.'[9]

This explanation from him was initially accepted, but created a storm later. Accusations began to be made against Krishnamachari on account of his business connections through his family. This was not the first time that Krishnamachari had to face such a situation. Even in April 1954, when he was the minister for commerce and industry, a communist leader and a member of the Lok Sabha at the time, A.K. Gopalan, had written to Nehru complaining that an import licence had been issued to TTK & Sons. Nehru had promptly sent the letter of accusation to Krishnamachari, who clarified his role in the matter to his prime minister. There indeed had been a decision to grant an import licence to TTK & Sons, but that decision was taken completely independently by the Chief Controller of Imports within the delegated powers he enjoyed. Armed with that reply, Nehru cleared the air for Krishnamachari. In December 1954, a former minister and a Congress leader from Uttar Pradesh, Mohanlal Saxena, wrote a letter to Nehru raising questions about the propriety of Krishnamachari's connections with industry. In his response, Nehru had given his commerce and industry minister a clean chit, saying that he had full faith in him and had no reasons to doubt his integrity.

Less than a year after he took charge of the finance ministry for the second time, S.M. Banerjee, a powerful trade union leader and an independent Lok Sabha member representing the constituency of Kanpur and supported by the Communist Party of India, had launched an attack against Krishnamachari for his alleged involvement in the grant of a licence to TV Sundaram and Company for the manufacture of sewing machine parts. The charge was made in April 1964, but the complaint pertained to the period when Krishnamachari was the minister for economic and defence co-ordination. There was indeed such a proposal for a foreign collaboration between Singer of the US and the TV Sundaram group. When the proposal was referred to Krishnamachari for his comments, he wrote on the file:

> I feel I should not take any decision on this file because the Indian participants of Singers happen to belong to a family with which I have close ties of friendship. I would, therefore, suggest to Secretary EAD (Economic and Defence Co-ordination) to refer this matter to the Prime Minister and request him to refer this file to some other minister for orders.[10]

After examining Banerjee's allegations, the government found that indeed the decision had been taken by the industry ministry, and not by either Krishnamachari or his secretary S. Bhoothalingam.

More attacks were made against Krishnamachari in the following months. In February 1965, some members of Parliament circulated a note referring to Krishnamachari's sons who owned business enterprises. There were no specific charges of impropriety or corruption, but merely the fact that he had business interests became a subject of political controversy. Krishnamachari clarified how he had dissociated from his sons' businesses since he had joined politics. But even senior political leaders did not hesitate from training their guns on him for his past business links. Socialist Party leader Ram Manohar Lohia, who had been elected to the Lok Sabha in a by-election in 1963, alleged that the financial position of the finance minister's family had seen an astronomical rise, from Rs 20–30 lakh at the time of Independence to Rs 3-4 crore. Lohia also alleged that the TTK group had been favoured by the grant of licences. Krishnamachari responded to what he thought was an outlandish charge with sarcasm and mockery. He said there were very few 'crore-patis' in south India and his sons were not worth more than Rs 30 lakh, and perhaps he was worth a little more before he got impoverished after having quit business and joined politics.

A rumour had also been floated that the Tatas were behind the campaign to tarnish Krishnamachari's image. J.R.D. Tata wrote to Krishnamachari to clarify that neither he nor his group had any role in such a campaign. The finance minister acknowledged the letter from Tata and expressed his gratitude for such a clarification, even though he did not believe even an iota of that rumour.

Sometime in April 1965, Krishnamachari's private secretary received two letters forwarded by the Lok Sabha Secretariat. Two members of Parliament had made similar charges as earlier once again, but not against the finance minister, but against his family business. Krishnamachari consulted Law Minister Asoke Sen and clarified to the prime minister that he could do very little about his family businesses, from which he had completely dissociated. He also sent a similar letter to the Lok Sabha Speaker, explaining in it his oft-stated position. Another storm was created in September 1965 around an old letter written by a foreign firm, Kalichemie, in 1955 to TTK & Co referring to Krishnamachari. Communist leader Bhupesh Gupta gave a copy of this letter to the finance minister for explanation. Krishnamachari explained he could neither do anything about it nor be charged with any impropriety if a foreign firm chose to mention his name in the mistaken notion that the head of the firm would also bear the same name as the firm itself.

The final straw that broke the camel's back was when as many as eleven members of Parliament presented a memorandum to the prime minister on 23 November 1965, raising their concerns over what they believed were conflicts of interest arising out of the finance minister's past links and

274   India's Finance Ministers

association with industry in general and his family business in particular. None of the allegations made in the memorandum was new. All of them had been raised earlier and Krishnamachari had responded to them individually as and when required. Parliament was in session. Without losing any time, Prime Minister Shastri forwarded the memorandum to the finance minister the very next day, on 24 November. A hurt Krishnamachari, who felt let down by his prime minister, wrote a detailed reply to Shastri on 27 November. He explained that all the charges were baseless and that the insinuations were aimed at tarnishing his image and ability to discharge his functions as the finance minister. He requested the prime minister to make a statement in Parliament to clear the air, attaching with his reply a draft statement for the prime minister's consideration.

There was silence from the prime minister's end for quite a few days. No statement was made by him when Parliament was in session. That gave rise to speculation over what the prime minister intended to do in response to the memorandum of charges against the finance minister. There were some suggestions in official circles that an inquiry could be instituted to look into the issues mentioned in the memorandum. Almost a fortnight passed and Krishnamachari thought of recording his deep disappointment with the way the prime minister had dealt with the charges made against him and offering his resignation so that he could explain his position to the people and Parliament.

In his letter of 14 December 1965, Krishnamachari referred to the many economic challenges the country faced and the need for a finance minister who could take 'unpleasant decisions', which he could do only if he had the 'full confidence and support of the Prime Minister and his colleagues'. He referred to the difficult foreign exchange situation and the suspension of foreign aid by the United States of America in the wake of India's war with Pakistan. Government finances too were under stress. He drew Shastri's attention to the 'weaknesses in the working of economic ministries' and the lack of co-operation from his colleagues. This, he wrote, made the job of the finance minister even more difficult, since he had to play the role of a coordinator among the various economic ministries, as also Planning Commission.

Elaborating further on the nature of his administrative difficulties, Krishnamachari noted in his letter that the imperatives of cutting down expenditure in view of the external and domestic financial troubles were not adequately appreciated by many of his ministerial colleagues. Shastri had set up a Committee of Secretaries, with the Cabinet Secretary heading it, to help Krishnamachari plan the nature and extent of expenditure cuts that were to be imposed on different ministries. However, almost every minister opposed such cuts and wanted the finance ministry's control over the expenditure provisions to be got rid of. Krishnamachari wrote: 'It is more than ever necessary that financial control should be adequate and effective in order to make the utilisation of the resources that we have to the fullest extent. I cannot see how I could frame a budget for next year and fulfil my responsibility under these conditions.'

The states too had begun making increased demands for resources from the Centre, which became an additional headache for Krishnamachari. He told the prime minister that in the prevailing situation of financial stringency he had to be tough while rejecting such demands from the states, and this would be possible only if the finance minister got the full support of the prime minister and if the other Cabinet ministers, belonging to different states, were made to fall in line. The details of states seeking recourse to financial indiscipline were quite alarming, Krishnamachari wrote in that letter:

> The States in the aggregate have a covered overdraft of Rs 50 crore as on 10th December, 1965. Their unauthorised overdraft is Rs 117 crore on that date – the exceptions to this being Bengal, Bihar and UP and the Punjab. At the best of times the Central Government cannot be a banker for the States to draw on as and when they feel the need. At the present moment, it is well-nigh impossible. I cannot expand currency and credit without going back on the understanding I have given to the IMF in respect of the ceiling. I have to keep within the limit because in March next year we have to repay the IMF $75 million and subsequent short-term advances that we may get will depend on our carrying out this understanding.

Krishnamachari noted with unconcealed regret and disappointment that his ministerial colleagues were carrying on a propaganda against him and the government's economic policies, holding him responsible for them. He told the prime minister that he had to ensure a 'proper orientation' of the country's economic policies, but 'the temper of some of our colleagues is very much against any change in a progressive direction in the matter of these policies'. Underlining the need for review of the government's economic policies, Krishnamachari wondered how he could continue to function if he were left in a 'vulnerable position in which neither our colleagues nor the country at large can judge whether I enjoy at least the confidence of the Prime Minister'.

The last few sentences in Krishnamachari's letter revealed how lonely he had become in the government. The prime minister, he noted, had not removed the doubts raised about him in the allegations made against him.

> With this uncertainty not removed and the atmosphere not cleared, you will appreciate why I cannot continue to function effectively. At the same time, it is now more than ever before that the country needs a strong Finance Minister. I would, therefore, ask you much as it pains me, to relieve me of my duties and leave it to me to explain my position to the people as best as I can and thereafter at a suitable opportunity to the Parliament.

Shastri took another fortnight to respond to Krishnamachari's offer of resignation. In between, the two had a few rounds of consultations on how to respond to the memorandum. On 29 December, the prime minister wrote to Krishnamachari to say he would not accede to the demand made by the signatories to the memorandum for appointment of a commission of enquiry to probe their charges. 'I do not consider that this obliges me to set up an enquiry because it is only when there is reason to believe that there is a prima facie case that such a step would be called for.' But Shastri also believed that there was a need to obtain a preliminary opinion on these charges from a person who would be seen as independent and objective. The prime minister told Krishnamachari that he, therefore, proposed to request the Chief Justice of India to 'study the papers' and give him an opinion confidentially. Krishnamachari was upset.

The next day he wrote back to the prime minister saying that the procedure of getting the opinion of the Chief Justice of India in confidence was 'wrong, which would also set up an unhealthy precedent for the future'. He, therefore, told the prime minister that he would be 'relinquishing charge as the Finance Minister on the afternoon of the 31st December, 1965'.

A day later, Shastri wrote back explaining why he needed to seek an independent and reliable opinion in the matter and how pained he was upon receiving his letter of resignation. But the same letter conveyed to Krishnamachari that the prime minister was recommending his resignation as the finance minister to the President for acceptance.

On the same day, 31 December 1965, which turned out to be his last working day in the government of India as its finance minister, Krishnamachari informed Shastri that he would like to explain his response to the memorandum to the public through the media and explain why he had resigned.

On 3 January 1966, Krishnamachari held a press conference where he released a detailed statement responding to each of the allegations levelled against him over the past few months. The most significant portion of his statement was at the end, where he accused a section of Indian industry for having supported the campaign to get him out of the finance ministry. The statement noted:

> It would . . . be clear that any Finance Minister who is compelled to take action even under the law of the land against the vested interests has to face heavy odds. The press statements during the last two-three days by leading businessmen indicate their jubilation over my relinquishing office. If I were to say more, I would be accused of being an enemy of the capitalistic system, which has not yet been outlawed under our Constitution.

Krishnamachari's final statement was equally significant: 'I can only hope that my successors will not be made to depend for their continuing in office on the goodwill of a small but selfish section of the population that may have cornered a large part of the tools of economic power.'

That was a telling comment from a finance minister who had to resign as the finance minister on two occasions under a cloud of controversy—once under the prime ministership of Nehru in the wake of the Mundhra scandal and the second time under the prime ministership of Shastri in the wake of unproven allegations against his industry links. But Krishnamachari's departure from the finance ministry was no less attributable to his opposition to some of the economic policy decisions that Shastri wanted to implement, including the controversial move to devalue the Indian currency.

Sachindra Chaudhuri (Finance Minister, 1966–1967)

Devaluing the Indian Rupee

The New Year's Day of 1966 saw the installation of a new finance minister at New Delhi. Sachindra Chaudhuri stepped into North Block, headquarters of the Union finance ministry, on 1 January 1966, a day after the resignation of his predecessor T.T. Krishnamachari took effect. Chaudhuri was an unexpected choice as the finance minister and would go down as the guardian of the central exchequer with a relatively short stint, but one who took one of the most dramatic economic policy decisions in pre-reforms India.

At the time he was invited by Prime Minister Lal Bahadur Shastri to join his Cabinet as the finance minister, Chaudhuri was a sixty-two-year-old first-time member of the Lok Sabha. A lawyer by training, Chaudhuri was yet to make a mark as a politician of high standing. After attending Presidency College, he had joined Fitzwilliam Hall in Cambridge and Lincoln's Inn in London. He had won the Lok Sabha seat of Ghatal, a place a little over 100 kms from Kolkata in West Bengal, in the 1962 general elections.

But Chaudhuri had many other attributes that helped Shastri and his secretary L.K. Jha opt for him. By then the government had already taken a decision, in principle, to take the extreme step of devaluing the Indian currency against the US dollar. One of the reasons for the vacancy in the finance ministry was that its incumbent, Krishnamachari, was not comfortable with the idea of devaluation of the rupee, for political reasons. Krishnamachari had quit almost in a huff, for a variety of reasons, including his differences with the prime minister over the direction of economic policies that needed to be pursued, and the proposal for devaluing the currency was certainly one of them. Shastri's advisers saw Krishnamachari's departure as an opportunity to bring into the finance ministry someone who would be agreeable to the idea of devaluing the Indian currency and taking a host of other reform measures necessary to gain full advantage of the currency value adjustment. Sachindra Nath Chaudhuri was an ideal candidate from that perspective.

Not surprisingly, I.G. Patel, who was the chief economic adviser in the finance ministry at that time, wrote in his memoirs that the choice of Chaudhuri as the finance minister was 'strange, but clever'. Patel listed some none-too-complimentary attributes of Chaudhuri's, which made him an ideal candidate as the next finance minister. He wrote in his memoirs, *Glimpses of Indian Economic Policy*,[1] 'As a political light-weight, economic illiterate, a thoroughly pleasant and agreeable professional with impeccable manners, he would be pliable and do what he was told by the PM and by his advisers.'

Chaudhuri had another qualification, which the political establishment at that time could not ignore. The RBI governor, P.C. Bhattacharya, was a good personal friend of Chaudhuri's. Given the past conflicts and tense relations between the RBI governors and the finance ministers, Shastri and his advisers found that to be a particularly important attribute. As Patel wrote, Chaudhuri would be 'pliable not just to the PM but to the RBI governor as well'. Having trained as a lawyer at Lincoln's Inn, Chaudhuri was also trusted as a finance minister who would be competent at international negotiations with multilateral bodies, as would be required for decisions like the planned devaluation.

But Chaudhuri had a mind of his own and he would exercise that to take a call on matters pertaining to his personal friends. S. Bhoothalingam, who was the Finance Secretary at that time, was also a good friend of the finance minister. The two had known each other since 1952, when Biren Mukherjee, the Bengal industrialist and steel baron, had introduced Chaudhuri to Bhoothalingam as his lawyer at the time. But, as Bhoothalingam would soon realize, Paresh C. Bhattacharya was a bigger friend of the finance minister.

In his biographical account of the developments in the 1960s *(Reflections on an Era: Memoirs of a Civil Servant)*, Bhoothalingam writes that sometime in 1962, he had been given the impression by the government that he would be the next Governor of RBI, after the incumbent Bhattacharya completed his five-year tenure in March 1967. Bhattacharya had taken charge of the RBI on 1 March 1962. But in January 1966, Chaudhuri, the new finance minister, called Bhoothalingam and said: 'At the end of this year you will retire. Therefore, I want to offer you the post of Auditor General on your retirement.'[2]

Bhoothalingam was in no mood to accept that post for two reasons. One, he was hoping to become the next RBI governor, after Bhattacharya completed his term in March 1967. Two, he believed that by temperament he would be unsuited to perform the role of an auditor general, whose tasks were to do a post-mortem examination of the financial activities by way of expenditure incurred by the government, its departments and other state-owned entities.

He also sensed why the finance minister had made that suggestion. Chaudhuri's friendship with Bhattacharya was one of the worst-kept secrets those days. Bhoothalingam was also aware of that special relationship. The finance minister wanted to extend Bhattacharya's term, according to Bhoothalingam. An astute civil servant, Bhoothalingam suggested to Chaudhuri that since he was not keen to become the Auditor General, the minister could consider S. Ranganathan for the job. A.K. Roy was due to complete his six-year tenure as the Auditor General in 1966. On Bhoothalingam's suggestion, the finance minister decided to appoint Ranganathan as the next Auditor General. But Chaudhuri also realized that Bhoothalingam too needed to be compensated, as he was being denied governorship of the central bank. As a compromise formula, Bhoothalingam was offered the post of India's ambassador at Brussels. Bhoothalingam accepted the offer. But the developments that would take place in the following months ensured that neither Bhattacharya got a fresh tenure as the RBI Governor nor Bhoothalingam shifted to Brussels as India's ambassador. A bigger tragedy and a little bit of political uncertainty engulfed India.

A New PM after Shastri's Sudden Death

Less than a fortnight after Sachindra Chaudhuri assumed charge as the finance minister, Prime Minister Lal Bahadur Shastri died while he was in

Tashkent on 11 January. Shastri had gone to Tashkent to have talks with Pakistan premier Ayub Khan after the war the two countries had fought in September 1965. But a day after the talks concluded, Shastri suffered a massive heart attack and passed away, leaving the country to face the shock of its prime minister meeting a sudden death for the second time in quick succession. Jawaharlal Nehru had died on 27 May 1964. Just as Shastri had begun to take charge of the government at the Centre, he too passed away, less than twenty months later, on 11 January 1966. Once again, the top Congress leadership had to look for a new prime minister. In May 1964, Shastri had got nominated to the post even though Morarji Desai was a strong contender. In 1966 as well, Desai was a strong contender, and this time he lost the race to Indira Gandhi.

For Chaudhuri, it meant he had to deal with a new prime minister. Indira Gandhi did not go in for any change in the existing team, either at the ministerial level or at the top bureaucratic level assisting her in the prime minister's secretariat. With less than a month remaining for the government to present the Budget for 1966–67, Chaudhuri got down to the task in right earnest.

The economic backdrop against which he began preparations for his Budget was hardly inspiring. Economic growth, measured by gross domestic product or GDP, had begun slowing down. As the figures would later show, GDP contracted in the full year of 1965–66 by 3.7 per cent. This was the second time that the Indian economy had contracted in the span of about ten years. GDP had shrunk in 1957–58 by 1.2 per cent, and once again in 1965-66. The pressure on the balance of payments and prices continued during the year. The foreign exchange reserves at the end of March 1966, however, had improved to $626 million, compared to $524 million the previous year, largely because of the squeeze applied to imports. The monsoon had failed, leading to crop failure, and food grain output once again suffered hugely, increasing the country's dependence on imports. Contributing to the grim outlook was the war that India had fought with Pakistan in September 1965, which too had an adverse impact on the country's resources and economic stability.

As Chaudhuri's Budget for 1966–67 would show, the government's finances were under stress during 1965–66, with the budget deficit to become as large as Rs 165 crore. This deterioration took place in spite of the supplementary Budget the government had presented in

August 1965 to mobilize additional revenues of about Rs 100 crore. The bulk of the increased deficit was on the capital account, mainly because of the government's higher borrowing. The revenue account showed a higher deficit because income and corporation taxes had shown a shortfall of Rs 73 crore even as customs and excise revenues had improved, thanks to the government's crackdown on imports using higher duties.

The state of India's food economy was perilous. Agricultural output in 1965 suffered as a result of poor rains. The United States and other friendly foreign countries had agreed to supply substantial quantities of food grain to meet the shortfall. The finance minister thought it necessary to acknowledge the nation's gratitude to these foreign countries for bailing it out. Industrial output also took a hit, and one of the factors responsible for this was the government's inability to compensate the shortage of domestic raw materials through higher imports. Fresh licensing for imports had been restricted in the wake of inadequate foreign exchange reserves. Exports too were sluggish, which put extra pressure on the country's balance of payments. Chaudhuri, therefore, continued the various schemes for tax credit certificates, import entitlement and national defence remittance in an attempt to promote higher exports. Under the national defence remittance scheme introduced earlier in October 1965, recipients of remittances in foreign exchange from abroad were extended the benefit of import entitlement licences.

Chaudhuri was clear in his mind that there was no running away from improving the country's ability to import more to meet domestic production of goods. In his Budget speech, he said: 'It is only on the basis of a more liberal import policy that we can hope to give a fresh momentum to industrial production and greater regard for efficiency all round in the immediate future.' The finance minister noted that higher imports were not possible without adequate external assistance, and he told Parliament how the government had planned to seek the help of international institutions and friendly foreign governments to reduce the 'severity of our present import restrictions'.

Chaudhuri's First and Only Budget

In the process, Chaudhuri's maiden Budget (and the only one he presented) struck a balance between tax reliefs and some new levies to raise government revenue. He increased the exemption limits on personal income tax and the limits on tax-free allowances. He abolished the expenditure tax his predecessor had imposed, giving a big relief to taxpayers. Equity shareholders too benefited from his proposal to levy the capital gains tax on bonus share allotments only when the gains were actually realized. The gift tax rates were brought in line with those of estate duty, as a result of which the taxation incidence came down a bit. But in order to strike a balance and to compensate for the revenue loss arising out of these reliefs, he levied a flat special surcharge of 10 per cent on personal income tax and increased the basic corporate tax rates by varying margins on different types of companies.

One of the factors for which Chaudhuri's Budget stood out was for the soft spot he had for the states. As the finance minister, he was acutely conscious of the states' financial problems, reflected in many of them seeking recourse to unauthorized overdrafts from the Reserve Bank of India. The Centre had to step in to clear the overdrafts, as a result of which its ability to provide more resources to help the states' plan activities was constrained. This required that the states kept a check on their deficit financing, without which they would run overdrafts with the RBI. Chaudhuri had decided that the finance ministry would hold consultations with the Planning Commission and the state governments to ensure that their financial mismanagement was brought under control.

In the same spirit of finding a solution to the states' financial problems, Chaudhuri announced two important decisions in his Budget. One, he increased the rate of central sales tax, levied on inter-state sales, from 2 per cent to 3 per cent so that the additional revenue generated from the move would augment states' revenues. Collections from the central sales tax used to be fully shared with the states. Two, the Budget raised the ceiling prescribed for sales tax on goods declared to be of special importance in inter-state trade from 2 per cent to 3 per cent. This move allowed the states to refix the rates of local sales tax on commodities like coal, cotton, cotton yarn, hides and skins, iron and steel, jute and oilseeds, within the ceiling of 3 per cent. This decision also helped the states garner some additional revenue to reduce their deficit financing.

That indeed was a different era. Almost half a century later, finance ministers would indulge in something opposite. Instead of helping the states earn some more revenues, they would increase surcharges and cesses on both direct and indirect taxes on a wide range of commodities and services so that the Centre is not obliged to share those revenues with the states. The divisible pool of taxes, which the Centre shares with the states, does not include surcharges and cesses. Consequently, the share of cesses and surcharges in total central tax collections would rise and the effective transfer to the states under the devolution formula would be much lower than what was mandated by the Finance Commission.

A Plan for Devaluation

In less than four months of Chaudhuri's Budget, the government of Indira Gandhi took her first bold step—devaluation of the Indian currency against the US dollar by over 57 per cent in one stroke. While the decision was announced by Chaudhuri in the first week of June, the moves for devaluation had begun many months earlier, when Lal Bahadur Shastri was the prime minister and T.T. Krishnamachari was in charge of the finance ministry.

It was in March 1965 that the government had to enter into a standby loan arrangement with the International Monetary Fund to augment its foreign exchange reserves to enable it to meet its demands for imports to keep the Third Plan expenditures going. The amount of the standby loan was $200 million. While the finance ministry team was holding these talks with the multilateral financial institutions, there was no suggestion of or reference to the need for devaluation as an instrument to get India out of the dire balance of payments situation faced by it. Yet, these institutions had quietly begun efforts to convince India to accept devaluation as a long-term solution to its chronic external payments problem. It is, however, significant to note that there was neither any reference to nor an inkling of the possibility of devaluation of the rupee when the IMF had concluded the standby arrangement in March 1965.

Developments Leading up to 1966

For the first few years after Independence, the Indian rupee was relatively stable. There was, however, a temporary problem in 1949 with the devaluation of the pound sterling with which the Indian currency was linked. This led to India too devaluing its currency. India's exports saw an improvement in the following couple of years, but inflation remained a cause for concern, so much so that by 1951 there was a demand for revaluing the Indian rupee. The demands were also triggered by Pakistan's refusal to devalue its currency against the pound sterling, which had an adverse impact on the volume of trade between India and Pakistan— particularly for goods exchanged on India's eastern borders with what was then known as East Pakistan. The bulk of the jute mills were situated in West Bengal, which depended on raw jute supplies from East Pakistan. But since Pakistan had not devalued its currency, India's imports of raw jute became costlier. India was not alone. Many European countries were also under pressure to revalue their currencies. But the International Monetary Fund argued that trade liberalization was a better instrument to tackle their problems instead of revaluation of their currencies.

In India, the most vociferous demand for a stronger rupee came from a business journal, *Eastern Economist*, which used to be published by the Birlas. But the Reserve Bank of India was completely opposed to the idea and found it 'devoid of economic justification'. It was argued that making the rupee stronger would harm India's trade. 'While the devaluation of 1949 was a compulsive necessity, revaluation in 1951 was not,' RBI History for this period noted.[3] The government accepted the RBI argument and C.D. Deshmukh, who was the finance minister at that time, had opined that 'revaluation . . . could be considered at leisure'.[4]

The campaign for revaluing the Indian rupee had gained momentum soon after it had been devalued in September 1949 by John Matthai, then the finance minister. Since he had devalued the currency, the demand for revaluation had received support from him. In his view, making the currency stronger would help India to counter inflationary pressures and reduce the cost of imports of food grains and capital goods needed for the country's development schemes. Two of India's major industries at the time, cotton textiles and jute (dependent on import of raw materials), also would have benefitted from a stronger currency. Matthai's keenness on revaluation, however, was resisted by others, and even the dominant opinion of the Reserve Bank of India was against it. Deshmukh, who succeeded Matthai in June 1950, was initially impressed with the idea of a stronger currency, but was later convinced by his successor at the RBI, the new Governor, Benegal Rama Rau, that India could consider revaluing its currency only after watching the impact of such a move on the economies of countries such as Australia and Sri Lanka.

During the mid-1950s, the tenor of the debate about the valuation of the Indian rupee changed. Instead of a revaluation, the idea of devaluing the the currency became a subject of debate in the wake of stagnating exports and shortage of foreign exchange, creating difficulties in making payments against imports. The Reserve Bank of India conducted a study in 1958 to examine the stability of the Indian rupee, with interesting findings. The study, done with the new governor, H.V.R. Iengar, and many other senior experts at the central bank, concluded that there was no decline in India's export competitiveness and that the weaknesses in the country's exports were on account of structural causes, which could not be addressed just by devaluation of the currency.

Until about 1962, there was no pressure on the government or the RBI to consider major steps like a currency devaluation, largely because it managed to secure long-term external assistance from multilateral financial institutions and friendly foreign countries. Nevertheless, delays in disbursal of foreign aid often created uncertainties and project-financing bottlenecks, all of which triggered the need for the Reserve Bank of India to conduct another study in June 1962 to evaluate if there was any need for a change in the rupee's exchange rate. The RBI study once again concluded that the benefits of any exchange rate adjustments were limited and almost non-existent. Any such policy step could make sense only if India's neighbouring countries like Pakistan and Sri Lanka too embarked on such a valuation change in their respective currencies. Such a view was endorsed by the finance ministry too, with Finance Secretary Laxmi Kant Jha arguing that India's exports were largely price-inelastic. Devaluation under such circumstances could actually reduce India's export earnings. Instead, it was argued, selective subsidies were a better option to boost exports and earn foreign exchange. The Bank of England also believed that devaluation could cause instability, while the International Monetary Fund came up with an idea which had no takers. The Fund suggested that India and Pakistan could jointly devalue their respective currencies, but the proposal did not make any headway.

The First Moves on Devaluation

By the summer of 1965, there was widespread expectation in government and political circles of a possible devaluation of the Indian rupee in response to the external account challenges the economy was facing. What also triggered such speculation was the India visit of a mission of the World Bank, headed by Bernard Bell, during 1964–65. Bernard Bell was a former chief economist of the Export-Import Bank in the US and had worked with different consulting firms from 1953 to 1965. The objective of the Bell mission was to evaluate the Indian economy and advise the World Bank and members of the Aid India Consortium on the challenges India faced. At that time, India was the largest debtor of the International Bank for Reconstruction and Development, or the World Bank. It was also indebted to other development agencies and a few foreign governments. Hence the urgency of the Mission was to find out what needed to be done to help the Indian economy. The Bell Mission Report was a huge document, consisting of fourteen volumes, and was submitted to the World Bank in October 1965. Among the key recommendations the report made for India included introduction of intensified agricultural production and devaluation of the Indian rupee. The Bell mission also endorsed India's request for more external assistance if the Indian government implemented these reforms.[5]

The recommendations of the Bell Mission came at around the same time that India's external account vulnerability increased. In spite of accessing the International Monetary Fund for assistance (a drawing of Rs 24 crore in the first quarter and another Rs 12 crore in the second quarter of 1965–66), India's foreign exchange reserves during the year saw no improvement. India had to even to seek a postponement of its obligation to repurchase $25 million from the IMF by the end of September 1965, which was duly approved by the Fund.

But the Bell Mission's recommendations for steps like devaluation of the currency triggered an internal discussion within the government of Lal Bahadur Shastri. RBI Governor P.C. Bhattacharya, Finance Secretary S. Bhoothalingam and Principal Secretary in the Prime Minister's Office, L.K. Jha, along with Chief Economic Advisor I.G. Patel, prepared a report for Shastri that outlined an agenda for reforms. However, it did not talk about devaluation. Instead, it suggested steps to restrict imports and monitor remittance of export receipts and outflows on account of invisibles. The objective was to somehow apply the brakes on any disguised flight of capital out of the country. These suggestions were also seen as the government response to the Bell Mission's recommendation for devaluation of the Indian rupee.

The month of July 1965 saw a series of significant developments on the devaluation front. The IMF was scheduled to hold a meeting of its board in the first week of the month to discuss the report on Article XIV Consultation with India. Under Article XIV, the IMF is required to hold an annual review of the state of the economy of all its member countries. The question of devaluing the Indian rupee was expected to figure in that review. But the Indian government's reluctance to agree to devaluation or similar bold moves, as suggested by the Bell Mission, created uncertainty, forcing the IMF to postpone that meeting.

India's response to suggestions for devaluation of its currency further hardened even as the World Bank and the IMF dropped hints to the effect that if India refused to devalue its currency, further aid to the country could be suspended. That hugely upset Finance Minister T.T. Krishnamachari, who as a result toughened his stance. He decided to reject the advice on devaluation and also succeeded in bringing Shastri around to his view, although the prime minister looked at this issue a little differently, as subsequent events would show.

S. Bhoothalingam, the finance secretary at that time and a strong proponent of devaluation, had a slightly more nuanced assessment of why Krishnamachari opposed any downward adjustment in the value of the Indian rupee. In his memoirs, *Reflections on an Era*, Bhoothalingam writes:

> And strange as it may seem, the dual personality of TTK stood in the way. He was I can say even today intellectually quite convinced (of devaluation), but because of the political side of his personality, he would not agree to it. He would go along with me 90 per cent of the way and after that he would quickly turn round and say,'You can call it what you like, but for heaven's sake don't use the word 'devaluation'.[6]

In a broadcast to the nation on 17 July 1965, Krishnamachari made it abundantly clear that devaluation in his view was no solution to India's economic problems. 'Indeed, it (devaluation) might well serve as an opiate by creating the impression that by taking what is generally considered a drastic action, we have really done all that needs to be done to correct the imbalance in our external payments position,' he said.[7] The finance minister's analysis and assessment of the state of the Indian economy and the strategy to overcome the challenges it faced were different from those of the World Bank and the Bell Mission. Krishnamachari feared that India's task of enlarging the domestic production base might be undermined by any 'sharp, sudden and indiscriminate, across-the-board increase in the price of all imports – even of those items, which could not conceivably be produced at home in the immediate future'.[8] He was also of the view that the lowering of export prices of jute or tea as a result of the devaluation would not benefit the country, as the overseas demand for these commodities was inelastic to price movements. He, therefore, recommended in his national address on radio that the government would rather adopt a selective approach by deploying other policy instruments. The prevailing structural rigidities did not make a general instrument like currency devaluation suitable for the Indian economy, he argued, while nevertheless calling for discipline and determined action through the Budget and credit policies as also in the way development plans were to be framed.

The obvious consequence of Krishnamachari's categorical rejection of devaluation also resulted in a significant review of the government's thinking on what ought to be the size of the Fourth Plan, which was to begin from April 1966. Without devaluation, the government could not rely on a sustained flow of higher external assistance to finance its development projects. Earlier plans for a substantial increase in the outlay for the Fourth Plan, therefore, had to be shelved. Instead, the board of the IMF discussed the report that Bhattacharya, Bhoothalingam and Jha had prepared on an alternative policy package to address India's economic woes. IMF Managing Director Pierre-Paul Schweitzer, along with his senior team of officials, held a meeting with Bhattacharya and Bhoothalingam in Washington in September 1965 to discuss those options. The Fund officials showed some appreciation of the Indian point of view, but they were also keen on alternative measures that the government should adopt.

Another meeting between Patel and the Fund officials, held later in the same month, discussed the possibility of replacing the existing scheme for import entitlement licences, issued against exports, with a new arrangement for issuing tax credit vouchers whose value would be determined as a percentage (ranging between 10 and 15) of the foreign exchange surrendered by the exporters as well as by recipients of foreign exchange remittances from abroad. This would have cost the government an estimated amount of Rs 250 crore, but the IMF officials were not satisfied with the tax credit voucher scheme alone. They were also keen that the government should levy a price equalization tax on imports, whose revenue could be used to finance the tax credit voucher scheme.

The World Bank's Inflexibility

Interestingly, the response from the World Bank to India's difficult financial situation was quite different from that of the International Monetary Fund. While the World Bank, led by George David Woods, was keen on India devaluing its currency, the IMF, led by Pierre-Paul Schweitzer, had a more nuanced approach to such a currency value adjustment move and was open to consider alternative policies. According to B.K. Nehru, India's ambassador to the US at that time, Schweitzer had told Nehru that even though the Fund's first preference was for devaluation, it was 'not "dogmatic" and would be willing to accept a "well-coordinated set of measures for exports, imports and invisibles . . . which would yield the same results as a straight devaluation"'.[9]

I.G. Patel, who was then the chief economic advisor, had an interesting explanation for why the World Bank had adopted a more inflexible line in its negotiations with the Indian government on policy reforms like devaluation and its need for external assistance. In his memoirs, *Glimpses of Indian Economic Policy*. Patel writes that the World Bank leadership underwent a change in 1963, which gave rise to an unusual problem in the relationship between the World Bank and India. While Eugene Black, the president till 1963, was a 'civilized and urbane southern gentleman with gravitas', his successor George David Woods was 'a New York banker of no great pedigree'.[10] Patel also notes that Woods, as a banker, was earlier employed by nobody else but the Indian government as a consultant and financial advisor. In that capacity, Woods would naturally be deferential to his employers, namely Finance Minister T.T. Krishnamachari. But once Woods became the World Bank President, his approach to Krishnamachari and the Indian government changed and the new chemistry was, Patel writes in his memoirs[11] . . . just not right. George Woods was also perhaps a little manipulative by nature: instead of straight but friendly talk, he seemed to relish strategies, more like a chess player than an ally; and he seemed to have made up his mind who needed to be checkmated. TTK, on his part, was at his acerbic best in referring to Woods.

That shed a lot of light on why the World Bank's approach to India was almost adversarial, even though Woods was keen that Indian policymakers quickly adopted the much-needed economic reforms.

The reputation of the Indian policymakers, including the officials, also complicated this worsening equation between the World Bank and the Indian government. The manner in which Indian officials would respond to suggestions from the World Bank officials was forthright and far less deferential than that of Pakistani officials. This was noticed and often commented on by foreign countries and World Bank officials, as Patel noted in his memoirs. For instance, Indian government officials made a strategic shift in their negotiations on the exchange rate adjustment plan. They would deal with the IMF on this matter rather than with the more difficult World Bank, on the ground that exchange rate was the Fund's remit and not that of the Bank.

India Veers towards Devaluation

An equally interesting development within the Indian government, and within the finance ministry in particular, was the gradual recognition of the need for doing away with selective controls and moving away from a system of multiple exchange rates to unify them into a single exchange rate through devaluation. The tough approach the World Bank had adopted by suggesting, in the words of B.K. Nehru, that India either devalued or got no more money, had of course created a political problem. Nehru, who was India's ambassador to the US at that time, writes in his memoirs:

> When I was leaving for India in December 1965 I called, as usual, on these two gentlemen (George Woods of the World Bank and Pierre-Paul Schweitzer of the IMF) and was left in no doubt, though on polite terms, that if there was no devaluation, there would be no money for the Fourth Plan.[12]

But by December 1965, the overall thinking within the government had also veered round to the view that a devaluation would be an opportunity to put an end to the many problematic and flawed policies that had been followed in the past few years. The top economic policy team in the government and the RBI—L.K. Jha, S. Bhoothalingam, I.G. Patel and Paresh Bhattacharya—were broadly of the view that the controls regime had imposed huge costs on the Indian economy and the various subsidy and import entitlement schemes had failed to achieve the desired goals. It is this team (Patel was not visibly identified as a member of the team, although he provided the necessary intellectual support to this shift) that began the process of gradually discarding the system of controls and incentives to put in place a more realistic exchange rate and a liberalized trading system. One of the notes prepared by the finance ministry in the winter of 1965 had commented that the 'current method of taxing imports and subsidising exports had a number of loopholes'.[13] In view of the country's external imbalances, many other economists too were articulating the need for adjusting the exchange rate in a way that more rupees were available against the dollar.

Two significant political developments completely changed the course of the debate in favour of devaluation. Finance Minister T.T. Krishnamachari resigned at the end of December 1965 over his differences with the prime minister. Among the many issues over which the differences arose, the proposal on devaluation was what made the rift between the finance minister and the prime minister complete and irreconcilable. Evidence of that lies in the recounting of a meeting that B.K. Nehru had with Lal Bahadur Shastri in early January 1966. Nehru had landed in Bombay on 1 January 1966 and was greeted by his son at the airport holding up a newspaper with a headline saying: 'TTK Resigns'. He also received a message from L.K. Jha that he should be in New Delhi at the earliest. On reaching Delhi, he was told that he must meet Prime Minister Lal Bahadur Shastri. As he entered 10 Janpath, Shastri met him in his room and asked him: 'How did you like the New Year's present I gave you?'[14] Nehru was not very pleased with the suggestion that a finance minister had to be eased out because of his opposition to devaluation and other differences with the prime minister. B.K. Nehru was somewhat unhappy at this remark and thought Shastri too was in favour of devaluation, but he had nothing personal against Krishnamachari.

Deliberations before the Devaluation

The vacancy caused by Krishnamachari's resignation had been quickly filled by the appointment of Sachindra Chaudhuri as the new finance minister. But before he could settle down in his new job and less than a fortnight after his appointment, Prime Minister Shastri died in Tashkent. Before the end of January 1966, there was a new prime minister in Indira Gandhi, who was quickly convinced of the need for a currency devaluation by her advisers.

In February 1966, RBI Governor Paresh Bhattacharya and Chief Economic Adviser I.G. Patel left for Washington to meet officials at the IMF and the World Bank. Little did Patel know then that a decision in principle on devaluation had been taken at the highest level. Patel took an Air India flight from New Delhi and Bhattacharya was to join him on the same flight from Bombay. Just a few hours before he left, Finance Minister Sachindra Chaudhuri handed over to Patel a sealed envelope, with the instruction that this be given to Bhattacharya when they met in Bombay. The envelope contained the brief on the basis of which the two would hold their discussions with the IMF. Patel writes in his memoirs:

> The 'brief' in fact was a letter from the FM to our Executive Director in the Fund, J.J. Anjaria, authorising him to inform the Managing Director of the Fund that the Government of India was prepared to devalue the Indian rupee in due course after discussions about possible Fund assistance and about the extent of devaluation.[15]

Indeed, given the backdrop of this promise of devaluation of the rupee, Patel and Bhattacharya during that trip explored the possibility of additional loans from the Fund and discussed with the World Bank a schedule for the next meeting of the Aid India Consortium. India had exceeded the domestic assets ceiling under that year's standby arrangement with the Fund and needed some additional drawing arrangement in the wake of its foreign exchange reserves ruling at low levels and some major forex payments likely to fall due in the coming months.

The meeting with IMF Managing Director Pierre-Paul Schweitzer went off very well, even though the initial terms and conditions that the Fund tried to impose on India in return for extending financial assistance to the country were not easy. Schweitzer offered temporary assistance, either in the form of a postponement of India's immediate repurchase obligations or an emergency assistance of $100 million linked to the adverse impact of drought on the Indian economy. Such immediate assistance was to be followed by a $300–400 million credit line to India on the basis of an agreed programme of assistance, Schweitzer explained.

Bhattacharya and Patel wanted something different. They wanted the IMF to offer a long-term loan of about $200 million for about three or five years, since a one-year loan would not solve India's problems. Also, a large loan of $300-400 million would put pressure on India to devalue the currency and establish a linkage between policy changes and the loan—a situation that India wanted to avoid, although a decision in principle to devalue the Indian rupee had already been taken by that time.

On 23 March 1966, the IMF board gave its approval to the loan programme, allowing India to draw $187.5 million. The deputy managing director of the IMF, Frank Southard, clarified at the board meeting that the loan was intended to help India meet an emergency situation and an exception was being made. The board members, however, expressed concern that the loan to India had been granted without the member-country agreeing to a policy reform plan, including the need to devalue its currency.

It was significant that Bhattacharya and Patel had left for Washington with the clear brief that India was willing to devalue its currency by June 1966. They were authorized to inform Schweitzer that 'the Government of India have decided in favour of a formal change in the par value of the Indian Rupee to be made in June 1966'.[16] But since the talks with Schweitzer for a loan went off successfully without the need for committing the country to a currency devaluation, the Bhattacharya–Patel pair chose not to make any reference to such a decision. After the loan amount was approved, Bhattacharya asked J.J. Anjaria, who was at that time India's executive director at the IMF, to orally inform Schweitzer of the following: 'The Government of India have accepted the advice of the Governor, Reserve Bank of India that the official par value of the rupee has to be changed, and that the timing of this will be around June this year.'[17] Meanwhile, they also succeeded in obtaining from the World Bank a loan of $50 million to finance India's import of industrial components and materials, with the repayment obligations to be fulfilled only after five years. That was also seen as smart and prudent economic diplomacy at work.

The pre-Budget Economic Survey, presented on 15 February 1966, a few days before the Budget, was quite candid about the precarious situation with regard to the country's balance of payments. The cat, however, was almost let out of the bag because of a specific paragraph in the Survey and that became a subject of heated discussion in Parliament and outside.

The paragraph, appearing in Part II of the Survey, was quite candid:

> The pressure on the balance of payments during the current year (1965–66), caused by continuing factors such as growth of imports, relative stagnation in exports and the mounting burden on debt service charges, was further increased following the Indo-Pakistan hostilities. While further restrictions on imports became necessary, Government also took positive measures to increase the foreign exchange availability. These include the issue of gold bonds to mobilise the idle holding of gold from within the country as also the National Defence Remittance Scheme which sought to give incentives for remittances from abroad through banking channels. The problem of achieving viability in the balance of payments is, however, a more basic one and requires continuing effort on a variety of fronts.[18]

The last sentence, where the government hinted at the possibility of initiating effort on 'a variety of fronts', gave rise to speculation about devaluation. Many members in Parliament quizzed the finance minister on whether the government meant devaluation when it referred to the need for policy options on various fronts. Neither the finance minister nor the minister of state for finance gave any clear answer, although the Planning Minister Asoka Mehta denied that there was any government move on devaluation. Ironically, however, it was Mehta and his Cabinet colleague, Agriculture Minister Chidambaram Subramaniam, who were then among the chief votaries of the idea of devaluation.

Before Indira Gandhi accepted the whole idea of devaluation, as proposed by Bhattacharya, Jha, Bhoothalingam and Patel, she of course had a series of discussions with leading economists and sought their views on what the implications of such a major step could be. The eminent economists consulted on this matter included Jagdish Bhagwati and K.N. Raj. Prof. D.R. Gadgil, who would later join the Planning Commission, was also consulted. A core group was set up in the government to oversee execution of the devaluation plan. The core group included both ministers and senior bureaucrats. There was, of course, the prime minister, Indira Gandhi, along with three other ministers—Finance Minister Sachindra Chaudhuri, Planning Minister Asoka Mehta and Agriculture Minister Chidambaram Subramaniam. The senior civil servants in this core group included RBI Governor Paresh Bhattacharya, Finance Secretary S. Bhoothalingam, Principal Secretary to the PM Laxmi Kant Jha, Economic Secretary Govindan Nair, Chief Economic Adviser I.G. Patel and Economic Adviser V.K. Ramaswami.

It was this core group that Finance Minister Chaudhuri referred to when B.K. Nehru had called on him before he returned to Washington. Nehru wanted to know from the finance minister if there was any communication on devaluation that the government wanted to share with the International Monetary Fund chief. Nehru recalls in his memoirs that Chaudhuri casually told him a committee had been formed based on the decision to devalue the Indian currency. He even asked Nehru whether the latter had seen the report prepared by L.K. Jha in this connection. 'When I said that I had not, he (Chaudhuri) went to his desk, fumbled in his drawer and produced a piece of paper which he said was the report,'[19] writes Nehru. According to Nehru, that report had recommended devaluation and the finance minister gave him the go-ahead to inform Schweitzer accordingly. Nehru insisted on a written note from the government indicating its decision. Chaudhuri wrote a note on the government's decision to devalue the currency and handed it over to Nehru. The Indian Ambassador then told Schweitzer about the decision. This was followed up by a formal communication from the RBI to S.S. Anjaria, India's executive director at the IMF.

But outside this small group, nobody had an inkling of what was being debated and what policy step was being examined. It was this core group that finally came out with the recommendation for rupee devaluation, along with the steps to be taken to liberalize trade. Not surprisingly, the Budget that Chaudhuri presented on 28 February 1966 gave no indication, let alone make any mention, of the devaluation decision that had already been taken in principle.

The secretive nature of the discussions within the government on devaluation also meant that the secretaries included in the core group had to tread a tightrope. Apart from the prime minister, only three ministers were in the loop—the finance minister, the planning minister and the agriculture minister. Ideally, Manubhai Shah, the commerce minister at that time, also should have been part of the core group. But Bhoothalingam had made it clear to Indira Gandhi that given Shah's personality and his views on such matters, he could not be trusted to keep the information on devaluation a secret. Gandhi had agreed to that arrangement and Shah got to know of the devaluation plan only when it was discussed at the Cabinet meeting for approval. Even the Commerce Secretary was not involved in the discussions. Instead, for all trade policy issues arising out of the proposed devaluation, Bhoothalingam worked in close consultation with the economic adviser in the commerce ministry, S.S. Marathe (who later went on to become the Industry Secretary in the late 1970s). [20]

Sometime in March 1966, a technical mission visited Washington to hold discussions with the International Monetary Fund and the World Bank on devaluation. The mission included Patel, Manu Shroff, an economic adviser in the finance ministry, and Ramaswami. An embarrassing situation arose when a news report in the *New York Times* stated, quoting a senior US government official, that the US and other donor countries were of the view that the Indian currency was overvalued and that this issue was being discussed with the Indian government. This gave rise to some speculation in India about devaluation of the rupee.

Perhaps in response to that news report and also by way of abundant caution, the government decided that when Indira Gandhi visited Washington later in March, she would not have the entire top finance ministry team with her. Only the economic secretary, Govindan Nair, an official with a relatively low public profile, went to the US along with the prime minister. In the normal course, Bhoothalingam would have gone to Washington along with Gandhi, but in a bid to allay any such speculation or apprehension of the decision on devaluation coming to public knowledge, Bhoothalingam stayed back and it was Govindan Nair who accompanied the prime minister on that important visit to the US.

During the discussions on the extent of devaluation, the view in India was that 50 per cent should remain the upper limit for adjustment in the value of the Indian rupee. Two major considerations played a role in this assessment, according to RBI History for the period between 1951 and 1967. One, the devaluation should result in such an increase in the rupee receipts of exporters that it would allow the government to abolish the various export subsidies and still retain the extra edge to Indian exporters' competitiveness to help them face new challenges in the future. Two, the devaluation should result in such an increase in the rupee cost of imports that it would require the government to reduce customs duties by a margin which, however, should not adversely affect the government's revenue position. The negotiating tactic was to offer devaluation by a third, but at the same time not resist an adjustment by up to 50 per cent, if there was no alternative to it.

The exchange rate of the Indian rupee at that time was Rs 4.76 to the US dollar. There are no official records of how the final revised exchange rate was arrived at. According to an account in *The Reminiscences of Gregory Votaw* (Votaw was an economist working with the World Bank as chief of its India division around that time and, therefore, was presumably present at the crucial meeting between Indira Gandhi and Pierre-Paul Schweitzer), the discussion turned out to be quite dramatic.

Gandhi told Schweitzer:

I don't know anything about economic matters. It was not a very good subject of mine at Oxford. But my technicians tell me that you're very concerned about this. I trust you. I trusted your uncle who was one of the great men of our century. What should I do?[21]

This was not only dramatic but also a class act in economic diplomacy. Here was a freshly appointed prime minister of a newly independent country negotiating with the IMF chief about the extent of currency devaluation it should agree to in return for continued external aid to keep domestic investments continuing at the planned pace. Gandhi also made a friendly gesture by referring to Schweitzer's famous uncle. To be sure, Schweitzer had two famous uncles—Albert Schweitzer, who won the Nobel Peace Prize in 1952, and Charles Munch, the conductor of the famous Boston Symphony Orchestra. But it seems Gandhi was referring to Albert Schweitzer in her conversation with the IMF managing director.

Schweitzer, who already had a soft spot for India, told Gandhi that the decision on devaluation rested with her, but his view was that India must devalue its currency. Without a pause, the Indian prime minister asked him how much India should devalue its currency by. Gandhi was at her innocent best and Schweitzer too was supremely diplomatic.

The conversation, reportedly, went like this:

Schweitzer: 'Six would be good. Seven would be better. Seven and a half would be fantastic.'

Gandhi: Okay. I'll do 7.5. Whatever you say.[22]

And that indeed turned out to be the new exchange rate for the Indian rupee after the devaluation.

Soon after the meeting between Indira Gandhi and Pierre-Paul Schweitzer at the end of March 1966, India's Planning Minister Asoka Mehta was in Washington to discuss with the World Bank the volume of assistance that India could expect from the Aid India Consortium meeting to be held later that year. That was necessary for finalization of the size of the Fourth Plan, which was due to begin in April 1967, and internal discussions were going on to finalize the growth and investment parameters. That meeting between Mehta and George Woods, the World Bank president, was nothing short of a disaster. At that April meeting, Woods, who was also chairperson of the Aid India Consortium, raised the issue of India's defence spending. Coming as it did after India had fought a war with Pakistan in September 1965, following which foreign aid had been suspended and food shipments had become a cause for concern, Mehta recognized that the World Bank's attitude to India had become tougher and that its approach would also influence other donor members of the Consortium. In his meeting with Schweitzer, Mehta raised a different issue. He underlined the importance of India continuing to get assistance, without which political stability in India could be in jeopardy, it becoming a 'major destabilising force in the world'.[23] This created some avoidable confusion about the purpose of Mehta's visit to Washington and his meetings with the Fund-Bank officials. Mehta's request for assistance to help India liberalize imports confused the Fund on whether the assistance should precede or coincide with the devaluation.

Although this particular meeting was a disaster, it was but a minor hiccup in the negotiations between India and the Fund, and everything else moved as per plan. By May 1966, the Indian government had prepared a package of measures to be implemented. These included devaluation of the currency, abolition of export subsidies, fiscal consolidation and imports relaxation.

But the plan for devaluation was still a well-guarded secret. Even within the Reserve Bank of India, nobody other than the Governor knew of it. Sometime in May 1966, two senior officials of the RBI, M. Narasimham, the head of the banking research division at the RBI (he later became the governor) and V.G. Pendharkar, an economic adviser, happened to be in New Delhi. RBI governor Paresh Bhattacharya also was in the Capital at that time. The governor called the two for a meeting, and that was the first time anybody outside the core group got a clear inkling of the government's decision to devalue the Indian rupee. Narasimham's account of this meeting in his memoirs reveals how the die had been cast by then:

> He [Bhattacharya] mentioned that he had been engaged in the preceding days in intense discussions in Delhi on the exchange rate and that it had been decided to devalue the rupee early in June 1966. Pendharkar mentioned that we were on the threshold of the monsoon and asked whether the decision could wait until we knew what sort of monsoon we would have. The Governor said that the decision taken was final and that the IMF had also been kept in this picture.[24]

Instead, Bhattacharya was focused on the need for rolling out a restrictive monetary policy to reduce liquidity and keep a check on inflation after the devaluation, as already the need for reining in their deficits had been impressed upon the governments at the Centre and the states. The RBI governor was certainly in the loop as far as the government's plans to devalue the currency was concerned. But the country's central bank as an institution was kept in the dark. Narasimham's regret was that this was not the first time that the country's central bank was institutionally ignored in a key decision concerning its functions, and nor was it going to be the last.

The Union Cabinet was to meet on 5 June 1966 to decide on the devaluation. But a day earlier, B.K. Nehru received a personal secret communication from L.K. Jha asking him to tell the IMF to hold all operations as the decision to devalue the currency was being reconsidered. Nothing much is known about why the Indian government had a second thought and what the nature of the reconsideration was. But a worried Nehru wrote back a telegram to Jha to say that to go back on devaluation was now too late. He wrote in that note:

> Two Ministers of the central government during the last few months, C Subramaniam and Asoka Mehta, had discussed the financing of the Fourth Plan with the World Bank and the IMF. The entire discussions were held on the clear understanding on both sides that the rupee would be devalued. I had myself, on the authorisation of the Finance Minister, told the Managing Director of the IMF that we would devalue. Our Director had, on instructions, formally so assured him. The tranche of our drawing rights which we needed had been released to us on this understanding. To go back on this decision would now make the Government of India look ridiculous and its word not worth believing. Furthermore, we should, if we did not devalue, write off all external finance for the Fourth Plan as also any further short-term support from the IMF.[25]

Nehru believed that his note prevented a last-minute change of mind on devaluation of the currency.

After this mild hiccup, the Union Cabinet met on 5 June 1966 and approved a 57 per cent devaluation of the Indian currency. It was a Sunday. The Cabinet meeting was not without some debate on the proposal. As expected, Manubhai Shah, the commerce minister, opposed the proposal as he realized that he would lose all his discretionary prerogatives of arriving at multiple exchange rates for the rupee in the days to come. But eventually it went through—the exchange rate for the US dollar went up from Rs 4.76 to Rs 7.50 and for the pound sterling from Rs 13.33 to Rs 21. Simultaneously, export duties on several commodities were abolished and the schemes for import entitlement and tax credit certificates were discontinued. This was done to soften the relatively higher impact of the devaluation on exports, compared to imports.

Immediately after the Cabinet meeting, the Union finance ministry sent out its officials as emissaries of the Prime Minister to all the state capitals to leave a sealed envelope with their governments, marked 'top secret', with the instruction that it could be opened only after 6 p.m. that evening. The government did not want the information to be leaked out before it actually took effect on the midnight of June 5 and June 6. J.B. Kripalani, a noted political leader, whose wife Sucheta Kripalani was at that time the chief minister of Uttar Pradesh, recalls in his memoirs that on that Sunday Sucheta was informed of a sealed envelope that had been received in Lucknow, to be delivered to her only after sunset:

> Why this 'after sunset' instruction? The letter must have reference to some economic matters and, therefore, it must be delivered after sunset, when the share markets everywhere would be closed. I told Sucheta that there was a rumour afloat in Delhi about the devaluation of the rupee. It was an unpopular move. It was vehemently denied by the Government. When governments think it fit to be vehement in their denial, it generally means that they want to take the step.[26]

Kripalani was not wrong. That envelope indeed carried the communication to the chief minister of the state about the government's decision to devalue the Indian currency. By the time Sucheta Kripalani decided to hold a Cabinet meeting of the Uttar Pradesh government in Lucknow, Patel and P.N. Dhar had reached the venue and were stationed in the ante room to explain, if needed, the rationale of the decision to devalue the Indian rupee.

India's executive director at the IMF, S.S. Anjaria, was also informed of the decision so that he could apprise the IMF Managing Director Pierre-Paul Schweitzer of it, who in turn could convene a special board meeting and take note of the decision made by the Indian government. Schweitzer was generous in his comments at the Board meeting and he expressed the hope that the 'momentous decision would pave the way for the foreign aid necessary for trade liberalization'.[27]

Some anxious moments preceded the scheduled national broadcast announcing the devaluation. I.G. Patel and V.K. Ramaswami were in Bhoothalingam's room waiting eagerly for the phone call from S.S. Anjaria in Washington about the outcome of the IMF Board meeting. There were disturbances in telephone line. Hence, the conversation was unclear. Patel and Ramaswami could hear Anjaria's voice but the reception at Anjaria's end was poor. Anjaria 'kept asking whether we had got the coded message about the Board's approval. After a while we had to end the conversation without worrying about Anjaria as what mattered was that we had heard . . .' Patel recalls in his memoirs.[28] Immediately thereafter, Patel rushed to the finance minister who, as earlier planned, was at dinner with some friends. Patel told Chaudhuri that he could leave for All India Radio and read out the speech that had been prepared in advance and was kept safely in his pocket.

At around 9 p.m. on Sunday, 5 June 1966, Finance Minister Sachindra Chaudhuri announced the devaluation in a special broadcast on radio. The new exchange rates took effect from 2 a.m. on 6 June 1966 and the Reserve Bank of India ordered the closure of banks for the public for two days.

That was how the sharpest devaluation of the Indian currency took place, just about two months after that famous conversation between Indira Gandhi and Pierre-Paul Schweitzer in Washington at the end of March. The special meeting of the IMF board, which took place on 5 June 1966, a day before the devaluation was to become effective, specifically noted that the decision followed discussions with the Indian government, which had agreed to the advice of the Fund, and that the new exchange rate was not a compromise. Nobody else in the RBI, apart from the Governor, had been in the loop. And the only substantive role that the reigning finance minister played in the entire devaluation episode was to simply read out a script prepared by others.

The Aftermath

The decision on devaluation of the rupee took the ordinary people by surprise. The media had its own reservations. RBI History gives an account of the many headlines on the devaluation decision that appeared in the financial newspapers, describing it as an 'ill-advised plunge' or a 'leap in the dark' or even an 'escape from reality'. The general commentary expressed fears of inflation, and even uncertainty as to whether the move would help boost exports.

Industry representatives expressed their concerns over the cost of imports their projects would have to bear. Senior government officials and RBI officials, including Governor Bhattacharya, began making public statements arguing that increased imports would make more raw materials available, helping increase domestic production, improve availability of goods and, therefore, dampen inflationary expectations. Industry leaders were also asked not to raise the prices of goods that were imported during the pre-devaluation period. On the whole, the government had a lot on its hands to manage a difficult situation.

Politically, too, the situation became a little problematic for the government. Within the Cabinet, Commerce Minister Manubhai Shah, who was kept completely in the dark about the talks on devaluation, opposed the proposal and criticized it after it was announced. Former Finance Minister T.T. Krishnamachari criticized the move from Madras. Even Kumaraswami Kamaraj, a grassroots Congress leader from the south, was opposed to the idea and eventually condemned it as a 'sell-out to the Americans'.[29] The rift between Kamaraj and Indira Gandhi had just begun to take place and the devaluation exercise was just the first glimpse of that conflict between the two leaders.

Global Impact of the Devaluation

The government decision to devalue the Indian rupee in June 1966 had impacted two different regions in the world in different ways. One was the Eastern Bloc, including the Soviet Union, with which India had a long-standing bilateral rupee trading arrangement. The second region consisted of the Gulf countries, which had continued to use the Indian rupee as legal tender. A 57 per cent devaluation of the Indian rupee had serious implications for the trade between India and the East European countries, and for the value of the rupee as legal tender in the Gulf region.

With eastern Europe, India had a payment agreement that also included a gold clause, under which the exchange value of the rupee was fixed in terms of the gold reserves. This effectively guarded the holders of rupees against any devaluation. Not surprisingly, the Soviet Union and other east European countries insisted on enforcement of the gold clause to protect themselves against the adverse impact of the devaluation of the Indian currency. This was a cause for great concern in India as well, since this meant disruption in India's exports to the Eastern Bloc. The gold clause, in particular, worked against Indian exporters, since their rupee realizations were protected at the pre-devaluation level.

Talks continued to be held between officials of the east European countries and India for months after the June 1966 devaluation. An arrangement was worked out by which Indian exporters to the Eastern Bloc were assured of higher rupee payments, reflecting the devaluation impact, over future trade transactions. But a tricky issue arose over trade contracts that had been entered into before the devaluation but executed after it. Undeniably, the devaluation had an adverse impact on the nature of rupee trade agreements in general, an issue that continued to bother trade relations between India and the east European bloc, until the early 1990s, when rupee trade arrangements were dismantled.

For the Gulf countries, the devaluation of 1966 had kicked off a different controversy. During the 1950s and early 1960s, several Gulf countries used the Indian currency as legal tender. However, they had begun gradually phasing out the rupee through ongoing negotiations that were not fully concluded when devaluation of the Indian rupee was announced in June 1966. At that time, Muscat and Oman were the only Gulf territories where the Indian currency was legal tender. Discussions continued between a delegation from the Gulf kingdoms and Indian authorities for some months to resolve the tricky situation following devaluation.

It was only in March 1968 that an agreement to resolve the dispute over devaluation was reached with the Gulf countries. RBI History notes:

> After further discussions, the two sides came to an agreement in March 1968 by which the total liability resulting from the repatriation of the rupee notes was put at Rs 12.88 crores. Besides a down payment of a fifth of the resulting sterling liability, £7.2 million was treated as a sterling loan carrying an interest rate of 5.5 per cent per annum, repayable in eleven equal annual instalments commencing January 1969.

Was the Devaluation a Success or a Failure?

The most illuminating commentary on the loans to India promised against the devaluation came from the *New York Times*. In a longish dispatch published on 12 June 1966 with the headline 'Mrs Gandhi Gambles with a Cheaper Rupee', the leading publication wrote the following:

Here she (India) must depend largely on the promises she evidently has received from the United States and the International Bank for Reconstruction and Development. For whatever other long-range benefits may stem from devaluation, its chief short-run benefit is expected to be the long awaited first infusion of Western aid for India's fourth Five-Year Plan.

India is unlikely to get what she asked for: $1.6 billion a year. However, there are indications that she will get – probably in two stages – about $1.3 billion. This is an increase of about 30 per cent over the annual level of Western aid during the third Five-Year Plan.

Even more important is that $900 million to $1 billion of this – twice the Third Plan rate – will be non-project aid for imports of raw materials, spare parts and components. India's liberalisation of imports will permit it to use these funds quickly.

The government hopes this massive infusion will allow plants which have been running well below capacity because of the foreign-exchange shortage to boost production substantially. Eventually, they are confident, increased production will bring prices down.[30]

Gamble it was, as subsequent events would show. And the gamble, it seemed, did not pay off. What became clear after about a few months of the devaluation is that Gandhi's expectations of more assistance from the US and other countries were belied. Making matters more complicated were the developments on the macroeconomic front, with growth not picking up, inflation rising and dependence on food imports becoming even more crucial after the failure of the monsoon.

Thus, measured against the goals that the devaluation was expected to achieve, the move could not be described as a success. RBI History's entry for the period indicates that the central bank also saw the devaluation as a failure. It observed:

By common consent, the devaluation of 1966 failed, or it did not immediately achieve its objectives. According to the Reserve Bank's explanation at the time, the 'adjustment in relative prices, costs, and pattern of investment' necessitated by the devaluation proved 'even more difficult because of the serious drought' which affected the Indian economy for the second year in succession.[31]

The World Bank did not disagree with such an assessment. It had concluded that the Indian economy could not positively respond to devaluation because of the recession caused by two successive years of drought, a decline in foreign aid and the delays in negotiations for and release of concessional loans for India from its soft-loan window, the International Development Association.

The process of reviving the external aid process, which had slowed down after the war with Pakistan, did get reactivated after the devaluation. But the volume of aid that was promised to India before the devaluation was far less than what the requirement was. The apprehensions in the dispatch from the *New York Times* were not an exaggeration. 'India is unlikely to get what she asked for: $1.6 billion a year,' it had said.

Having got wind of the possibility of the aid promise remaining unfulfilled, the Indian government engaged in a diplomatic counter-offensive, which made the situation even more complicated. Already, Indira Gandhi's stop-over at Moscow in April 1966, on her way back from the US, had upset the Americans. She had met Soviet Premier Alexei Kosygin, who had assured India more aid for its industrialization programme. In July 1966, after the devaluation debacle, Indira Gandhi visited Moscow again and met Leonid Brezhnev, who was then the general secretary of the Communist Party of the Soviet Union. She joined Brezhnev in 'condemning "imperialists bombing and aggression in Asia"', a clear reference to the US attacks on Vietnam, which were on the rise.[32] This infuriated the US President Lyndon B. Johnson. The promised first instalment of $900 million of aid was delayed and the aid package for 1966–67 was announced only after November 1966, upsetting the government's plans. Johnson made things worse by deciding to include the value of the food aid being given under Public Law 480 or PL480 within the overall consortium assistance to be extended to India.

RBI History captures this predicament of India quite vividly:

World Bank records suggest that its officials expected India to require aid of the order of $900 million each in the first two years, and a billion dollars in the third. But when non-food imports fell as a result of the recession induced by the drought and the decline in public expenditure, these amounts were scaled down to $600 million in the second year (1967-68) and $900 million in the third. At the November 1967 consortium meeting, the World Bank presented an aid estimate of $750 million for 1967-68 and $820 million for 1968-69. While members of the consortium felt this was reasonable, chances of achieving this level of commitment for 1967-68 receded with every delay in IDA replenishment.[33]

The slow disbursement of aid during this period had its expected fallout for the Indian economy. India's trade deteriorated, with the deficit widening and an external account crisis looming on the horizon. India's trade deficit widened from $1.22 billion in 1965–66 to $1.47 billion in 1966–67. In spite of the promise of more aid, net external assistance to India saw only an insignificant rise, from $0.99 billion to $1.34 billion in this period. Foreign exchange reserves, after having dipped by $0.1 billion in 1965–66, made a marginal recovery, by $0.06 billion. Finance Minister Sachindra Chaudhuri spent the months following the devaluation mainly managing these adverse consequences for the economy. There were fears that India's foreign exchange reserves would decline precipitously by the end of 1966–67 if import controls were not reimposed. In December 1967, India had to draw $90 million under the new Compensatory Financing Facility and convinced the IMF Board to agree to a postponement of the repayment schedule. The external economic situation remained tense even in 1968, when in May that year the Aid India Consortium meeting could provide only $295 million of non-project assistance. This raised questions on whether the hard negotiating stance, which the World Bank adopted on its consortium commitments, would derail the government's liberalization process.

There was understandable disappointment among the senior policymakers in the government who had backed the devaluation plan in the hope that it would push the economy towards embracing more reforms and rescue it from a tight external account situation. Bhoothalingam noted in his memoirs with regret that the idea of going in for devaluation was to remove discretion and control wielded by any one individual in the government over economic policy matters:

> Now I won't go into detail, But I will just say that even within the next
> three or four months, while I was still in office, the erosion started. After
> my retirement (March 1967), the erosion was swifter, so that by the time
> of the next Budget there were hardly any traces of devaluation in the

policies of the Government of India. On top of the devaluation, it had restored all the subsidies, incentives and controls one by one, besides all the direct incentives, replenishment licences and so on.[34]

To the question on whether devaluation had worked or not, Bhoothalingam was fairly categorical in his assessment that devaluation was not allowed to work as all the old policies had been restored. It was an idea whose implementation was flawed, the idea as a result getting a bad name, ending in India getting the worst of both worlds, Bhoothalingam concluded.

The reputation of the World Bank and the US also took a hit as they were seen to have ditched India by not fulfilling their promises in spite of the latter having devalued its currency. But Bhoothalingam had a different perspective on that. The two institutions had promised more assistance to help India overcome its financing problems. But the reintroduction of controls gave them an excuse. 'They could turn back and say: What is this kind of devaluation? You have restored controls; on what grounds can we give more aid? It is clear why despite devaluation the level of aid did not increase very much,' Bhoothalingam observed.[35]

It seemed nothing went right for India's devaluation plan. In the words of I.G. Patel, one of the officials who worked on the devaluation proposal,

> Admittedly, there was great anger at the fact that the Consortium meeting that followed the devaluation was a big disappointment and indeed a betrayal. The much-advertised non-project assistance of a billion dollars did not materialise and there was the usual wrangling about projects and denial by delaying. The hoped-for liberalisation of imports could not be attempted with the result that there was no spurt in growth from greater utilisation of capacity. The Fourth Plan which should have begun in 1966 had to be abandoned and we had a plan holiday for three years, when we had only annual plans.[36]

What complicated the situation further was the failure of the monsoon in 1966, for the second year running. Industrial growth fell from 3.4 per cent in 1965–66 to 2.3 per cent in 1966–67 and further down to 1.4 per cent in 1967–68. Merchandise exports did not record any significant increase—going up by just 7 per cent from $1.65 billion in 1965–66 to $1.77 billion in 1966–67, on account of a variety of factors, including weak international demand for commodities like tea and pepper. But imports rose by 13 per cent, from $2.87 billion to $3.25 billion in this period, as a result of relaxation of the import policy. However, the increase was still muted as higher prices of imports, following the devaluation, made imported raw materials or components costlier. Also, a reduction in public investments by the government also meant reduced demand for import of capital goods. The external account improved from 1968–69 with the help of modest public investments, the revival of the monsoon and an increase in agricultural output as a result of the Green Revolution. The devaluation had failed to yield the desired results, but a short-term relief was that the Indian economy was spared any further setbacks during the next two years.

For Finance Minister Sachindra Chaudhuri, devaluation remained a dominant, disruptive factor during the entire course of his short tenure at the Centre that lasted a little less than fifteen months. General elections were held in February 1967. The Congress returned to power with a reduced majority in the Lok Sabha. But Chaudhuri's ministerial career had ended as he had not fought the general elections in 1967 and was not a member of the fourth Lok Sabha. In any case, the need for a soft and pliable finance minister was over. Indira Gandhi decided to look for a new finance minister in March 1967. A new saga of India's finance ministers who changed the country's economic fortunes was about to begin.

Morarji Desai (Finance Minister, 1967–1969)

A Failed Crusade for Social Control of Banks

The gap of four years between Morarji Desai's two terms as finance minister saw major political and economic developments in the country. India had earlier fought a war with Pakistan in 1965 under the leadership of Prime Minister Lal Bahadur Shastri. Tragedy struck India when Shastri died in Tashkent in January 1966, after signing an accord with Pakistan after the war, necessitating a leadership change in the Indian government and triggering fresh political turmoil. Eventually, Indira Gandhi succeeded Shastri as the prime minister even as the Congress party was strained because of internal dissent and fighting among senior leaders. The rise of the Syndicate, led by Kumaraswami Kamaraj, kept Desai out of the race for prime ministership, but Indira Gandhi, after assuming charge as the prime minister, decided to assert herself and was not unduly influenced by the Syndicate and its wishes.

The Indian economy faced a major downturn with its foreign exchange reserves once again turning precariously low and inadequate to meet the country's growing import needs. Gandhi, under advice from her top economic policy team, agreed to devalue the Indian rupee by 57 per cent, and the consequences for the economy were huge, with import costs skyrocketing and inflation spurting. General elections were due to be held in 1967 and Indira Gandhi led the Congress during those polls. The Congress did emerge as the single largest party in the Lok Sabha, but it became clear that the party had begun losing its national appeal among people across the country, which was reflected in its substantially reduced majority of only 283 seats in the 523-seat Lok Sabha. This was a big drop in seats for the Congress from the previous general elections of 1962, when it had bagged 361 out of 508 Lok Sabha seats. In addition, the state assembly elections also brought no cheer as the Congress lost power in as many as seven states in different parts of the country.

It was under such difficult political circumstances that Desai got an invitation from Indira Gandhi to join her government in 1967. Given Desai's strained relationship with Indira Gandhi, he was not expecting any such invitation. So he was surprised when he received a phone call from Indira Gandhi, three days after she was elected as leader of the Congress Parliamentary Party. Gandhi sought Desai's cooperation and invited him to meet her at her residence. Desai was unmoved and blunt as ever. He told her that he could not meet her at her residence lest her party colleagues should get the impression that he was canvassing for his inclusion in the Union Cabinet. That was Morarji Desai!

Indira Gandhi deferred to Desai's wishes and presented herself at Desai's residence at around ten next morning. At the meeting, Gandhi came to the point without beating about the bush. She said she needed Desai's cooperation in running the government and wanted him to join her Cabinet. But Desai was not an easy person. He set some tough conditions before accepting Gandhi's offer. In his autobiography, *The Story of My Life*, Desai provides a graphic account of his meeting with Gandhi. He says he told her:

> I have been noticing since 1962 that you are prejudiced against me and I talked to you about it at the end of 1962. If this prejudice still continues, it would be futile for me to join the Cabinet as I would not be able to function usefully under those circumstances. If I am not able to talk to you very frankly and clearly now in this discussion, the discussion is not likely to be of much use. I should, therefore, like to know whether this prejudice still persists and whether, if I talked very frankly and you did not like some of my arguments, you would take it ill. I would not like to take that risk as I do not want to spoil our relations further. I would, therefore, request you to answer me very frankly.[1]

Desai's Trust Deficit

The suspicion of prejudice against him had been a running issue with Desai. He had accused Nehru of being prejudiced against him when the latter was the prime minister. Nehru had denied that he was prejudiced in any way against him, but for Desai the feeling persisted. With Indira Gandhi, too, Desai had a similar problem. Gandhi told Desai that he should forget the past and even assured him that she held no prejudices against him. It was at this point that Desai set his first condition for joining Gandhi's Cabinet: 'If I can speak with authority in your absence on your behalf, I can help you by joining your Cabinet. This will be possible only if I am given the position of Deputy Prime Minister.'[2]

The second condition Desai set was even more difficult to meet. Desai argued that with his vast experience in administration, he was more competent than even Gandhi to take on the challenge that would be put up by many Opposition stalwarts who had been elected to the fourth Lok Sabha. Ideally therefore, Desai, apart from being the deputy prime minister should be entrusted with the responsibility of the home ministry. Gandhi, according to Desai, did not give a firm response to his demands. She neither accepted them nor refused them categorically. Instead, she told Desai that Yashwantrao Chavan had been inducted into the home ministry in November 1966 and he continued to hold that ministry. Hence, it would be difficult to ask him to vacate that ministry to accommodate Desai, she argued. Desai countered this by saying that Chavan had been his junior in politics, had worked under him for several years and had succeeded him as the chief minister of Bombay. Hence, Chavan would hardly take it amiss if he were to vacate the home ministry for Desai. That ended the meeting without any settlement of the central issue of how Desai should be inducted into Gandhi's Cabinet.

Another meeting was to be held with Gandhi the same evening, and this meeting was to be attended by Kamaraj too. But during the day, much before the evening meeting, Desai was informed of a disturbing talk that was going on among members of the Congress party in Parliament's Central Hall. The speculation centred on Desai's reported comments suggesting that neither Gandhi nor Chavan were capable of heading the government as prime minister and home minister, respectively. Desai suspected that a political campaign had already been mounted among the section of the

Congress that was opposed to him. At the evening's meeting with Gandhi, Desai raised the matter of this political campaign against him and asked her if she had taken any part in those discussions that morning. Gandhi denied she had, but Desai was not convinced. Relations between Gandhi and Desai worsened further and the gulf between the two was getting wider. In an attempt to break the stalemate, Gandhi told Desai that he could join the Cabinet as the finance minister. Desai was not willing to join the Cabinet in that role as his experiences in that position, which he had held from 1962 to 1964, had not been happy.

A way out of that impasse was found with Kamaraj's decision to have a chat with Desai. Kamaraj told him about the need for a compromise deal—if Indira Gandhi accepted Desai's demand that he be made deputy prime minister, Desai too should agree to hold charge of the finance ministry. Desai had no way of wriggling out of that offer. The ball was now in the court of the Congress working committee where this matter was discussed, and the consensus was that Desai and Gandhi should settle for a compromise as suggested by Kamaraj.

After several rounds of deliberations, with emissaries like Chandra Bhanu Gupta and D.P. Misra playing crucial roles in support of Desai, a rapprochement looked likely. Gandhi invited Desai for a meeting to resolve the issue. But when Desai reached her residence, he found that Chavan and Jagjivan Ram were already seated in the room where the meeting was to be held. As soon as Desai arrived, Gandhi too did, making it obvious to all that the discussion would take place not just between Gandhi and Desai, but among all four present there. The manner in which the discussion began made it appear that Desai was being subjected to a cross-examination session. Gandhi asked him how he thought he would be able to strengthen the government by joining the Cabinet. Desai was curt in his reply when he said her question implied her deep prejudice against him as it presupposed that his joining the Cabinet would weaken the government. Gandhi was taken aback by such a counter from Desai and clarified that her intention behind asking that question was to remove all misunderstandings. After that it was the turn of Yashwantrao Chavan and Jagjivan Ram to ask Desai to explain what kind of powers Desai believed a deputy prime minister would enjoy in the Cabinet and in the government. Desai had sensed by now that there were serious apprehensions among the senior Congress leaders about his assuming the position of deputy prime minister. He said the deputy prime minister was senior in status to all other ministers in the Cabinet and this was obvious from the past precedent of Sardar Vallabhbhai Patel having been a deputy prime minister in the Nehru government. Chavan and Jagjivan Ram asked a few more searching questions, which made Desai even more uncomfortable. Chavan asked if the deputy prime minister could issue instructions to other ministers. Desai was quick to point out that there was no question of that, but certainly he could advise them and it was up to them to accept or reject such advice. Jagjivan Ram asked if the deputy prime minister's advice and consent were necessary for the prime minister to form or reshuffle the council of ministers. Desai reiterated that the deputy prime minister could offer his advice and that would not be an order.

At this point, Desai decided that it was beneath his dignity to subject himself to such cross-examination. He told Gandhi that the developments up to this point had showed that she had no confidence in him. Moreover, he felt insulted by the manner in which he was being questioned and, therefore, had no desire to join her Cabinet. Gandhi quickly intervened to say that she wanted him to join the Cabinet as deputy prime minister and finance minister. Desai decided to leave that meeting, saying he had to meet Kamaraj. It was at that meeting with Kamaraj that Desai reconsidered his stance. Kamaraj told him that he must join the government because if he stayed out of it the government and the Congress would not last for very long. Desai asked Kamaraj to check with Gandhi if she was honest and serious about having him in the Cabinet. Kamaraj obliged him, and after checking with Gandhi told Desai that he should join the government. In light of these discussion and in the larger interests of the organization and the future of the Congress government, Desai accepted the position of deputy prime minister and finance minister.

Senior economic advisors in the government also played a crucial role in ensuring that Morarji Desai and Indira Gandhi worked together in the government to face up to the immense economic challenges that lay ahead for the nation. I.G. Patel, who was then chief economic adviser in the finance ministry, had a discussion with Pitambar Pant, head of the Perspective Planning Division in the government, and P.N. Dhar, who would later join the prime minister's office under Indira Gandhi, believed that they should try to persuade the two to patch up their differences for the country's sake. Pant and Dhar were to meet Gandhi and Patel was to meet Desai, who as usual was inquisitive to know if the idea had come from someone else or was his own. Desai heard Patel out but did not respond to his suggestion.[3]

The next day, 13 March 1967, Desai got a call from Gandhi to meet her and discuss the formation of the council of ministers. Desai made some suggestions for changing the composition of the council. Gandhi did not accept all his suggestions. The same day the swearing-in ceremony was held at Rashtrapati Bhavan. A little later, Desai went to North Block and took charge of the finance ministry for the second time in his political career, and after a gap of just four years.

A Short-Lived Victory

Desai's second stint as finance minister was no less stormy or controversial than the first one. The Indian economy was still to emerge from the deep turmoil in the wake of a steep currency devaluation of 57 per cent. Its import bill for crude oil and petroleum products was threatening to go out of control. Food availability within the country was a major cause for concern. A drop in food grain production in the country led to an increase in food imports, whose value went up from $676 million in 1965–66 to $868 million in 1966–67. While imports had shot up, exports did not reflect any measurable increase in spite of the rupee devaluation. Gandhi was under attack even within the Congress and was desperately looking for support from within—support that came from a group of socialist Congress leaders, including Chandra Shekhar and Mohan Dharia.

Not surprisingly, therefore, a proposal for nationalizing a few banks and general insurance companies was brought before the Congress working committee sometime in May 1967. Along with that came a proposal to abolish the Privy Purses and privileges that the government had committed to providing the princes who had agreed to join the Indian Union at the time of Independence in 1947. Many Congress leaders openly supported the idea of nationalizing banks and general insurance companies. That was not surprising, as the Congress had taken a policy decision on pursuing a socialistic pattern of economic development and the Nehru government had already completed nationalization of Imperial Bank of India, rechristening it State Bank of India in 1955, and of the life insurance companies, resulting in the formation of the Life Insurance Corporation of India in 1956. But Desai's response to the idea of nationalizing banks and general insurance companies in 1967 was nuanced.

Desai made a subtle distinction between a principle and an instrument for policy change. His belief was that bank nationalization was not a matter of principle, but one of instrument to bring about a kind of economic development that policymakers desired. 'If the country benefits by nationalisation and the interest of the common man is served, it should be resorted to, but if that purpose is not served, there should be no nationalisation, just for the sake of nationalisation,' Desai declared at the Congress working committee meeting.[4] Having enunciated this basic distinction, Desai elaborated on why he believed bank nationalization should not be the preferred mode of policy instrument at that point in time. He referred to the economic distress that had prevailed since the Chinese aggression in 1962 and how the food shortage of two years had posed new challenges for the government. Inflation had reared its ugly head once again. Industrial growth had been suffering. The few public-sector undertakings that had been created were yet to become profitable or efficient. In such a situation, Desai argued, the proposal for bank nationalization would inflict more damage to the economy, and obtaining the required resources for boosting investment would become an even bigger challenge.

At that meeting, Desai also gave ample evidence of his understanding of the financial constraints that the Indian economy faced. After all, he had spent four years as the finance minister under the Nehru government and was now once again in charge of the exchequer. He recalled that most banks in India had been set up by industrialists. As a result, these banks would be focused on providing loans to big industry, and small entrepreneurs would suffer from paucity of funds to run their businesses even when they had a deserving case for obtaining bank loans. Similarly, the farm sector never got loans from commercial banks. But if the banks had not lent money to the farm sector, it was because the government policy was such, Desai argued. The government's policy did not specifically encourage commercial banks to lend to the agriculture sector as it wanted cooperative banks to play that role. So, why blame commercial banks for not extending adequate loans to the farm sector, Desai asked his colleagues at that meeting.

A way out, according to Desai, was not nationalization of banks but introduction of steps to exercise social control over commercial banks in the country, mandating them to channel a specific share of their total loans to agriculture. Social control of banks could be exercised, either through the Reserve Bank of India or through a legislative change. Laws could also be changed to reduce the dominance of industrialists on the boards and managements of the commercial banks, in a bid to ensure that they offered more loans for farming activities. Even a credit policy could be framed to meet the government's requirement of providing adequate loans to the farm sector. Those commercial banks that did not fall in line, did not implement the revised credit policy or did not channel more loans to agriculture could be taken over by the government, Desai declared.

What's more, Desai argued, while only a few commercial banks could be nationalized, his policy of social control could actually be enforced on the entire banking sector, including the foreign banks operating in India. In his arguments against nationalization of banks, Desai also said that substantial amounts of resources would be needed from the exchequer to compensate the owners of these banks for the change in ownership. This would be a burden on the government, which was already facing a resources constraint. Finally, nationalizing commercial banks would also breed inefficiencies, as once they become government undertakings the disease of red tape would infect their managements.

Desai was equally firm in his opposition to the proposal for nationalizing general insurance companies. He argued that this could not be justified just because life insurance companies were nationalized a few years ago, because the two were different kinds of businesses. General insurance companies in operation in the country at that time were very few, and nationalizing them would serve no specific national purpose except that their managements would suffer from bureaucratic inefficiencies and corruption. The manner in which these companies would be run under government control could be an additional headache. Instead of nationalizing the general insurance companies, Desai suggested that the existing weaknesses in their businesses could be removed and social control provisions could be enforced on them too.

His arguments against nationalization were strong and his alternative proposal for introducing social control over banks and general insurance companies was a viable idea. A few members present at the Congress working committee asked Desai how long the experiment of social control would have to be undertaken to see some positive results in the banks' lending patterns. There was also a question put to him on whether he would be prepared to nationalize the banks and general insurance companies if social control measures failed to secure for government the desired benefits. Desai clinched the issues under debate with a categorical response to those questions. He said, 'Social control will be more effective than nationalization, but if most of my colleagues are not convinced at the end of two years about the success of social control, I shall myself come forward with a scheme for nationalization without anybody asking for it.' After this there was no further debate. Desai's idea of social control for banks was accepted by the Congress working committee.

Abolishing the Privy Purses

On the question of abolishing the Privy Purses and other privileges for the erstwhile princes of India, Desai's arguments made only partial impact. He reminded the members of the Congress working committee that Privy Purses were part of the promises the government had made to the erstwhile princes. If these facilities had to be abrogated, the government must hold negotiations with those who were enjoying these financial privileges. Desai even offered his services for these negotiations. However, this view was accepted only partially. Desai was not asked to hold these negotiations with the erstwhile princes. Instead, a decision to discontinue the privileges was taken, but the Privy Purses were allowed to be continued. Privy Purses included an annual fixed tax-free amount paid to all the ex-princes by the Union government. In addition, certain non-financial privileges, like official recognition of the titles of the princes, were granted to them.

However, there was a volte-face on the Privy Purses issue subsequently at a meeting of the All India Congress Committee (AICC). Minutes before the end of the session, a resolution was moved calling for the abolition of Privy Purses and privileges. This was accepted by a majority. Desai had noted that since this resolution had come up for consideration at the fag end of the session, when attendance was thin, it perhaps facilitated approval of the proposal. But on the crucial question of bank nationalization, Desai held his ground.

Implementation of Social Control on Banks

Soon after the AICC meeting held in the summer of 1967, Desai asked V.A. Pai Panandiker, a young economist with the Planning Commission, to examine the idea of social control on banks and submit a report on how to implement it. The report was ready before Desai left in August 1967 for a tour of Japan. He studied the report during this trip. Although he returned from Japan in September, action on the report had to wait for some more weeks as Desai was scheduled to go on an overseas visit once again. He left for Rio de Janeiro in Brazil to attend the annual meetings of the World Bank and the International Monetary Fund, and from there visited Port of Spain to attend the meeting of the Commonwealth finance ministers. It was a long overseas tour for Desai and he returned to India in October 1967. Based on the report and other consultations Desai held, a scheme for social control of banks was prepared and sent to the Union Cabinet.

At the Cabinet meeting, the scheme triggered a lengthy debate. Desai argued there too for the need to introduce the scheme instead of nationalizing banks. The Cabinet approved his idea of social control over banks, though there were a few dissenting voices.

Once the Cabinet gave its stamp of approval to the scheme, Desai lost little time in starting the process of bringing about a major change in the banking sector. He told the Lok Sabha on 14 December 1967 that he planned to introduce a legislative bill for social control of banks, facilitating reconstitution of the bank boards, prohibiting advances or guarantees to directors and to the companies in which they had interests. In addition, Desai said the new bill would allow acquisition of the business of a particular bank by the government if the bank failed to comply with the provisions of the new legal framework. The Reserve Bank of India was to be given additional powers to facilitate such monitoring, supervision and enforcement of the new law. At around the same time, Desai met the top management of the commercial banks to discuss his proposals on social control for channelling more loans to the farming sector and the necessary changes in the management structure that would have to be made to achieve those goals.

In the winter session of Parliament in December 1968, Desai introduced the bill on social control of banks. The Banking Laws (Amendment) Bill, 1968 was primarily aimed at regulating the activities of commercial banks in the country. The objective was to help the economy attain optimum growth and at the same time prevent monopolistic trends, concentration of economic power and misdirection of resources. More specifically, the new law was expected to ensure a fairer and more equitable distribution of bank loans to priority sectors like agriculture, small-scale enterprises, the self-employed, and public sector undertakings. The bill was passed by Parliament in February 1969.

Just before the passage of the legislation on social control of banks, the proposal for bank nationalization had figured once again in early 1969. It was raised at a meeting of the National Development Council, a body of the Planning Commission where chief ministers of the states and important Union ministers and the prime minister are represented. A few chief ministers had expectedly raised the question of bank nationalization. But both Desai and Dhananjay Ramchandra Gadgil, the deputy chairman of the Commission, opposed the move and suggested that social control of banks must be given a fair trial before taking any steps towards bank nationalization. I.G. Patel, who by then had become Special Secretary in the Economic Affairs Department in the finance ministry, had advised Desai that the prime minister should be asked to make her stand clear on the question of bank nationalization. Desai, therefore, asked Gandhi to state her position on the issue. Gandhi said 'clearly that she was not in favour of nationalization of banks'.[5] Gandhi even said the country had not yet made a success of what had already been nationalized and the state taking on more responsibilities made little sense. Moreover, social control of banks as an idea should be given a fair trial, she said. But a few months later, Gandhi changed her mind completely and went in for bank nationalization. In his memoirs, I.G. Patel notes that the minutes of the Planning Commission recording Gandhi's views opposing bank nationalization were perhaps deleted in light of subsequent developments.

With the legal changes in place to usher in social control of banks, Desai got down to the task of bringing about the necessary changes in the boards of the banks and reducing the say of the banks' industrialist promoters on their lending decisions. Desai also set up a Credit Council, under his chairmanship, which had RBI Governor L.K. Jha, Planning Commission Deputy Chairman D.R. Gadgil, bank management representatives, industry leaders, small entrepreneurs, agriculturists and economic policy experts as its members. The primary task of the Council was to prepare a credit policy which the banks were obliged to implement. The new law was also expected to lead to changes in the management and administration of banks, the establishment of an institute for training bankers and the appointment of the Banking Commission. By March 1969, Desai had made sure that the National Institute of Bank Management was set up.

Foreign banks were not spared either. Desai met the top leaders of the foreign banks and told them that even though the new law on social control did not apply to them, they should fall in line with the overall objectives of the new legal framework. Many foreign banks set up special advisory boards and began changing the composition and focus of their top managements to give a fresh thrust to their lending operations so that they too began extending more loans to the farming sector.

However, the apparent success of the new law on social control on banks made little impact on the views of those sections within the Congress still wedded to the idea of nationalization of banks.

No Improvement in Gandhi–Desai Relations

Desai should have sensed that not all was well in his relations with Gandhi, and this was evident from the manner in which the two leaders would disagree on many issues, including even appointment of the deputy chairman of the Planning Commission. Soon after the formation of the new government in 1967, there arose the need to appoint a new deputy chairman for the Planning Commission. This was because the incumbent, Asoka Mehta, had been inducted into the Cabinet, and as per the recommendations of the Administrative Reforms Commission a minister could not be made deputy chairman of the Planning Commission. Mehta proposed Chidambaram Subramaniam as his successor, but Desai opposed the name on the ground that Subramaniam had lost the Lok Sabha elections in 1967. Desai had told Gandhi that no leader defeated in the elections should be appointed in key positions in the government—an idea with which Gandhi had concurred. When Gandhi sought Desai's views on the candidature of Subramaniam as the next deputy chairman of the Planning Commission, Desai opposed the idea on the ground that his appointment would be roundly criticized by everybody. Finally, Gandhi conceded Desai's point and asked him to suggest alternative names. Desai proposed two names—C.D. Deshmukh and D.R. Gadgil. Deshmukh was a former finance minister and Gadgil an accomplished economist with a record of unimpeachable integrity. Gandhi showed her willingness to consider Gadgil as the next deputy chairman.

Eventually, Gadgil's appointment was cleared by the government and Desai won that battle with Gandhi. But little did Desai sense that a larger battle was awaiting him on the question of bank nationalization—a battle which he would lose even before it actually began. A far worse fate would await Gadgil! Several months later, when banks would be nationalized and Indira Gandhi was the finance minister, the government would expect Gadgil to praise its move on bank nationalization. A principled man, Gadgil would not agree to praising a move that he believed was not correct. Gadgil would be made to feel unwelcome in the government, and in May 1971 he would pack up his bags decide to leave Delhi for Bombay. On the train to Bombay, Gadgil would die, with his wife beside him![6]

Desai Takes on Challenges of Deficit Financing

The ghost of deficit financing returned to haunt Desai soon after he rejoined the government of Indira Gandhi. The differences between the central bank and the finance ministry over how much leeway the Centre should get in its overspending drive to finance ambitious development expenditure also resurfaced. Similar problems had confronted him during his first tenure as the finance minister under the Nehru government. But the challenges now were more formidable, given the political forces he had to deal with within the ruling party, as also the external environment in the form of a rapidly deteriorating economy preceded by a 57 per cent devaluation of the Indian rupee against the US dollar.

The problems for the economy had begun getting worse a few years before Desai rejoined the finance ministry in March 1967. The actual numbers of the government finances for 1964–65 had shown that the deficit was much higher than the revised estimates presented by Finance Minister T.T. Krishnamachari in February 1965. RBI Governor P.C. Bhattacharya (a former secretary in the finance ministry), had lobbied hard with Prime Minister Lal Bahadur Shastri to speak to his finance minister Krishnamachari to maintain prudence. In a letter Shastri wrote to Krishnamachari in June 1965, there was a directive to the finance ministry to take advance measures to revise outlays on some items of expenditure so that the revenue shortfalls could be adequately adjusted without widening the deficit. Both the domestic food availability situation (dependence on imports was on the rise even as agricultural output within the country was not adequate to meet the rising demand) and the external security environment (the country had begun facing military aggression from Pakistan from April 1965, which culminated in a full-scale war in September that year) were critical. In 1967, Bhattacharya told Desai in no uncertain terms that the Fourth Plan, originally scheduled to begin from 1966, should be based on realistic estimates of both domestic and external resources. It was at the RBI's insistence that the size of the Fourth Plan had to be scaled down from the original estimate of Rs 23,750 crore to Rs 19,000 crore. However, the Fourth Plan was abandoned because of a combination of factors, including the food crisis, the impact of the war on the economy and the devaluation. A period pf three years of Plan Holiday began before the Fourth Plan was resumed in 1969.

Desai and RBI Differ over Deposits Collection

Differences between Morarji Desai as the finance minister and the Reserve Bank came to the fore soon after Desai returned to the government as deputy prime minister with added charge of the finance ministry in March 1967. By then the Reserve Bank of India had already put in place a revised policy framework for deposits collected by non-banking companies. The central bank had been a bit worried that companies were channelling a good part of the savings of people into their accounts as deposits by offering attractive interest rates. Its worry arose on account of its finding that many companies without strong balance sheets were raising these deposits and that the repayment risks could threaten the financial system in the country. Many companies were also offering attractive interest rates, often as high as 12 per cent, even as banks were finding it difficult to attract deposits at their relatively modest interest rates. A way out was to impose a cap on the deposits that non-banking companies could collect in a year. More curbs were also imposed on such deposits, including closer monitoring and supervision of accounts of non-banking companies. Trade and industry opposed these norms and the RBI was exploring options to relax them—a move that got further impetus from Desai in June 1967. Desai was of the view that the existing rules were 'onerous' on non-banking companies and that these restrictions, like the cap on the volume of deposits they could collect, should be further relaxed. However, the RBI did stay firm in its overall approach against dilution of the norms in view of the risks such a relaxation could entail for the financial system.

Desai's First Budget under Indira Gandhi

The first Budget Desai presented in his second stint as finance minister required the framing of policies against the backdrop of an economy that was in distress. The Chinese aggression in 1962 and the war with Pakistan in 1965 had adversely impacted the economy and government finances. The Indian economy had contracted in 1965–66 by 3.7 per cent, and in the following year the growth recovery was marginal, at just 1 per cent. India's foreign exchange reserves were not too healthy either. They were estimated at $626 million in 1965–66. The following year they rose to $638 million. But even this marginal increase was possible only on the strength of drawings from the International Monetary Fund—$100 million in 1964–65, $137.5 million in 1965–66 and $187.5 million in 1966–67. Putting pressure on the foreign exchange reserves was a widening trade deficit—up from Rs 583 crore in 1965–66 to Rs 906 crore in 1966–67. Both wholesale price-based inflation and consumer inflation had risen to an uncomfortably high level of 13–14 per cent in 1966–67. The task before Desai, when he rose to present his Budget in May 1967, was undoubtedly onerous.

In Desai's view, the urgent need was for him to present a balanced Budget that would recognize both the reality of reduced availability of resources in the prevailing situation of economic distress and the need for incurring enhanced expenditure on relief as well as support operations in view of runaway inflation. As a consequence, Desai's first Budget under Indira Gandhi as the prime minister had to concede a deficit of Rs 168 crore. The central objective of the 1967–68 Budget was to restore economic stability.

Thus, the finance minister underlined the need for increasing the country's self-sufficiency in food, which could reduce its dependence on imports, for introducing steps to revive industrial production, including measures such as relaxation in imports and higher allocations for the capital goods sector, schemes for exports promotion and dismantling of the many controls that had outlived their utility. In terms of taxation, Desai was quite restrained. He announced a series of direct tax concessions and announced small increases in excise and customs duties on a few commodities. The promises made while devaluing the Indian currency a few months ago had been largely forgotten.

But the unique feature of Desai's first Budget under Indira Gandhi was a novel element that was introduced for the first time. Unfortunately, that practice was not continued in the future. Desai accepted the idea of doing away with deficit financing. It was an idea mooted by his economic advisors and even though accepted in his Budget for 1967–68, in reality, the idea had few takers. I.G. Patel, the chief economic advisor at that time, wrote in his memoirs to capture this interesting development in Desai's first Budget:

> We had always justified some deficit financing on the ground that a growing economy which was also becoming more marketized needed a growing money supply. It was for the first time in a Budget speech that we confronted the question as to why this legitimate scope for money creation should be appropriated entirely by the public sector. After all, the demand for money arose largely in the private sector where the bulk of economic transactions took place. Why should the RBI not finance commercial banks rather than the Government to achieve the desired increase in money supply? There was also the consideration that the much-needed increase in foreign exchange holdings of the RBI would in any case add to money supply. A conscious decision was taken to have no deficit financing for the Government. This was a reflection of the spirit in which the new Government was to address its tasks. Alas, in the event, there was a deficit.[7]

Desai had a difference of opinion with Gandhi on the allocations made for the states in the Budget for 1967–68. Soon after the Budget was passed, the prime minister requested the finance minister to increase allocations for a couple of the states. Desai was in no mood to accept a request that was not only in violation of the spirit of decision-making, but also quite impractical, given the constraints on government resources. Desai pointed out that the Budget had been passed and it would be improper to reopen the question of increasing allocation for a few states. More importantly, the Centre was going through an acute scarcity of resources and any further increase in allocation to a few states would only make the burden on its finances unbearable. And the costs of increasing government expenditure would be huge for the price situation in the country as such demands could be met only through deficit financing. Such excesses in expenditure over revenues of the government are inflationary by nature, Desai warned his prime minister. Eventually, Gandhi saw reason in those arguments and did not press the issue further. Desai heaved a sigh of relief.

Desai's Second Budget as Economy Recovers

By the time Desai had to present his second Budget in his second stint as finance minister, the Indian economy had staged a smart recovery. That was the Budget for 1968–69. The Indian economy had expanded by 8.1 per cent, the highest growth rate seen since Independence. The wholesale price-based inflation had been brought down to just 0.88 per cent in 1967–68, even though retail inflation was still in the double digits. Trade deficit too was reined in, at Rs 788 crore, down 13 per cent from the level in 1966–67. Not surprisingly, foreign exchange reserves rose by over 12 per cent to $718 million in 1967–68, although the accretion in the reserves was helped by the withdrawal of $90 million from the IMF during the year. But the amount drawn from the IMF was less than half of what was borrowed in the previous year. All in all, Desai's Budget for 1967–68 was seen to have turned the Indian economy around, paving the way for him to take bolder steps in his Budget for 1968–69 to build on the growth already achieved.

The central thrust in the 1968–69 Budget, therefore, was to take advantage of the recovery and initiate further steps to improve the investment climate. The surtax on corporate taxes, which Desai had imposed a few years ago in his earlier stint as finance minister, was now reduced by him. The tax levied on dividends was removed completely. More support measures were taken for farmers so that agricultural output could get a boost and Indian companies could increase their exports. The income tax structure for individuals was simplified and exemption limits were relaxed. Steps to prevent evasion of tax payment were also announced, and these included imposition of limits on expenditure that could enjoy tax concessions. Tax exemptions on expenditure by companies were also restricted to only payments made by cheque. New schemes were introduced to encourage savings by the people, which would be exempted from taxes. A five-year fixed deposit scheme with income tax exemption and a public provident fund scheme with tax exemptions for those who did not have an opportunity to subscribe to such schemes were introduced. Additional tax mobilization through the Budget amounted to Rs 66 crore.

The Last Budget from Desai

Desai's third and final Budget in his second term as finance minister was presented on 28 February 1969. The focus was on raising capital investment in light of the recovery phase into which the Indian economy had already entered. Further simplification in the taxation structure was also introduced. In the hope that the economic recovery would result in higher tax collections, Desai went in for an increase in the Centre's overall expenditure outlay by Rs 177 crore, the bulk of which was on account of higher expenditure on development projects. Indeed, the Budget for 1969–70 proposed a cut in the outlay for subsidy of food grains and for relief expenditure to address food shortages in the economy. A significant move Desai initiated was the linking of excise duty rates on many items to their prices. The shift to ad valorem rates, instead of a fixed rate of duty levied on the volume, irrespective of the price, meant that the government's revenues from excise duty acquired added buoyancy. As and when prices of goods went up, the excise collections would automatically rise because the rate was ad valorem, or linked to the price of the product. The wealth tax policy was also tweaked to include agricultural land while calculating the wealth of a person for purposes of payment of wealth tax. The move was aimed at reducing evasion in payment of wealth tax.

The importance of the 1969–70 Budget also lay in the fact that it marked the resumption of the Five-Year Plans. The Third Five-year Plan was ambitious in its intent. It had projected an annual growth rate of 5.6 per cent for the five-year period beginning April 1961 and ending March 1966. Thanks to an acute resources constraint and the two wars India fought with its neighbours, China and Pakistan, and rising inflation, the Third Plan had ended with an annual growth rate of only 2.4 per cent. Stumped by this reversal and by the steady deterioration in the economy, a virtual Plan holiday had been declared from 1966 for about three years. Only in 1969 did the government muster the courage to return to the five-year planning schedule by deciding to roll out the Fourth Five-year Plan from April 1969 and set yet another ambitious growth target of 5.6 per cent.

Differences over Who Should Be the Next President

Less than three months of the presentation of Desai's third Budget under Gandhi, India's third President Dr Zakir Husain died following a massive heart attack. That was on 3 May 1969. Husain was the first Indian President to have died in office. While a period of national mourning had been declared and schools and offices were closed across the country, the Congress party went into a huddle to decide on who should succeed Husain at Rashtrapati Bhavan.

Desai had returned from an overseas visit to Australia and Singapore on the morning of 3 May 1969. Soon after he reached office, he was informed by the President's office that Husain had suffered a heart attack and doctors were attending to him. Desai rushed to Rashtrapati Bhavan and learnt from the doctors that they were trying to revive Husain, but to no avail. Indira Gandhi was not in the city as she was away on a tour of Rajasthan. Senior doctors were summoned, and when they examined the President and found there was no response, they declared that he was dead. The prime minister returned to New Delhi only by 5.30 p.m., and the funeral was planned for the next day.

The question as to who the next president should be had to be settled, and this became another bone of contention between Gandhi and Desai. A day or two after the funeral ceremony for Husain, Gandhi invited Desai for a meeting to discuss the issue of Presidential succession. Desai was clear in his point of view: the country was lucky to have for all its past Presidents persons of great calibre and of unimpeachable integrity—Rajendra Prasad, Sarvepalli Radhakrishnan and Zakir Husain. That tradition, he said, must be maintained and the President should be elected unanimously.

According to Desai, it was at this point that Gandhi asked if he would endorse the candidature of V.V. Giri for the post of President. Giri at that time was the Vice-President. A veteran politician and trade union leader, Giri had not endeared himself to many Congress leaders because of the manner in which he would take his entire family, which was quite large, as part of his entourage during his official visits. Desai was also one of his critics in the Congress party. So, when Gandhi asked Desai about considering Giri for the post, he did not mince words to express his opposition. Desai cited three reasons for his stand against Giri. One, he recalled that Gandhi herself was not greatly enamoured of his performance as the vice-president, thereby ruling him out for the proposed elevation. Two, Desai reminded Gandhi that she herself had expressed the view earlier that a vice-president should not always be automatically elevated to the post of President. And three, it was time that a candidate from a lower caste (Harijan) was nominated to contest in the election to become the next President. Desai named two Harijan candidates—Jagjivan Ram and Damodaram Sanjivayya, but rejected both too, revealing a lot on how he approached such issues. He told Gandhi that Ram had not submitted his tax returns for his additional income for the last ten years, which would debar him from qualifying as a Presidential candidate. And Sanjivayya was too young to be considered for the job as he had a bright political future ahead of him. Ram was a member of the first Nehru Cabinet after India gained independence and was the minister for food and agriculture in Gandhi's Cabinet at that time. He was sixty-one. Sanjivayya was just forty-eight and had done well as a Dalit leader. He was the second chief minister of Andhra Pradesh and the first Dalit head of any state. He served as a minister for labour and employment in Lal Bahadur Shastri's Cabinet, and in 1969 was a member of the Rajya Sabha.

In spite of Desai's reasons and reservations, Gandhi, however, was still keen on either Jagjivan Ram or V.V. Giri to succeed Zakir Husain as the next President. Desai and a few other Congress leaders proposed Lok Sabha Speaker Neelam Sanjiva Reddy as an alternative. Gandhi made no secret of her disapproval of Reddy as the Presidential candidate. She apprehended that if Reddy became the President, he could create difficulties for the government. Reddy was politically aligned with senior Congress leaders like K. Kamaraj, S Nijalingappa, S.K. Patil and Atulya Ghosh, who had formed their own group within the party and whose relationship with Gandhi was becoming strained. There was a logjam on this issue. Gandhi wanted either Giri or Ram, while others like Desai and Kamaraj preferred Reddy. The Congress Parliamentary Board finally resolved that the issue should be discussed at a meeting of the All India Congress Committee and the Congress working committee, which had been scheduled to be held on 9 July in Bangalore.

That meeting continued for two days. On the second day, Gandhi wanted to move a resolution that called for either nationalization of about half a dozen banks or release of more funds by commercial banks for industries in sync with the policy on social control of banks. Desai intervened and told the gathering that while the idea of bank nationalization had been accepted in principle, the modality and timing of implementing that decision would be decided by the Congress working committee after taking on board the views of all concerned. When the resolution was taken up for consideration, Desai addressed all the concerns over funds availability for industries, and the idea of bank nationalization did not get the nod of approval for implementation. Desai won the battle that day, but little could he anticipate that a bigger crisis was awaiting him in the next few days.

On 12 July, the Congress Parliamentary Board met to discuss the issue of who should be party's Presidential candidate. The stalemate continued as Gandhi and her followers (Fakhruddin Ali Ahmed, who was the minister for industrial development and company affairs, and Jagjivan Ram, who, along with Gandhi, was a member of the Board) were keen on Jagjivan Ram's candidature, while others on the Board (led by Congress president S. Nijalingappa, Home Minister Yashwantrao Chavan, S.K. Patil, Kamaraj and Desai) supported the candidature of Neelam Sanjiva Reddy. The eight members of the Congress Parliamentary Board were asked to give their votes in favour of the candidate they believed should be the Congress's Presidential nominee, choosing from Jagjivan Ram and Neelam Sanjiva Reddy. The voting results were in favour of Reddy—five in his favour and three in favour of Ram. Gandhi feared that Reddy's nomination would create difficulties for the government and refused to accept the verdict. By then she was convinced that the senior group of Congress leaders including Kamaraj and Nijalingappa could create problems for the government as they had begun opposing her politically. As a compromise formula, it was decided that Nijalingappa and Gandhi should hold a final consultation to decide the way forward. A day later, on 13 July, Reddy was named as the Congress candidate for the post of President.

An Unceremonious Exit for Desai

On 14 July, Desai learnt from officers close to Fakhruddin Ali Ahmed that he was being dropped from the Cabinet. The rumours were not entirely baseless. What followed in their wake pushed Desai out of the government eventually. On 16 July, a special letter from Gandhi was dispatched to Desai. The letter, handed over to Desai at 12.30 p.m. that day, informed him that he was being divested of his responsibility of the finance ministry. An hour later, an official announcement was made to the effect that Gandhi had taken charge of the finance ministry as an additional responsibility. Gandhi's letter told Desai that he could continue as the deputy prime minister and that she would discuss with him what work could be assigned to him later. But Desai replied to Gandhi saying that in view of the manner in which he was divested of the finance ministry, he would resign from her government. Gandhi insisted on a meeting with Desai to persuade him to stay on in the Cabinet. Desai met her the following day and told her that he could stay on in the Cabinet only if she agreed to retrace the steps she had taken—of divesting him of the finance ministry portfolio. Gandhi was categorical in her decision to take the finance ministry portfolio away from him and said that the step taken could not be retraced. The bitterness was not over yet. At the Congress Parliamentary Board meeting on 19 July, Gandhi explained why she chose to take away the finance ministry from Desai. The reason was that she wanted to gain experience of running the finance ministry. Moreover, she argued that everyone in the Cabinet must acknowledge her right to assign ministerial responsibilities to the person of her choice and that decision should be accepted by all. Once again, Desai launched a broadside against the prime minister, arguing that if she wanted to gain experience of handling the finance ministry, he would have gladly vacated the ministry, if only the prime minister had asked him. What she did instead was to send him a letter informing him of her decision to move him out of the finance ministry. Desai also questioned the absolute and unilateral right of the prime minister to shift any minister out of a ministry, instead of building an opinion on such an issue by consulting other team members.

At the end of a long debate, at around 3 p.m., Desai's resignation from the Union Cabinet was accepted, ending the Morarji Desai saga in a Congress government. The same evening, Indira Gandhi, the new finance minister, announced the government's decision to nationalize fourteen banks. But that is another chapter on how Gandhi as finance minister changed the course of the Indian economy.

Indira Gandhi (Finance Minister, 1969–1970)

The Architect of Bank Nationalization

Rarely do Indian prime ministers take additional charge of the finance ministry.

Only once up to 1969 had an Indian prime minister decided to take on the finance ministry as an additional responsibility. That was Jawahar Lal Nehru, in 1958. His finance minister, T.T. Krishnamachari, had to resign just about a fortnight before he was due to present the Union Budget for 1958–59.

The circumstances under which Krishnamachari resigned were controversial—a financial scandal had raised questions about his conduct. And even though Nehru was convinced of his finance minister's probity, he had to succumb to political and popular pressure to secure his finance minister's resignation. Nehru took upon himself the additional responsibility of the finance ministry and presented the Budget for 1958–59, but a month later he entrusted the responsibility of managing the central exchequer to Morarji Desai.

The second time an Indian prime minister decided to include the finance ministry as additional responsibility was in July 1969. That prime minister was Indira Gandhi. Coincidentally, the finance minister who was eased out by Gandhi before she assumed additional charge of the finance ministry was none other than Morarji Desai. And the circumstances under which the prime minister took upon herself this additional responsibility were even more complex and intensely political than in 1958.

The relationship between Indira Gandhi and Morarji Desai was always tense. There was mutual lack of trust between the two. Yet, Desai was accepted by Gandhi as a member of her Cabinet, mainly because of political compulsions. She may have sensed that Desai was not one among her arch rivals forming the nucleus of the Congress Syndicate. She also needed the administrative experience of Desai to run her government. On the other hand, Desai saw this as an opportunity to become the deputy prime minister as well as the finance minister in her government.

But this relationship did not last long, for two reasons. One, Gandhi soon found that Desai was not helping her in her battle with the old guard in the party—the Congress Syndicate led by K. Kamaraj, S. Nijalingappa, S.K. Patil and Atulya Ghosh, among others. Two, Gandhi found to her dismay that Desai was not willing to play along with her idea of bringing about a socialistic shift in the economic policies of the government.

While Gandhi was keen on nationalizing the private banks in the country, Desai was opposed to the idea, pointing out that instead of nationalizing them it would be better to introduce social controls for banks. Indeed, Desai had moved quite rapidly in ensuring social controls for banks. This essentially meant that the government's objective of ensuring more equitable growth in the rural pockets of India had to be achieved by setting lending targets for banks to meet its socio-economic goal of greater financial inclusion. But Gandhi was unhappy with this idea and was keen on bank nationalization instead.

What complicated the political situation at the time was the sudden death of President Zakir Husain in May 1969. V.V. Giri, the Vice-President at that time and a close associate of Indira Gandhi, was made the acting President until the elections could be completed to find Husain's successor. The process of finding a candidate who could take over from the acting President posed yet another challenge for Gandhi. While the Congress Syndicate leaders wanted Neelam Sanjiva Reddy, who was at the time the Lok Sabha speaker, Gandhi was keen on Giri becoming the next President. This issue also became a bone of contention between Gandhi and Desai. The stalemate continued for more than two months.

Turbulent July

The month of July 1969 turned out to be hugely eventful for India's politics and economy. In the second week of July 1969, a series of meetings of the

Congress party in Bangalore highlighted the widening differences between Gandhi and Desai. At these meetings, Gandhi once again tried to push for bank nationalization, but Desai held his ground. In the final round of these meetings, Gandhi seemed to have lost her other battle as well, with the Congress party deciding to nominate Sanjiva Reddy to be the party candidate for the post of President. But, as it eventually turned out, she managed to achieve both her goals.

On 9 July, Gandhi dispatched a note to the Congress working committee. The note, sent through Fakhruddin Ali Ahmed, who was then the minister for industrial development and a close ally of Gandhi's, recommended nationalization of the major commercial banks in the country. With that note, Gandhi sprang a big surprise on Desai. The law on social control of banks had been passed and its implementation was taking place at a healthy pace. And just about four months before Gandhi's note, the National Credit Council, a body set up under the law on social control for banks to ensure the desired direction of credit allocation, had held its third meeting. The third volume of the history of Reserve Bank of India says:

> Indira Gandhi had, by then, decided to confront the Syndicate in what was a bid to wrest control of the party. She needed a dramatic issue and bank nationalization fitted the bill. Accordingly, she decided to precipitate matters. Indeed, hindsight as well as oral evidence from the main dramatis personae suggest that she had already decided upon nationalization. Only the details were left to be worked out by the Finance Ministry.[1]

What did Gandhi's note dated 9 July to the Congress working committee contain? She made no bones about her intentions. The note said:

> There is a great feeling in the country regarding the nationalization of private commercial banks. We had taken a decision at an earlier AICC, but perhaps we may review it. Either we can consider the nationalization of the top five or six banks or issue directions that the resources of banks should be reserved to a larger extent for public purposes.

Not mincing words, Gandhi provided a policy rationale for the need for bank nationalization:

> Even after the new policy of social control and reconstitution of boards of directors, the former industrialist chairmen of the banks still continue on the board and naturally influence the present chairmen who had previously been general managers. We may examine whether through legislation or otherwise we can prevent these men from continuing on the boards. The chief executive of the banks will not then feel obliged to the former Chairman and may be expected to take an independent line in regard to lending.

Morarji Desai fought tooth and nail against the move, arguing that the legislation on social controls for banks had been introduced only about five months ago, and any step towards bank nationalization at that stage would undermine the people's confidence in the banking system. Bank nationalization as an idea could be discussed only after a couple of years, after judging the effectiveness of the law on social controls for banks, he pointed out. But just as Desai was backed by the Syndicate, as also by the moderates within the Congress, Gandhi's note on bank nationalization was supported by members of the Congress Forum for Socialist Action, also known as the 'Young Turks', like Chandra Shekhar and Mohan Dharia.

The note was discussed at the All-India Congress Committee session in Bangalore on 10 July. Expectedly, the Syndicate, ably supported by Desai's arguments, ensured that the resolution on economic and social policy made no reference to bank nationalization, even though it talked eloquently on issues such as food supply, tenancy security and rural development.

But high drama followed soon thereafter, altering the actual course of the debate. The official draft, which had not mentioned bank nationalization, was challenged by Gandhi at the discussion stage. Her loaded question, referring to the official draft, was: 'This is all right as far as it goes. The question is whether it goes far enough?'[2] That question triggered a heated debate. Desai argued that there were no essential differences between the objectives of social control of banks and bank nationalization. The minimum amount that banks had to invest in public securities had already been raised—from the earlier mandatory level of 25 per cent to 29 per cent—and this share could be raised to even 30 per cent, Desai pointed out, noting in addition that the newly created National Credit Council was meeting regularly and its next meeting scheduled at the end of July could take a decision on that.

Gandhi had also made a stinging attack on the nexus between the top bank managements and the banks' industrialist-owners or chairpersons. She had said the industrialist owners of banks were influencing the lending decisions of the bank managements. In defence, Desai said allegations of such a nexus were being examined, with both the government and the RBI closely monitoring the situation to prevent the exercise of any such influence; many steps had been taken to make sure no such influence could be exercised, and indeed the composition of many bank boards had already been diversified by including economists and representatives from the domains of agriculture, cooperatives and small industries.

Y.B. Chavan Bats for Bank Nationalization

A key and almost decisive role was played by Y.B. Chavan, who was then the home minister in the Gandhi Cabinet and was not seen to be on the side of Gandhi in her battle with the Syndicate. But, surprising many observers, Chavan remained apparently ambivalent, but his intervention in the debate seemed to strengthen the lobby in favour of bank nationalization. He made a rather cryptic comment that social control without nationalization was not possible, just as nationalization without social control would amount to a great fraud. In his view, nationalization of banks was only a matter of time, and he rejected the idea that the proposal was politically motivated in any way. Not entirely unrelated to this development, less than a year later, Chavan would be rewarded by Gandhi. He would succeed her as the finance minister in June 1970.

But on that day—10 July 1969—Gandhi used a clever ploy. The AICC session's economic resolution made no categorical reference to bank nationalization, but Gandhi's original note sent by her to AICC on 9 July was appended to the resolution. The resolution also pointed out that the note contained details of the policies to be followed to improve the economy and urged the governments at the Centre and the states to take steps to implement them. Surprisingly, the Syndicate members made no noise about it and let the resolution be adopted in that fashion.

A couple of days later, on 12 July, Bangalore saw the Congress Parliament board meet and, much to Gandhi's consternation, the board decided to nominate Neelam Sanjiva Reddy, who was then the Lok Sabha Speaker, as the official Congress candidate for the Presidential election. The Syndicate had ceded ground to Gandhi in the matter of the economic resolution by agreeing to appending to it Gandhi's note on bank nationalization, but made sure that Gandhi's candidate, V.V. Giri, did not get the nod to be the official Congress candidate for the post of President. Of the eight members who were to decide on the nomination, two chose to abstain, two voted in favour of Giri and four cast their votes in support of Reddy.

Desai Quits as Finance Minister

A mildly disheartened Gandhi returned to Delhi on 14 July, a day after the Congress nominated Reddy. The same day, Desai learnt of a possible move to remove him from the Cabinet. Indeed, on 16 July, Gandhi divested Desai of the finance portfolio even while retaining him in the Cabinet as the deputy prime minister. Deeply hurt by Gandhi's move, Desai sought an explanation for her decision to remove him from the finance ministry. Gandhi was reticent, choosing to explain casually that she had wanted to gain the experience of running the finance ministry. In protest, Desai decided to quit the government.

Of course, the real reason for her decision to get rid of Desai was to move fast on bank nationalization, without his becoming a hurdle in the way, and get that proposal through with the help of an ordinance, which could be signed by acting President Giri.

In the back of her mind was the ten-point agenda for action she had unveiled about two years ago, in June 1967, which, among other things, had promised social control of banks, nationalization of general insurance, introduction of state trading in imports and exports, state trading in food grains, expansion of cooperatives in the processing and manufacturing industries, effective steps to curb monopolies and concentration of economic power in light of the Monopolies Commission report, provision of minimum needs to the people, restrictions on unearned increase in urban land value, a plan for a rural works programme, quicker implementation of land reforms and removal of the privileges enjoyed by princes and ex-rulers of states that had acceded to the Union of India after Independence in 1947. Some steps, like the abolition of special privileges enjoyed by the ex-rulers and princes of states, had been discussed internally, but no concrete action had been initiated yet. They would have to wait for more than a year.

Significantly though, bank nationalization was still to receive the assent of the Congress party and the government. But Indira Gandhi had made up her mind on it. Helping her in this mission and thought process were a clutch of senior government officials led by her Principal Secretary, P.N. Haksar.

On the other hand, there were quite a few of her officials, and of course her finance minister, Morarji Desai, who did not favour bank nationalization. Desai had made his opposition to it quite clear on more than one occasion. RBI governor L.K. Jha was of the view that social control of banks was a better tool with which to achieve the goals of financial inclusion and expansion of financial access in the country. Gandhi's economic affairs secretary in the finance ministry, I.G. Patel, also was not in favour of bank nationalization.

Gandhi wanted to either remove those in the government who did not see eye to eye with her on bank nationalization or side-line them. Not surprisingly, Desai was divested of the finance ministry on 16 July and both Jha and Patel were kept in the dark about her plans for bank nationalization till the final stages of planning, just before the announcement was made on All India Radio on the evening of 19 July 1969. Desai's resignation from the government had been accepted by Gandhi just a few hours earlier that same day!

For Gandhi, time was of the essence if she were to succeed in executing her plan. She wanted the bank nationalization order to be passed before the electoral battle for the new President began. After having lost the presidential nomination battle to the Congress Syndicate, which had chosen Neelam Sanjiva Reddy the party's candidate, she had made up her mind on V.V. Giri for the post and was hoping to secure support for Giri from all her followers. It was a move that would eventually lead to the splitting of the Congress.

After her return from Bangalore on 14 July 1969, Gandhi first made sure that Giri was on board to become an independent candidate for the post of President of India in the election that was to be held on 16 August. On 16 July, the same day Desai was divested of the responsibility of the finance ministry, Giri announced his candidature for Presidency and informed Gandhi of his intention to resign from his twin offices of acting President and vice-president, in the 'best traditions of democracy and to uphold the dignity of the two offices he was currently holding'.[3]

Since Giri had to file his nomination papers by 20 July and the monsoon session of the fourth Lok Sabha was to start on Monday, 21 July, Gandhi had reckoned that both the bank nationalization decision and Giri's nomination as a Presidential candidate had to be made by Saturday, 19 July. Gandhi had just about five days to complete the challenging task—get the bank nationalization ordinance promulgated by the acting President before he resigned on 20 July.

It is not entirely clear when Gandhi gave the green signal to P.N. Haksar, secretary to the PM, to go ahead and plan the bank nationalization ordinance. But it is reasonable to conclude that divesting Desai on 16 July of the finance ministry was the first big move in her grand plan. Haksar had already advised Gandhi to take some bold economic measures to strengthen her political base. Bank nationalization was one such measure.

Industry and Bank Nationalization

Gandhi had begun consulting leading industrialists, politicians and economists to seek their views. G.D. Birla and J.R.D. Tata, two doyens of Indian industry, had told her in clear terms that bank nationalization would be a bad idea. They were, of course, interested parties, as they would be among those to lose their banks if nationalization were to happen. Haksar met Krishna Menon, former minister of defence in the Nehru government, who made an astonishing and simplistic suggestion that bank nationalization would put an end to all the worries of the government when it came to mobilization of resources. Gandhi also had the benefit of the views of Kakkadan Nandanath Raj, a brilliant economist who had helped the Nehru government draft its First Five-Year Plan at the young age of twenty-six. Haksar had invited home both Raj and P.N. Dhar, another economist—who would later, in November 1970, join the Prime Minister's Secretariat—for a discussion on the move.

What transpired at this meeting is quite revealing. Dhar believed that bank nationalization could be a 'powerful weapon in the factional fight against the Syndicate, but if it was just a flash in the pan, unaccompanied by constructive steps to accelerate growth, it would yield no long-term economic and political benefits'.[4] Indeed, Dhar's fears came true in the years after bank nationalization. However, 'Raj was wholeheartedly for nationalisation and said it would take at least six months to prepare for it and that it should be done as an elaborate but secret exercise'.[5] Three days after this meeting, Gandhi got the ordinance on bank nationalization promulgated.

Two Days before Bank Nationalization

Even as letters were exchanged between Gandhi and Desai the next couple of days, Gandhi told Haksar on 17 July to move fast to finalize the ordinance on bank nationalization. The very same day, Haksar got in touch with Dhruba Narayan Ghosh, who was then a Deputy Secretary in the banking division of the Economic Affairs Department in the finance ministry. Ghosh was a little surprised when he received that call from Haksar on the night of 17 July. The two were not very close to each other and had met only on a couple of occasions at the residence of A. Bakshi, who had served at the banking division for many years before becoming chairman of the Industrial Finance Corporation of India, and later the Deputy Governor of the Reserve Bank of India. Indeed, after being tasked by Indira Gandhi with the preparation for bank nationalization, Haksar had initially thought of consulting Bakshi. But that evening Bakshi was at Tirupati. When the two talked, Bakshi said he could come to Delhi by the next flight from Madras, and in the meanwhile Haksar could consult Ghosh. Haksar made sure that the Indian Airlines flight from Madras that evening took off only after Bakshi was on board, even if that meant delaying the flight.[6]

That night, Ghosh met Haksar at the latter's Race Course Road residence. The meeting was long, ending only in the early hours of Friday, 18 July, by which time they had come to grips with the broad contours of the plan for bank nationalization. Bakshi had joined them late in the night after reaching Delhi by the Indian Airlines flight from Madras.

Earlier, K.V. Raghunatha Reddy, minister of state for company affairs, had entered the room where Ghosh, Haksar and Bakshi were deliberating on the plan and volunteered his suggestion that all banks should be nationalized. Haksar paid no heed to that suggestion and actually told the minister of state to leave him and Ghosh alone. To be sure, even Bakshi was a little ambivalent on whether the bank nationalization plan could be implemented with an ordinance in the next two days. But Ghosh made a political argument, pointing out that the prime minister was using a short window of opportunity to make a decisive impact on both the politics and economy of the country. Haksar was convinced by that argument, and the three got down to the task of finalizing the details of the ordinance. But one issue remained to be settled: how many banks were to be nationalized?

What Happened on 18 July

By the time the three ended their meeting, it was early morning of 18 July. Haksar told Ghosh to meet him at his South Block office at around 8.30 a.m. Haksar was to see the prime minister at 7.30 a.m. at her residence. Ghosh reached Haksar's office a little before 8.30 a.m., after collecting the latest RBI statement that had detailed the amount of deposits with the major banks in the country at the end of that week. That document would prove to be useful in determining the number of banks to be nationalized. Haksar returned from the prime minister's office and informed Ghosh that the nationalization plan was cleared and they had to move fast on it to complete the exercise before 20 July so that the Vice-President could sign the ordinance before tendering his resignation to contest the Presidential elections.

A strange but not entirely unexpected development took place at this point. Haksar told Ghosh that the unofficial interactions between them had ended and that soon the latter's services would be requisitioned through the normal official channel, in keeping with his hierarchy in the bureaucracy. Ghosh realized that nothing of what had transpired till then was official, nor would any of his interactions on the matter remain in the records. But before Ghosh could leave for his office, Haksar said he would need to understand a few more things 'unofficially' from Ghosh.[7]

This was about resolving the crucial question on the number of banks to be nationalized. Ghosh's calculations, based on the RBI data on credit allocations as at the end of that week, had shown that the top fifteen banks accounted for over 85 per cent of the total commercial bank deposits in the country. Ghosh was of the view that only one foreign bank, National & Grindlays Bank, figured on that list and that it was better to keep it out of the scope of nationalization to minimize the political repercussions.

Haksar seemed to be in agreement with that view. Once again, a suggestion from K.V. Raghunatha Reddy, the minister of state for company affairs, figured in the discussions. Hailing from Andhra Pradesh, Reddy was keen to include Andhra Bank in the list of banks to be nationalized, as he thought such a move would win him some political mileage. Ghosh was opposed to the suggestion, as he sensed that this would mean including a bank for nationalization on a discretionary basis, and not on the basis of a principle or a criterion, which was at the time the top Indian banks with deposits of Rs 50 crore and above. Haksar decided to consult the Attorney General, Niren De, who too advised against tinkering with the list. Thus, Andhra Bank was left out of it. According to RBI History, there was a proposal for the cut-off level of Rs 100 crore in deposits for nationalization of a bank. But this would have meant the exclusion of a few banks with large deposits, including Dena Bank, which had a deposit base of Rs 98 crore. Hence, the threshold was brought down to Rs 50 crore.[8]

The drama was not over even after the list was finalized. Haksar had gone to meet the prime minister to seek her clearance for the proposed number of banks to be nationalized. Ghosh was waiting in Haksar's room. The prime minister's secretary did not take long to return from Gandhi's room and told Ghosh that the decision to nationalize fourteen banks had been approved. But the prime minister wanted to have a meeting with Ghosh, the man who would be entrusted with the responsibility of drafting the ordinance on nationalization.

Ghosh was ushered into Gandhi's room without any further delay. It transpired that Ghosh had interacted with the prime minister sometime back, when she had accepted his suggestions for the redrafting of a reply to one of the questions she had to answer in Parliament. With these pleasantries over, Gandhi asked him bluntly if he would be able to maintain secrecy and complete the assignment of producing an ordinance draft before the deadline. Ghosh explained that he already had a rough draft on nationalization of five banks, a proposal that had been mooted at the end of 1963 by the then finance minister, T.T. Krishnamachari, and which had not made much headway and was dropped. Ghosh told Gandhi that it would be possible to tailor that draft to meet the requirement of bank nationalization now. Gandhi looked reassured. Quiet and confident, Ghosh gave her his assurance that what she wanted could be done, and the prime minister seemed to heave a sigh of relief and let him get back to his office to complete the task. As he returned to Haksar's room, he was once again reminded by the principal secretary: 'All the incidents since last evening have vanished from history,' and that from now on, Ghosh's services would be 'commandeered officially'.[9]

Some more drama was to follow. Ghosh returned to his office in North Block in room number 68 on the ground floor at around 10 a.m. As soon as he settled down, he got a call from S.S. Shiralkar, Additional Secretary in the banking division. Ghosh was told by Shiralkar that there was a directive that he should present himself before Haksar to help him answer some Parliament questions. Ghosh realized that the official commandeering of his services had begun. 'You are now under my custody,' Haksar told Ghosh as soon as he entered the room of the Principal Secretary to the prime minister. Haksar had asked Attorney General Niren De to be present in his room that morning. De vetted the nationalization proposal from the legal angle and endorsed the idea. A relieved Haksar asked Ghosh what kind of assistance he would need to draft the ordinance.

In his candid autobiography *No Regrets,* Ghosh recalls how Haksar gave him an almost free hand in deciding on the team he would like to have for the drafting of the ordinance in about a day's time. Thus, he got Haksar to requisition the services of S.K. Maitra, a Joint Secretary in the law ministry who had earlier helped Ghosh draft many banking laws, including the one on social controls for banks. Ghosh also requested for the services of R.K. Seshadri, who was earlier in the banking division and was now an executive director at the Reserve Bank of India. As will be revealed later, Economic Affairs Secretary I.G. Patel too would ask for Seshadri's presence in New Delhi to decide on the legal draft of the ordinance; he had remembered that Seshadri had been involved in the drafting of an earlier proposal on nationalization of five banks, which could not be implemented.

Two Crucial Meetings on 17 and 18 July

In a parallel and significant development, Gandhi had two meetings within days of her writing to Desai that he would no longer be the finance minister. A day after 16 July, when she had sent that letter to Desai, Gandhi asked Economic Affairs Secretary in the finance ministry, I.G. Patel, to meet her.

Patel's relations with Desai had been healthy and cordial, and even as Desai received the dismissal letter from Gandhi, Patel, along with other finance ministry Secretaries, were with the finance minister and discussing what course of action he should take. 'While we were with Morarji, the news came that Mrs Gandhi had assumed charge as the Finance Minister. Some people present tried to advise Morarji that there must have been some misunderstanding and that he should call on Mrs Gandhi and clear the air,' Patel recalls in his autobiography.[10]

Patel's own view conveyed to the finance minister was that since Gandhi wanted Desai out of the finance ministry, the honourable course for him would be to quit the government. Desai accepted that logic and packed his belongings in his North Block office and vacated it the same evening. Patel was both sad and angry at the course of events. The same evening, P.N. Dhar, who was yet to join the government but had a close relationship with Haksar, as also with Gandhi, came to meet Patel and discussed the developments of the day. Patel made no secret of his dejected state of mind. Another important visitor to Patel's residence that evening was Pitambar Pant of the Planning Commission. Pant, a brilliant officer who helped the government set up its statistics department, and Patel had worked hard to bring Desai and Gandhi together in the government so that the Indian economy got the benefit of better governance and sensible economic policies. But Desai's departure from the finance ministry in about two years' time under the circumstances that drove him out had undone the good work they had begun.

The next morning, on 17 July, Patel met Gandhi at her office. The meeting was not unusual. It was customary for the new finance minister, who also happened to be the prime minister, to meet the Secretaries in the ministry and get a briefing. Patel played a key role in the finance ministry as Secretary of the Economic Affairs Department. Patel explained to her the functioning of the finance ministry and promised Gandhi that he would not burden her with too many files. Only the important ones would be sent to her for her comments and approval. When Patel asked Gandhi how long she intended to retain the ministry of finance as an additional responsibility, she stumped him with a counter question. She asked if it was true that Patel was contemplating resignation from his post after the departure of Desai. Patel made no secret of his disappointment at what had happened, knowing full well that since Dhar had met him the previous evening it was likely that Gandhi had been briefed about the conversation they had had. Also, Gandhi was aware that Patel was close to Desai.

Patel made no bones about what he felt. He said he had no plans to leave the finance ministry as long as two conditions were met: that his 'bona fides' were not doubted and that he was taken into confidence as far as the government's economic policy intentions were concerned, without which he could not perform the key function of advising the finance minister. Gandhi gave him no assurances. Nor did she criticize Patel for his comments and the conditions he had demanded. Instead, she praised Desai, even though she said he was rigid and had not changed with the times. She asked Patel to send as many files as possible to her so that she could be trained to understand the finances of the government. At the end of that brief meeting, Gandhi surprised Patel again. She said: 'You asked me how long I propose to keep this portfolio. As long as it takes you to initiate me into the intricacies of finance. I do not want anyone to say that the PM of India knows nothing of finance.'[11]

The following day, 18 July, Gandhi again asked Patel to meet her. Gandhi was alone in her room, and as Patel sat down she asked him if the Department of Banking came under his jurisdiction. Patel nodded in affirmation. What Patel heard from Gandhi sounded like the dropping of a bombshell: 'For political reasons, it has been decided to nationalise the banks. You have to prepare within 24 hours the bill, a note for the Cabinet and a speech for me to make to the nation on the radio tomorrow evening. Can you do it and make sure there is no leak?' Gandhi said all this with a straight face.[12] The message from the finance minister was clear: a political decision had been made and there was no need for any debate on it as a final decision had already been taken. In spite of that, Patel ventured to suggest to Gandhi that the scope of nationalization should cover only the large private-sector banks and that foreign banks should be left alone. Gandhi agreed to those two suggestions.

It is reasonable to assume that when Gandhi told Patel on 18 July about her 'political' decision to nationalize the nation's top banks, she had already met Haksar several times and had been briefed by Ghosh on the modalities of drafting the required ordinance for it. What Gandhi achieved in that meeting with Patel on 18 July was to bring her top Secretary in charge of banking into the loop so that a decision that had already been taken could be implemented without any hiccup.

Fast-Forwarding Bank Nationalization

The first thing that Patel did on his return from that meeting on 18 July was to get the RBI governor L.K. Jha to New Delhi and get him into the loop. Jha was summoned to Delhi without any explanation as to why he was being called. Jha had not publicly aired any views against bank nationalization. Neither had he shown any laxity or dilly-dallying in the matter of introduction of the norms mandated under the law on social control of banks. But his earlier stint in the Lal Bahadur Shastri government and his association with the reforms that it had mooted in 1965–66 led to his being bracketed with those who were not part of the left economists' group and therefore as someone opposed to bank nationalization. Jha's predicament on being called to New Delhi on 18 July was understandable. Just a day earlier, he had presented a note to Gandhi endorsing the idea of social controls for banks. But Gandhi was clearly unimpressed with the RBI governor's note.

   While preparing his action plan, Patel also remembered that the bank nationalization move had been debated earlier too, when T.T. Krishnamachari was the finance minister. R.K. Seshadri, a senior officer in the finance ministry, and Patel had prepared a draft legislation for nationalizing the top five banks in the country. But that proposal had made no headway at the time. Seshadri was now in the RBI in Bombay. So he asked Jha to bring Seshadri along, in the hope that Seshadri would still have the draft legislation for the nationalization of five banks made some years ago, which would come of use in preparing the ordinance now. The RBI Governor was puzzled by the sudden summoning. But since Seshadri too had been asked to come along, he soon reasoned that something serious was being planned for the banking sector.

After ensuring that Jha and Seshadri would be in Delhi by evening, Patel called Ghosh at around 3 p.m. and told the young deputy secretary in the banking division that the government had decided to nationalize fourteen banks. Ghosh recalls that on being told that nationalization of fourteen banks all at once would be a difficult challenge, Patel had said that Haksar was quite adamant about that decision.

Patel and Ghosh agreed on having S.K. Maitra, joint secretary in the law ministry, to help with the drafting of the legislation. In a secret noting on his official file, Maitra had written: 'Shri Haksar told me that the Prime Minister has directed that an Ordinance for the nationalization of certain banks should be drafted by me immediately. He also instructed me to keep the matter completely secret and told me that I should not disclose my movements to anyone.'[13] According to Maitra, he had the services of the personal secretary of the RBI governor and of the personal assistant of Patel.

That Friday night was long. Jha and Seshadri landed in Delhi by 10 p.m. Patel decided that he should work on the Cabinet note and the speech that Gandhi would be delivering to the nation on All India Radio on Saturday evening. To ensure confidentiality of the operations, Patel decided to work from home, while Seshadri, Ghosh, Maitra and a couple of other assistants worked at the RBI guest house in New Delhi to prepare the draft ordinance and the legislative bills that would have to be presented to Parliament to replace the ordinance. The RBI Governor was staying at the guest house and told them that he would be joining them for their consultations on drafting the ordinance.

The RBI guest house that night was witness to the most secretive operations to be held on its premises. It also saw heated arguments over how the ordinance should be drafted. The fourteen banks shortlisted for nationalization accounted for over 70 per cent of the total bank deposits and 60 per cent of the total advances in the country. The most difficult issue pertained to the compensation to be provided to those bank owners who would lose their businesses and banks after the nationalization. The earlier compensation methods adopted in the nationalization of Imperial Bank was used as the model for calculating the compensation to be made to the owners of the fourteen banks to be nationalized. Thus, the compensation amount was to be payable in the form of government securities, to be converted at the market rate of exchange. The banking business would be carved out of the existing banking companies and nationalized, leaving the existing companies as mere shell entities.

Heated arguments ensued after Seshadri joined Ghosh and Maitra in the drafting exercise. Seshadri had different views from the others on how the ordinance should be as comprehensive as possible, including even on issues such as the composition of the boards of the new nationalized companies. Ghosh and Maitra had earlier decided that such issues would be determined by the rules to be framed under the legislation. This became a bone of contention between them, and only after Bakshi's and Jha's intervention was a middle path chosen to complete the drafting exercise.

Once the drafting of the ordinance was over, Ghosh got five copies of that document and destroyed all the other papers by going up to the terrace of the RBI guest house and burning them. By 9 a.m. on 19 July, Ghosh handed over the first copy of the draft ordinance to Patel. Ghosh, Seshadri and Maitra kept a copy each for themselves, and the fifth copy was given to Bakshi to hand over to Haksar. According to Maitra, who was also involved in the drafting exercise, the first draft of the legislation was later discussed at a meeting in Haksar's room in the presence of Jha, Bakshi, Patel, Shiralkar, Seshadri and Ghosh. RBI History believes that the draft must have undergone some more changes during the day before being presented to the Cabinet.

By this time, Patel had also completed the task of preparing the Cabinet note and the national address Gandhi would deliver over All India Radio later in the day. The Cabinet note had to be carefully drafted. Patel made sure that the note contained all the reasons and justifications for the government having taken such a major step, so soon after the launch of the law on social control of banks.

With his vast administrative experience and understanding of how a move such as the one on bank nationalization would play out on the minds of the people of the country, the domestic industry and the international community, Patel decided to apply the necessary balms to soften the blow of the drastic step. On his own, Patel inserted a crucial sentence in the draft speech that Gandhi was expected to read out. It said: 'This is not the first step in a new wave of nationalisation. This, in fact, is the culmination of the process which began with the nationalisation of Life Insurance and the Imperial Bank to occupy the commanding heights of finance.'

Neither Haksar nor Gandhi changed or modified the draft speech. Patel believed that the above-mentioned assurance he had inserted in the speech and the decision to exclude foreign banks and small banks from nationalization had softened the decision's adverse impact on the economy and policy. Patel explains in his autobiography why he introduced that element in Gandhi's speech: 'The idea was to link with the past to take away the revolutionary edge, and even more to assure that no more nationalization would follow.' This was Patel's fond hope. That such assurances did little to restrain Gandhi from initiating more nationalization moves in other sectors became evident in the first half of the 1970s.

The Union Cabinet met at 5 p.m. It was a mere formality. All the senior officials involved in the exercise of drafting the ordinance were seated outside the room where the Cabinet met. While discussions were going on in the Cabinet, Ghosh was summoned. Gandhi motioned him to explain some matter to Defence Minister Swaran Singh, who had some questions about the compensation to be paid to the owners losing their banks to nationalization. Ghosh explained to him that the compensation model was the same that had been followed in the earlier nationalization of Imperial Bank.

But Singh was not satisfied. In order to reduce the financial burden on the government, he wanted the compensation for land and buildings to be determined on the basis of their book value instead of their market value. Singh was supported by Law Minister P. Govinda Menon. Ghosh explained to them that not following a precedent set in the past could make the law vulnerable to legal challenge. Gandhi intervened to say that if there are issues that needed to be sorted out, they could be looked at while converting the ordinance into a law. That settled the debate and the Cabinet gave its stamp of approval to the ordinance. As subsequent developments would show, the flawed approach to determining the compensation package did create legal hurdles as the apex court challenged it.

But immediately after the Cabinet meeting that day, Haksar asked Ghosh to meet him in his room. He prepared a quick note addressed to the Secretary to the Acting President, Giri, informing him about the Cabinet approval of the ordinance and seeking his assent for it. Ghosh took with him the Cabinet-approved copy of the ordinance and Haksar's letter to the Acting President's office. In less than five minutes, Ghosh returned after getting the approval. The deed was done.

Gandhi addressed the nation on the evening of 19 July 1969, informing the people of the decision to nationalize fourteen banks. She said:

> As early as December 1954, Parliament took the decision to frame our plans and policies within a socialist pattern of society. Control over the commanding heights of the economy is necessary, particularly in a poor country where it is extremely difficult to mobilize adequate resources for development and to reduce inequalities between different groups and regions . . . [and, also expressed the hope that the nationalization of banks would herald a] new and more vigorous phase in the implementation of our avowed plans and policies.

The legitimate credit needs of industry and trade would also be met, she said.

What the Ordinance Outlined

What Giri signed that day—the Banking Companies (Acquisition and Transfer of Undertakings) Ordinance—envisaged the acquisition and transfer of fourteen banking companies to help serve better the needs of development of the economy, 'in conformity with national policy and objectives and for matters connected therewith or incidental thereto'. The fourteen banks listed in the ordinance had deposits of not less than Rs 50 crore each as on 27 June 1969, the last Friday of that month. The ordinance stipulated that the chairman of each bank would become the custodian of the respective nationalized bank, unless another person had already been appointed by the Centre for that position. An advisory board was to be appointed to advise the custodian of every nationalized bank, which was to be dissolved once a board of directors was set up. On the crucial question of compensation to those who lost ownership of the banks following their nationalization, the ordinance provided for an amount equal to the total value of the assets of the existing bank as on the date of nationalization, after deducting its total liabilities and obligations.

Two days later, at the start of the monsoon session of Parliament on 21 July, Gandhi made the following statement:

Nearly 15 years ago, Parliament approved that we should set before ourselves the goal of a socialist pattern of society. Since then Government have taken several measures towards the achievement of this goal. Public ownership and the control of commanding heights of national economy and of its strategic sectors are essential and important aspects of the new social order which we are trying to build in the country. We regard this as particularly necessary in a poor country which seeks to achieve speedy economic progress consistent with social justice in a democratic political system, one which is free from the domination of a few and in which opportunities are open to all.

The caveats that Patel had introduced in the address Gandhi would make to the nation—like the bank nationalization being the culmination of the process that began with nationalization of life insurance and Imperial Bank—had been set aside. Instead, the prime minister, with the additional responsibility of the finance ministry, outlined the political and social reasons for bank nationalization. Indeed, in the next couple of years, Gandhi would nationalize more industries, including general insurance, coal, textiles and oil.

By December 1969, she would get Parliament to pass the Monopolies and Restrictive Practices Bill to regulate expansions, mergers, amalgamations and appointment of directors in companies that were dominant by size and market share. All companies with more than Rs 1 crore in assets and all interconnected undertakings with a combined asset size of Rs 20 crore were brought under the draconian provisions of this law. These companies were to seek government permission before setting up new subsidiaries or projects. The Monopolies and Restrictive Practices Act, which came into force from 1 June 1970, was in pursuance of the recommendations made by the Monopolies Inquiry Commission, which had submitted its report in October 1965.

In addition, the privy purses for the former rulers of provinces that had acceded to newly formed independent India would be abolished by December 1971, and a new, draconian law curbing freedom of use of foreign exchange resources would be passed. Indeed, Gandhi would go for another round of bank nationalization about eleven years later, taking over the ownership of six more banks in 1980.

A Series of Reactions

Bank nationalization evoked sharp reactions from different sections of society. Trade and industry were understandably upset over the nationalization of the country's top domestic banks. Equally understandable was the support bank nationalization received from the then, left and socialist parties because of their political beliefs. Jyoti Basu, who was then the deputy chief minister of West Bengal, welcomed the move, just as the Swatantra Party leader, Chakravarti Rajagopalachari, expressed serious apprehensions over the manner in which it was implemented, using the ordinance route. Sarvodaya leader Jayaprakash Narayan said the step was wrong and unwarranted. But the most surprising reaction came from a few members of the Congress Syndicate, which had been opposed to Gandhi. K. Kamaraj and Atulya Ghosh welcomed the move and justified it, saying that it had already been accepted by the All-India Congress Committee. It was a tactical move on their part, and a deeply political one.

A day after the ordinance was promulgated, RBI Deputy Governor B.N. Adarkar held an impromptu discussion with the local representatives and custodians of the nationalized banks. It was a Sunday. RBI Governor Jha was still in New Delhi and Adarkar did not want any uncertainty to grip the banking sector in the wake of the ordinance. Instructions were issued at this meeting asking the nationalized banks to ensure that normal business activities should continue, that the banks should maintain their independent identities and go ahead with their branch expansion plans, as approved by the RBI. On Monday, 21 July, the nationalized banks dropped the suffix 'Ltd' and their chairpersons were now their custodians and treated as public servants.

Gandhi's political astuteness was once again on display when, in the fourth week of July, she decided to hold a public meeting of bank employees in Bombay just outside the headquarters of the RBI, to explain the government's intent behind nationalizing fourteen banks and to quell rumours of any further changes or of any vindictive action to be taken against those in the banking system who had opposed the move. There was a huge roar of approval from the assembled employees when Gandhi outlined the reasons behind bank nationalization.

Gandhi's performance in Parliament in defence of bank nationalization was equally spirited. The propriety of issuing an ordinance just two days before Parliament was to start its monsoon session came under attack. The issue was raised by the fiery Jana Sangh leader, Atal Bihari Vajpayee, who would later steer the Central government as prime minister from 1998 to 2004. Gandhi justified the ordinance route on the ground that the possibility of manipulation had to be avoided as there was speculation about bank nationalization. She also explained that foreign banks had been excluded as they functioned in India only to facilitate foreign trade and tourism as part of their international operations.

Morarji Desai, although he still was a member of the Congress, gave vent to his ire at the ordinance and recalled before the Lok Sabha the circumstances under which he was divested of his responsibilities as the finance minister. Since he realized that he could continue to be part of the Cabinet only at the cost of his self-respect, he had decided to quit the government, he said. In response, Gandhi used a clever ploy. She explained that since Desai had expressed his serious reservations about the direction of the government's economic policy, she had no desire to burden him with the responsibility of implementing decisions like bank nationalization.

The Legal Drama

The 1969 legislation on bank nationalization, however, faced a roadblock when the Supreme Court struck it down on the question of how the compensation for those who had lost ownership of the nationalized banks had been decided. This was a temporary setback. The apex court had declared invalid the principles and procedures used to determine the amount of compensation to be paid to the owners of the banks. Since the compensation procedures were part of the main legislation, the Supreme Court decided to strike down the entire law. The government under Gandhi made changes to the compensation package and formula and presented a modified bill to Parliament, which was passed by it on 31 March 1970.

In the interim, however, there was no delay on the part of the RBI in enforcing bank nationalization. Two days after Gandhi made a strong case and rationale for bank nationalization, the department of banking operations and development (DBO&D) of the RBI sent a circular to all the fourteen nationalized banks directing them to consult it before approving any loans, guarantees or other proposals that in the normal course would have required the sanction of its board of directors. That was on 23 July, and the central bank under Jha had wasted no time in enforcing the writ and intent of the Union government. Of course, these restrictions remained in force till the legal uncertainties were temporarily cleared. On 10 September, the RBI asked the banks to form internal management committees in place of the board of directors. The committees would discharge such supervisory functions (as mentioned earlier), including clearance of loans or investments, as would have required the approval of the board of directors before the banks' nationalization. RBI representatives, along with a nominee of the government, began attending the meetings of these banks, which were held every week.

Once the legal roadblocks to implementing bank nationalization had been temporarily removed, Jha convened a meeting of the custodians of the fourteen nationalized banks and the chairman of State Bank of India. That meeting, held in Bombay on 14 August 1969, helped chalk out the steps needed to implement the objectives of the banks' nationalization. The RBI Governor told the nationalized banks that they should retain their separate identities so that they could compete among themselves in offering better services to customers and achieve greater efficiency. RBI History for this period noted:

> The meeting lasted for five hours and discussed the responsibilities of the public sector banks in the new scenario, including the fresh orientation to be given to the banking business, and ways to achieve better distribution of credit, improvement in banking services and profitability. The Governor exhorted the banks to pare their advances to big business houses and examine the scope for contracting large share advances, to aim at better distribution of credit with emphasis on small borrowers, to lay stress on banking operations in the non-urban areas, and to share the SBI's burden of financing the Food Corporation of India's food procurement operations.[14]

In a related development, which brought some cheer to the Gandhi camp, on 20 August, V.V. Giri was declared elected as the next President by a narrow margin of victory over the official Congress candidate, Neelam Sanjiva Reddy. A former finance minister, C.D. Deshmukh, was also in the electoral fray. Deshmukh's candidature was supported by the Swatantra Party and the Jana Sangh, and he came third in the elections. Gandhi had got a president of her choice. In addition, fourteen banks had been nationalized.

A Temporary Setback for Nationalization

What turned out to be a temporary setback for Gandhi's bank nationalization plan was the Supreme Court's 22 July interim stay order against the ordinance, just three days after its promulgation. The stay was in response to two writ petitions filed in the apex court by a few persons, including Rustom Cavasjee Cooper, a leading financial consultant, and Minocher Rustom Masani, popularly known as Minoo Masani, who was at that time a member of the Swatantra Party. But since the stay only barred the government from appointing any boards of advisers, from removing the chairmen of the banks and from issuing any directions contrary to the Banking Regulation Act, the government went ahead with the planned nationalization while making sure that no changes to the boards of these banks were made.

The ordinance faced another hurdle when, at the time of passing the law, there was a suggestion from a section of members that it should be referred to a select committee of Parliament. If that suggestion had been accepted, there would surely have been delays in implementing the nationalization. D.N. Ghosh recalls in his autobiography that Finance Secretary T.P. Singh did indeed suggest to him that the bill could be referred to a select committee. Ghosh had informed Gandhi about this, after which such a suggestion was never heard of again. A move to set up an apex body to supervise the fourteen nationalized banks was also scotched, with Gandhi categorically asserting in Parliament that there was no plan for a monolithic machinery to monitor the banks.

After the nationalization ordinance was converted into a law, a few more petitions were filed before the Supreme Court. But the apex court only partially stayed the law. There was no stay on enforcement of the law, barring a directive disallowing the government from changing the custodians of the nationalized banks. The real setback came on 10 February 1970, when the Supreme Court struck down the nationalization— although it upheld the legislative power of Parliament on the question of the government acquiring banking companies—saying the norms for compensating the owners of the nationalized banks were not valid and that the banking companies which held the banking businesses had been discriminated against by being debarred from carrying on any banking business. There was a dissenting note from one of the judges, A.N. Ray, who would later figure in a bigger controversy when he was appointed as the Chief Justice of the apex court in 1973, in supersession of his seniors on the bench.

The very next day, 11 February, the RBI Governor approved a decision taken by the Department of Banking Operations and Development to appoint its officers as directors of the fourteen banks in order to protect the interests of depositors and address the uncertainty caused by the Supreme Court's order. This became necessary as after the apex court's order, the banks had to be technically restored to their old owners.

The government also lost no time in reissuing a fresh ordinance on 14 February to take over ownership of these fourteen banks with retrospective effect from 19 July 1969. The big difference this time was that instead of laying down a principle for providing compensation to the owners, the fresh ordinance fixed a specific amount of compensation for each of the nationalized bank owners.

The total compensation value was Rs 87.4 crore, which was to be paid to the owners to all the banks within sixty days after the application for compensation was received by the government. The ordinance was followed up with a revised bill on bank nationalization, which was introduced in Parliament on 27 February, a day before Indira Gandhi would present her first and only Budget. The bill was passed without any amendment by both houses of Parliament by the end of March 1970. 'The Bill received the assent of the President on 31 March, 1970,' RBI History noted.

Fallout of Bank Nationalization

There were at least three major consequences of nationalization of the country's top banks. One, it launched Gandhi's political career on a strong and almost unassailable footing. Bank nationalization was a decision that Gandhi took in the face of tremendous opposition from within a large section of the Congress. In this move, she was supported by the relatively younger members of the Congress (the Young Turks), who had grouped under the Congress Forum for Socialist Action (CFSA). The leaders of this group included Chandra Shekhar and Mohan Dharia. Gandhi's decision on bank nationalization was hailed as a pro-poor step, helping banks serve the rural economy more effectively and addressing the credit needs of a large number of unbanked people living in villages across the country.

In terms of the nationalized banks' operations too, the banks did well for the economy in the first couple of years after nationalization. Popular confidence in the banking system increased; mobilization of private savings by banks was on the rise; and more bank branches were set up in different parts of the country. The problem with nationalization began a few years later. National trade unions, with support from political parties, secured increased salaries and perquisites for workers without a corresponding increase in productivity. There was overstaffing, growing indiscipline and inefficiency. And there was no accountability.

The second consequence was that after bank nationalization, all hopes of restructuring Indian banks were dashed. Just before bank nationalization, the finance ministry, under Patel's guidance, had prepared a note on the restructuring of banks to make them more efficient and more empowered to respond to the social need of financial inclusion. The proposal envisaged allowing only one or two major banks to operate on an all-India basis to meet the requirements of a wholesale market for credit and foreign exchange. This would make these banks big enough to compete with the foreign banks. They would also be able to use technology and better work methods to become more effective financial intermediaries. The remaining banks were to be reorganized and merged into several bigger entities geared towards meeting the requirements of specific regions in the country, of agriculture, small industry, trade and other sectors that were earlier ignored by the larger banks. A competitive spirit was to be encouraged by ensuring that more than two or three small banks operated in a region. With bank nationalization, these ideas were simply dropped.

Three, bank nationalization led to the creation of a new department in the ministry of finance—the banking department. Earlier, banking was looked after by the banking division within the finance ministry, which was part of the Economic Affairs Department. After bank nationalization, the government reckoned that there needed to be a banking department within

the finance ministry as the workload had increased. As the shareholder of
these fourteen banks, the government had to build administrative capacity
to help it supervise their operations. The new banking department was
headed by A. Bakshi, who had earlier worked in the finance ministry but
was now with the RBI. Bakshi was a competent officer, but his other
qualifications too made him suitable for the job. He was a leftist and a
friend of Haksar's. Not surprisingly, the initial plan was to empower the
banking department with an enlarged jurisdiction. This meant that the
Economic Affairs Department would cease to oversee the government's
relations with the Reserve Bank of India or the conduct of the monetary
policy. Such responsibilities were proposed to be vested with the newly
created the banking department, which was also to get more powers to
decide on key appointments in the central bank. Naturally, Patel was
unhappy. Even the cabinet secretary, D.S. Joshi, was surprised by the move.
But when Patel objected to the proposed arrangement, Haksar quickly
revised the work allocation and responsibilities of the new department.
Accordingly, the RBI continued to be the responsibility of the economic
affairs department and its Secretary continued to be on the board of the
central bank. The secretary of the banking department, however, was
made a permanent invitee to the RBI board meetings. Responsibilities
such as the oversight of monetary policy implementation, management
of government debt and foreign exchange continued to be under the
economic affairs department. The banking department was entrusted with
the responsibilities of overseeing the nationalized banks' management and
their credit allocation. The formula used for carving out responsibilities
for the new department was simple: the new responsibilities after bank
nationalization were entrusted with the banking department, and whatever
was already being handled by the economic affairs department remained
with it. It was also decided that the chief economic adviser in the finance
ministry would be responsible for ensuring coordination between the two
departments. Ashok Mitra (who would become the finance minister of
West Bengal under Jyoti Basu a few years later) had just joined the finance
ministry as the chief economic adviser, and he began his stint with the
additional responsibility of acting as the coordinator between the banking
department and the economic affairs department. Mitra had succeeded
V.K. Ramaswami, who met with a tragic death—his chair had caught
fire at night, most likely from a spark from his cigarette. Ramaswami was

not aware of it, and even as he went to bed, the fire spread slowly and asphyxiated him to death.

Indira Gandhi as FM

Indira Gandhi's first and only Budget bore the imprint of her economic policy thinking in no small measure. Committing herself to achieving the goal of equitable growth, she told Parliament that it was necessary to frame policies that reconciled 'the imperatives of growth with concern for the well-being of the needy and the poor'. Her prescription was: 'Any severance of the vital link between the needs of growth and of distributive justice will produce stagnation or instability. Both must be avoided.'

Small enterprises played an important role in her economic vision. She was of the view that small enterprises and new entrepreneurs must be encouraged as that could nurture managerial and entrepreneurial talent. At the same time, she was in favour of restraint on urban land values and individual ownership of urban property, a sign of her socialistic bent of mind. 'Without some restraint on urban land values and individual ownership of urban property, we cannot adequately develop housing and other amenities necessary to wrest the maximum benefit from the vast productive investments already made in our over-crowded towns and cities,' she argued.

In her Budget speech, Gandhi painted a rosy picture of the economy. She began with an account of the performance of the Indian economy during 1969–70, when economic growth was estimated at between 5 and 5.5 per cent. 'The modernisation of Indian agriculture is well on its way and it has led to a substantial recovery in industrial production. There has been a welcome increase in foreign exchange reserves and the general level of prices over the past two years has been relatively stable,' she said. Clearly, the positive effects of the Green Revolution were becoming evident as the country's reliance on food grain imports was coming down.

But Gandhi also made it clear that she was a strong votary of higher outlays for development projects to ensure higher but also more equitable growth. She believed that an increase in the Plan outlay for the public sector would have a positive knock-on effect on the private sector, whose investments too would see an increase. The Budget for 1970–71, therefore, was framed with a view to allocating adequate resources for many schemes that would be aimed at ensuring both social welfare benefits for the people and growth for the entire economy. Three key policy steps taken by her government were mentioned in this context: bank nationalization, the framing of the monopolies law to prevent concentration of economic wealth in the hands of a few companies, and the promotion of industrial development in selected backward areas in the country.

The Fourth Five-year Plan, which had been launched in April 1969 after a gap of about three years, when there were only annual plans, received due emphasis in Gandhi's Budget. She informed Parliament that the Fourth Plan was being revised so that it paid special attention to meeting socio-economic requirements like 'the development of suitable techniques for dry farming areas, greater employment opportunities for landless labour, the adequate supply of drinking water and the improvement of urban environment in many of our congested metropolitan areas'.

The impact of the recommendations of the Fifth Finance Commission, headed by Mahavir Tyagi, was evident in the Union government's Budget numbers for 1969–70. The budgeted deficit of Rs 254 crore had risen to Rs 290 crore, according to the revised estimates, largely because of the increase in the transfer of taxes to the states. In addition, the states also had to be provided with higher non-Plan assistance so that they could implement their Plan programmes. The Fifth Finance Commission had recommended for the states a higher share of the Centre's revenues from income-tax, excise duties and additional duties of excise. This had been accepted by the government through an explanatory memorandum on the action taken on the recommendations of the Fifth Finance Commission by the end of August 1969, as a result of which the total volume of Union tax revenues that the Centre had to share with the states had gone up.[15]

Quite apart from the increased transfer of Central taxes to the states, Gandhi's Budget also showed how she was acutely conscious of the need for providing higher assistance to the states. It is not clear if this was in response to a foreboding she may have had that the states needed to be wooed a bit if she had to keep her party's popularity intact. Indeed, an additional amount of Rs 175 crore was provided to the states to cover the gaps in their resources, without which many of them would not have been able to implement some of the Plan programmes. Gandhi announced in her Budget speech:

Provision for Plan assistance to the states is also being increased from Rs 615 crore this year to Rs 635 crore next year. If state governments are able to raise additional resources and keep a careful watch on non-Plan expenditure, it should be possible for them to increase their Plan outlay from roughly Rs 950 crore this year to about Rs 1,150 crore next year i.e. an increase of the order of 20 per cent.

While the Central Plan outlay went up by 15 per cent, the total Plan expenditure for the Centre and the states for 1970–71 was raised by 18 per cent. A big push was given to rural development programmes, with a special emphasis on schemes for small farmers, for drinking water and for a minimum pension and family pension for employees of the Union government. In addition, Gandhi announced her plan to set up the Urban Development Corporation, which could implement schemes in the areas of slum clearance, housing and urban land development.

The focus on the health of the central public sector undertakings (PSU) was no less important, from Gandhi's perspective. She ensured that the internal resources of the Central PSUs increased by about 25 per cent. A key initiative of hers in the financial sector was to start the era of administered interest rates for banks. Having nationalized fourteen banks already, she took the next step by mandating that these banks would have to offer more attractive interest rates for their deposits, particularly for the rural population, for whom tax concession was no incentive for savings through the various Post Office schemes. Inaugurating a highly harmful culture of state mandating of bank interest rates, which would take many decades to be rolled back, she announced:

> Accordingly, it is proposed to introduce a new series of time deposits, recurring deposits and savings certificates, which will carry higher rates of interest without any special tax concessions. The present tax-free facilities will also be continued with slightly higher rates of interest. The rates of interest on contributions to the General Provident Fund and the Public Provident Fund are also being enhanced slightly.

Indira Gandhi's only Budget as the finance minister had a fair dose of her fiscal policy vision, as also of fresh taxation. She made no secret of her belief that the Union Budget must generate substantial surplus revenue to meet its requirements on the capital account, largely because it was the government that was expected to bear the responsibility for capital formation in the economy. This became all the more necessary as the country's net receipts of foreign aid and import of food grains on concessional terms were declining as a result of the government's pursuit of economic self-reliance as an important goal.

Gandhi was also worried about the fall in the tax-GDP ratio. The share of Central taxes in GDP had risen from 9.78 per cent in 1964–65 to 10.43 per cent in 1965–66 and stayed in the double digits, at 10.28 per cent, in 1966–67, the year of the rupee devaluation. But since then, this share fell below the 10 per cent mark in the next three years that followed—to 9.3 per cent 1967–68, to 9.56 per cent in 1968–69 and to 9.7 per cent in 1969–70. 'At existing rates of taxation, the revenue account for 1970–71 will yield only a nominal surplus. The ratio of taxation to national income in India is among the lowest in the world and over the recent past, it has declined . . .' she said, arguing that, therefore, the tax base needed to be enlarged to meet the requirements of 'growth and social welfare'.

Outlining a Six-Pronged Taxation Strategy

Gandhi's only Budget listed six major priority areas for taxation. One, there must be steps to plug the loopholes in the taxation system that led to both tax avoidance and evasion, resulting in revenue loss. Plugging loopholes meant, among other things, withdrawal of concessions that had outlived their utility.

Two, she believed that taxation was an instrument with which to achieve greater equality of income and wealth. Therefore, she proposed to make direct taxes progressive—by increasing income tax at higher levels of income and also by imposing higher rates of taxation on wealth and gifts.

Three, she was of the view that taxation on urban land and buildings should be substantially increased, as part of a strategy to curb speculation on urban land and property.

Four, she believed tax concessions should be rationalized to stimulate savings and that marginal relief in tax rates should be offered to low-income groups.

Five, she spared the corporate sector from any significant changes in income tax in order to encourage higher production and investment. The existing structure of corporate taxation was left largely unchanged, in a bid to maintain 'a stable climate for investment decisions'. The only change introduced in the area of corporation taxes was to disallow expenditure incurred by companies in India on entertainment or on maintaining guest houses (other than for employees) for computing their taxable profit.

And finally, Gandhi was aware that excessive dependence on indirect taxes for garnering revenues was not fiscally healthy. As much as three-fourths of the total Central tax revenues came from duties like customs and excise. But, at the same time, raising indirect taxation to meet revenue requirements could not be ruled out, she argued, if the government had to bolster its finances to meet the requirements for its development outlays.

Her socialistic inclinations were again evident when she said that the proposals on indirect tax increases were 'designed primarily to raise additional resources in a manner which helps our progress towards self-reliance and restrains the consumption of certain commodities'. The increases in indirect taxes, however, were restricted only to those goods that did not constitute the common consumption basket of the poorer sections of the people. The objective was that the government's tax increases should not hurt the poor.

On direct taxes, Gandhi followed the principles of progressive taxation—the higher the income level, the higher the tax rate. The marginal rate of income tax was increased progressively on all personal incomes above Rs 40,000 per year. This took the country closer to the peak levels of taxation on individual incomes that would eventually prevail a few years later. But in Gandhi's Budget, the maximum rate of income tax went up to as high a level as 93.5 per cent for those earning annual income of over Rs 2 lakh. The higher tax incidence included the impact of a 10 per cent surcharge added by the finance minister. Earlier, the tax incidence on incomes above Rs 2.21 lakh a year was 82.5 per cent.

Gandhi's socialistic credentials were in evidence once again when she raised the wealth tax rates. From the existing rates, varying from 0.5 per cent to 3 per cent, they were raised to 1 per cent at the lowest slab to 5 per cent at the highest slab. A significant change in the wealth tax regime was removal of the difference between the taxability of owners of a single residential house located in a place with a population of less than 10,000 and that of owners of corresponding residences in the larger towns. The prevailing rules stipulated that one residential house, irrespective of its value, would be exempted from tax if it was situated in a town with a population of less than 10,000. The new wealth tax regime did away with that distinction and levied tax on residential houses whose value was higher than Rs 1 lakh, irrespective of where it was located. Additionally, the rate of wealth tax on urban lands and buildings was raised. Depending on the location and the value, the rate was raised by 1–4 percentage points to 5 per cent for urban lands and buildings exceeding Rs 5 lakh in value, and to 7 per cent on such properties valued in excess of Rs 10 lakh.

That sufficient planning and thought had gone into the making of Indira Gandhi's only Budget was clear from the manner in which she tried to crack down on tax evasion and tax avoidance through the creation of private trusts. The taxation policy until then was to tax all discretionary trusts on their income and wealth at the same rates as were applicable to individuals. Since the tax rates for individuals were a little lower than for corporate entities in general, there was a marked tendency among many Indian industry houses and corporate groups to set up discretionary trusts to take advantage of the tax arbitrage. In a bid to curb the proliferation of such trusts, Gandhi decided to tax them at a flat rate of 65 per cent on their income and at 1.5 per cent on their wealth. The loophole in the entire taxation policy change was that a few types of existing discretionary trusts were exempted from the flat rate of taxation. It was a loophole that remained a bone of contention in the matter of taxation of trusts for many decades hence.

The exemptions introduced by Gandhi were for charitable and religious trusts if their income was actually used for the stated purpose of the trust in the same year or within three months of the close of the year. Such trusts were to forfeit the tax exemption they had if their funds constituting their corpus or income were invested in an entity in which the creator or the founder of the trust or any of his or her relatives had substantial interest, and if the amount of such investment exceeded 5 per cent of the capital of that entity. The obvious intention of the change in the taxation laws for charitable trusts was to curb the use of their funds to acquire control over industry and business. 'Some changes are also being made to prevent indirect benefits being enjoyed by the authors or founders of such trusts,' Gandhi clarified in her Budget speech.

On the direct taxes front, the Budget for 1970–71 made a few more important changes. These included rationalization of the gift tax rates to bring them in line with the rates of estate duty. The exemption limit of Rs 10,000 for the value of gifts to attract tax was lowered by half, to Rs 5000 a year, once again in a bid to plug what the Gandhi government believed to be loopholes in the taxation system. The rules on taxability of income from investment in various types of instruments were also rationalized. Gandhi removed the distinction, in terms of taxation, made between income from investment in Unit Trust of India and shares of Indian companies and income from other financial assets, like securities of the Union or state governments, bank deposits, small saving schemes and Post Office deposit accounts. Instead, she exempted from tax all income up to Rs 3000 in a year from investments in Unit Trust, from shares in Indian companies or from any other savings schemes and bank deposits. In the same spirit, the finance minister abolished the system where income-tax exemption was related to the number of dependants in a family. At that time, the income-tax exemption limit varied from Rs 4000 to Rs 48,000 a year, depending on the number of dependants in the family of the taxpayer. Gandhi decided to end all that and imposed a uniform exemption limit of Rs 5000 for all non-corporate income-tax assessees, irrespective whether they were married or had any children. In retrospect, this was a major simplification in the taxation laws, introducing greater administrative simplicity.

The changes in indirect taxes were on expected lines. The customs duty on machinery, with some exceptions, was raised steeply, from 27.5 per cent to 35 per cent, in an attempt to encourage import substitution, which had become a policy talisman of the Gandhi government's economic philosophy. The import duty on motor vehicles parts, pharmaceutical chemicals and non-electrical instruments, apparatus and appliances, was also raised by 10 per cent. Emphasizing her socialistic credentials yet again, she also increased the customs duty on imported whisky, brandy, gin and wines.

The scope of excise taxation was widened to cover almost the entire range of manufactured products with a low rate of about 10 per cent. Items whose excise duty went up included synthetic rubber, sanitaryware and glazed tiles of porcelain, refrigerators and their parts, air-conditioning plants and machinery, and polyester fibre of certain varieties. Reflective of the times the Indian economy was going through, Gandhi raised the excise duty on tea 'in order to release larger quantities for export particularly of quality teas'. Similarly, the duty on free-market sugar, accounting for about 30 per cent of the market, was raised by a hefty 63 per cent, the assumption being that it was only the rich and businesses classes that purchased free-market sugar. Of course, the excise duty on cigarettes and petroleum products too was raised, triggering an immediate increase in the retail selling price of cigarettes, petrol, diesel and kerosene from the very evening of 28 February 1970, when the Budget was presented.

Quite apart from the new tax initiatives, Indira Gandhi's only Budget had brought about a significant directional change in the state of the Centre's public finances. True, her Budget had imposed an additional tax burden on the economy of about Rs 170 crore, almost 0.37 per cent of GDP that year. But more importantly, her Budget ensured a perceptible rise in tax buoyancy. The nominal size of the Indian economy rose by less than 7 per cent in 1970–71 over the previous year. But the Centre's total tax revenue jumped by 13 per cent. This meant that Gandhi's Budget proposals saw the Centre's overall tax buoyancy rise to a healthy level of 1.91 in 1970–71, much higher than the 1.16 recorded in 1969–70.

Yet, the pressure of expenditure was such that Gandhi had to concede a budgetary gap of about Rs 225 crore. The gap (calculated after the government's borrowings from the RBI) was 0.49 per cent of GDP. Although it was lower than the gap of Rs 290 crore (0.67 per cent of GDP) in 1969–70, Gandhi was still concerned about the adverse impact such a gap would have on prices. A wider budgetary gap leads to more borrowing and increased money supply creating inflationary pressure in the economy. She conceded the need for a reduction in deficit financing, though the favourable food grains supply situation was a source of comfort and the deficit level of that order was considered to be manageable. The finance minister also drew comfort from the fact that adequate transfers of resources to the states were being made to help them finance their development plans.

In all this, however, Gandhi was influenced by her overall economic philosophy of growth with inclusion. She said:

If the requirements of growth are urgent, so is the need for some selective measures of social welfare. The fiscal system has also to serve the ends of greater equality of incomes, consumption and wealth, irrespective of any immediate need for resources. At the same time, the needs of these sectors of our economy, which require private initiative and investment must also be kept in mind in the interest of the growth of the economy as a whole.

I.G. Patel, the Economic Affairs Secretary who drafted Gandhi's Budget speech, recalls in his memoirs that none of the proposals she made in her Budget speech had to be withdrawn or modified.[16] This was rare, given the political challenges she faced in 1970. There was an occasion when Gandhi realized that she might have to amend one of her proposals, but Patel advised her to assert her position as the prime minister and not allow a roll-back of her announcement. Gandhi insisted on an alternative, which Patel had prepared. But eventually, Gandhi succeeded in averting the political pressure for a change in the Budget, which was passed without any modification.

Gandhi had taken up the finance ministry portfolio as part of a grand design to politically neutralize her opponents within the Congress and to implement socialistic economic policies like bank nationalization. There was elaborate planning behind her decision to become the finance minister. But her departure from the finance ministry was swift. Less than a year after her assuming additional charge of the finance ministry, she decided at the end of June 1970 to get her home minister, Y.B. Chavan, to take charge of it.

Y.B. Chavan (Finance Minister, 1970–1974)

Dealing with War and Economic Crisis

The elevation of Yashwantrao Chavan as the finance minister on 26 June 1970 was sudden, but not entirely unexpected.

Indira Gandhi had taken charge of the finance ministry less than a year ago, on 16 July 1969, in a move that killed quite a few birds with one stone. She sidelined Morarji Desai, a political thorn on her side, eventually forcing him to quit her government. Simultaneously, she steered the country's economic governance policy towards socialism through bank nationalization. With that, she also managed to isolate the Congress Syndicate and expand the popular base of the faction of the Congress she was leading.

Once she formally split from the Congress, leading her own faction in November 1969 and completing the process of bank nationalization by the end of March 1970, Gandhi began toying with the idea of relieving herself of the finance portfolio. She had already presented the Budget for 1970–71, which too had a good dose of socialistic economic policies.

Her choice of Chavan as the next finance minister was significant. Chavan was earlier seen to be close to the Congress Syndicate. But later he distanced himself from it, and his support of bank nationalization was a clear signal showing his support for Gandhi. Not surprisingly, therefore, Chavan, who was at that point the home minister, was shifted to the finance ministry. It was a swap of sorts. Gandhi handed over the finance ministry to Chavan and took over the home ministry from him. Chavan had held charge of that ministry for many years, from 1966, when Gandhi became the prime minister.

Chavan at that time was one of the tallest leaders from the state of Maharashtra. He was the first chief minister of Maharashtra after the creation of the state in 1960. The Nehru government had hived off the Saurashtra region and rechristened it as Gujarat, a separate state. But Chavan's tenure as the chief minister of Maharashtra was short—just about two years. He was summoned to New Delhi by Jawaharlal Nehru in 1962, soon after the reverses India faced in its war with China. A reluctant Nehru had to sacrifice V. Krishna Menon as the defence minister. And Chavan filled the vacancy, which he retained for about four years—even in the government led by Lal Bahadur Shastri and when India fought a war with Pakistan in 1965. After Gandhi became the prime minister in January 1966, Chavan continued to remain the defence minister for about ten months. But in November 1966, Gandhi faced her first big political challenge from outside her party—a procession of Hindu religious fundamentalists, supported by the Rashtriya Swayamsevak Sangh and its political wing, the Bharatiya Jana Sangh, demanding that laws be framed to ban cow slaughter in the country. The government's intelligence apparatus had failed to anticipate the momentum the movement had gained to have succeeded in mobilizing such a large gathering right inside the heart of New Delhi near the Indian Parliament. The failure of the law enforcement agencies in controlling the rioting mob which ransacked many offices of the Union government forced the police much later to open fire on it. An estimated eight persons were killed, hundreds injured and over 1500 demonstrators arrested. Gandhi came under attack for having failed to prevent the breakdown of law and order. There were charges that her home minister, Gulzari Lal Nanda, was sympathetic to the cause of the demonstrators and had not taken the required preventive steps. Gandhi defended Nanda to the hilt, but about a week later she removed him from the home ministry. Chavan was brought into the ministry, while she herself took the additional responsibility of the defence ministry. General elections were held in 1967, and even after the elections Gandhi retained Chavan as the home minister till June 1970, when she made him the finance minister.

So, when Gandhi chose Chavan to lead the finance ministry, the two had already developed a relationship of trust and understanding. Gandhi's decision to nationalize banks and secure the victory of V.V. Giri in the Presidential election had intensified the rift between her and the Congress

Syndicate. Giri fought the election as an independent and won it after defeating the official Congress candidate, Neelam Sanjiva Reddy. A point came when Gandhi began touring the country to mobilize support for herself within the party, simultaneously insisting that the Congress chief, S. Nijalingappa, should convene a session of the All-India Congress Committee. The objective was to elect a new president for the party to further marginalize the Congress Syndicate leaders. Nijalingappa retaliated by accusing Gandhi of destroying internal democracy in the party. On 1 November 1969, two meetings of Congress leaders took place at around the same time—one at the Congress office on Jantar Mantar Road (led by Nijalingappa, along with the Congress Syndicate leaders) and the other at Gandhi's residence on Safdarjung Road. The official Congress meeting decided to move against Gandhi by removing her from the primary membership of the party and urging the party to elect a new Parliamentary leader of the Congress. Within days, Gandhi mobilized the support of many members of the Congress party. In retaliation, the Congress leadership expelled Gandhi from the party on 12 November. This meant freedom for Gandhi from the Syndicate leaders as she formed her own breakaway Congress party.

During this period, Chavan stood by Gandhi. Writing for the *New York Times* in February 1971, Dom Moraes, a leading journalist and poet, described Chavan's role during the days of the Congress split in these words:

> We talked about the Congress split, and whether Mrs. Gandhi had caused it. 'I wouldn't think so,' he (Chavan) said. 'It was a sad and sorry business, but it was inevitable. Circumstances were leading that way. She was very close to events, and she was not prepared to compromise on specific issues. The moment of split came when the resolution to expel her was passed. But it was very difficult to think of splitting a party which was a century old. She told me to try to patch things up. She even helped me draft a unity resolution. That's positive proof that she did not cause the split.'[1]

Chavan in North Block

As finance minister, Chavan inherited an economy that had begun doing well. The Indian economy had grown by 6.5 per cent in 1969–70.

Agricultural growth had contributed significantly to the overall revival of the economy. But inflation was a cause for concern, as wholesale prices rose by over 7 per cent in 1969–70. With money supply growing at a rapid pace, the Reserve Bank of India had used monetary policy instruments to halt that growth by raising interest rates.

Politically, however, the Indira Gandhi government had run into some problems. Less than three months after Chavan took charge of the finance ministry, the government faced an unexpected setback while implementing its plan to abolish the privy purse—a fixed payment being made to the erstwhile rulers of provinces and estates as part of an arrangement following their accession to the Union of India. The Lok Sabha passed the legislation, but the government failed to garner the required two-thirds majority in the Rajya Sabha (remember that it was a Constitutional amendment) as it fell short of that number by a single vote. An attempt to get a Presidential order to abolish the privy purse failed; the order was challenged by the princes and ex-rulers, and the Supreme Court's verdict went against the government. The privy purse would eventually be abolished, but only in December 1971, after Gandhi returned with a thumping majority in Parliament after the general elections in March 1971.

In the normal course, Chavan would have presented his first Union Budget in February 1971. That would have been the fifth and final Budget of the Indira Gandhi government that began its term after the general elections in 1967. The split in the Congress party and her less-than-comfortable majority in Parliament forced her to rethink her plans. Her move to nationalize banks had begun to yield benefits in terms of more branches being opened by them. Between July 1969 and December 1970, for instance, the state-owned banks, including State Bank of India, had opened 145 new branches every month, against only eighty branches per month opened in the first six months of 1969 and forty-seven branches during the whole of 1968. Almost 70 per cent of the new branches were opened in the rural areas. To capitalize on these economic gains and enhance her government's majority in Parliament, Gandhi decided to advance the general elections by a year. Gandhi called for elections to be held in the first week of March 1971, instead of in February 1972. The Congress, led by Gandhi, returned to the Lok Sabha with a huge majority, winning two thirds of the seats in the lower house. Not surprisingly, Gandhi used bank nationalization and her promise of pro-poor policies (the famous *Garibi Hatao* campaign) to win the confidence of the people and marginalize those elements in the old Congress who were ideologically opposed to her. Chavan would thus present an interim Budget for 1971–72 on 24 March 1971, and would return to Parliament again on 28 May 1971 to present the full Budget for 1971–72.

The preoccupation with the pursuit of politics and electoral gains, however, did not have any significantly adverse effects on the economy. The Indian economy's growth decelerated marginally to 5 per cent in 1970–71 even as Indira Gandhi's Congress tasted unusual political success. Food grain output rose by 5.5 per cent to 105 million tonnes in 1970–71, and the country's food grain stocks exceeded the reasonably healthy level of 5.5 million tonnes, against just 4 million tonnes a year ago. By the time Chavan rose to present the Budget for 1971–72 in the newly elected Lok Sabha, the fifth after Independence, the Indian economy seemed to be brimming with confidence.

If there were areas of concern, they sprang from inflation and the balance of payments situation.

In the second half of 1970, the wholesale price index stayed at an elevated level of over 7 per cent and moderated to about 4 per cent in the early months of 1971. But Chavan did not mince words when he told Parliament in his interim Budget speech on 24 March 1971 that 'the price situation warrants continued vigilance and we propose to take vigorous measures to ensure a reasonable degree of stability in the prices of essential good, which enter into mass consumption'.[2] One of the reasons for the spike in inflation was the unrestrained growth in money supply, made worse by the substantially large budget deficit of the government. The Reserve Bank of India had responded to the challenge by raising the bank rate from 5 per cent to 6 per cent in January 1971. The increase in the interest rate was accompanied by several other measures to encourage savings, boost deposit mobilization and discourage bank borrowing, except for priority purposes.

On the balance of payments front, the situation was hardly inspiring. A big increase in import licences issued during 1970–71 to help meet the economy's consumption needs had an adverse impact on the country's foreign exchange reserves. Promoting exports in such a situation acquired an urgency that could not be easily ignored. During this period, India did repay all its outstanding drawings from the International Monetary

Fund (made during the crisis years of 1966 and 1967), but did this without a significant increase in its exports. This had put avoidable pressure on the country's balance of payments. Since jobs and poverty were two major challenges, Chavan's interim Budget speech underlined the need for new employment-oriented schemes somewhat on the lines of the Calcutta-headquartered Industrial Reconstruction Corporation, the new development financial institution created to help revive industries and drive more sustainable investment and employment.

Chavan and His Four Budgets

During his tenure as the finance minister between June 1970 and October 1974, Chavan presented four Budgets. This period coincided with one of the most turbulent times for India. Economic growth was modest, at just 1 per cent in 1971–72, only to get worse in the following year, when the Indian economy contracted by 0.3 per cent. That was only the second time India had experienced a decline in national economic output, the first time having been in 1965–66, when the contraction was 3.7 per cent. The economy bounced back somewhat in 1973–74, but the growth was marginal, at just 4.6 per cent. Inflation had reared its ugly head. From 5.6 per cent in 1971–72, the wholesale price index galloped to a double-digit rise, at 10.1 per cent in 1972–73, and worse, doubled to 20.2 per cent in 1973-74. Not surprisingly, Chavan produced not just four Budgets in this period, but in addition presented two more statements that sought to mobilize more revenues through additional taxation measures. Those were difficult days, and Chavan was the only finance minister who, in his four-year tenure, imposed two doses of taxation in addition to his four Budgets.

India's economic plight was not entirely unconnected with what was happening in the region, in particular with regard to its immediate neighbour, Pakistan. There was political turmoil in Pakistan, with one of its major political parties, the Awami League, seeking secession of East Pakistan and declare it as an independent country. The Pakistani authorities decided to launch a military crackdown on the people of East Pakistan, leading to large influx of refugees into India's eastern states from March 1971. India carried the burden of millions of refugees from East Pakistan for several months, until the Indian Army decided to intervene in the matter. A war with Pakistan ensued in December 1971. India's economy suffered, both from the refugee influx and the war with Pakistan. The 1971–72 Budget had provided for an extra expenditure of Rs 60 crore to provide relief to the evacuees from what was then East Pakistan. This amount was not considered adequate; the estimate had been based on the assumption that international assistance would also flow in to help the Indian government carry the refugee burden. Chavan's Budgets and his two additional tax-revenue mobilization statements were a reflection of these developments across India's eastern and western borders. While Bangladesh was born and Pakistan was humbled, the economy had to bear the consequences.

Chavan's First Full Budget

Undeterred by the hugely increased financial burden created by the refugee influx, Chavan rededicated the Central exchequer to the task of providing a higher outlay for developmental and social welfare projects in his Budget for 1971–72. The prevailing political ideology behind economic development also was in evidence. The Budget reminded everyone of the need for renewing import substitution efforts, promoting the small-scale sector, increasing public investments and boosting exports. Not surprisingly, the fall in food grain prices was countered by an aggressive farm-price support operation. But higher imports of commodities like steel, cotton, oils and oilseeds became necessary to meet their domestic demand, which exerted pressure on the balance of payments.

Chavan interpreted the massive victory of Indira Gandhi in the March 1971 elections as a mandate for socialism, rapid economic growth and increased delivery of social justice. Thus, he announced special work programmes to improve job opportunities in the countryside, which would particularly help small farmers and small entrepreneurs in the backward areas. The finance minister left no one in doubt that without increasing the Plan outlay, the goals of stepping up the tempo of economic activity would not be achieved. A milieu of relative price stability was also a key requirement, he believed. No less important were the public-sector enterprises, which were given the task of deepening and widening the industrial base of the economy to achieve the country's basic social objectives. Now that more than a dozen commercial banks had become part of the public-sector stable, Chavan underlined the need for ensuring the cooperation of trade union leaders to improve the efficiency of the entire government system, including the banks. Already, the nationalized banks had been asked to formulate annual credit plans to ensure that credit meant for specific sectors did get disbursed to them without, of course, violation of the monetary expansion norms—for inflation management also was a concern of the government. Similarly, differential lending rates for small borrowers and the weaker sections of society were under consideration; a Credit Guarantee Corporation had already been set up and was in operation from April 1971 to underwrite the advances offered by banks to small borrowers. The finance minister also recalled how the government had decided some months earlier to enforce conversion of loans offered by state-owned financial institutions into equity. This, Chavan pointed out, 'should go a long way to promote the establishment of a joint sector to which we attach considerable significance'. Economic policymaking was following a new path to achieve socialism, economic growth and social justice.

In terms of fiscal policy measures, Chavan's first Budget was quite conservative. He mooted the idea of a new law to enable the government to acquire properties that had changed hands at prices much higher than recorded in the actual transaction documents. This understatement of property transaction values was aimed at saving on taxes. Hence, Chavan decided to empower the government to take over properties that were thus undervalued in sale deeds. The government's powers to acquire properties whose sale deeds reflect a much lower price than the actual transaction or market value remains even now in the statute book, as there has been no end to the need for cracking down on black-money generation through real-estate deals.

Interestingly, Chavan in his very first Budget had mooted the idea of a service tax, although he could not levy it. He referred to the fact that there were Constitutional limitations on the powers of the Centre to tax services. Chavan believed that since the Centre could not easily levy the tax on services, he should advise the states to consider levying the service tax and meet their revenue needs. The Constitution did not specifically bar the states from imposing a tax on services. Chavan made no progress in persuading the states to consider levying a tax on services. The idea of a service tax was picked up by Manmohan Singh and introduced by him from July 1994, when he was the finance minister.

Several taxes were raised in 1971. The surcharge on income-tax for individuals was raised from 10 per cent to 15 per cent, just as capital gains tax was also increased. On top of an increase in the rates of additional wealth tax on urban property, announced by Indira Gandhi in her Budget in 1970, Chavan increased the wealth tax rates steeply—to 8 per cent on wealth above Rs 15 lakh. Earlier, the wealth tax rate was 4 per cent on net wealth between Rs 15 lakh and Rs 29 lakh, and 5 per cent on net wealth above Rs 20 lakh. The new rates from 1971 were to apply on net wealth above Rs 1 lakh for individuals and above Rs 2 lakh for Hindu undivided families (HUFs). But this was not an exemption slab. Anyone holding wealth above Rs 1 lakh or HUFs holding wealth above Rs 2 lakh would have to pay tax on the entire value of their wealth. Approved financial investments, one owner-occupied houses and agricultural assets continued to be exempted from wealth tax.

On indirect taxes, Chavan simplified the rate structure for import duties by reducing the number of bands—from seven ad valorem rates to only four. Effectively, however, the customs rates were increased as the new band of four rates ranged between 30 per cent and 100 per cent, while the earlier seven-band rate structure ranged between 15 per cent and 100 per cent. Chavan introduced a new tax to be levied at the rate of 20 per cent on all transportation tickets purchased in rupees for foreign travel. The total additional tax revenue mobilization was not much—about Rs 177 crore—which would have reduced the pre-tax deficit of Rs 397 crore to Rs 220 crore.

A Mini-Budget after the War

Seven months after Chavan presented his first full Budget, the country saw a major upheaval. The refugee problem on India's eastern border went from bad to worse and by early December, India was engaged in a fortnight-long war with Pakistan, from 3 to 16 December 1971. The Indian economy had taken a big hit on account of the refugee problem and the war. The provision of Rs 60 crore made in the Budget in May 1971 for meeting the costs on account of the refugee burden had proved to be woefully inadequate. By August 1971, the provisions under this head had to be raised to Rs 260 crore and a demand for an additional amount of Rs 100 crore had been put up before Parliament for approval. Defence expenditure was also on the rise, since what was provided for in May 1971 was inadequate to meet the costs of a war. In addition, a major tropical cyclone had hit Paradip on the coast of Orissa on 29 October 1971, devastating that region with its fury, which lasted just about a day. Relief and rehabilitation work in the wake of the cyclone imposed an additional financial burden on the Centre and the state of Orissa. The government needed more resources to finance all these additional expenditures.

Thus, even before the war with Pakistan came to an end, Chavan decided to seek Parliamentary approval for raising additional resources of about Rs 135 crore for the full year. Remember that this effort was as large as three-fourths of the amount his Budget had proposed to mobilize in the full year. He levied a surcharge of 2.5 per cent on income tax payable by all Indian and foreign companies, fetching for the Centre an additional revenue of 10 crore in the full year. On indirect taxes, he sought recourse to Section 4 of the Finance Act, 1971 (under which the Budget for 1971–72 was passed) to impose a regulatory duty of 2.5 per cent on all imports, with the exception of a few items, including food grains and books. A similar regulatory duty by way of additional excise duty was levied on commodities like iron and steel products, copper, zinc, aluminium and unmanufactured tobacco. The export duty on carpet backing and hessian was raised steeply, by Rs 400 per tonne, and the excise duty on sacking was raised by Rs 175 per tonne in light of the buoyancy seen in jute products with respect to both exports and domestic sales.

Additionally, the finance minister also dangled the stick of enforcing the Defence of India Rules, which allowed the government to keep a tight check on pricing and distribution of essential goods. Fears of shortage of essential goods, their hoarding and a rise in their prices had provoked the finance minister to issue the threat of using such draconian provisions under the law. Of course, he hoped that he would not be required to use these provisions. But the fact that he issued the threat was an indication of the government's concern about price rise and shortage of essential goods after the war. While expressing the hope that people would contribute to the National Defence Fund to help the government in the wake of the war, Chavan announced the decision to float a new series of National Defence Loans, into which banks and other financial institutions would be able to channel resources. The need for introducing economy measures and curbs on imports to conserve resources was also underlined by the finance minister.

On the expenditure side, Chavan subjected the government's non-Plan expenditure to scrutiny. As a consequence, guidelines were issued to the Central ministries to curtail their non-obligatory and non-contractual non-Plan expenditure by at least 5 per cent. The expected savings were to the tune of Rs 50–60 crore. Chavan also decided to effect selective cuts in expenditure on a few Plan schemes and the Board of Direct Taxes was asked to expedite collection of income and corporation tax arrears.

Chavan's Second Budget

By the time Chavan came before Parliament to present his next Budget for 1972–73, the Indian economy had already begun showing signs of increased stress and a slowdown. The rate of growth for 1971–72 had slumped to about 1 per cent. Inflation was rising and would be estimated at 5.6 per cent by the end of March 1972. The finance minister had become acutely conscious of the need to increase investments for building new capacities to sustain growth. Another area of concern was foreign trade, where exports did not do well even as imports spurted, widening the trade deficit at a time when the country's foreign exchange reserves were not too comfortable, at just about $1.2 billion. The burden of refugees had meant an additional expenditure of Rs 325 crore, against the provision of Rs 360 crore made earlier. Foreign assistance of Rs 120 crore had become available, aiding the Indian government in its refugee relief efforts, and this would eventually alleviate the country's overall expenditure burden. Thanks to the war with Pakistan, defence expenditure, at Rs 1411 crore, increased by 14 per cent over what was budgeted for in 1971–72. Plan outlay suffered a shortfall and the government's borrowings were higher; and even though corporation tax, excise and customs duties increased, the government's Budget deficit ballooned to Rs 385 crore in 1971–72—a slippage of 66 per cent from the Budget estimate of Rs 232 crore. Early signals of a brewing economic trouble were too obvious to be ignored.

Recognizing the need for increased investments, Chavan announced a 25 per cent rise in the outlay for the Central Plan and for Centrally sponsored Plan schemes to Rs 1787 crore. This was the sharpest-ever increase in Plan outlay in a single year. The biggest increase under the Centrally sponsored schemes was for those schemes aimed at providing social welfare for the people and small farmers.

On taxation matters, Chavan was rather conservative. The report of the Direct Taxes Enquiry Committee, headed by K.N. Wanchoo, former chief justice of India, was with the government. The finance minister proposed that a new legislation would soon be introduced in Parliament to give effect to many of the reformist recommendations made by the committee. He spared individual income-tax payers from any change in the tax rates or the surcharge on them. But that also meant that the marginal income tax rate in the highest slab continued to stay elevated at a record high level of 97.7 per cent including surcharges. He did not change the corporation tax rate, although he doubled the surcharge on it from 2.5 per cent to 5 per cent. Customs duties were raised and excise duties on many items were either rationalized or increased. Total additional tax revenues as a result of his efforts were expected to amount to Rs 133 crore, which in 1972–73 was expected to bring down the deficit to Rs 242 crore.

Chavan Delivers the FERA Jolt

A key legislative change in India's economic policy governance was brought about by Chavan in 1972. This was the dreaded and highly restrictive Foreign Exchange Regulation Amendment Bill, which Chavan introduced in the Lok Sabha on 24 August that year. The new law was part of Indira Gandhi's socialistic regime, marked by a control-permit rule to keep a tight check on flows of foreign resources into and outside the country. The amendment bill had as many as seventy-three clauses, reflecting the range of the overhaul of the law, principally aimed at regulating dealings in foreign exchange, which was scarce those days. The key objectives of the amendment included plugging of foreign exchange leaks arising from invoice manipulation in trade and property deals, and placing of foreign exchange curbs on foreign companies, including branches of foreign firms engaged in trading. An important provision in the amended law was to ensure that foreign firms converted themselves into Indian companies. While introducing the bill in the Lok Sabha, Chavan noted that cases of foreign investment which were operational without prior permission or were functioning in non-priority areas would be reviewed on a case-by-case basis. However, cases of recent approvals, specifically in high-technology or export-oriented sectors, were to be exempted from such reviews.

Politically, the FERA amendments were explosive. Chavan had anticipated that there would be political reactions to the changes and that the government must be ready to deal with them. Immediately after the amendment bill's introduction, it was referred to a Joint Select Committee of Parliament to examine the provisions proposed in it. The committee had as many as forty-five members of Parliament and was presided over by Satish Chandra, a Congress member of the Lok Sabha from Bareilly in Uttar Pradesh. The committee had many high-profile parliamentarians, including left leader Jyotirmoy Basu and Indrajit Gupta, Piloo Mody, Manubhai Shah and, of course, Chavan himself. Industry leaders, including representatives of the national chambers of commerce and industry, made representations before the committee and sought clarifications on many issues. It was clarified that the responsibilities of the Reserve Bank of India were mainly regulatory, while the enforcement provisions of the amended law would be implemented by the relevant government department, like the Enforcement Directorate.

Almost seven months later, after deliberations by the committee, the government decided in March 1973 to introduce some significant changes in the proposed FERA amendments. The most important change was in the ceiling to be imposed on foreign equity in Indian companies. The new amendments clarified that any company with more than 40 per cent of foreign equity would have to seek clearance from the Reserve Bank of India for continuing business until such time as it diluted its foreign equity below 40 per cent. Not surprisingly, industry had become deeply apprehensive of the deleterious impact of these changes on foreign investment and on operations of foreign companies in India. In response, the central bank was given powers to provide general or special exemptions.

Another five months later, Chavan revised the amendment bill and introduced a revised law in Parliament on 24 August 1973. Left members of Parliament, like Jyotirmoy Basu, attacked the provisions in the law on the ground that they were not stringent enough to prevent misuse of the foreign exchange laws. After some debate, the bill was passed by Parliament and received the assent of President V.V. Giri. The new regime received a mixed response. While business houses were unhappy, sections of the media expressed apprehensions that the new provisions had many loopholes in the regulation and would be unable to prevent the repatriation of excessive profits and dividends. But the fact of the matter was that the FERA amendments damaged the confidence of Indian and multinational companies in doing business in the country. It had introduced many draconian steps. Violation of a few of the new FERA rules attracted provisions under the criminal law, which meant anyone accused or found guilty could be arrested during trial or punished with imprisonment. India's turn towards greater state control of businesses was expedited by these amendments in FERA, a direction that was changed many years later with the introduction of the Foreign Exchange Management Act in 1999.

Guiding Credit Allocations

Another important policy initiative that Chavan took in collaboration with the Reserve Bank of India was in June 1972, when the central bank was persuaded to issue guidelines for the Differential Interest Rates Scheme or DIRS. This was in pursuance of the finance minister's announcement in Parliament in March 1972 of the government's policy decision on public-sector banks for launch of a scheme to lend to low-income-earning customers engaged in productive enterprises at concessional rates of interest. But a review of the scheme, as announced in June 1972, showed that it had failed to make much of an impact among its intended beneficiaries. In his Budget for 1973–74, therefore, Chavan announced many changes in DIRS. Its coverage was expanded from the earlier 163 industrially backward districts to 265 such districts, accounting for three-fourths of all the country's districts. Of course, districts already covered by the Small Farmers Development Agency and the Marginal Farmers and Agricultural Labour Schemes continued to benefit from DIRS. Even institutions for physically handicapped persons, orphanages and women's homes, irrespective of their location, were made eligible for assistance under DIRS. More importantly, the income limit for eligibility for the scheme was generously enhanced by 50–67 per cent to an annual family income of Rs 3000 in urban and semi-urban areas and to Rs 2000 for families in rural areas. The ceiling for working capital loans too was raised, from Rs 500 to Rs 1500, and for term loans from Rs 2500 to Rs 5000. DIRS made some progress as the government had set a minimum quantum of lending under the scheme for each public sector bank at 1 per cent of its total advances in the previous year. But the big hurdle in the implementation of the scheme was the failure of the banks in ensuring proper identification of beneficiaries from among a large number of eligible borrowers.

It was a difficult time for the nationalized banks. The idea of defining what constitutes the priority sector and therefore who was eligible for receiving preference in securing loans from the banks was formalized in 1972. Initially, there was no minimum target set for lending under the priority sector scheme. Chavan as the finance minister oversaw the launch of this initiative. After he left the finance ministry, public-sector banks were told in November 1974 that priority-sector lending should account for as much as one third of their total outstanding credit by March 1979. Subsequently, the priority-sector lending target was set at 40 per cent of the nationalized banks' total credit, while the private-sector banks were told to lend at least a third of their credit to the priority sector. What Chavan had begun in 1972 became a major socio-economic obligation for the banking sector in the next few decades.

Tweaks in Industrial Policy

Days before Chavan presented his Budget for 1973–74, the government modified the contours of the industrial policy, which essentially redefined the scope and freedom of large industrial groups and companies in their operations. This was in tune with Indira Gandhi's policy tilt towards socialism, a greater role for the public sector and more restrictions on the private sector, but in effect it also meant greater clarity and marginal relaxations. The industrial licensing policy of 18 February 1970 had imposed restrictions on activities like expansion or fresh investment by undertakings belonging to large industrial houses with assets exceeding Rs 35 crore. This was not in tune with the asset limits of Rs 20 crore, prescribed under the Monopolies and Restrictive Trade Practices Act of 1969.

Thus, on 2 February 1973, the government aligned the definition of large industrial house under the industrial licensing policy with what was prescribed under the MRTP Act. This meant that the industrial licensing policy also began treating companies and groups with assets exceeding Rs 20 crore as large industrial houses. A list of industries that were of basic, critical and strategic importance for the growth of the economy and had long-term export potential was prepared and classified as Appendix I. The modified policy ensured that MRTP companies (with assets of over Rs 20 crore) and foreign companies could take up manufacturing of goods mentioned in Appendix I, as long as these were not reserved for the public sector or the small-scale sector (with investment in plant and machinery of up to Rs 7.5 lakh and up to Rs 10 lakh for ancillary undertakings). The revised policy gave preference to small and medium entrepreneurs, just as cooperatives, small and medium undertakings would be encouraged to produce goods of mass consumption. By way of concession, exemption from licensing provisions for substantial expansions and new undertakings was provided, but only for a small set of applicants. Units that had fixed assets in land, building and machinery worth more than Rs 1 crore, companies that fell under the MRTP Act and foreign companies were not entitled to such exemptions. Even companies with existing licences with fixed assets of over Rs 5 crore were not eligible for such exemptions. Only a tiny number of small units could claim to be outside the purview of licensing.

The licensing policy change was hardly a recipe for encouraging more investments on the part of the private sector. Not surprisingly, the unemployment problems in the Indian economy were becoming worse. But Chavan was determined to address the challenge of creating more jobs. In his Budget for 1973–74, Chavan launched a new programme to generate employment opportunities for an additional half a million educated persons in various fields. The scheme was also aimed at creating durable assets, collection and compilation of valuable data and training of an adequate number of persons to help in the implementation of new programmes and projects. Chavan kept a Budget provision of Rs 100 crore to launch an employment-creation scheme.

Chavan's Third Budget

A year later, Chavan presented his next Budget for 1973–74 amidst fears of a contraction in the economy in 1972–73. Indeed, economic data available later would show that the Indian economy did contract by 0.3 per cent. Chavan had noted two factors contributing to the output decline: the financial burden of the refugees from East Pakistan and the failure of the monsoon in the summer of 1972. For the second year running, kharif output in India had faced a major setback. Inflation was back, unleashing its fury; between April 1972 and end-January 1973, the wholesale price index had risen by 9.1 per cent, against the mild rise of 3.7 per cent in the same period of 1971–72. By the end of March 1973, the full year's inflation was up at 10 per cent, driven largely by prices of food products.

The drought after the failure of the monsoon had seen the government strengthen its public distribution system for food items. A country-wide emergency programme was launched to raise agricultural production in the rabi season of early 1973 to offset the losses in the preceding kharif season. By way of precaution, Chavan had already arranged for imports of about 2 million tonnes of food grains in early 1973 to manage any adverse fallout of a crop output shortage on the price situation. At the same time, Chavan was becoming acutely conscious of the need for reducing the dependence of Indian agriculture on rains—a thought that gave a push to the building of irrigation infrastructure over the next several years. In the next few decades, the dependence of Indian agriculture on rains would decline, but the progress would be painfully slow. A little less than a fourth of India's total cropped area would be irrigated in 1972–73, and in the next fifty-odd years that coverage would still be less than half of India's cropped area. In other words, the dependence of Indian agriculture on rains came down from 75 per cent of its total sown area to just about 50 per cent by 2020.

An aspect of the Indian economy that did well in 1972–73 in an otherwise gloomy situation was the sharp pick-up in exports of merchandise goods. In 1972–73, exports had grown by 19 per cent to $2.6 billion—a healthy increase by any yardstick, even though its share in India's gross domestic product was a measly 3.7 per cent. Not surprisingly, Chavan exuded no great satisfaction over the country's export performance, underlining the need for giving exports a further boost to help finance the country's needs for foreign exchange to meet its import requirements.

Another positive development was the finance minister's commitment to taking the country on a higher growth trajectory. In spite of the gloomy economic scenario, Chavan announced in his Budget for 1973–74 the government's intention to fix an annual growth rate target of 5.5 per cent for the Fifth Five-year Plan beginning from April 1974 and ending in March 1979. In retrospect, it became clear that Chavan was a little

overambitious in setting such a goal. In the next few months, the Fifth
Plan would be finalized with the growth rate scaled down to 4.4 per cent
for the five-year period. Eventually, the achievement in those five years
exceeded the target, the Plan clocking an annual growth rate of 4.8 per
cent, but not before the entire Plan exercise was modified to suit the
political exigencies of the day.

The Fifth Plan was the brainchild of Planning Minister Durga Prasad
Dhar, a close confidante of Indira Gandhi. The challenges before Dhar were
many: faltering growth, skyrocketing inflation and a spurt in oil prices. The
government's attempt at taking over the wholesale trade in wheat to keep
a check on food prices made no headway. The Fifth Plan had two planks:
removal of poverty (inspired by the famous and electorally successful
Garibi Hatao campaign of Indira Gandhi's) and attainment of self-reliance.
Chavan's Budgets had underlined both these goals. But the goals were not
easy, as high inflation led to the cost calculations for the Plan outlay going
haywire. The outlay had to be revised. Two major political developments
took place even before the Fifth Plan could complete its first year. D.P.
Dhar was shifted to Moscow in early 1975 as India's Ambassador, and on
12 June 1975, days before Gandhi promulgated Emergency, Dhar died
of a heart attack in Moscow. During the Emergency regime, the Fifth
Plan's focus shifted more towards achieving the Prime Minister's twenty-
point programme. Worse, the Congress under Gandhi lost the elections in
1977, and one of the first decisions of the Janata Party government led by
Morarji Desai was to terminate the Fifth Plan a year before its scheduled
end. The Fifth Plan continued only till March 1978.

One of Chavan's major achievements with regard to fiscal management
was the manner in which he dealt with the states' overdraft problem and
persuaded them to enter into an arrangement that could bring them back
on the path of fiscal rectitude. For some years, states had been running
substantial overdrafts with the Reserve Bank of India. These overdrafts
were used by the states to finance their expenditure. Chavan got the states
and the central bank together to thrash out the tricky issues between them.
A scheme was put into operation from 1 May 1972. This meant that the
states' overdrafts, amounting to about Rs 642 crore as at end April 1972,
would be cleared by providing the states ways and means advances. These
ways and means advances were to be recovered in small instalments over
the following few years. The recovery process began in 1972–73. The

states agreed to the new arrangement and came on board as the Centre, under Chavan's leadership as finance minister, agreed to take over the past deficits of the states on its books, with corresponding adjustments being made in the books of the state governments. There was thus a notional increase in the Central government's deficit, which was to be pared down over the following few years. That was a classic example of Centre-state cooperation for management of government finances in the quasi-federal governance structure that prevailed in India. Many decades later—during the Modi regime—economic policy commentators would pine for such a collaborative relationship between the Centre and the states in fiscal and other economic policy reform matters!

Contours of Chavan's Fiscal Policy

In 1973–74, Chavan implemented many recommendations made by the Direct Taxes Enquiry Committee headed by K.N. Wanchoo, a former chief justice of India, and those of the Committee on Taxation of Agricultural Wealth and Income, which was headed by the eminent economist Dr K.N. Raj. This resulted in many new taxation initiatives in Chavan's third Budget. The Raj Committee's recommendation that agricultural income should be taken into account while determining the rate of tax applicable to the non-agricultural income of taxpayers led to a new provision in the tax laws. The Budget mandated aggregation of both the agricultural and non-agricultural components of a taxpayer's income for purposes of determining the rates of income tax that would apply to the non-agricultural portion, in cases where the taxpayer had non-agricultural income exceeding the exemption limit. The exemption limit for non-agricultural income in this provision was set at Rs 5000 in a year. The new provisions would apply to individuals, HUFs, unregistered firms, associations of persons, bodies of individuals and artificial juridical persons under the Income Tax Act.

Chavan's taxation policy also targeted HUFs, which in his view had indulged in tax avoidance. Thus, he mandated separate rate schedules for both income tax and wealth tax for them. These schedules fixed higher tax rates for HUFs with one or more members with independent income or wealth exceeding the exemption limit. Similarly, the capital gains taxation provisions were tweaked to prevent tax avoidance. Thus, concessional tax treatment was made applicable to capital gains tax only when the capital assets were held for a period exceeding sixty months, instead of the earlier period of twenty-four months. In other words, the concessional tax rate on long-term capital gains would be available only if an asset was held for more than five years. To encourage more savings under insurance schemes launched by the Life Insurance Corporation, Chavan made the scheme for allowable tax deduction more attractive for investment in such life-insurance policies. There was also a slew of measures that provided fiscal concessions to encourage investment in selected sectors located in backward areas. On excise, Chavan plugged the exemption gaps in many sectors, including the textiles sector, raised the rates for oil products to garner revenues for the exchequer and increased duties on many items that were used by the rich, like refrigerators and air-conditioners. As expected, customs duty was raised on a wide range of imported items in a bid to raise resources and conserve foreign exchange by discouraging imports.

It is remarkable that Chavan had imposed a good dose of additional taxation on companies, individuals, manufactured goods and imports during his tenure as the finance minister. It was probably because the government needed more resources, particularly at a time when the economy was facing headwinds creating obstacles in its growth path. In the Budget for 1973–74, for instance, Chavan had estimated a deficit of Rs 335 crore at the existing levels of taxation. At the end of his new taxation proposals, he had imposed fresh taxation of about Rs 250 crore. In 1972–73, the annual additional revenue mobilization was Rs 133 crore; in the previous year's Budget for 1971–72, Chavan had sought to raise additional tax revenue of Rs 177 crore. But it was not just in the Budget that Chavan raised taxes; he followed it up with a mini-Budget in December 1971 to raise additional tax revenues of Rs 135 crore.

Chavan was acutely conscious of his revenue-raising initiatives, which he said gave him no pleasure. At the end of his 1973–74 Budget speech, he said:

Sir, before concluding I would like to point out that this is the third regular Budget that I have been privileged to present to this august House. During each of these Budgets, I have had to come forward with proposals for significant amounts of additional taxation. This was not a pleasant task. It was, however, inevitable in the light of resources required to meet our basic commitments to the people and the unprecedented challenges of the difficult times we have lived through . . . It is in this context of our firm commitment to socialism, rapid economic growth and a self-reliant economy that the Budget proposals must be appraised. The building-up of a socialist society requires a sustained multi-dimensional effort to transform our social and economic structure . . . Fiscal policy must assist in this process. This is the vision I have kept in mind in formulating this year's Budget.

Chavan's Last Annual Budget

During the one year that followed after Chavan's third Budget, the Indian economy was in deeper trouble. The international oil shock, triggered by the decision of the Organisation of Petroleum Exporting Countries, or OPEC, to regulate and raise prices of crude oil, implied a huge increase in India's oil import bill. Making the economic situation worse was a decline in agricultural production by over 9.5 per cent in 1972–73. The kharif crop in 1973 was expected to be better, but that comfort was not sufficient to rein in food prices. In short, both domestic inflation and the country's external economic security were immediate casualties. Chavan had also reckoned that the Fourth Five-year Plan was coming to an end with an annual average growth rate of just 3.3 per cent, against the target rate of 5.7 per cent to be achieved during April 1969–March 1974. The war with Pakistan, the refugee problem on the country's eastern borders, the oil shock raising fuel prices and the monsoon failure of two successive years had contributed to the low growth. Wholesale price index-based inflation had crossed 20 per cent in 1973–74, even though the country's economic growth rate had inched up to 4.6 per cent. But the spectre of inflation rising further in 1974–75 was causing Chavan sleepless nights. It was against this background that he presented his fourth and what would turn out to be his last Budget, on 28 February 1974.

The increased burden on government finances was an additional cause for concern. The Third Pay Commission had already queered the pitch for Chavan. In 1973–74, he was aware of the need for implementing the recommendations of the Third Pay Commission, but his budgeting exercise did not reflect this. At the start of 1974–75, he estimated the additional burden on account of higher wages for government employees at Rs 150 crore. This was almost double the Budget deficit of Rs 85 crore he had projected for 1973–74. Indian Railways' finances were under strain, thanks to continued industrial unrest among large sections of the railway employees. Indian Railways had created an additional financial burden of Rs 109 crore on the central exchequer. As 1973–74 ended, the actual Budget deficit had ballooned to Rs 650 crore, against a projected figure of Rs 85 crore.

Yet, for 1974–75, Chavan was in no mood to curtail expenditure. He raised the Central outlay for the first year of the Fifth Plan. Acknowledging that oil prices had risen, he advocated a shift away from oil and a move towards greater dependence on coal, allocating a higher outlay for creating coal-production facilities.

On taxation efforts, Chavan was quite bold and pleased individual tax payers no end. In one stroke, he reduced the maximum marginal income tax rate from 97.7 per cent, including surcharges, to 77 per cent. He also extended the scheme for development rebates for companies by another year. But there was also a big increase in the wealth tax rate, which went up from 2 per cent to 3 per cent on the lower wealth slab of between Rs 5 lakh and Rs 10 lakh, and from 3 per cent to 4 per cent for wealth above Rs 10 lakh. A big change for salaried taxpayers was the introduction of standard deductions up to a maximum of Rs 3500 a year, instead of separate deductions allowable on travel, books, taxes on professions and expenditure incurred in the performance of duties. This was a reform that has stood the test of time. Excise duty increases were mainly on items consumed by the rich, like passenger cars and air-conditioners or television sets. This was in line with the government's overall socialistic mindset. The bulk of the additional revenues were to come from indirect taxes, as part of the government's policy of taxing consumption items of the rich.

The state of the Indian economy worsened rapidly in the few months after the presentation of the Budget for 1974–75. Inflation rose at a menacing pace. The rise in the general price level in the three months between April and June 1974 was 7.8 per cent. For the full year of 1974–75, inflation would be estimated at over 25 per cent, against 20 per cent in 1973–74. According to the government's internal assessment, the rising inflation rate was 'basically rooted in the sluggishness of agricultural production'. The wheat crop was below expectation, leading to producers holding back supplies. Procurement of food grains had not picked up in spite of a sizeable increase in procurement prices. Cash crops like oilseeds had not done well, fuelling a price rise in the vegetable oils sector. The government had come round to the view that it must take a series of tough measures to keep prices under check.

The Reserve Bank of India played along with the finance ministry in managing the adverse conditions in the economy. The credit needs of the priority sector were being met. But the implicit goal of the central bank's policy approach was to tighten money supply to contain inflation. However, differences between the central bank and the finance ministry surfaced. The share of food procurement credit, export credit, credit to public sector undertakings and credit to priority sectors together amounted to about 55 per cent of gross bank credit, significantly up from 32 per cent earlier. The slack season credit policy for 1974, announced in April that year, recognized that the refinance and rediscount policies would continue to be selective and discretionary. RBI Governor S. Jagannathan advised banks that their next expansion of credit should be about 33–35 per cent of their incremental deposits. In addition, in order to aid credit flow into the system, the cash reserve ratio was lowered from 7 per cent of net demand and time liabilities of banks to 5 per cent and the statutory liquidity ratio was raised from 32 per cent to 33 per cent. These rates took effect from 1 July 1974.

Yet, an upset Banking Secretary Nirmal Chandra Sengupta wrote to Jagannathan in May 1974, drawing the latter's attention to the unintended adverse impact that the new policy had on small borrowers in the priority sector, particularly agriculture. Earlier, at the RBI's central board meeting too, Sengupta had underlined the need for the central bank to frame some schemes for banks to ensure a sustained flow of priority-sector lending. It was at that meeting that Sengupta handed over to Jagannathan a note from Finance Minister Chavan. The finance minister had pointed out that 'small borrowers and priority schemes like the half-a-million-jobs programme and the DRI scheme were being denied credit while the organised sectors received enough funds, especially through relaxation in individual cases and by way of the New Bill Market Scheme'.[3] RBI History notes that it was surprising that Chavan, who was a votary of a tight money policy to check inflation, would want credit flows to be increased at all, leave alone in a selective manner. What emerged in the following weeks was a difference of opinion within the finance ministry—the Department of Economic Affairs was in tune with the RBI, while the Banking Department wanted a stepping up of credit flows to the priority sectors. Eventually, the differences were resolved at a high-level meeting, which was attended by the RBI governor, the finance minister, Chief Economic Adviser Manmohan Singh, Banking Secretary Sengupta and member of the Planning Commission Sukhamoy Chakravarty. There was no concrete decision after the meeting but the finance minister appeared to be convinced by the arguments on credit restraint put forward by the Department of Economic Affairs.

Three Ordinances

Thus, Chavan got three ordinances promulgated. These led to the imposition of temporary curbs on declaration of dividend by companies, immobilization of 50 per cent of additional dearness allowances of government employees and an increase in the compulsory deposits to be made by income tax payers from the higher-income-earning groups. The objective of these measures was to reduce the imbalance between the aggregate demand and supply in the economy, thereby reducing the pressure of demand as also decelerating the rate of growth of money supply. An alternative that the government avoided under such a situation was a cut in developmental expenditure, which it feared would have a far more adverse outcome for the economy.

Chavan had also got the Reserve Bank of India to introduce measures to tighten its credit controls. The central bank had asked all commercial banks to scrutinize their top 50 accounts to ensure that bank credit was not used for excessive accumulation of inventories or diverted to non-productive uses. On 22 July 1974, the RBI also increased the policy interest rate at that time, the bank rate, by a steep margin of 2 percentage points from 7 per cent to 9 per cent. Once again, the objective was to reduce incentives for accumulation of inventories with the help of bank credit and to help increase bank deposits.

The government's assessment then was that the only way the imbalances in supply and demand could be addressed was by means of a sustained increase in agricultural production. This was a formidable task, given the domestic shortage of fertilizers, the demand for which could be met only through higher imports, entailing precious foreign exchange outgo. Foreign exchange reserves were still maintaining a stable level of about $1.3 billion and were used to finance import of food grains. The export outlook was a little uncertain, as prices of a few of the country's main export products had declined and the high inflation rate had undermined the competitiveness of India's exports.

Clearly, demand-compression measures were not going to be enough. The rapid rise in the inflation rate was threatening the government's fiscal stability as well. The original calculations on the Budget deficit for 1974–75 had gone completely awry. The government had to increase the issue prices of wheat in a bid to scale down the burden of food subsidy on its finances. The weak finances of Indian Railways, made worse by the recent railway strike and the burden of higher wages for railway employees, had meant an increased burden on the Central exchequer. Rising inflation also implied that the government's expenditure on higher dearness allowance for its employees would be more than what had been budgeted for during the year. Projects also suffered from cost escalation, increasing the government's capital expenditure. The government had already subjected its non-developmental expenditure to scrutiny to effect some savings. But Chavan reckoned that the deficit of Rs 126 crore that he had budgeted in February 1974 would be exceeded quite easily and he needed to raise more resources to rein in the deficit level. The additional resources mobilization initiative he planned had three major features: avoidance of new taxes on basic necessities; discouragement of conspicuous consumption; maximum economization of use of scarce materials; and mopping up of the windfall gains being made by producers and middlemen in certain sensitive commodities.

In a statement made before Parliament on 31 July 1974, Chavan announced the government decision to levy a tax on the gross amount of interest received by scheduled banks on loans and advances made in the country. This was a measure with far-reaching impact in both the fiscal and monetary policy spaces. This was a controversial move, as a fiscal policy measure would once again encroach into the territory of monetary policy supervised by the Reserve Bank of India. Such a tax had earlier been mooted by Finance Minister T.T. Krishnamachari and had created a rift between him and the then RBI Governor Benegal Rama Rau, which eventually led to Rau's premature exit from the central bank. But this time the idea was mooted by M. Narasimham, who was an Additional Secretary in the finance ministry at that time and had been brought to the ministry from the RBI. In his memoirs, Narasimham, who would later become the RBI governor, wrote:

> I put it to the Finance Minister, Shri Y.B. Chavan, that while interest rates could be put up as proposed, there was no reason why such an increase, which was part of broader policy, should benefit only one particular segment of the economy, namely, the banking system by helping to increase its earnings profits.[4]

Narasimham had argued that the government too should benefit from an increase in the interest rates, and a tax on interest would have the same effect as raising the cost of money, but the benefits would accrue to the government. Chief Economic Adviser Manmohan Singh had reservations about the move and the RBI too was opposed to the proposed tax. But Chavan eventually agreed to the new tax and announced its levy. As a result, the cost of borrowed funds went up on average by 1 percentage point, as the tax rate was 7 per cent of the gross interest earned by banks, according to calculations made by the finance ministry. Chavan raised the tax on long-term capital gains. On indirect taxes, he raised excise rates on a wide range of items, including copper, copper alloys, zinc, rayon and synthetic fibres and yarn, tyres, cement, cigarettes, pig iron, asbestos cement products, electric lighting bulbs, steel ingots, iron or steel products, paper and paper board, plastics, paints, varnishes, di-methyl terephthalate or DMT and caprolactam.

Chavan's new tax proposals would get the government an additional revenue of about Rs 210 crore in the full year, of which Rs 147 crore would come from indirect taxes and the remaining from direct taxes. The 31 July statement of Chavan's was no different from his Budget speech, at least in terms of its revenue-raising implications. His last Budget, presented on 28 February 1974, had imposed an additional annual tax burden of Rs 186 crore. The 31 July imposts were larger than what was announced five months ago.

Chavan Shifted out of North Block

How would Chavan be remembered as a finance minister? There can be little doubt that he steered the Indian economy when it, as well as the polity, was facing one of its most formidable challenges. As finance minister, he had to withstand the economic impact of a war and the huge refugee crisis that imposed additional costs on the exchequer. He took charge of the Indian economy just about a year after the Indira Gandhi government had nationalized fourteen banks in 1969. Keeping in tune with the socialist turn in the government's economic ideology, he had to manage the impact of many other similar steps, like the introduction of many stringent provisions through an amendment in the Foreign Exchange Regulation Act, or FERA.

Inflation was rising and growth remained tepid; during one of those years the economy had even contracted. The Indian economy had also weathered the shock of a sharp rise in the international prices of crude oil. The adverse impact of the increase in oil prices on the country's foreign exchange reserves was as telling as it was on its inflation trajectory. All in all, it was no fun to be the finance minister of the country during that period. Chavan faced a difficult time. And in spite of those adverse challenges, he did his best, reducing the overall incidence of taxation by slashing the maximum marginal rate of income tax, including surcharge, on individuals from 97.7 per cent to 77 per cent in those four years. That was a big relief, reflecting Chavan's belief in the principle of achieving tax buoyancy through reduced tax rates and increased compliance. But at the same time, Chavan raised the wealth tax rates during his four-year tenure in North Block.

Chavan had built a solid reputation as a finance minister among his senior staff in the ministry, even though he did not have any flourish in his personal dealings or in his overall personality. I.G. Patel, the economic affairs secretary during that time, recalled that Chavan was regarded as a 'colourless person'. But he had many other qualities. The finance minister, according to Patel, was 'able, quick to grasp and, while attentive to our advice, not devoid of political sagacity or practical wisdom to put his own stamp on the decision-making process'.[5] Chavan, according to Patel, may have functioned with a handicap, although he was a gentleman and accessible to his staff and not known for shirking his responsibilities. 'What gave an impression of insipidity was that he was shy and a man of few words. He must have also been inhibited by the fact that Mrs Gandhi did not trust him fully and he could not have been sure of his position or independence,' Patel wrote.[6]

Here was one instance showing how Chavan would resist political pressure and shield his senior officials against it: just before the general elections of 1972, the Congress treasurer, L.N. Mishra, began asking for all kinds of special financial favours to be showered on selected parties, in an apparent bid to secure electoral dividends for the party. Patel was at the receiving end of this pressure. When it became difficult for him to resist this pressure, Patel informed Chavan about the matter and asked him if he could forward those files containing requests for political favours from Mishra to the finance minister so that he could decide what should be done. Patel writes in his memoirs:

> His response was forthright. He said I should carry on with the way I was handling matters. If I wanted to for any reason, I could also send a file to him for clearance. But in that case, I should on a separate piece of paper express my views and the reasons thereof. There was, he added, a third way. I could lock up the files till the elections are over.

This was a rare display of political courage, contrary to the impression created in the public mind at the time that Chavan was a pliable finance minister; and also quite contrary to what Indira Gandhi's Principal Secretary P.N. Haksar was reported to have said to Patel about Chavan: 'Chavan will do anything to remain in power. He likes to eat a chicken at every meal. Who is going to provide him that when he is not in power?'[7]

The departure of Chavan from the finance ministry was quite sudden. But given the manner in which the state of the Indian economy was worsening, Prime Minister Gandhi perhaps realized that she must be seen to be taking some big steps to make a change in the leadership of the finance ministry. An overhaul of the Union council of ministers was effected on 10 October 1974, leading to a reshuffle of many senior ministers.

It all began with veteran Congress leader Uma Shankar Dikshit being divested of the home ministry. He was not removed from the Cabinet but was retained as a minister without portfolio. K. Brahmananda Reddy was brought in to succeed Dikshit in the home ministry. Another big change was the shifting of Jagjivan Ram from the ministry of defence to the ministry of agriculture. The defence ministry was taken over by Swaran Singh, who was earlier the minister for external affairs. That change made room for Chavan. From the finance ministry, Chavan was shifted to the external affairs ministry. And the vacancy caused by Chavan's move to external affairs was filled by Chidambaram Subramaniam, who at that point had been the minister for industrial development.

Significantly, the reshuffle also meant that the finance ministry now had a completely new team. Along with the departure of Chavan, the minister of state for finance, K.R. Ganesh, was also shifted out. Instead, there were two fresh incumbents: Chidambaram Subramaniam as the Cabinet minister for finance and Pranab Mukherjee as the minister of state for finance.

C. Subramaniam (Finance Minister, 1974–1977)

The FM during the Emergency

On 15 October 1974, the Cabinet Secretariat issued a memorandum detailing the portfolio changes after Prime Minister Indira Gandhi's major reshuffle of her ministry five days earlier, on 10 October. As a result of that reshuffle, all the key ministries of home, defence, external affairs, agriculture and finance had new incumbents. Scanning the list, one notices that the ministry of finance had somehow been relegated to the side in terms of seniority. In the past, all finance ministers would regularly figure among the top four or five Cabinet ministers mentioned on the list. But in that seventeen-member Cabinet, including the prime minister, C. Subramaniam figured at number sixteen as the finance minister. Chavan continued to occupy the number two slot in that list, indicating that even though he was shifted out of the finance ministry, he had not yet lost his political importance in the ministerial pecking order.

That list also included two other names—Pranab Mukherjee and Vishwanath Pratap Singh. Mukherjee was elevated to the position of minister of state for finance and later given independent charge of revenue and banking, while Singh was inducted into the Union ministry as a deputy minister for commerce. Over the next few years, both would become finance ministers and steer the Central exchequer under different governments.

For Subramaniam, however, the corner seat in North Block at the head of the Union government's finances was a big opportunity. He was stepping into the big shoes of Chavan to continue the job of repairing the

Indian economy, begun by the strongman from Maharashtra. Subramaniam had already made a name as a successful minister for agriculture, having helped usher in the Green Revolution a few years earlier and aiding the country's march towards self-sufficiency in food grains, obviating the need for their imports. It was now his turn to do something similar—a rescue operation for the Indian economy.

Baptism by Fire

Subramaniam's entry into the finance ministry was almost a baptism by fire. Such was the state of the economy that on the very first day of his taking over as finance minister, Subramaniam held a meeting with bankers and representatives of financial institutions. The message to them was clear and stern. They must make sure that they adhered strictly to the existing credit policy to keep a tight lid on liquidity. The busy season credit policy announced in the last week of October continued with the selective credit controls for sensitive commodities like food grains, cotton, oilseeds and oil, sugar and textiles. The objective was to discourage speculative hoarding of these commodities with the help of bank credit. The tenor of the policy was influenced by rising prices. Inflation, measured by the movement of the wholesale price index, had spurted to over 27 per cent by the end of October 1974.[1] It was clear that the 31 July package of measures announced by Chavan to contain prices was yet to make an impact on inflation. The credit policy was expected to make that impact. But, as a commentary in the January 1975 edition of the *Economic and Political Weekly* pointed out, demand for credit was high even at a higher rate of interest, and this neutralized the effects of a tight credit policy.[2]

The challenges for Subramaniam acquired a new dimension as tensions between the finance ministry and the Reserve Bank of India escalated from November 1974. The trigger was a letter from RBI Governor S. Jagannathan sent to Finance Secretary H.N. Ray, with a copy marked to the finance minister. The letter was quite candid: 'We in the Reserve Bank would like to convey our congratulations to the government and the ministry of finance in particular, on their success in bringing down the government deficit.'[3] The Governor went further to say: '. . . there is no doubt that fiscal correctives are essential and monetary measures can only support but cannot wholly substitute for action in the fiscal field.'

Nobody in the finance ministry liked what appeared to be gratuitous piece of advice and what seemed like a grudging accolade. The finance ministry had already acquired a stance vis-à-vis the RBI, where the central bank was expected to comply with what the government expected it to do as far as credit or monetary policies were concerned. A week later, the finance ministry informed the RBI that it was accepting the recommendation made by Parliament's Estimates Committee to earmark 33.3 per cent of lending for the priority sector. It was yet another instance of the government letting the RBI know who called the shots in such matters.

By December 1974, Subramaniam had to deal with the consequences of another major economic policy move initiated by Indira Gandhi. After a brief discussion, Parliament passed the Sick Textile Undertakings (Nationalisation) Bill on 21 December. This law allowed the government to acquire sick textile units and rehabilitate them after subjecting them to a reorganization process. The stated objective of the law was to 'subserve the interests of the general public by the augmentation of the production and distribution, at fair prices, of different varieties of cloth and yarn'. The new law resulted in the nationalization of as many as 103 sick textile mills, and their ownership was transferred to a newly created state-owned enterprise—the National Textile Corporation, or NTC. The total compensation paid to the private mill owners who lost their mills was a relatively small amount of Rs 39.15 crore. The compensation amounts for some of the individual owners of the mills ranged from as low a figure as Rs 1000 (for as many as twelve mills) to more than Rs 1 crore (for about seven mills); as many as twenty-four mill owners got compensation amounts of between Rs 50 lakh and Rs 1 crore and the remaining received compensation of less than Rs 50 lakh.[4] This was a classic display of Indira Gandhi's socialistic turn in her economic policies after the lack of modernization and violent trade union activism had sent these mills into sickness. At the same time, the nationalization move showcased how private loss-making and sick mills were being nationalized for what was politically justified as a public good. Over the next few decades, even the textile mills that remained under private ownership would experience serious financial difficulties and many of them would be allowed to monetize their land and make use of real estate opportunities in many parts of the country, most notably in Mumbai. Many of these mills have ceased to exist now.

The Budget before the Emergency

Even as Subramaniam was dealing with the rapid turn in India's economic policies and learning to manage a slightly stressful relationship with the RBI governor, he had to pay more attention to the process of preparing the next annual Budget, for 1975–76. He began preparing the Budget in the backdrop of an Indian economy that had been buffeted by developments, external as well as internal. On the internal front, the economy had slowed considerably, adversely impacted by the railway strike, rising inflation and erratic agricultural output. On the external front, there was the rise in international crude oil prices and India's uncomfortable foreign exchange reserves situation. Thus, Subramaniam's first Budget—for 1975–76, presented on 28 February 1975—focused on both the internal and external concerns for the economy. Inflation management was his immediate concern, as critical as the need to 'devise ways and means of stimulating production from the available capacity, and of adding to that capacity in sectors considered vital for improving income and consumption levels of the poor'.[5]

A special area of attention for Subramaniam was the agricultural sector. This was only to be expected. Subramaniam had the past experience of having successfully overseen the transformation of Indian agriculture through the Green Revolution. But, as the finance minister, he recognized that a lot more had to be done for sustaining growth in Indian agriculture. He would lay emphasis on four specific areas to give Indian agriculture a fresh boost: launch of a national seeds project for large-scale production of quality seeds to help Indian farmers access high-yielding varieties of good-quality seeds; increase in the domestic capacity to produce more fertilizers in the public, cooperative and private sectors; introduction of programmes to ensure optimum use of surface and ground water, along with a boost to build major irrigation projects; and organization of farmers' service societies, which could provide credit to farmers in time, arrange for inputs and help in the processing as also marketing of their produce.

Subramaniam identified three key segments of the energy sector that he believed should receive the government's policy attention: coal, crude oil and electricity. He was of the view that the decision to nationalize the coal industry about two years ago in 1973 had begun to yield results in the form of higher output, at about 88 million tonnes in 1974–75, which showed an annual increase of about 13 per cent. Coal nationalization, according to the finance minister, also helped in reorganization of the management of mines and supply of equipment and technical expertise, which laid a strong foundation for increasing coal output. Shortages in railway transport and power—two constraints in raising coal production—had been largely removed. Not surprisingly, Subramaniam announced in his Budget speech in February 1975 that the country's coal output in 1976–77 would rise again, by over 11 per cent, to reach 98 million tonnes. This would be an achievement, as at this level of output the country would not only meet its domestic demand for coal but could also undertake some exports.

What worried Subramaniam were the developments in the petroleum sector, where international crude oil prices had risen sharply, straining the balance of payments and pushing up the inflation rate. In just about six months—between October 1973, when OPEC decided to curtail oil production, and April 1974—the price of crude oil in the international markets spiked by over 300 per cent. Almost 65 per cent of India's total petroleum product requirements were met through imports. This meant huge pressure on India's balance of payments. For instance, India's crude oil import bill almost trebled, from $266 million in 1972–73 (pre-OPEC hike) to $719 million in 1973–74. The challenge for Subramaniam was that crude oil prices kept rising in 1974–75, as a result of which the country's oil import bill rose further, to $1.5 billion. Since exports were not rising, India's trade balance saw a sharp deterioration. A trade surplus of $136 million in 1972–73 had turned into a trade deficit of $554 million in 1973–74.

When Subramaniam took charge of the finance ministry in October 1974, he had reckoned that 1974–75 would witness a further worsening of the trade balance. Indeed, that year ended with the deficit almost trebling, to $1.4 billion. Seen from another perspective, the scale of the challenge before Subramaniam would become more clear: India's total oil import bill was only 10 per cent of its total exports of about $2.6 billion in 1972–73. That was before oil prices went up. The ratio of the oil import bill to total export earnings rose to 22 per cent in 1973–74 and to 35 per cent in 1974–75. Subramaniam reckoned that with the foreign exchange reserves coming under pressure, India's ability to finance its imports would be under strain. He sought the help of the International Monetary Fund and secured a loan of $640 million (about Rs 485 crore) under its special oil facility. This helped stabilize the country's foreign exchange reserves at around $1.4 billion by the end of March 1975. For Subramaniam, it was a conscious reminder that the country had sought recourse to assistance from the IMF for the second time in less than seven years; it had got assistance from the IMF's compensatory financing facility in November 1967.[6]

The only silver lining on the oil front was the step-up in domestic oil exploration activity as a result of the OPEC oil price increase. Just about four months after the oil shock delivered by OPEC, the Oil and Natural Gas Corporation (ONGC), a state-controlled enterprise, had discovered the Bombay High oilfield. That discovery on 19 February 1974—about 160 kilometres from the shores of Mumbai and at depths of about 75–90 metres—turned out to be the biggest oil discovery in India. Even without the Bombay High discovery, there was greater urgency and momentum to increase indigenous production of oil from the existing sources. Domestic oil production eventually went up from 7 million tonnes in 1972–73 to 8 million tonnes in 1974–75, and further up, to about 9 million tonnes in 1975–76. In his 1975-76 Budget speech, Subramaniam said:

> The ONGC is expected to establish the first stage of production from Bombay High in the second half of 1976 with a yield of about 1 million tonnes per year. By 1980 production from this source might well reach the level of 10 million tonnes, though one may have to wait a little before making firm estimates.

Subramaniam was not far off the mark. By 1981–82, India's indigenous crude oil production had reached a level of 20 million tonnes and kept rising for the next few years.

As for the third segment of the energy sector, Subramaniam gave a big push to electricity generation and distribution. The accent was on restructuring the electricity industry, with more stress on professionalism, efficiency and competence. This led to a distinct improvement in power generation and in the performance of the state electricity boards. Plans to set up super-thermal power projects near the pitheads of the major coalfields in the country were prepared at this time.

Subramaniam's economic philosophy as finance minister identified two clear priorities for the country—food and energy. His Budgets reflected these two concerns as he earmarked more funds for their development. Additionally, promotion of backward areas became an article of faith for him. Subramaniam believed that development plans must be drawn up on the basis of a 'careful analysis of local needs, potentialities and resources'. In order to deal with the challenges of scarce domestic financial resources and the strained balance of payments situation, Subramaniam showed his faith in higher exports, optimum use of scarce imported inputs, higher investments which were to be financed in a non-inflationary manner, increase in the rate of savings and introduction of a rational and a more equitable wage and salary structure. He also made no secret of his commitment to expansion of the public distribution system, backed by an efficient and strong procurement infrastructure.

By the end of February 1975, the rate of inflation had slowed a bit, but not enough to provide any reason for Subramaniam to relax some of the harsh steps that his predecessor Chavan had introduced in July 1974. The wholesale price index-based inflation would decelerate to about 25 per cent by the end of the year, a little lower than the 27 per cent mark it had reached at the end of October 1974. Chavan had curtailed non-developmental spending, frozen increases in wages and a part of additional dearness allowance, reduced the increase in the rate of money supply, and decided on stringent action against hoarders and smugglers. Seven months later, even though the inflation rate had marginally slowed, his successor finance minister Subramaniam decided to continue the same policies.

At the same time, however, Subramaniam recognized the need for stimulating investment. He had thus got an ordinance issued to provide tax relief for investment in the stock markets and also announced a plan to give companies the freedom to announce higher dividends, a facility that had been curbed earlier. Subramaniam also reiterated the government's commitment to 'root out the evil practices of smuggling, hoarding, black marketing and tax evasion' and announced in his Budget for 1975–76 that a separate law to deal with such economic offences with a severe hand would be introduced.

The 1974–75 Budget presented by Chavan in February 1974 had imposed additional annual taxes of Rs 186 crore, by which the deficit was expected to be brought down to Rs 126 crore. But in July Chavan realized that there was a need to raise more resources and thus went in for additional measures to raise an annual revenue of Rs 210 crore.

Tax collections during 1974–75 did improve, but not enough to keep the deficit under check. Instead of the budgeted deficit of Rs 126 crore, 1974–75 ended with a revised deficit of Rs 625 crore.

The stressed finances of the Centre meant that the finance minister's fiscal headroom became a little more restricted. The Fifth Five-Year Plan, which began from April 1974, did not get the extent of additional funding that the government considered necessary. For the Central Plan, Subramaniam's Budget for 1975–76 made a provision of Rs 2558 crore, which was a 20 per cent increase over what was allocated in 1974–75. But Subramaniam was not elated over the extent of the increase. He said:

> I am conscious that a more substantial step-up in the Plan investment to provide for achievement of a draft Fifth Plan targets in all sectors would have been desirable from the long-term perspective of the economy. But we cannot forget that large-scale deficit financing leading to further price increases will substantially erode the real content of the Plan and cause more damage to the programme of planned development.

But within the Central Plan outlay of Rs 2558 crore, the finance minister made sure that the allocations for his priority areas like agriculture, fertilizers, rural electrification, coal, petroleum and petrochemicals were raised handsomely.

On the taxation front, Subramaniam did not make any significant changes in the basic rates of tax on individuals and companies. Individual income tax rates had been cut sharply by Chavan in the Budget for 1974–75, and no further reduction was mooted. There were tax incentives to encourage investment so that savings could be channelled into high-priority industries. Thus, Subramaniam decided to exempt from tax all inter-corporate dividends derived by domestic companies from new companies engaged in the manufacture of fertilizers, pesticides, paper and cement. Higher tax deduction was allowed on various instruments of long-term savings so that people saved more to support higher investments. An important legislative change pertained to exempting from income tax compensation amounts of up to Rs 20,000 received by workers retrenched under the Industrial Disputes Act or other similar laws.

The indirect tax changes were essentially aimed at raising the levies on items of consumption and use by the rich or the upper middle-class sections, or which were considered luxury and demerit goods. The items whose excise duty went up included free-sale sugar in the open market, tea, cement, petroleum products, tobacco products, air conditioners and their parts. The total annual additional revenues—both from direct and indirect taxes—was estimated at Rs 239 crore, which was expected to bring down the deficit to Rs 225 crore. The proposed deficit was expected to be substantially less than the Rs 625 crore of 1974–75.

RBI Governor Cuts Short His Tenure

Subramaniam's Budget had a special provision that could well have further roiled the government's relationship with the Reserve Bank of India. In the 1974–75 Budget, Chavan had levied a tax on interest earnings received by scheduled banks, which had raised the cost of borrowings from banks by about 1 percentage point. This move had encouraged the non-banking non-financial companies to raise deposits from the public, which became more attractive than deposits received by banks from the public. Subramaniam had become apprehensive that this would not be in conformity with the government's overall focus on selective credit control measures being imposed by the central bank. As a corrective, Subramaniam proposed that while computing the taxable income of non-banking non-financial companies, only 85 per cent of the interest paid by them on public deposits would be allowed as expenditure for tax purposes. This would facilitate a level playing field among scheduled banks and non-banking non-financial companies. At the same time, the measure would fetch an additional revenue of Rs 10 crore in a full year.

It is reasonable to conclude that this issue may have exacerbated the already strained relationship between RBI Governor S. Jagannathan and the government. What created a bigger problem was the change in the political landscape of New Delhi—the rise of Sanjay Gandhi as a power centre. His Maruti car project required financial assistance through loans, calling for a special dispensation by banks. The RBI under Jagannathan had enforced strict control over credit allocations by banks, and the Maruti project did not qualify for a loan under those circumstances. But Jagannathan was under pressure to make a concession for Maruti. If Sanjay Gandhi's Maruti project had to receive bank loans, then the RBI Governor had to agree to a selective relaxation.[7] Quite understandably,

Jagannathan was most reluctant to make that exception and shower favours on a company promoted by a man who was politically the most powerful person at that time. Naturally, he earned the wrath of the powers that be, and Subramaniam was relatively powerless to intervene.

Jagannathan was a career civil servant, having joined the Indian Civil Services many decades ago. For two years—between 1966 and 1968—Jagannathan was a secretary in the economic affairs department of the finance ministry before he joined the World Bank, representing India as an executive director there. In June 1970, he came back from Washington to hold the reins of the RBI in Mumbai, succeeding B.N. Adarkar who had stepped in to fill the vacancy created by the departure of L.K. Jha in May 1970.

At the time that Jagannathan came under such pressure from the government, he was close to the end of his tenure and was to retire in June 1975. He also had an offer to become an executive director at the International Monetary Fund. Jagannathan decided to accept that offer and cut short his tenure at the RBI by a month. It was a resignation, but the government presented it as a situation where the RBI governor had left when he was close to the end of his tenure. Nevertheless, this was a resignation, and the third time an RBI governor had quit before the end of his term. The previous ones who had quit before completing their tenure were Sir Osborne Smith and Sir Benegal Rama Rau. Subramaniam had to suffer the fate of being the finance minister when the country saw its third RBI governor quit before the end of his term. He sent Banking Secretary N.C. Sengupta to take charge of the RBI as its governor for a period of three months, from May 1975. The expectation was that the government would be able to find a suitable candidate for the job in three months' time. Indeed, the government had found Sengupta's successor in K.R. Puri, who was then chairman and managing director of the Life Insurance Corporation of India. Puri joined the RBI as its twelfth governor on 20 August 1975.

A few months prior to Puri's appointment, the political situation in the country had begun to heat up. About a month after Sengupta took charge of the RBI in May, Indira Gandhi declared a state of internal emergency in the country. It was an unprecedented political situation and Subramaniam's challenges of managing the economy under those circumstances acquired a new dimension. The finance ministry became overactive against economic offences, in a bid to establish that the government was firm in its resolve against corruption and black-money generation. For the Reserve Bank of India, the appointment of Puri as the governor signified yet another stage in the central bank's relationship with the Centre. Already, the government, through the finance ministry, had managed to assert itself over how the RBI should act on a variety of monetary and credit policy issues or with regard to the management of banks. With Puri in the corner room of the RBI, whatever little resistance the central bank had been putting up against the Centre's growing interference disappeared.

Quite ironically, the finance ministry actively colluded in the destruction of RBI's independent functioning. According to T.C.A. Srinivasa Raghavan, who edited one of the volumes of the history of RBI, monetary policy during those days had given way to credit rationing to ensure that credit went to those who needed it the most.[8] That need was decided by the government, and the secretaries in the finance ministry played a key role in determining the priority list. RBI was obviously not pleased, but the finance ministry stepped in whenever the central bank tried to assert its independence in matters of credit allocation. Economic affairs secretary Manmohan Singh, who would become the RBI governor a few years later, was quite firm in ensuring that the government had a say over the way the RBI decided credit allocation issues. Singh told the RBI's top executives that there should be prior consultation with the government before the central bank announced its credit policy on 8 May 1976. And when there was only a verbal communication to the finance ministry on what the RBI governor intended to announce at his meeting with the bankers, Manmohan Singh said quite firmly that such matters from the RBI should be communicated in writing. This was a clear suggestion to the RBI that its policies should be framed after a formal consultation with the government. Not surprisingly, the RBI raised margins on credit for raw cotton in July 1976 after being told to do so by Manmohan Singh. Once again, the RBI had to supply additional credit of Rs 250 crore to Food Corporation of India—since FCI could not repay this amount to the government—for which the Budget for 1976–77 had taken credit. The RBI, after all, was seen as an arm of the government, and the former acted after consultations with the latter.

Finance Ministry under the Emergency

The Emergency was declared on the midnight of 25 June 1975. At a meeting with senior officials of the revenue department on 27 June, the finance ministry worked out a game plan for necessary action. By 1 July, an ordinance was promulgated to amend the Conservation of Foreign Exchange and Prevention of Smuggling Activities (COFEPOSA) by removing a few loopholes in the law pertaining to the detention of those accused of having committed economic offences under the law. The very next day, a Cabinet committee constituted to deal with smuggling and other economic offences issued a series of directives. These included immediate arrest of smugglers ordered to be detained but absconding, no unauthorized concessions for smugglers who were jailed but were carrying out their activities even while in detention, and strengthening of the apparatus to detect smuggling by the sea route by recruiting crew to operate boats on the seas. In the next couple of days, over a dozen notorious smugglers were arrested in Mumbai, Delhi and Chennai, including those who had been released by the courts earlier. Another legislation was passed by January 1976, allowing the government to confiscate properties belonging to the smugglers. Such laws also helped get a large number of professionals and self-employed persons under the tax net.

Another area of focus was facilitation of procedures for remittances by non-resident Indians. The finance ministry, in consultation with the Reserve Bank of India, simplified the norms and the route by which Indians living abroad could transfer their foreign exchange savings back home. This was one way of diverting this money being routed to the country by means of illegal, or hawala, transactions. Two deposit schemes were introduced. In one scheme, non-resident Indians could make deposits in foreign currency with Indian banks, and the principal amount as well as the interest, earned at the prevailing rates, was repatriable. The other scheme allowed NRI depositors to receive Indian rupees against their foreign currency deposits with Indian banks, along with interest. Both schemes had a lock-in period to prevent speculation. NRIs were also incentivized to invest in India, including in real estate.

The central objective was to prevent diversion of foreign exchange inflows through illegal routes like hawala. In subsequent years, the NRI investment and deposit schemes would provide the platform for one of India's most celebrated corporate controversies. But the short-term impact of these schemes on the country's foreign exchange reserves was positive. Remittances through legal channels rose to Rs 441 crore in the fourteen-month period from October 1974 to November 1975. Monthly remittances during this period went up by a whopping 63 per cent, from Rs 41 crore before the crackdown on tax evasion to Rs 67 crore. In two years after the imposition of the Emergency, the country's foreign exchange reserves increased at a rapid pace. Foreign exchange reserves $2.17 billion at the end of March 1976 jumped by 57 per cent over March 1975 and the increase was even sharper by 72 per cent at $3.7 billion at the end of March 1977. In contrast, foreign exchange reserves rose by just 9 per cent to $1.32 billion at the end of March 1974 and the annual increase at the end of March 1975 was even lower at 4 per cent.

The big increase in the number of income tax raids against tax evasion and black-money operations (the number of such raids was estimated at over 3500 between April 1974 and November 1975) and the consequent rise in the value of assets seized during such operations gave rise to the idea of introducing yet another scheme to allow tax evaders and black-money holders to come clean through a voluntary disclosure of concealed income, on which taxes could be paid at the prevailing rates without payment of any penalty and without attracting penal provisions of the law. In other words, these taxpayers would enjoy immunity from the law even though they had violated it, if they paid up taxes on their undeclared income at the prevailing rates. This idea was strongly backed by the minister of state for finance, Pranab Mukherjee, although the Wanchoo Committee on Direct Taxes, whose report the government had received just a couple of years ago, had warned that such action rewarded dishonesty and penalized the honest taxpayer. Mukherjee was initially opposed to such a voluntary income disclosure scheme, but was persuaded by a forceful plea from his senior officials in the tax department. They argued that the potential for unearthing concealed income, securing revenues and ensuring a higher tax base for the future were gains that neutralized the moral-hazard problem cited by the Wanchoo Committee.

Such schemes launched by former finance ministers, including C.D. Deshmukh, T.T. Krishnamachari and Morarji Desai, had failed to elicit a good response. The challenge before Mukherjee and Subramaniam was to make the scheme a success. Once Prime Minister Indira Gandhi gave her approval to the scheme, Subramaniam gave it the green signal and Mukherjee oversaw the rollout of the scheme from October 1975 for a period of three months. During those three months, Mukherjee addressed twenty-seven meetings across the country asking taxpayers to take advantage of the scheme. There was no extension of the last date of the scheme, although there were requests to that effect.

The Voluntary Disclosure Scheme (VDS) of 1975 was a success, dispelling earlier apprehensions about it among sections of the finance ministry. On 2 January 1976, Mukherjee announced on All India Radio that total disclosures under the scheme were estimated at Rs 1450 crore, of which income disclosures amounted to Rs 700 crore and wealth disclosures to Rs 750 crore. For 1975–76, an additional revenue of Rs 250 crore on account of income tax and wealth tax was secured. An additional amount of Rs 40 crore was invested in government securities by tax evaders who wanted to come clean, as under the scheme those who declared income and wealth were required to pay tax at the prevailing rates and invest 5 per cent of the disclosed income and wealth in notified government securities. About three months later, when Subramaniam presented the Budget for 1976–77, it turned out that the additional tax revenue for the government as a result of the VDS was a higher amount—Rs 660 crore—than estimated. A large part of these gains—an estimated Rs 226 crore—went to the states under the prevailing devolution formula.

Mukherjee listed many gains from the VDS. Prevention of tax evasion was one of them. But a more enduring gain, according to the minister of state for finance, was the reduction of the government's budget deficit from the extra revenue and creation of a wider base for taxation following conversion of black money, which would sustain revenue growth the coming years. The most interesting feature of Mukherjee's announcement on All India Radio was the offer to taxpayers to declare their undisclosed income or wealth even after the VDS had ended, if they so wished. They could approach the tax authorities to make a clean breast of their concealed income and wealth. There would be no special tax treatment for such disclosures, but the government had the power to grant immunity to these taxpayers from penalty and prosecution.

Over to a New Exchange Rate System

Within weeks of promulgation of the Emergency, the Indian economy began facing a new challenge on the exchange rate management front. After the breakdown of the Bretton Woods system in the early 1970s, the Indian rupee began experiencing sharp depreciation vis-à-vis the British pound sterling. This was also because of declining share of the UK in India's trade and the weaknesses in the British economy, which was affecting the sterling's exchange rate vis-à-vis other major international currencies. The rupee depreciation against the pound sterling became too sharp by the middle of 1975. At that time, the Indian rupee was fixed in terms of the British pound sterling and moved with respect to other currencies, depending on how the pound sterling moved against them. Thus, any depreciation or appreciation of the Indian rupee depended less on domestic circumstances like inflation, trade or the foreign exchange situation and more on how weak or strong the pound sterling became vis-à-vis other currencies.

Subramaniam was unhappy with this arrangement and wanted a technical solution to what he believed was a problem. Chief Economic Adviser Manmohan Singh was given the responsibility of working out an alternative arrangement. Those days, Vijay Joshi, a professor at Oxford and an eminent economist, had been requisitioned by Manmohan Singh to work in the finance ministry as an officer on special duty. Additional Secretary in charge of banking, M. Narasimham, and Joshi 'discussed the possibility of moving out of the sterling link and moving to a trade weighted basket as was then the widespread international practice'.[9] Joshi and Narasimham worked on this proposal and presented a detailed paper to Finance Minister Subramaniam. More discussions within the finance ministry followed. Manmohan Singh supported the idea and argued that the weights to be assigned to each of the currencies should not be fixed and instead be determined by the value of India's trade with each of the countries to whom these currencies belonged.

RBI Governor S. Jagannathan, however, had a different view. He opposed the proposal on the ground that it would be a 'leap into the unknown' and that the central bank did not have the requisite technical staff to operate such a scheme. An argument ensued between Narasimham, who hailed from the RBI, and Jagannathan. Eventually, since the finance minister was batting for the switch, Jagannathan withdrew his opposition. Two more expert views were sought—those of B.K. Nehru, who was then India's high commissioner in the United Kingdom, and L.K. Jha, who was at the time the governor of Jammu and Kashmir. Both endorsed the idea. Emboldened by these responses to the proposed exchange rate management system, Subramaniam decided to meet the prime minister, Indira Gandhi. He took along with him Narasimham, who could explain to the prime minister in plain and simple language what the proposal would mean. Even before Narasimham could finish his explanation, the prime minister asked whether the new system would lead to devaluation of the Indian currency. This was a politically loaded question. Gandhi had to face a political backlash after the devaluation of the Indian rupee in 1966 and she was careful to avoid a repeat of that. Narasimham explained that there would be no devaluation and it was most likely that the Indian rupee would actually appreciate vis-à-vis the sterling. Gandhi nodded her head and said '*Theek hai*', according to Narasimham.

Thus, from September 1975, the Indian rupee got delinked from the British pound sterling. The exchange rate of the rupee was officially determined by the RBI within a nominal band of +/- 5 per cent of the weighted basket of currencies of India's major trading partners. It was a significant step, aimed at imparting greater stability to the effective exchange rate of the rupee and to the country's foreign trade, which in effect was expected to help promote exports. That system continued till 1992, when a new liberalized exchange rate management system was introduced.

Organizational Restructuring at North Block

In December 1975, an organizational restructuring took place in the finance ministry. While Subramaniam continued to function as the finance minister, Mukherjee was given the responsibility of heading the Department of Revenue and Banking as a minister of state with independent charge. Earlier, from October 1974, Mukherjee was only the minister of state for finance.

While the two departments of revenue and banking remained within the finance ministry, Mukherjee began enjoying greater power, becoming in charge of them as minister of state with independent charge. For all effective purposes, the Banking Department and the Revenue Department had an independent ministerial boss. This curtailed Subramaniam's powers as the finance minister. In the past, such attempts to vest a minister of state for finance with independent charge of a few departments had been made, but they had not succeeded. Mukherjee's elevation was thus unique and has remained unique, as even though such an idea of bifurcating the finance ministry in the following decades was mooted, they were given up as unworkable.

Birth of Regional Rural Banks

Even before the restructuring of the finance ministry, Subramaniam had initiated action on expanding and strengthening the reach of banking in rural India. Bank nationalization had helped the move towards such a goal to some extent, but increasing credit allocations to villages of India to an optimum level still appeared a mirage more than anything else. Subramaniam had a long discussion with his additional secretary in the finance ministry, M. Narasimham, and asked him to head an experts group to examine ways to increase provision of institutional credit to rural areas.[10] The committee relied on the available data to show how poorly served India's rural pockets were in terms of credit availability. Quoting an RBI study, it was pointed out that the existing financial intermediaries could offer only Rs 800 crore to rural India, against an annual requirement of Rs 3000 crore. The unmet rural credit demand was more than 70 per cent of the annual requirement. This led to a large number of rural artisans, shopkeepers, agricultural workers, sharecroppers and farmers depending on moneylenders and their usurious practices, which for many of them turned out to be financially ruinous. The Narasimham Committee recommended that the government should set up regional rural banks, or RRBs, to provide credit to save the rural population from the clutches of moneylenders. The proposed RRBs were expected to operate as low-cost lending institutions, combining in them the efficiency of commercial banks with the flexibility of cooperative credit societies. Mukherjee, who championed the cause of RRBs, believed that they were to be built as 'local institutions steeped in the area's cultural ethos and manned by people possessing intimate knowledge of the local economy and culture'.[11]

M. Narasimham, who headed the experts' group that recommended the establishment of RRBs, was not happy about the way some of the recommendations made by him were ignored by the government. For instance, the Narasimham Committee had suggested that there should be local equity participation in the RRBs by local individuals or institutions and that a pilot scheme should be launched first so that the necessary changes could be made to the structure after observing the gaps in the proposed institutional framework.[19] The government went ahead with the RRB plan without incorporating these suggestions, and on 26 September 1975, the President promulgated the ordinance for setting up RRBs.

There was quick follow-up action. In less than a week, five RRBs were launched, on 2 October 1975, coinciding with the birth anniversary of Mahatma Gandhi. Each RRB was sponsored by a nationalized bank and had an authorized share capital of Rs 1 crore and a paid-up capital of Rs 25 lakh. The Union government held 50 per cent of the shares, while the remaining 35 per cent and 15 per cent were, respectively, held by the sponsoring bank and the government of the state of location of the individual RRBs. By March 1977, as many as forty-eight RRBs had been established.

The ordinance on RRBs was made into a law after Parliament passed it in 1976. The President gave his assent to the Regional Rural Banks Act, 1976 on 9 February 1976. A few weeks later, on 16 February, another organizational change took place. The Industrial Development Bank of India was delinked from the RBI, and the Unit Trust of India, which since its inception in 1963 had remained an associate institution of the RBI, was converted into an associate institution of the IDBI.

Mukherjee had lost little time in taking full advantage of the new powers he had begun enjoying as a minister of state for finance with independent charge. He had convened a meeting of the chief executives of all the nationalized banks about a fortnight before Subramaniam was due to present the Union Budget for 1976–77. It was a high-level meeting, convened on 14 February 1976 and attended by the CEOs of the nationalized banks, the RBI governor, the RBI deputy governor, the banking secretary and the chief economic adviser. Significantly, the finance minister, C. Subramaniam, was not present at this meeting. The meeting discussed advances to be made to the priority sector, branch expansion, deposit mobilization and tackling of banks' bad investments by paying more attention to sick industries. Mukherjee had noted that in the twenty-point programme introduced by the Indira Gandhi government during the Emergency, about a dozen objectives pertained to the banking sector. Hence, he wanted greater emphasis to be given by banks to their rural lending operations, particularly in the handloom sector. A decision was taken by banks to devise a suitable information system to ensure early detection of incipient sickness and thereby address the banks' stickly loans portfolios.

The Indian economy had begun to turn in improved results during 1975–76. Instead of the 25 per cent inflation of 1974-75, the wholesale inflation turned into deflation in 1975–76, and there was a price decline of 1.1 per cent. Economic growth spurted by 9 per cent (up from 1.2 per cent in 1974–75) and foreign exchange reserves had stabilized at a much more healthy level of $2.17 billion, representing a hefty rise of over 57 per cent in just one year. Stocks of food grains, a marker of the government's ability to deal with any failure of the monsoon and any adverse impact on agricultural output, rose to a high level of 11 million tonnes. Thanks to enforcement of strict discipline in the government administration, public-sector enterprises too showed higher growth as their production went up by 15 per cent. Subramaniam attributed some of these gains to the imposition of the Emergency from June 1975.

On the investment front, the 25 per cent increase in the annual Plan outlay during 1975–76 was bearing fruit for the Indian economy. Enthused by these encouraging results, Subramaniam made sure that the annual Plan outlay for 1976–77 was raised by about 32 per cent, to Rs 7852 crore, to sustain higher production and availability of key resources for investment. At the same time, the increased Plan outlay was expected to help industries improve their capacity utilization and meet domestic demand. However, Subramaniam was still not completely confident that he had gained control of inflation. Thus, measures aimed at securing economic discipline and the checks on non-developmental expenditure saw no relaxation, even after March 1976. Since a higher Plan outlay would mean an expansion of money supply, Subramaniam decided to keep a tight leash on inflationary forces and extended the decision to impound half of the dearness allowance increases for government employees for one more year, beyond July 1976. The impounded deposits of dearness allowance were to earn interest at 12.5 per cent, to be repaid in five equal annual instalments into the employees' Provident Fund accounts from July 1978.

Subramaniam's economic policy priorities for 1976–77 saw no significant change from earlier. The foremost priority was accorded to schemes intended to speed up agricultural development and to strengthen sectors such as power, irrigation, seeds, fertilizers and pesticides, so that an effective attack could be launched against rural poverty. There was special focus on launching an integrated rural development programme, backed by a special financial allocation in the Budget for 1976–77. Rollout of the National Seeds Project was expedited, inter-state river disputes were resolved speedily, fresh fertilizer capacity was being created and, most importantly, steps were taken to improve the fertilizer mix to enhance land fertility. Thus, prices of urea, phosphatic fertilizers and muriate of potash were reduced to encourage a balanced use of nitrogen, phosphorus and potash in the fertilizer mix used by Indian farmers. Investment in the energy sector rose as the government decided to set up more super-thermal power stations and increase onshore and offshore oil exploration activities in order to address power and petroleum shortages in the country.

An attempt was made by Subramaniam to encourage private-sector investment in a few priority industries by making the pricing policy more flexible. The idea of decontrolling prices in some sectors and introducing dual pricing in others was mooted, although it made slow progress. The specific provisions requiring the permission of the Controller of Capital Issues before companies under the MRTP Act could issue bonus shares were relaxed. Permission was now required only if the amount of issue exceeded Rs 50 lakh, up from the earlier limit of Rs 25 lakh. The state-owned Industrial Development Bank of India was entrusted with the responsibility of providing adequate financial assistance to industries to undertake modernization and expansion of their capacities. An exports package was unveiled to help industry sustain its exports growth and earn precious foreign exchange for the country. Export procedures were simplified and liberalized, with the announcement of more attractive rates for cash assistance for exports. Additionally, modernization programmes for jute, textiles and sugar were introduced to improve these industries' export competitiveness.

The twenty-point Economic Programme was launched after the promulgation of Emergency. Subramaniam ensured that measures to secure social justice under the 20-point Economic Programme were launched. These included redistribution of surplus land, provision of house sites for the poor and socialization of vacant urban lands. All these steps were expected to have a favourable impact on the structure of income distribution. Construction of low-income houses and family planning to help improve the standard of living of the people were also part of this agenda of the government.

A major governance reform was decentralization of the government accounts and payments system. Until then, the accounts of different central ministries were maintained by an independent audit department outside the administrative control of these ministries. Over the years, this system came to be considered as not conducive to effective financial management, as accounts and finance should form an integral part of the overall management of ministries. In a bid to integrate the ministries' accounts into their own administration and departments, Subramaniam decided to separate accounts from audit and institute a departmentalized accounting system. Audits, under the new system, would be done by an external agency in the government, but the accounts would be maintained by individual ministries. Subramaniam got two ordinances issued by the President after securing the necessary approvals from the Cabinet. The ordinances were expected to ensure that the necessary expert manpower was available to the government for discharging the new responsibilities and that the Comptroller and Auditor General was able to discharge his functions without disruption.

The new scheme, introduced from October 1976, meant that administrative ministries began taking full responsibility for arranging for payments and timely compilation and rendering of accounts. It was a big administrative reform that resulted in timely receipt of information on the progress of expenditure and enabled a proper analysis of expenditure trends, facilitating correct decision-making and adoption of remedial steps when required.

Another accounting reform, which became hugely popular, was the rationalization and modernization of procedures pertaining to claiming of dues, including pension and gratuity, and payment of salaries. The new system was aimed at eliminating the existing delays in the preparation of pension papers and the sanctioning of pension and gratuity. Procedures for payment of salaries and allowances of government officers were also simplified, and nationalized banks were used for carrying out financial transactions between the government, its employees and private citizens. This put an end to the monopoly enjoyed by the limited number of treasuries or banks in the disbursement of such dues. Simultaneously, a new social security scheme was announced, which was to provide insurance to workers without any payment on their part.

Subramaniam's Last Budget

Subramaniam's Budget for 1976–77, the last of his two Budgets during his stint as finance minister, would be remembered for continuing the process of reducing the income tax rates, begun by his predecessor, Chavan. Encouraged by the positive response to the Voluntary Income Disclosure Scheme (VIDS), Subramaniam decided to cut the tax rates on personal income and wealth. He announced:

> The maximum marginal rate of income-tax including surcharge will be reduced from 77 per cent to 66 per cent and will be applicable on the slab of income over Rs 1 lakh in the case of individuals and Hindu undivided families, other than those having one or more members with independent income exceeding the exemption limit.

Interestingly, Subramaniam expected tax buoyancy to improve as a result of this reduction in the tax rate and budgeted for no revenue loss as a result of the concession. Similarly, the wealth tax rates were reduced, but the coverage was increased. The Compulsory Deposit Scheme for income tax payers, however, was continued for another year. The rate of such deposits was retained at 4 per cent for incomes up to Rs 25,000 a year, but there was an increase in the rates for other income slabs—from 6 per cent to 10 per cent on annual incomes between Rs 25,001 and Rs 70,000, and from 8 per cent to 12 per cent on incomes above Rs 70,000 per annum. An additional revenue of Rs 80 crore was estimated from this measure, the single biggest impost in a Budget that provided for total net additional tax revenue mobilization of only Rs 80 crore.

For industries, Subramaniam introduced a scheme of investment allowance for the priority sector. The existing scheme of depreciation allowance was replaced by a system of investment allowance, to be available at the rate of 25 per cent of the cost of acquisition of new machinery and plants installed after 31 March 1976. This would apply for a list of industries that was expanded to include sectors such as those producing carbon and graphite products, inorganic heavy chemicals, organic heavy chemicals, synthetic rubber and rubber chemicals, including carbon black, industrial explosives, basic drugs, industrial sewing machines and finished leather and leather goods, including footwear made wholly or substantially of leather. Foreign companies too were given a relief. Income tax for them was fixed at a flat 40 per cent on the gross amount of royalties received by them from Indian concerns under approved agreements made after 31 March 1976. Lumpsum payments received by them for providing technical know-how outside India was to be charged to at a flat rate of 20 per cent.

One of the tax law changes Subramaniam introduced received little attention at the time. It was about protecting the taxman's rights to tax on the basis of where income is generated. An amendment to the direct tax law was carried out to introduce what is known as source-based taxation. This clause came in handy many decades later, in 2012, when the government decided to levy tax on capital gains earned as a result of an ownership-change transaction that took place outside India, but where the business underlying that income was located in India and the resultant capital gains made in India. In what became known as the 'Vodafone tax', the government went ahead with a taxation law change to reiterate the principle of source-based taxation. It became controversial because it was amended retrospectively. In 2021, the government amended the retrospective nature of the law of 2012, but retained the principle of source-based taxation, enunciated first in 1976.

Major changes in the indirect taxes regime were introduced by Subramaniam from 1976–77. A committee was set up to review the existing structure of the indirect tax system and advise the government on the steps to be taken. This was an early indication of the government's thinking on transitioning to a value-added taxation system to replace the excise duty structure. Another change was to switch over to an ad valorem system of excise from a specific duty rate system for more items like textiles, paper and paper board. Most significantly, reversing the earlier trend of raising excise on luxury goods, Subramaniam announced steep reductions in excise duties on a range of items, including television sets, refrigerators, air-conditioners, water coolers, small passenger cars and jeeps, ambulances, pick-up vans and other such vehicles of lower engine capacity. With an eye on exports, Subramaniam took a bold step to abolish excise duty on readymade garments, and in a bid to promote the use of computers, he reduced the basic import duty on computers and computer sub-systems from 60 per cent to 40 per cent.

Subramaniam ended his Budget speech exuding confidence in the Indian economy, saying it was poised for a surge forward and that the Emergency, along with its New Economic Programme, would usher in a qualitative change in the economic environment of the country. Although inflation during 1976–77 would be brought down to about 2 per cent—a major achievement—economic growth would see a marked deceleration, to just about 1.2 per cent, even though foreign exchange reserves would maintain a robust momentum, rising by 72 per cent, to $3.7 billion.

Subramaniam as FM

Subramaniam was a finance minister in the Union government for a little less than two and a half years, from October 1974 to March 1977. Compared with most of his predecessors, he was not a political heavyweight. He was a reformer at heart but lacked the necessary clout to overcome political resistance to change. One such case pertained to his passionate plea for creating a far more effective system for clearing investment projects. He made this suggestion at one of the regular meetings in the finance ministry reviewing the functioning of the Public Investment Board, the body entrusted with the task of evaluating public-sector projects and clearing them. Subramaniam decided that this idea should be evaluated by a group of officials, to be headed by the Additional Secretary in the banking department, M. Narasimham. The group deliberated on the relevant issues and recommended an alternative to the PIB system, suggesting that an institution like a National Development Bank be set up. This body would be run by professionals and would undertake an unbiased and apolitical techno-economic appraisal of projects. This process would end the practice of many Central ministers and state chief ministers proposing projects under some local or national-level political pressure, without any economic rationale. The group was of the view that the proposed National Development Bank was to be funded out of the Central Budget, along with resources to be raised through market borrowings. The new body should also be eligible to draw on external sources of funding. As a bank, it could then lend for infrastructure projects on the basis of professional appraisals based on commercial and financial viability. Subramaniam found the recommendations in the report of the group worthy of further evaluation. He called a meeting where the then Planning Commission Deputy Chairman P.N. Haksar was to examine the proposal. Haksar was brief and appreciated the rational approach of the group in suggesting creation of the new body. But he rejected it on the ground that it had little scope for success in the 'real world of chief ministers'.[20] The idea was given a quiet burial after that.

Subramaniam's equations with his senior officials in the finance ministry were marked by mutual respect and trust. The manner in which he dealt with the clearance of the Kudremukh iron ore project, which was in collaboration with the government of Iran, was an example of how sensitively and respectfully he dealt with his senior officers. Kudremukh Iron Ore Company, a state-owned enterprise of the Union Steel Ministry, was set up in Karnataka in 1976. But the project was conceived on the basis of a memorandum of understanding signed between the governments of Iran and India. The idea was for the Indian company to produce iron ore concentrates. The pelletized iron ore would then be exported to the National Iranian Steel Company. This meant that a financial agreement, including a sale-and-purchase contract, had to be concluded between the two governments. The contract was to envisage that the Iranian government would extend credit up to US$630 million, and in return its iron ore company would receive 150 million tonnes of pelletized iron ore from August 1980. In early November 1975, a team led by the then Steel Secretary Wadud Khan concluded the negotiations with the Iranian team, which ended late at night. The Iranian team had to return to Teheran the next morning to report to the Shah of Iran about the deal. The Indian Cabinet had to consider and approve the proposal that had been finalized by the Indo-Iranian team of negotiators. A Cabinet meeting had been scheduled to be held at 9 a.m. the next morning.

The Union finance ministry was fully involved in the exercise as it had to give its nod of approval for a deal that involved a credit line from Iran. Additional Secretary in the finance ministry, M. Narasimham, received the final proposal, which was cleared by the Indo-Iranian team of negotiators at

around 5 a.m. Narasimham reckoned that Finance Minister Subramaniam
was due to leave for Madras by an early morning flight. He quickly finalized
a note, on the basis of the communication he had received from Wadud
Khan. With that note, he presented himself at Subramaniam's residence
quite early in the morning, when the finance minister was busy in his yoga
session. Narasimham informed the minister about the proposal and sought
his approval. In an action that surprised Narasimham, the minister did not
even read the note but signed on it, indicating his approval. Narasimham
asked him why he would not read the note before signing it. Subramaniam
said he believed that the note contained what Narasimham had briefed
him about and felt it was therefore not necessary to read it. 'Narasimham,
if a minister has not that much confidence in his secretary and his secretary
not that much confidence in his minister, neither of them deserves to be
where they are,' Subramaniam had told him, with a disarming smile. With
that note containing the minister's signature, Narasimham went to the
Cabinet meeting, where Indira Gandhi commented that she had received
the proposal on the deal with Iran on the Kudremukh project only that
morning and that the finance minister was unfortunately not at the meeting
since he was heading for Madras. Narasimham pointed out from the side-
lines that he had the minister's signature approving the proposal. Gandhi
quipped with a smile, 'You do not spare your ministers.' Not letting go
an opportunity for a repartee, Narasimham replied, 'Madam, we did not
spare ourselves either; we worked through almost the whole night.'[21]

Subramaniam's relationship with Narasimham was special. That also
showed how the finance minister was transparent and open about helping
his senior officials plan their careers to their satisfaction. Sometime in the
middle of 1976, Subramaniam sent for Narasimham. The finance minister
told him he had a few proposals from RBI Governor K.R. Puri for the
appointment of two Deputy Governors at the central bank. Subramaniam
had some knowledge of the background of one of the nominations, but
he asked Narasimham to shed more light on the second nomination.
Even as they discussed the aptitude of the two candidates for the post,
Subramaniam asked Narasimham if he would like to be considered for
the same job in Bombay. Narasimham could not make up his mind. He
saw the opportunity as a way of getting back to the RBI, from where he
had been sent to the finance ministry on deputation. At the same time,
he was not sure if it was a good move on his part to leave the Central

government at that stage. So he asked the finance minister what his opinion in the matter was. Subramaniam explained to Narasimham that the rank of deputy governor was almost on a par with that of an additional secretary; the position of banking secretary was going to fall vacant in a few months and the minister was going to consider Narasimham for that job. Narasimham's confusion was resolved. He decided to stay back, and he became the Banking Secretary in November 1976.

Even with respect to I.G. Patel, Subramaniam showed his magnanimity. Patel had joined the United Nations Development Programme (UNDP) as its deputy administrator on a three-year term, which was coming to an end in December 1975. Patel had made a request for his leave of absence from the finance ministry to be extended by another two years. Subramaniam granted him that request. Patel returned to India only after the end of the Emergency and eventually became Governor of the RBI.

Subramaniam could not present his third Budget in 1977 as the political situation changed dramatically and Indira Gandhi decided to call for general elections. The decision to hold general elections was taken in January 1977. There was no question of Subramaniam presenting a Budget for the next year—1977–78. Elections were held between 16 and 20 March. To Indira Gandhi's shock and horror, the Congress party was completely routed in north India and reduced to a minority in the Lok Sabha. The newly cobbled-together Janata Party won a comfortable majority in the Lok Sabha. She lost her own seat in Rae Bareli. On 21 March, Gandhi and her government, including Subramaniam, resigned soon after she had revoked the Emergency.

A new prime minister and a new finance minister were sworn in the last week of March—Morarji Desai and H.M. Patel, promising to usher in a new economic order. Both had been earlier involved in India's economic administration—one as finance minister in two separate tenures, and the other as finance secretary. A new era in Indian politics with the first non-Congress government at the Centre was about to begin.

Acknowledgements

The idea of this book took shape initially as a single-volume project. But as I began delving into the details of how all the finance ministers of India steered the economy over the last several decades, the original idea had to be revisited. It became clear to me that the story of India's finance ministers over a period of seventy-five years since Independence cannot be told in a single volume. Instead, a three-volume project looked more appropriate. Manish Khurana, my editor at Penguin Random House India, was initially disappointed and even worried that the project would get delayed. But over time I could convince him that a three-volume project could do justice to the original idea. He was patient, understanding and appreciative of my efforts. I am grateful to Manish.

I must also acknowledge my debt of gratitude to Kripa Raman, who painstakingly went through the manuscript, highlighting many gaps in the narrative and plugging them.

I am thankful to Vineet Gill, who kindly agreed to incorporate last-minute changes in the manuscript and took care in meeting the book's publication deadline.

I am indebted to *Business Standard* and its editor, Shailesh Dobhal, who allowed me to use the sketches of the finance ministers published in this book. The sketches have been drawn by Binay Sinha, and I am grateful to him for producing these masterly portraits in just about a week.

I have benefitted immensely from the knowledge of several authors, whose books I read while working on this project. They have been acknowledged in Notes.

I will be failing in my duty if I do not record my deep gratitude to all the members of my family for their support while I was busy writing the manuscript.

Notes

Chapter 1: A Victim of a Procedural Lapse

1 Source: https://madrascourier.com/insight/did-shanmukham-chetty-indias-first-finance-minister-meddle-with-tax-investigations/
2 M.O. Mathai, *Reminiscences of the Nehru Age*, Vikas Publishing House, New Delhi, 1978.
3 Source: https://www.geni.com/people/Justice-Sir-S-VARADACHA RIAR/6000000013432326272
4 Durga Das, ed., *Sardar Patel's Correspondence 1945–50. Volume VI*, Navajivan Publishing House, Ahmedabad, 1973.
5 Ibid.
6 Ibid.
7 Ibid.
8 Ibid.
9 M.O. Mathai, *Reminiscences of the Nehru Age*, Vikas Publishing House, New Delhi, 1978.

Chapter 2: The Finance Minister Who Quit over Planning Commission

1 Source: https://www.britannica.com/topic/sterling-area
2 V. Haridasan, *Dr John Matthai 1886-1959: A Biography*, University of Calicut, 2000.

3 S. Bhoothalingam, *Reflections on an Era: Memoirs of a Civil Servant*, Affiliated East-West Press, New Delhi, 1993.

4 V. Haridasan, *Dr John Matthai 1886–1959: A Biography*, University of Calicut, 2000.

5 S. Bhoothalingam, *Reflections on an Era: Memoirs of a Civil Servant*.

6 V. Haridasan, *Dr John Matthai 1886–1959: A Biography*.

7 Ibid.

8 Sarvepalli Gopal, *Jawaharlal Nehru: A Biography, Vol II*, Oxford University Press, Delhi, 1979.

9 Ibid.

10 Ibid.

11 V. Haridasan, *Dr John Matthai 1886–1959: A Biography*.

12 S. Bhoothalingam, *Reflections on an Era: Memoirs of a Civil Servant*.

Chapter 3: A Former RBI Governor Steers the Economy

1 C.D. Deshmukh, *The Course of My Life*, Orient Longman Ltd, July 1974.

2 Ibid.

3 Ibid.

4 Source: https://indianexpress.com/article/explained/september-2-when-indias-interim-govt-was-formed-in-1946-5959889/

5 Source: https://thecommonwealth.org/about-us/history#11

6 C.D. Deshmukh, *The Course of My Life*.

7 Ibid.

8 Ibid.

9 Ibid.

10 Ibid.

11 Ibid.

12 Jairam Ramesh, *A Chequered Brilliance: The Many Lives of V.K. Krishna Menon*, Penguin, 2019.

13 Ibid.

14 Ibid.

15 C.D. Deshmukh, *The Course of My Life*.

16 Ibid.

17 Ibid.

18 Source: https://theprint.in/forgotten-founders/harekrushna-mahatab-the-man-who-started-the-merger-of-princely-states-with-india/106792/

19 Source: http://ashwinnaik.com/blog/2005/11/22/history-of-airlines-in-india/

20 C.D. Deshmukh, *The Course of My Life*.

21 Ibid.

22 Source: https://shodhganga.inflibnet.ac.in/bitstream/10603/43939/6/06_chapter%201.pdf

23 Source: https://adrindia.org/sites/default/files/FAQ%20-%20Donations%20to%20political%20parties.pdf

24 Source: https://rbidocs.rbi.org.in/rdocs/content/PDFs/90028.pdf

25 Ibid.

26 C.D. Deshmukh, *The Course of My Life*.

27 Source: https://rbidocs.rbi.org.in/rdocs/content/PDFs/90028.pdf

28 Ibid.

29 C.D. Deshmukh, *The Course of My Life*.

30 Neelima Dalmia Adhar, *Father Dearest: The Life and Times of R.K. Dalmia*, Namita Gokhale Editions/Roli Books, 2003.

31 Kamal Gupta, *Contemporary Auditing*, Tata McGraw-Hill Publishing Company Limited, 2005, p. 1032.

32 Source: https://www.irdai.gov.in/ADMINCMS/cms/NormalData_Layout.aspx?page=PageNo4&mid=2

33 A.K. Bhattacharya, *The Rise of Goliath: Twelve Disruptions that Changed India*, Penguin Random House, July 2019.

34 Source: https://ccs.in/internship_papers/2003/chap32.pdf

35 *Economic Weekly*, 1 October 1949. Source: https://www.epw.in/system/files/pdf/1949_1/40/devaluation_of_the_rupee.pdf

36 Durgabai, *India International Centre Quarterly*, vol. 22, no. 4, *C.D. Deshmukh: Life and Times*, published by India International Centre, 1995, pp. 79–93.

37 Durgabai Deshmukh, *Chintaman and I*, Allied Publishers Private Limited, 1980.

38 C.D. Deshmukh, *The Course of My Life*, Orient Longman Ltd, July 1974.

39 Ibid.

40 Source: https://www.mha.gov.in/sites/default/files/State%20Reorganisation%20Commisison%20Report%20of%201955_270614.pdf

41 C.D. Deshmukh, *The Course of My Life.*
42 Durgabai Deshmukh, *Chintaman and I.*
43 Durgabai, *India International Centre Quarterly*, vol. 22, no. 4, *C.D. Deshmukh: Life and Times.*
44 C.D. Deshmukh, *The Course of My Life.*

Chapter 4: Singed by the Mundhra Scandal

1 R. Tirumalai, *TTK: The Dynamic Innovator*, TT Maps & Publications/ Rupa & Co, Madras, 1988.
2 Source: https://www.nytimes.com/1974/03/08/archives/t-t-krishnamachari-74-dead-was-finance-minister-of-india-cleared-in.html
3 Source: https://www.financialexpress.com/india-news/tt-vasu-son-of-legendary-finance-minister-tt-krishnamachari-was-an-early-business-pioneer-in-india-heres-a-brief-look/539006/
4 Source: https://www.financialexpress.com/india-news/tt-vasu-son-of-legendary-finance-minister-tt-krishnamachari-was-an-early-business-pioneer-in-india-heres-a-brief-look/539006/
5 B.K. Nehru, *Nice Guys Finish Second: Memoirs*, Penguin, 1997.
6 Ibid.
7 R. Tirumalai, *TTK: The Dynamic Innovator.*
8 Ibid.
9 Ibid.
10 Source: https://www.economicsdiscussion.net/india/planning/the-second-five-year-plan-with-critical-assessment/21276
11 G. Balachandran, *The Reserve Bank of India 1951–1967*, Oxford University Press, Delhi, 1998.
12 Ibid.
13 Ibid.
14 B.K. Nehru, *Nice Guys Finish Second: Memoirs.*
15 G. Balachandran, *The Reserve Bank of India 1951–1967.*
16 Ibid.
17 B.K. Nehru, *Nice Guys Finish Second: Memoirs.*
18 Ibid.
19 R. Tirumalai, *TTK: The Dynamic Innovator.*
20 Ibid.

21 B.K. Nehru, *Nice Guys Finish Second: Memoirs.*
22 Source: https://www.hindustantimes.com/columns/a-haunting-memory/story-QftyfD30mjf6k6v096imbO.html
23 G. Balachandran, *The Reserve Bank of India 1951–1967.*
24 Ibid.
25 Ibid.
26 Ibid.
27 Ibid.
28 Ibid.
29 Ibid.
30 Ibid.
31 Ibid.
32 Source: http://archive.indianexpress.com/news/the-mundhra-affair/397317/
33 Source: https://www.pressreader.com/india/gfiles/20190115/282162177384182
34 Source: http://archive.indianexpress.com/news/the-mundhra-affair/397317/
35 M.C. Chagla, *Roses in December: An Autobiography*, Bharatiya Viddya Bhavan, Bombay, 1973.
36 G. Balachandran, *The Reserve Bank of India 1951–1967.*
37 Source: http://archive.indianexpress.com/news/the-mundhra-affair/397317/
38 Source: https://www.hindustantimes.com/columns/a-haunting-memory/story-QftyfD30mjf6k6v096imbO.html
39 M.C. Chagla, *Roses in December: An Autobiography.*
40 Ibid.
41 Source: https://www.epw.in/system/files/pdf/1959_11/28-29-30/afterthoughts_on_the_mundhra_affair.pdf
42 M.C. Chagla, *Roses in December: An Autobiography.*
43 Ibid.
44 Ibid.
45 Ibid.
46 G. Balachandran, *The Reserve Bank of India 1951–1967.*
47 Source: https://www.epw.in/system/files/pdf/1959_11/28-29-30/afterthoughts_on_the_mundhra_affair.pdf

48 Source: http://archive.indianexpress.com/news/the-mundhra-affair/397317/0
49 G. Balachandran, *The Reserve Bank of India 1951–1967*.
50 Ibid.
51 Madhav Godbole, *The God Who Failed: An Assessment of Jawaharlal Nehru's Leadership*, Rupa, Delhi, 2014.
52 *Selected Works of Jawaharlal Nehru*, second series, Jawaharlal Nehru Memorial Fund, vol. 41, New Delhi, 2010.
53 Ibid.
54 Ibid.
55 Ibid.
56 B.N. Mullik, *My Years With Nehru 1948–1964*.

Chapter 5: Presiding over Aid India Club and Bank Failures

1 Morarji Desai, *The Story of My Life*, Macmillan India, 1976.
2 Ibid.
3 Ibid.
4 Source: https://www.indiabudget.gov.in/doc/bspeech/bs195859.pdf
5 Morarji Desai, *The Story of My Life*.
6 Ibid.
7 Source: https://rbidocs.rbi.org.in/rdocs/content/PDFs/90038.pdf
8 Source: https://rbidocs.rbi.org.in/rdocs/content/PDFs/90038.pdf
9 Source: https://rbidocs.rbi.org.in/rdocs/content/PDFs/90038.pdf
10 Source: https://rbidocs.rbi.org.in/rdocs/content/PDFs/90038.pdf
11 Source: https://niti.gov.in/planningcommission.gov.in/docs/plans/planrel/fiveyr/index5.html
12 Source: http://mospi.nic.in/sites/default/files/Statistical_year_book_india_chapters/Five%20Year%20Plan%20writeup_0.pdf
13 Morarji Desai, *The Story of My Life*.
14 Ibid.
15 Source: https://www.inc.in/en/congress-sandesh/tribute/anecdotes
16 G. Balachandran, *The Reserve Bank of India 1951–1967*, Oxford University Pres, Delhi, 1998.
17 Source: https://rbidocs.rbi.org.in/rdocs/content/PDFs/90038.pdf
18 Source: https://www.bloombergquint.com/opinion/yes-bank-crisis-rbis-trysts-with-large-private-bank-failures#:~:text=Palai%20

Central%20Bank%20%E2%80%93%201960,K%20Joseph%20
Augusti%20from%201931.
19 Source: https://www.thehindu.com/opinion/lead/A-Kamaraj-Plan-
for-our-times/article12715025.ece
20 Morarji Desai, *The Story of My Life.*
21 Source: https://www.thehindu.com/opinion/lead/A-Kamaraj-Plan-
for-our-times/article12715025.ece

Chapter 6: Clouded by Differences with Shastri

1 R. Tirumalai, *TTK: The Dynamic Innovator,* TT Maps & Publications/
Rupa & Co, Madras, 1988.

2 Ibid.
3 G. Balachandran, *The Reserve Bank of India 1951–1967,* Oxford
University Press, Delhi, 1998.
4 Ibid.
5 R. Tirumalai, *TTK: The Dynamic Innovator.*
6 Source: https://www.jstor.org/stable/4357961?read-
now=1&seq=4#page_scan_tab_contents
7 Source: https://taxindiainternational.com/columnDesc.
php?qwer43fcxzt=NzU#:~:text=Voluntary%20Disclosure%20
Scheme%2C%201965&text=This%20came%20to%20be%20
known,two%20instalments%20over%20six%20month
8 S. Bhoothalingam, *Reflections on an Era: Memoirs of a Civil Servant,*
Affiliated East-West Press, New Delhi, 1993.
9 R. Tirumalai, *TTK: The Dynamic Innovator.*
10 Ibid.

Chapter 7: Devaluing the Indian Rupee

1 I.G. Patel, *Glimpses of Indian Economic Policy: An Insider's View,* Oxford
University Press, New Delhi, 2002.
2 S. Bhoothalingam, *Reflections on an Era: Memoirs of a Civil Servant,*
Affiliated East-West Press Pvt Ltd, Delhi, 1993.
3 G. Balachandran, *The Reserve Bank of India 1951–1967,* Oxford
University Press, Delhi, 1998.
4 Ibid.

5 Source: http://documents1.worldbank.org/curated/en/2820114680
00299920/pdf/104705-WP-PUBLIC-2010-11-Report-to-the-
PResident-on-Indias-Effort.pdf

6 S. Bhoothalingam, *Reflections on an Era: Memoirs of a Civil Servant.*

7 R. Tirumalai, *TTK: The Dynamic Innovator*, TT Maps & Publications, Madras, 1988.

8 Ibid.

9 G. Balachandran, *The Reserve Bank of India 1951–1967*, Oxford University Press, Delhi, 1998.

10 I.G. Patel, *Glimpses of Indian Economic Policy: An Insider's View*, Oxford University Press, New Delhi, 2002.

11 Ibid.

12 B.K. Nehru, *Nice Guys Finish Second: Memoirs*, Penguin Books, Delhi, 1997.

13 G. Balachandran, *The Reserve Bank of India 1951–1967.*

14 B.K. Nehru, *Nice Guys Finish Second: Memoirs.*

15 I.G. Patel, *Glimpses of Indian Economic Policy: An Insider's View.*

16 G. Balachandran, *The Reserve Bank of India 1951–1967.*

17 Ibid.

18 Source: https://www.indiabudget.gov.in/budget_archive/es1965-66/PART_II.pdf

19 B.K. Nehru, *Nice Guys Finish Second: Memoirs.*

20 S. Bhoothalingam, *Reflections on an Era: Memoirs of a Civil Servant.*

21 Robert W. Oliver, *George Woods and the World Bank*, Lynne Rienner Publishers Inc., USA, 1995.

22 Ibid.

23 G. Balachandran, *The Reserve Bank of India 1951–1967.*

24 M. Narasimham, *From Reserve Bank to Finance Ministry and Beyond: Some Reminiscences*, UBS Publishers, New Delhi, 2002.

25 B.K. Nehru, *Nice Guys Finish Second: Memoirs.*

26 J.B. Kripalani, *My Times: An Autobiography*, Rupa & Co, New Delhi, 2004.

27 G. Balachandran, *The Reserve Bank of India 1951–1967.*

28 I.G. Patel, *Glimpses of Indian Economic Policy: An Insider's View.*

29 G. Balachandran, *The Reserve Bank of India 1951–1967.*

30 Robert W. Oliver, *George Woods and the World Bank*, Lynne Rienner Publishers Inc., USA, 1995.
31 G. Balachandran, *The Reserve Bank of India 1951–1967*.
32 Robert W. Oliver, *George Woods and the World Bank*.
33 G. Balachandran, *The Reserve Bank of India 1951–1967*.
34 S. Bhoothalingam, *Reflections on an Era: Memoirs of a Civil Servant*.
35 Ibid.
36 I.G. Patel, *Glimpses of Indian Economic Policy: An Insider's View*.

Chapter 8: A Failed Crusade for Social Control of Banks

1 Morarji Desai, *The Story of My Life*, Macmillan India, Madras, 1974.
2 Ibid.
3 I.G. Patel, *Glimpses of Indian Economic Policy: An Insider's View*, Oxford University Press, New Delhi, 2002.
4 Morarji Desai, *The Story of My Life*.
5 I.G. Patel, *Glimpses of Indian Economic Policy: An Insider's View*.
6 Ibid.
7 Ibid.

Chapter 9: The Architect of Bank Nationalization

1 *The Reserve Bank of India*, Volume 3, 1967–81, RBI Central Office, Mumbai, 2005.
2 Ibid.
3 Source: https://www.tribuneindia.com/news/archive/this-day-that-year/giri-to-resign-twin-offices-803095
4 P.N. Dhar, *Indira Gandhi, the 'Emergency', and Indian Democracy*, Oxford University Press, New Delhi, 2000.
5 Ibid.
6 D.N. Ghosh, *No Regrets*, Rupa Publications, New Delhi, 2015.
7 Ibid.
8 *The Reserve Bank of India*, Volume 3, 1967–1981, RBI Central Office, Mumbai, 2005.
9 D.N. Ghosh, *No Regrets*, Rupa Publications, New Delhi, 2015.
10 I.G. Patel, *Glimpses of Indian Economic Policy: An Insider's View*, Oxford University Press, New Delhi, 2002.

11 Ibid.

12 Ibid.

13 *The Reserve Bank of India*, Volume 3, 1967–1981.

14 Ibid.

15 Source: https://fincomindia.nic.in/writereaddata/html_en_files/
oldcommission_html/memorandum/fifthemod.htm

16 I.G. Patel, *Glimpses of Indian Economic Policy: An Insider's View.*

Chapter 10: Dealing with War and Economic Crisis

1 Source: https://www.nytimes.com/1971/02/14/archives/indira-gandhi-
is-either-hated-or-adored-indira-gandhi-is-either.html

2 Source: https://www.indiabudget.gov.in/doc/bspeech/bs197172(I).pdf

3 *The Reserve Bank of India*, Volume 3, 1967–1981, RBI, Mumbai, 2005.

4 M. Narasimham, *From Reserve Bank to Finance Ministry and Beyond: Some
Reminiscences*, UBS Publishers, New Delhi, 2002.

5 I.G. Patel, *Glimpses of Indian Economic Policy: An Insider's View*, Oxford
University Press, New Delhi, 2002.

6 Ibid.

7 Ibid.

Chapter 11: The FM During the Emergency

1 *The Reserve Bank of India*, Volume 3, 1967–1981.

2 Source: https://www.epw.in/journal/1975/4/uncategorised/cause-
concern.html

3 *The Reserve Bank of India*, Volume 3, 1967–1981.

4 Source: https://legislative.gov.in/sites/default/files/A1974-57.pdf

5 Source: https://www.indiabudget.gov.in/doc/bspeech/bs197576.pdf

6 A.K. Bhattacharya, *The Rise of Goliath: Twelve Disruptions That Changed
India*, Penguin, New Delhi, 2019.

7 T.C.A. Srinivasa Raghavan, *A Crown of Thorns: The Governors of the RBI*,
Westland, Chennai, 2016.

8 Ibid.

9 M. Narasimham, *From Reserve Bank to Finance Ministry and Beyond: Some
Reminiscences.*

10 Ibid.
11 Pranab Mukherjee, *The Dramatic Decade: The Indira Gandhi Years*, Rupa, New Delhi, 2015.
12 M. Narasimham, *From Reserve Bank to Finance Ministry and Beyond: Some Reminiscences.*
13 Ibid.
14 Ibid.